List of illustrations

x

New Unesco Source Book for

Geography Teaching

New Unesco Source Book for
Geography Teaching

edited by

Norman J Graves
*Chairman of The Commission on Geographical Education
of the International Geographical Union 1972–1980*

Members of the Commission 1976–80
Paul Claval, University of Paris
Robert Geipel, Technical University, Munich
Vladimir Pavlovich Maksakovskiy, Lenin Moscow State Pedagogical Institute
Joseph Paul Stoltman, Western Michigan University
Juan Vila-Valenti, University of Barcelona

LONGMAN/THE UNESCO PRESS

First published 1982
by the United Nations Educational,
Scientific and Cultural Organization,
7 Place de Fontenoy, 75700 Paris, France

and

LONGMAN GROUP LIMITED,
Longman House, Burnt Mill,
Harlow, Essex

ISBN Cased: 92 3 101 934 1 (The Unesco Press)
       Paper: 92 3 101 935 X (The Unesco Press)
ISBN Cased: 0 582 36121 4 (Longman)
       Paper: 0 582 36122 2 (Longman)

Set in 10/11 pt Times New Roman
by Tradespools Limited, Frome, Somerset

Printed in Hong Kong by
Wilture Enterprises (International) Ltd

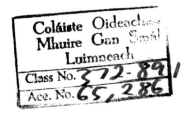

ERRATA

Pages 65-6: The list of world nations in Table 3.1 should read as follows:

Section A: United States, Kuwait, United Arab Emirates, Sweden, Switzerland, Canada, New Zealand, Luxemburg, Australia, Denmark, Libyan Arab Jamahiriya, Iceland, France, Norway, Federal Republic of Germany, Belgium, United Kingdom, Finland, Qatar, Netherlands, German Democratic Republic, Brunei.

Section B: Israel, Austria, Puerto Rico, Italy, Czechoslovakia, USSR, Japan, Ireland, Venezuela, Hungary, Argentina, Poland, Cyprus, Greece, Romania, Uruguay, Spain, Trinidad, Bulgaria, Singapore, Hong Kong, Rep. of S. Africa, Chile.

Section C: Yugoslavia, Panama, Lebanon, Mexico, Jamaica, Costa Rica, Mongolia, Portugal, Suriname, Nicaragua, Cuba, Guatemala, Peru, Albania, Colombia, Guyana, Malaysia, Turkey, S. Salvador, Iraq, Dominican Rep., Iran, Gabon, Brazil, Saudi Arabia, Taiwan, Ghana, Algeria, Ivory Coast, Honduras, Jordan, Liberia, Senegal, Zimbabwe, Paraguay, Tunisia, Ecuador, Democratic People's Republic of Korea, Syrian Arab Republic, Zambia, Angola, Morocco, Bolivia, Philippines.

Section D: Egypt, Sri Lanka, Republic of Korea, Sierra Leone, New Guinea, Mauritania, Thailand, Congo, Democratic Kampuchea, Republic of Viet Nam, Cameroon, Central African Republic, Indonesia, Mozambique, Sudan, Togo, Uganda, India, Democratic Republic of Viet Nam, Kenya, Madagascar, Pakistan, Yemen, China, Dahomey, Guinea, Niger, Nigeria, United Republic of Tanzania, Afghanistan, Chad, Haiti, Lao People's Democratic Republic, Nepal, Burma, Zaire, Ethiopia, Mali, Bangladesh, Burundi, Malawi, Somalia, Upper Volta, Rwanda.

Any reference to these nations in the text should read likewise.

Page 254: Line 11 should read 'University of New Mexico'.

Page 318: Line 28 should read 'influenced similar projects in the United Kingdom and in the Federal Republic of Germany'.

Page 392: The reference to 'population, control theme' should refer to pages 310-12.

Preface

As part of its programme to promote education for international understanding, peace and respect for human rights through the improvement of curricula, teaching methods and materials, Unesco has produced a number of handbooks and guides designed to provide curriculum planners and classroom teachers with useful information and suggestions based on international expertise and experience.

The present publication was prepared by the Commission on Geographical Education of the International Geographical Union under contract with Unesco. The original manuscript was written by ten co-authors and some 100 copies of a draft edition were sent for comment to specialists and geographical institutions throughout the world. The final version was then prepared on the basis of comments received.

A large part of the book is devoted to practical suggestions and information on ways and means of improving strategies and methods at both the primary and secondary school levels. The text encompasses a wide range of topics and issues such as the aims and value of geographical education, mental development and the learning process, teaching and learning strategies and techniques, resource material, course planning and evaluation.

The book supersedes Unesco's earlier publication *Source Book for Geography Teaching*, first issued in English in 1965, and followed by eleven editions in other languages, (Arabic, French, Hindi, Italian, Japanese, Korean, Polish, Portuguese, Slovenian, Spanish and Thai).

It is hoped that this publication will help to raise the standard of geography teaching and at the same time enlarge the contribution of this important subject, either as an autonomous discipline or in the context of social studies, to better international understanding, co-operation and peace.

Grateful acknowledgement is made to Professor Norman Graves, Chairman of the Commission on Geographical Education of the International Geographical Union from 1972 to 1980, and his colleagues in the International Geographical Union who have helped to draft the text, as well as to all those who provided comments and suggestions. Although the final work is in every sense a co-operative effort it should be clearly understood that any opinions and points of view expressed by the authors are their own and do not necessarily reflect the views of Unesco. Furthermore, the designations employed and the presentation of material do not imply the expression of any opinion whatsoever on the part of Unesco concerning the legal status of any country, territory, city or area or of its authorities, or concerning the delimitation of its frontiers or boundaries.

Contents

List of tables

The authors

Dr Donald Biddle is Principal of Sydney Teachers College, Australia

Dr Norman Graves is Professor of Geography Education and Head of the Geography Department at the University of London Institute of Education, UK

Dr Clyde Kohn was (until he retired) Professor of Geography at the University of Iowa, USA

Mr Michael Naish is Senior Lecturer in Education at the University of London Institute of Education, UK

Dr Olatunde Okunrotifa is Professor of Education at the University of Ibadan, Nigeria

Dr Philippe Pinchemel is Professor of Geography at the University of Paris, France

Mr Benoit Robert is Professor of Education at Laval University, Quebec, Canada

Dr Chandra Pal Singh is Lecturer in Geography at the Delhi School of Economics, India

Dr Frances Slater is Senior Lecturer in Education at the University of London Institute of Education, UK

Mr Brian Spicer is Senior Lecturer in Education at Monash University, Melbourne, Australia

Acknowledgements

We are grateful to the following for permission to reproduce copyright material:
Journal of Philosophy and the author, Prof. Lawrence Kohlberg, for an extract from the article 'The Claim To Moral Adequacy Of A Highest Stage Of Moral Judgment' in *Journal of Philosophy* Vol. LXX, No. 18 (25 Oct. 1973), pp. 631–2.

Photographs:

Australian News and Information Bureau, fig 7.35; V C Browne and Son, figs 7.19 and 7.22; J Allan Cash, fig 1.1; Michael Hellyer, fig 1.2; New Zealand High Commission, figs 7.17, 7.20, 7.21 and 7.23; Nigel Press Associates, figs 7.1, 7.2a, b, c and 7.3.

Artwork which first appeared in the following publications:

F. Stuart Chapin Jr, *Urban Land Use Planning*, University of Illinois Press, 1965, fig 7.29; Yves Lacoste, *Geographie du Sous-Developpement*, Presses Universaires de France, figs 3.3, 3.4 and 3.5, tabs 3.2b and c; K Lynch, *Image of the City*, The MIT Press, fig 7.4; Novosti Press Agency APN, Intourist Brochure, fig 7.5; Jean Piaget and Barbel Inhelder, *The Child's Concept of Space*, Routledge and Kegan Paul Ltd, 1966, fig 2.6; Port of London Authority, *Martech Report* 1964, fig 10.4; Schools Council Working Paper 43, *School Resource Centres* by Norman W Beswick, Evans/Methuen Educational, 1972, fig 8.4; J Thompson, *Urban Geography*, Pergamon Press, 1967, figs 10.2 and 10.3.
We would be grateful for information concerning © holders not acknowledged.

Introduction

NORMAN J. GRAVES

Change

In the present world nothing stands still for any length of time. If you miss listening to the radio, viewing the television or reading the newspapers for a week, you may be surprised to hear subsequently that a government has changed; that an oil tanker has broken up on rocks and caused beaches to be polluted; that unusually wet weather has resulted in floods in low-lying river valley lands; that the price of coffee has risen yet again; that an earthquake has caused extensive damage in Asia; and so on. But it is not only such newsworthy events that occur, there are also changes which are less obvious unless they are noted after some considerable period of time, such as changes in attitudes, changes in policies and changes in knowledge which involve looking at the world in a somewhat different light. One need only call to mind the changes in attitude towards ethnic minorities, changes in the policies of certain governments towards the Israel/Palestine issue and changes in our understanding of the problems of space travel, to be conscious of the nature of these less spectacular but nevertheless significant changes.

This book is a manifestation of change. In 1965, the *Unesco Source Book for Geography Teaching* was published, representing a compendium of ideas concerning what was then considered good practice in the teaching of geography, and examples of such practice. At that time the conceptual revolution in geography had made little impact on schools in most parts of the world, and the implicit assumption was that the main purpose of geography was to describe the various cultural and physical landscapes of the world in a manner that would prove educative for the students concerned. Today we are facing a situation in which not only is the conceptual revolution being absorbed in schools, but ideas on the geography of perception and on what is commonly called 'welfare geography' are also being assimilated.

By the 'conceptual revolution' is meant a change in both the philosophy and methodology of geography. Geography is now seen as having the objective of developing a series of laws, theories and principles concerned with the spatial aspects of human behaviour on earth. Its methodology is much more openly that of the social and physical sciences, in other words it is using both scientific method and those methods which derive from a phenomenological view of society, i.e. a view which suggests that, in many circumstances, an observer can only acquire knowledge through being part of the process he is observing; the process then has meaning for him. Recently research in geography has espoused a field broadly known as 'environmental perception' which is concerned with the way people subjectively perceive their habitat, including its resources. Another aspect of geographical research to develop recently, is one dealing with spatial aspects of welfare or social justice.

The educational disciplines have also made substantial progress in their understanding of the process of education. Not only are teachers now more aware of Piaget's and Bruner's models of mental development in children and adolescents but they have been introduced to the problems of curriculum development and curriculum planning; they are more aware of the variety of teaching styles which are available and they are conscious of the complex nature of classroom interactions. Consequently, this book does not attempt to be simply an updated version of the former *Source Book*. It assumes that the professional development of teachers has made necessary a different style of approach. It is therefore less prescriptive than the former book, but suggests strategies that teachers may decide to adopt, depending on the circumstances of their schools and environments.

The book's approach

What is this approach? Strangely in an educational book, the approach is less didactic, that is, the authors are not suggesting that the teacher should go about his job in any one particular way. Rather they are indicating the range of possible teaching strategies, objectives and content, from which the teacher may pick out what best suits him or her in the context of local circumstances. The authors recognize that in any teaching–learning situation there are numerous variables, of which the most important are: the *students* (their values, attitudes and existing knowledge); the *teachers*; the *school resources* and those of the local area; the *society* of which the school system is a part; and the *content* (knowledge or attitudes or values) which is to be taught. It is impossible, therefore, to prescribe a course of action, a teaching strategy, that will fit all circumstances. What is appropriate in a Lagos school may not be appropriate in a school in Nairobi. What may be done in a small French provincial town may not be possible in downtown New York. This does not mean that geography teachers the world over may not share certain basic aims, but it does mean that the way in which they attempt to reach these goals may have to be very different from one part of the world to another. Inevitably some aims will be different, or the emphasis put on them will differ from area to area. In developing countries, aims will tend to be much more instrumental in the sense that education is seen as a means of increasing the rate of economic development and of raising the national income per head of the population. In heavily industrialized areas like the Ruhr in the Federal Republic of Germany, the accent may be on environmental education given the pollution problems of the Rhine. In yet other areas, the emphasis may be on geography's contribution to thinking skills and to international understanding.

But whatever the aims, it is certain that the teaching process will vary considerably from one part of the world to another. What this book provides, then, is a variety of ideas, from which the teacher may choose in the light of his own circumstances. It does not seek to impose any one particular set of procedures or practices. Although teachers in colleges of education and in secondary schools are likely to be the main users of this book, it is hoped that all teachers, whatever their situation, may derive some benefit from its contents.

The nature of the book's offerings

In Chapter 1, Philippe Pinchemel takes a critical look at some of the changes in geography and education mentioned earlier. He admits that since the rate of change is a high one, it is not always clear what is the best course for action for an educator who is also a geographer. He does, however, commit himself to certain basic values which he affirms are promoted by geographical education. It is here that teachers may agree or disagree, for what is valued by one society may not be valued by another. Obviously, however, something worthwhile or of value should result from geographical education since otherwise all the teacher's efforts would be in vain. The teacher must make up his mind as to which values he feels are important to his students as well as to himself. Pinchemel's 'Credo' is neatly summed up in his concluding paragraph in which he suggests that ultimately all autonomous and responsible citizens should have geographical 'reflexes' about environmental and spatial organization issues.

In the process of teaching and learning the teacher is often looked upon as a manager. He manages his class, the resources at his disposal and the learning experiences which he plans. But in this job of management he needs to be aware of the kind of learning problems that his students face. Michael Naish, in Chapter 2, examines these learning problems in the light of evidence provided by such masters of their trade as Piaget and Bruner. Broadly, he describes Piaget's model of mental development and shows its relevance to learning problems in geography, especially in view of research undertaken in the field of geographical education. Attention is concentrated on the nature of concepts and their acquisition by learners and the function of language in this process. Inevitably, however, the perception of phenomena is an important variable in the same learning process. It is here that modern research in environmental perception is brought to bear on the problem along with research in psychology.

In structuring learning experiences for his students, the teacher uses certain teaching strategies. Benoit Robert, in Chapter 3, outlines some of these teaching strategies and gives examples of the way in which they have been put into operation. He suggests that most teaching methods may be divided into two broad groups – expository methods and inquiry methods – but notes that teachers normally use both though some tend to lean more heavily on one than the other. His illustrations are derived from various French and North American sources, such as the High School Geography Project, a Canada Studies Foundation Project and a programmed learning sequence on elementary relief features devised for schools in Nigeria. Teachers will be able to judge how far these examples and/or their strategies could, with due modification, be used in their schools.

In Chapter 4, Clyde Kohn indicates that a problem-solving approach has often been found profitable in the teaching of geography because it exercises the thinking skills of the students as well as their memory. He insists that the problems posed should be real problems, and by this he means problems having meaning for the students and in which they can feel involved. He accepts that geography has several traditional concerns: earth science, man–land relations, regional or areal differentiation and spatial organization, and he gives illustrations of the ways in which real problems may be drawn from each tradition. Kohn also suggests ways in which students and teachers may go about the business of tackling and solving the problem posed. He makes certain recommendations to teachers of a general nature based on his own experience of undertaking such problem-solving exercises with his own students.

One aspect of the conceptual revolution in geography is the application of scientific method to the solution of geographical problems. In Chapters 5 and 6, Olatunde Okunrotifa describes how such a method involves gathering information or data and then processing these. In Chapter 5, he concentrates on data gathering and examines such issues as the need to decide on the problem, the selection of information to be collected, sampling procedures, the collection of information in the field and from secondary published and unpublished sources. In Chapter 6, he suggests ways in which data may be described graphically and analysed statistically by standard methods. At present such statistical methods are not widely found in school geography, though they are increasingly being used with senior students as teachers become familiar with the techniques.

Chapter 7 examines further the possible use of some of the geographer's main sources of documentation, namely topographical and other maps and photographs, particularly aerial photographs. Frances Slater and Brian Spicer demonstrate how such basic tools may be integrated into the process of geographical education, with special reference to methods of map analysis and of processing remotely sense data.

The teacher, as indicated earlier, is now seen among other things as a manager of resources. Chandra Pal Singh, in Chapter 8, examines how resources for geography teaching can be organized. First he looks at the organization of the geography room, then at the resources centre, since many schools now tend to centralize their learning resources rather than have them dispersed in various departmental cupboards. Different aspects of collecting, storing and retrieving resources are discussed and to some extent evaluated, including the use of computer terminals.

Chapter 9, by Donald Biddle, is an attempt to throw light on the problem of curriculum planning and construction. It makes use of curriculum theory as well as recent advances in geographical education. Biddle draws on his own research and long experience as a teacher in schools and colleges of education, and on his involvement in curriculum and examination development in Australia.

In Chapter 10, the present writer looks at the problem of evaluating geographical education. In particular, attention is given to the problem of curriculum evaluation as against the evaluation of student learning. In other words, the concern is to determine how some means may be found of describing how the curriculum has worked rather than simply finding out what knowledge students have gained. It is important to find out what students and teachers feel about the curriculum as well as what students have learned in cognitive terms. Nevertheless, one needs to be a realist, and since tests and examinations are likely to remain an important aspect of curriculum evaluation for a long time to come, a good deal of attention is paid to these, particularly to course work assessment as well as objective tests, open-ended questions and essay examinations. Various types of objective tests are considered and guidance is given on item analysis and on ways of assessing the validity and reliability of tests. Lastly, some thought is given to the problem of moderating marks or grades given by different examiners or teachers in different schools for the same examination.

How to use this book

This is not intended to be a 'cook-book'. The authors do not guarantee that if you adopt its ideas, procedures and evaluation techniques all will be well with your teaching. It is best to look upon it as a handbook to be used from time to time. For example, if a problem arises concerning the organization of resources, then Chapter 8 and its references may furnish useful suggestions. In most cases it will probably be necessary to modify what is suggested to suit particular circumstances. Further, certain strategies suggested in Chapters 3 to 7 may not work the first time. They should be tried again and if they do not then come up to expectations, should be abandoned in favour of other procedures. It is important, however, not to expect too much. If there are thirty students in a class, it is unlikely that they will all react enthusiastically to an attempt to undertake group discussion work or a geographical simulation. Students, after all, are individuals with their own ideas and preferences. Changing attitudes is often an uphill task. But many of the ideas suggested in this book have been tried with various classes successfully.

Acknowledgements

In editing this book, I have had not only the willing co-operation of the authors, but also that of various members of the Commission on Geographical Education of the International Geographical Union and in particular of Dr Joseph P. Stoltman of Western Michigan University. I should also like to thank all those geographers and education specialists from all parts of the world who freely gave of their time to comment on the draft manuscript.

CHAPTER 1

The aims and values of geographical education

PHILIPPE PINCHEMEL

Introduction

In most countries of the world, geography is, in some form or other, part of the total curriculum from primary school to university. Depending on the nature of the education system, geography is taught sometimes as a discipline on its own, sometimes in association with other disciplines (like history or natural science) and sometimes as part of a group of allied subjects (like the social sciences or environmental studies). But, whatever its situation in the total curriculum, it is recognized as an essential aspect of the education of children and adolescents. This may be seen as the result of a long tradition, which for the Western nations is centuries old, and which corresponds to an almost innate desire of human beings to understand their terrestrial habitat, be this the local environment or more distant regions. This is why in schools the teaching of geography began before the teaching of many other social science subjects and developed a privileged position in the different stages of education.

But the privilege of being an old-established subject is currently resulting in certain questions. First by those practising other sciences who ask: why should geography continue to be taught even if this was once justified; has it not been overtaken by the development of other disciplines? Secondly, from within the subject itself: an 'ageing' discipine must of necessity question its values and its content which may need renewal. Unfortunately, the curriculum is enshrined in institutional structures which tend to become ossified, and a risk exists that too great a rift may develop between geographical research in universities and geography teaching in schools.

Two broad questions need therefore to be posed: what should be the nature of geographical education in the last quarter of the twentieth century, and what should contribute to the education of students who will be living, working and assuming responsibilities in the years between 2000 and 2050? What, in other words, should be the aims and values of such teaching?

Changes in geography teaching

The scientific attempt to understand the geography of the world is less than a century old. It is not surprising that geography should have evolved and developed as people spread over the world and took possession of its various parts. Since these times, the world has changed as well as the educational milieu in which geography is taught.

Changes in the teaching environment

A century ago, the teaching of geography was aided by wall maps; photographs were not normally available. Thirty years ago audio-visual aids, including aerial photographs and television, were in their infancy. Today potential resources seem almost unlimited in number, from census data to computerized data banks, from maps to various visual illustrations, such as aerial photography from remote sensing equipment (see Fig. 7.2). At the present time we can look at photographs which show us the earth as a whole without needing the mediation of a cartographer. We are now, therefore, much more familiar with such views of the earth, from which results a new relationship between man and his planet, whether or not he is conscious of this. To see the earth as a whole, to see it daily being transformed, change in colour in a way that one is used to seeing the moon, will be events as familiar to the pupils of tomorrow as is today their view of the street outside their home; all this owing to satellite photography.

Changes in the students

The students and pupils of today live in a cultural context very different from that of 20 years ago, let alone 50 years ago. School, the teacher, the textbook and teaching aids are no longer the only sources of information; numerous channels of information are available and used outside the school: magazines and newspapers, radio, television, all bombard the students each day with a mass of information, to such an extent that sometimes their reaction is to reject it. Such information consists either of descriptions of events which have been consciously or unwittingly distorted, or of interpretation of these events containing value judgements. Such interpretations clearly mediate the reality that the reader or viewer would have perceived and judged. It is therefore necessary to teach the young to examine such information critically, to get them to sort out facts from opinion, which can only be done through their having a wide cognitive perspective.

But students, the world over, have an unequal experience of space and spatial relations. Millions of children have never seen the sea, a mountain, a cliff, a glacier, a skyscraper or, more prosaically, a farm. In adult life, however, many young people will experience varied environments, for example the rural and urban landscapes experienced by migrants. Visits to relations in other parts of the world, holidays, school journeys, travel grants – all are now facilitating the acquisition of knowledge about a world which is becoming more and more accessible for some students. Yet, it is still true that a gulf is growing between the vicarious experience of the world made possible by the mass media and direct experience made possible by travel. Further, such direct contact with distant parts is becoming more discontinuous. Because it is possible to fly from one place to another rapidly, personal knowledge of places separated by long distances may be better than knowledge of intervening areas, including areas close to one's home. Direct experience of the world is also made unequal by income differences, whether these be on a national scale or at the individual scale within a nation.

Geographical education must be seen, therefore, as an integral part of the process of education, since such an education must make the student better able to understand life on earth by making evident spatial relations and the organization of space by man. Geographical education cannot be limited to those who in some form or other hope to practise geography professionally. It seems normal to us that all children should learn to read, to write, to count and calculate, that is to acquire the means of communicating with others, so that they may ask questions and give answers, that they may listen and also be heard, so that they may cope with daily life, so that they may exploit their aptitudes and develop their personalities. Is it less natural that students should learn to operate competently in space, to develop the habit of looking at the spatial aspects of problems, in order that they may better understand the environments in which they live?

Changes in geographical knowledge

A little more than a century ago, men were still exploring the coasts of certain continents and wondering about the possible existence of an Antarctic land mass. The interiors of Africa, Australia and South America were little known to geographers. Little by little, they discovered the nature of their rocks, their flora and fauna; they developed methods for measuring altitudes, they invented contour lines to represent relief, they described landscapes and the distribution of the world's population. Now that the world has been largely mapped, and photographed; now that its population has been more or less accurately counted and a rough inventory of its resources made, the geographer's task is no longer that of discovering a new land, of naming a peak, of listing the nations and empires of this earth; it is to understand how human societies can solve the many problems of spatial organization posed by the peopling of the earth and its development. This theme is elaborated below.

(a) First let us be aware of the huge quantity of information made available each day by the mass media, of the diversity of places from which this information emanates. To compare the present situation with that of 20 years ago, is to realize that world events may, each day, impinge on the mental consciousness of each student. Events and information coming from numerous varied and distant parts of the world are no longer sorted, classified and filtered by the friction of distance; whatever their locational origin they are placed in the limelight by the media because they may have a dramatic impact, or they may involve large numbers of human beings, or they may be expected to have a great influence on public opinion.

(b) Geography is no longer simply a listing of the facts and features of the various parts of the earth. It now makes use of facts to study the problems of spatial relations on earth, problems which are made manifest by overpopulation, underdevelopment, urban sprawl, regional planning, agrarian reform and land-use policies. Today, events in the news are not very intelligible if they are not seen in a geographical or environmental context, that is, unless the spatial implications can be understood.

These geographical aspects of current happenings are closely linked to the population explosion in which certain areas are becoming 'saturated' with people, and to urban growth; these phenomena highlight such processes as population migrations and concentrations; the absorption of available space; and competition for land and resources. All this is happening in a 'shrinking' world in which the means of communication have made most areas of the world familiar, in which no region is really very distant.

Two problems, those of the localization of economic activity and of environmental quality, are sufficient to show that most phenomena are linked and interdependent. The organic unity of the world, perceived over a century ago by Alexander von Humboldt in his *Kosmos* is being rediscovered by man, albeit by different means and at different scales. The evolution of geography as a science since the 1950s, the so-called 'new geography', has been marked by a concern for theory, for deductive methods, for quantitative techniques and for helping to solve practical spatial problems. These changes have often been labelled a conceptual revolution in geography, in which a new discipline is seen to replace a more traditional descriptive and encyclopaedic subject no longer relevant to present-day needs. As a result, deep cleavages have appeared among the international community of geographers: among researchers as well as among teachers. Traditionalists opposed innovators, and those favouring qualitative studies confronted those whose predilection was for quantitative studies. In fact, geography was simply evolving in the same way as most social sciences, in changing its methodology and its objectives.

The aims of geographical education

Given the context which has been described, the way in which geographical education should be developing is not always clear. Should it be a part of a larger course on the behavioural sciences (not yet generally taught in secondary schools) and therefore as a subject much more limited in extent than at present, or should it be the basis of an integrated course incorporating these behavioural sciences? Whatever the situation within a national education system, the choice to be made is a difficult one in which a risk exists that the aims of geographical education may be distorted, particularly if geography is seen not as a discipline of the mind, but as a purveyor of information to give future citizens a factual background to world events. This image of geography often acquired at school is why young people may not consider it as an autonomous discipline, and may see the geographer in terms of the teacher who taught them rather than as a professional attempting to deal with the spatial aspects of society's problems.

It would, nevertheless, be dishonest to ignore the diverse conceptions of geography which exist at present. While agreement may exist on certain words and concepts used in geography, agreement does not yet exist on a precise definition of the subject as a whole. Diversity is also evident in the kinds of research and teaching undertaken. It is possible to welcome this diversity and see within it a sign of conceptual vigour and creativity. On the other hand, it is also possible to consider this as a sign of the dismemberment of a discipline which has refused to define its bounds precisely, and which holds on nostalgically to the concept of a synthetic discipline attempting to encompass all terrestrial phenomena, to present a total view of societies and their environments.

Moving from the general to the particular, from large-scale concepts to small-scale concepts, there follows a list of the principles about which there is some consensus, which appear best to typify geographical thought and which therefore might be used to structure its teaching.

The analysis of locations and distributions

All earthly phenomena, visible or invisible, controlled or spontaneous, are localized. This localization is manifest as 'points' (a farm, a town, a factory), as lines (canals, roads, railways), as areas (cultivated land, urban areas), which result in *spatial differentiation* on the earth's surface. Considered separately and at different scales, each phenomenon makes a characteristic pattern of distribution which is not entirely due to chance but which is related to social and economic processes. Geographical analysis is concerned with the description and explanation of these patterns, searching out for the multiple causes which may be found among physical and human factors and whose origins may be recent or ancient. Such distributions are not static but in evolution, consequently geographic analysis must be dynamic.

Environmental analysis

Particular environments result from the co-existence of several phenomena in one area. This *spatial association* and the interdependence of environmental phenomena, such as olive groves and Mediterranean climatic conditions, contributes to spatial differentiation and gives a certain character to particular places.

Such characteristic environments may be 'natural' environments like the hot desert areas, the savannas, equatorial forests, though few are natural in the sense of being untouched by man, and indeed men and animals operate within such an environment as part of a total ecosystem which may or may not be in equilibrium. Human societies have established complex relationships with the physical and biotic environment, largely through the exploitation of natural resources such as animal husbandry, the clearing of vegetation to grow crops, the establishment of farms, plantations, small settlements and towns. Man is constantly interacting with his environment, though the extent of his impact depends on his needs, his technology and his perception of what makes up his milieu. This perception is itself influenced by the economic, political and social system within the society in question. The extent and degree of population pressure also affects man's appreciation of his environment.

Human societies act upon space in numerous ways. For example, they divide space into political and administrative areas with frontiers and limits within which laws, practices, jurisdictions and economic development differ. Further, men appropriate space, whether this be for private or public ownership, and this results in a visible pattern of land-ownership which itself is a manifestation of the workings of an economic system, in which certain social classes may exert great

power or in which the state effectively controls the market for land.
Land-use patterns, whether these be arable, pastoral, forest, industrial, residential, service or transport, also reflect the structures and
policies of each socio-economic system. For example settlement
patterns in the St Lawrence Valley are very different from settlement
patterns in the prairies. (See Figs 1.1 and 1.2.)

Fig. 1.1 Settlement pattern in the St Lawrence valley in Quebec Province,
Canada

The result of the varied geographical (or spatial) influences is a
cultural landscape. Without wishing to return to a conception of
geography as a discipline providing 'explanatory descriptions of
landscapes', it is possible, nevertheless, to accept that cultural
landscapes, even if they cannot provide all the clues, do give useful
indications of the way in which natural and man-made influences
interact and have interacted. The very archaic nature of certain
landscapes and the malfunctioning of the system within which they
exist are themselves significant. Men's lives are framed within an

Fig. 1.2 Settlement pattern in the prairie provinces of Canada

environment whose visible emanation is the cultural landscape. Although geographers in highly developed industrial countries tend to play down the relationship between man and his physical environment, many human communities still live in conditions where their links with nature are close. The severance of these links and the growing artificiality of man's environment have in the last few decades ceased to be looked upon as a sign of human progress or an indication of man's dominance over nature. Experience has taught us that it is wise to work with, rather than against, nature and to take note of the delicate equilibrium achieved in natural ecosystems.

In the ultimate analysis men can never be detached from their environment even if they proclaim their independence from it. All cultures or civilizations draw some strength and derive characteristics from the physical environments from which they evolved.

The study of spatial organization

Spatial organization is an expression used more and more by geographers, and it is important to reintroduce the notion of space in geographical discussion. While geography remained the study of the interaction of man and his environment, the latter tended to be conceived as the natural environment, or natural regions. Yet man's impact on the landscape does not occur anarchically, spontaneously and haphazardly. Rather does it result in certain spatial patterns. Environments are not just perceived in terms of their relief, soils and climate, but also by their size and shape, they are evaluated in terms of their accessibility in time and by cost. Individuals, families, villagers, citizens and nations tend to perceive, build and divide environments into regions whose poles of attraction are population centres which, themselves, are the basis of spatial organization and consequently of spatial differentiation.

Let me elaborate. A farmer who is pioneering new lands is likely to decide on his land-use according to the market's needs in a nearby town, according to transport facilities to the town and according to the town's facilities for transforming his produce into manufactured or semi-manufactured goods. His land-use is also going to be affected by the distance of each field from his farmhouse. Towns are themselves spatially structured partly by the functional specializations which occur within them (central business districts, industrial areas, residential areas) and partly by the transport networks which radiate out from them.

However, in spite of the generalized nature of the processes which result in spatial organization, the patterns differ markedly. They vary in accordance with the different levels of development, and with the different historical evolutions of societies. This is evident if one considers the many different cultural landscapes in the world.

The organization of space around an industrial centre or a service centre results in a *regional division of space*, though regions are of different sizes and may nest into one another in a hierarchical manner. The area of each functional region corresponds theoretically with the zone of influence of each town, which in fact means that their limits are movable and imprecise. In reality, regions are made evident by administrative divisions, by the pattern woven by their infrastructure (roads, railways, pipelines, sewerage, etc.) and by the flows which run along such an infrastructure. As these physical manifestations of regions are evident in the landscape, there results a great diversity of different regions.

These three major concepts cover broadly the nature of modern geography. They do not, however, do away with all ambiguities, some of which it is necessary to point out.

First, it is increasingly difficult to reconcile the dual character of geography as an earth science and as a social or behavioural science. The general tendency is for most sciences to become specialized and geography has not escaped this tendency given its antiquity. For the last 50 years, increasing subdivisions of the field has been a hallmark of geography, many regional geographers believing that the successive detailed descriptions of relief, climate, soil, agriculture, industry and communications, sufficed to draw up a regional description of an area. This is why such a specialization makes more necessary than ever a holistic approach to the study of spatial organization. Hence the dual character of geography results in geographers being trained in a rich and wide field.

Secondly, geography is constantly being pulled in different directions by the content that the subject studies, be this population, communities, landscapes or spatial organization. For example, it is true that people are the main agents of geographical or spatial change and that consequently it is important to study population structures and population dynamics. Unfortunately, population study often becomes an end in itself rather than a means of understanding one of the causes of spatial differentiation and organization. There is a need, therefore, to keep a balance between what is purely demography and what are the geographical consequences of demographic processes; otherwise geography might be reduced to a kind of 'demo-geography' consisting of comments on distribution of population maps and on various population indices. Yet the causes and manifestations of man's occupation of environmental space are basically the results of man's actions in, for example, shaping rural, urban and industrial landscapes. Thus it is human behaviour, attitudes, perceptions, beliefs, symbols about the environment, that is, all that constitutes a culture, which is at the heart of geographical analysis as elements of an explanation of spatial organization rather than as content.

Thirdly, geography as a discipline is often torn between explaining something unique and exceptional and dealing, like the natural sciences, in generalities. Some geographers are tempted to describe the character of each region, to concentrate on regional analysis, instead of trying to compare and bring out what are the universal characteristics of areas, noting at the same time what may slightly modify the general pattern from one area to the next. Science must be comparative and must bring out what is universal. Fortunately, the spatial analysis of the 'new geography' is more concerned with these general concepts which tended to be forgotten by the regional geographers.

Fourthly, geographers do not always distinguish clearly enough between different scales of analysis, yet data change their significance according to the scale at which they are being examined. The geographical analysis of the rearing of cattle for beef and of the trade in meat linked to it, cannot be done in the same way as that of an Argentine *estancia*. Similarly, the analysis of the distribution of urban central places in Europe cannot be done in a manner appropriate to the analysis of the structure of an old town central core. Yet geographers are sometimes guilty of not realizing that tackling problems at different scales requires an adjustment in concepts and terminology.

The values of geographical education

It is possible to look upon geographical education as having:
1. absolute value, that is, values inherent in geography as a discipline of mind;
2. relative value, that is, values which reside in geography's association with other disciplines, whether these are taught separately or in some integrated scheme of natural or social sciences. Let us deal with this aspect first.

The relative value of geographical education

(a) Learning geography depends on the analysis of data, some of which are concentrated and visible, such as what is directly observable in the field or indirectly observable through maps and photographs. Geography can therefore be anchored in the reality of the student's environment. But this reality is common also to the economist, the artist, the geologist and the novelist or poet. Thus a theme like towns is capable of evoking a number of lines of inquiry and the student can become aware how different disciplines structure the reality around him. Teachers can therefore use such themes for a multi-disciplinary approach to education. Geographical education can contribute to such an approach by its concern with spatial matters and the skills it employs, such as quantitative methods, games and simulations and field techniques.

(b) Geography may make students aware how complex the causes of events really are, it may show them that in the search for the explanation of phenomena, the interaction of various factors is the norm. All spatial structures, all regional patterns are the result of natural and human factors, of a succession of events often going to the distant past, whose traces remain unevenly distributed as relics over the landscape. The human factors may be political, historical, economic, sociological or psychological. This spatial analysis helps to make students aware that 'nothing is simple', but rather that simplistic explanations and simple cause-and-effect interpretations of events are rarely correct.

(c) The learning of geography contributes to the student's understanding of his habitat and of near and distant environments; it is important that he should not be immersed in a world of shapes, sizes and colours which have no meaning for him. It is essential that pupils be introduced progressively to the problems posed by man's occupation of his earthly habitat, e.g. his role, his powers, his weaknesses; the influence of world population growth, the nature and effects of irregular climatic variations.

(d) Through geography, students may discover man's prodigious creative ability. Those who view collections of aerial photographs are always amazed at the cultural landscapes which they portray; for example, rice terraces in South-east Asia, intensive poly-culture areas, the rectilinear patterns of North American plains. They may view critically, and with some anxiety, shanty towns, suburban sprawl, old industrialized areas in need of renovation and coastal areas disfigured by excessive urbanization. Thus by making evident the diversity of man's actions on the landscape, geography may motivate students to query the present state of things.

In associating the concepts of time and space, geography teaching can introduce young people to the idea that situations evolve over time, that is, they involve duration and trends.

(e) Geography can demonstrate that different civilizations have had different ways of structuring space, and that each way could be understood and therefore respected. This is vital in a world tending to be organized according to a model provided by Western post-industrial societies. By reconsidering its relationship to its past and present environment, each nation can rediscover its own virtues and its own solutions to the problem of organizing its space.

(f) Geography may also contribute to the understanding of the basic interdependence of all nations and the need for each individual to see himself as dependent also on neighbours near and far, to be conscious also of the differing levels of development in different regions, countries and continents.

In order that these aims might be achieved, considerable thought needs to be given to the way they can be translated into more specific educational objectives. This is illustrated in Chapters 9 and 10.

The values inherent in geography

Geographical analysis is of little use if it does not lead ultimately to an evaluation of the results of men's actions, since the objectives which lead to the peopling of certain areas and the exploitation of resources are an expression of certain values held by men.

The different values to be considered are:

(a) *Economic values* which often lead exclusively to the exploitation of mineral, agricultural, industrial and even touristic resources. The main aim is to make a profit with a minimum of investment, and the minimum cost location is sought. Such values are often the only ones evident when countries and regions are beginning their economic development. They have often resulted in the birth of industrial blight, of exclusively industrial towns, of concrete ribbons of tourist housing along coastlines. It is these values which have led to ugly conurbations, where the services are often inadequate and green spaces non-existent.

(b) Social values which aim to limit the spatial inequalities and injustices by seeking to prevent major disparities between regions, such as by the avoidance of ghettos and shanty towns through the provision of real investments.

(c) Ecological values which take note of the concept of dynamic equilibrium in nature and its application in situations where human intervention occurs. If such values exist in the minds of men responsible for development, then they can respect such ecological thresholds as are known to enable waste products to be absorbed through natural processes without destroying an equilibrium which it would prove difficult to restore.

(d) Spatial values which are positive values concerning all aspects of space; when for example decisions are taken to locate a factory, a motorway or a new town; then not only the advantages of each location are noted but also the impact of such a decision on other elements in the landscape, the social and environmental consequences and costs, so that ultimately a harmonious environment is created.

Young people are prone, given their idealism and their priorities, to seek what seem to them simple direct solutions to problems. It is therefore important, by means of case studies, of simulation exercises and games, to make them aware of not only the difficulties of the choices to be made but also of the relative nature of the values expressed in a choice, values which are relative to the cultures where the choices are made, to the precise situation of the choice and to the nature of the economic development of the society concerned.

It is nevertheless through these values that the cultural landscape is created through the intermediary of political, economic, cultural and social forces. Unfortunately such values are often based on a regrettable ignorance of the nature of the environment.

Education for spatial competence

Such research as has been undertaken seems to reveal a considerable inability on the part of the average man to operate effectively in a spatial context. Thus, while the citizen and worker are, to a greater or lesser degree, aware of such social and economic realities as their relationship to their firm, to their local authority and to their government, they seem to be but faintly aware of their environment: that is, of their spatial relationships with all that surrounds them, and consider these to be given and immutable. They do not seem to consider such relationships as simply the result of decisions taken by private individuals or organizations or public bodies.

Geographical education can therefore be looked upon as education for spatial awareness, carried out through training in the field and in the laboratory with maps, aerial photographs and other resources. This 'graphicacy' is a necessary complement to education for literacy and numeracy. Too many people suffer from a form of graphical illiteracy and spatial incompetence.

Conclusion

The aims and values of geographical education are not negligible even if they appear relatively simple. No inhabitant of this earth is truly educated, that is, he has not become an autonomous and responsible citizen until he has acquired a geographical education, not to say geographical 'reflexes'.

To have geographical 'reflexes' is:

- to perceive one's environment in the multiplicity and complexity of its constituent parts, to perceive it and not simply to look at it without really seeing it;
- to understand what one sees in terms of the locations, the relationships, the networks; that is, not to submit passively to the sense impressions of the world as it evolves, but to understand the world in terms of one's knowledge, in terms of models, in terms of analogies and previous points of reference;
- to be able to operate in space, by being able to locate one's position and orientate oneself, whether inside a town, or a rural area, or on a mountainside and to be able to read the landscape and assess the forces which have shaped it;
- to be able to seek explanations of what appears to be surprising and strange and to know roughly from where these explanations may come;
- to know that spatial phenomena are not just the result of a multitude of formless chance events to be considered as given, but that all such phenomena by their location, shape and spatial interactions result from socio-economic and cultural processes which are replicable and therefore may be predicted;
- to know that all locations and all organization or space whether controlled or spontaneous are manifestations of values whether these be social, economic, cultural or ecological values.

It is such geographical 'reflexes' which will help to develop in men a greater consciousness of their responsibility for human communities and their habitat. Geographical education should also help to clarify current issues. Only too often current world problems have been dramatized and orchestrated by the mass media. This has resulted in a sense of culpability with respect to nature as well, and a sense of the hopelessness of a struggle against inexorable demographic pressures, associated with an ignorance of the main issues. Geography can help to place such problems against a realistic background and therefore contribute modestly to a constructive solution. It also contributes to general literacy and numeracy and graphicacy.

The history of man's interaction with his environment is a long one. If man's folly seems to obsess certain commentators, one must not forget that in the cultural landscape of today one can also read the results of secular adjustments, of a kind of geographical wisdom not to say 'geo-sophy'.

CHAPTER 2

Mental development and the learning of geography

MICHAEL C. NAISH

Introduction

This chapter is concerned with the consideration of certain psychological variables which may influence the teaching and learning of geography. It is necessarily selective, since this is a complex and substantial area of study. The basic idea is that it is possible to apply the findings of psychological research to the particular problems of the study, teaching and learning of geography. In this introduction an attempt is made to substantiate this idea, thus introducing the selected areas of psychological study.

The development of children's thinking

The idea of children as empty vessels, waiting to be filled with knowledge by the teacher, is no longer acceptable. It assumed that children were miniature adults with the same level of development of mental faculties as their elders, and that they simply needed to be provided with information so that these faculties might be 'exercised'. The logical teaching strategy for this model was that of the teacher acting as the fount of knowledge, pouring it out for the children to absorb.

This limited understanding of children's mental make-up must be discarded in the light of evidence from studies in child development led by the work of the Swiss psychologist, Jean Piaget. These studies show that children's thinking develops as they mature and gain experience of their environment. It is qualitatively different from the thinking of adults, and passes through a series of developmental stages. One of the most fundamental questions for the geography teacher must be: 'Just what sort of thinking are these children in this particular class capable of achieving?' His or her problem is made more difficult by the fact that different children in the class may have reached different stages in the development of their mental operations, but at least the work of Piaget and others provides us with a general framework within which we can structure our understanding of children's thinking. Obviously our approach to teaching a particular group of children will be influenced by our understanding of the nature of their mental operations.

The shift to a conceptual basis for geographical study

These developments in our knowledge of children's thinking have been accompanied by important changes in geography in schools. One of the most significant of these is the shift in objectives away from explanatory description of parts of the world towards the understanding of the central concepts and principles of geographical study. The emphasis in the early regional work was on description rather than explanation, since teachers were constrained by attempts to study extensive areas of the world. This led to rather superficial study, mainly involving verbal skills, and laying stress on the learning of factual information.

Efforts are now being made to concentrate on the understanding of the key ideas of geography. This is based on the notion that each discipline has certain key concepts which form the core of the subject, and to which all studies are related. There have been many attempts to classify these concepts. In one such study, Catling (1976), considers such attempts and suggests that the central ideas of geography can be reduced to three 'distinct but fundamentally interrelated concepts'. These are 'spatial location', 'spatial distribution' and 'spatial relations'. He calls these the fundamental organizational concepts in geography, and argues that various ideas about the nature of geography such as those concerned with the relationships between man and his environment, an ecosystem approach or a regional viewpoint, may be reduced to these three basic concepts. It could be argued even that current developments in radical and humanistic geography must still be concerned with these fundamental concepts if researchers wish their work to be accepted as geographical in nature. Indeed, if we accept that a key question for radical geography is 'who gets what, where?', and that one for humanistic geography is 'how do individuals develop a sense of place?', then we can see that modern developments in geography are still concerned, at their core, with certain fundamental ideas about space and place. An early example of the application of the idea of key concepts to a geography curriculum is provided in Table 2.1, where the curriculum is based on a number of themes, including farming, settlement and environmental problems, through which key concepts are progressively developed.

Table 2.1 A conceptual syllabus in human geography. (*Source:* From Walker 1976. *See also:* Walker 1975)

Themes	Concepts		
	Location	*Interaction*	*Distance*
Local area and land-use in Britain	Location of points (co-ordinates, grid refs, latitude and longitude); location of areas, types of towns, zones in towns, land-use zones, spheres of influence	Factors influencing zoning in towns and countryside, need for conservation	Straight line, road and time distance; route planning (shopping and road journeys)
Farming	Agricultural land-use patterns	Factors influencing land-use: relief, soils, climate, distance, scale of operations, demand, government actions and human attitudes and knowledge; trade	Effect on land-use, both on a farm and in terms of distance to a market
Industry and communications	Location of industry	Factors affecting location of industry: raw materials, power, labour, markets, capital, individual and government actions and chance	Effect on least-cost locations
	Networks	Factors influencing types of networks: distance, type of goods, etc; trade	Accessibility; route efficiency; time and cost distance

Scale	Change	Representation
Measurement of scale, use of scale on maps, Hierarchy of shopping centres	Changing patterns of land-use and building styles	Maps, graphs, photographs, diagrams
Scale of operations, e.g. size and organization of farms	Changing patterns of agricultural land-use	Maps/topology, graphs, photographs, diagrams, models
Economies of scale influencing location	Changing patterns of industrial location; industrial inertia	Maps/topology, graphs, diagrams, models
Size of flows and routeways	Changing networks	

(vertical axis label between Scale and Change columns: ▸world ... EXAMPLES ON VARIOUS SCALES: Local)

table continues overleaf

Themes			**Concepts**
	Location	*Interaction*	*Distance*
Settlement	Types of settlements; siting, urban zoning, spheres of influence	Factors influencing siting of settlements, and functional zoning: resource availability, chance, association and segregation, distance, government and individual actions etc.	Effect on spacing of settlements, range of goods and services, etc., efficiency of route
Environmental problems	Location of developed and developing countries; distribution of population, location of productive and unproductive land, areas subject to natural disasters, areas of natural beauty, etc.	Man as a part of the ecosystem, need for conservation; factors influencing the stage of development; aid	Effect on diffusion of ideas and level of knowledge

Source: Based on Walker 1976

Conceptual learning and perception

Analysis of the conceptual structure of geography has thus led to attempts to base school learning on the understanding, not only of key concepts, but also of those less fundamental concepts which hang upon them. At the same time, more emphasis is being placed on the practice of skills, as students are encouraged to employ 'research' techniques to investigate the principles which underlie geographical study.

It is thus obvious that as teachers, we need to know about the nature of concepts. Are they concrete or abstract? Can they be

Scale		Change	Representation
Hierarchy of settlements	→world	Changing functions of settlements; changing patterns of urban land-use	Maps, graphs, diagrams, photographs, models
Scale of world problems – of population and food supply, pollution, etc.	EXAMPLES ON VARIOUS SCALES: Local	Changing technology; changing attitudes	Maps/topology, graphs, diagrams, photographs, models

arranged in a hierarchical order? What is their level of difficulty for children's understanding? How do children come to acquire understanding of concepts? Our approach to teaching geography will need to be specially geared to achieve effective learning of concepts, principles and skills. Since this approach will be based on inquiry learning, we shall also need to consider the perceptual difficulties which children find when faced with resources for geographical study: the environment, maps, pictures and other sources of data.

These, then, are the psychological questions which we shall now attempt to explore further: the development of children's thinking, conceptual learning and perception.

The development of children's thinking

When planning classroom or field experiences for children, the geography teacher needs to consider a variety of factors concerning the nature and state of his pupils (see Ch. 9). He obviously wishes to plan work, or provide the opportunity for work at a suitable level for their present understanding, and in such a manner that they will be challenged and stretched to a new level of understanding. Among the factors to be considered, therefore, are their previous learning, their level of motivation and their general mental ability. As was suggested earlier, the work of Piaget and other developmental psychologists provides us with a framework within which we can appreciate the stage of mental development of our pupils in general terms. A generalized outline of some of the findings of Piaget will now follow.

Piagetian theory

The work of Jean Piaget has been described as a clinical approach to the understanding of children's thinking. In essence his technique has been to engage in face-to-face questioning of and talking with children to discover the nature and quality of their conceptual understanding at different ages from birth to adolescence. The main concepts involved in these studies are number, time, velocity, space, geometry, chance and morality. As Child (1973) suggests, the theories which emerge from this work are genetic, maturational and hierarchical in nature: genetic in that they suggest that higher processes evolve from 'biological mechanisms which are rooted in the development of an individual's nervous system'; maturational in that conceptual understanding grows through a number of distinct phases; and hierarchical in that the individual must pass through one stage before the next becomes possible. While biological factors and educational transmissions are important in the development of conceptual understanding for Piaget, he stresses the active exploration by the child of his own environment as of key significance in cognitive growth.

Piaget has coined certain technical terms which he employs to describe the process of concept development. Some of the most important of these are included in the following attempt to explain the way in which the child makes use of his exploratory activity in building his mental image of his world.

As the child registers new experiences, these are measured against what he already knows, and *assimilated* to his previous learning. If there is a mismatch between the past and the new experience, then he will adjust, or *accommodate* the previous learning so as to assimilate the new, thus moving towards *equilibration*. The new learning disturbs his state of mental equilibrium, and accommodation is compensation for this external disturbance. Equilibration is putting experiences into relation with one another so as to achieve a system which is stable, consistent and non-contradictory (Piaget 1962). Piaget calls such a system a *schema* (pl. *schemata*), and we can say that through assimilation and accommodation, experiences are organized into schemata, which are patterns of knowing, and therefore act as guides for appropriate behaviour. In this way, experiences become *internalized* so that the child can represent his world mentally. Thought, for Piaget, is internalized action, and he uses the term *operation* to describe the carrying-out of activities in one's imagination, that is mentally.

Perhaps an example may help to make all this more clear. Imagine that a child gains the idea of the placing of dwellings in his home village through his own experience. He then visits a neighbouring village where groupings of dwellings are very different, and so he has to accommodate his earlier idea of the spatial arrangement of dwellings in a village by assimilating this new experience. In doing this, he is moving towards equilibration with this idea, balancing one experience against another to modify the general notion which he holds of dwellings and the way they are grouped in villages. He now has a new schema for viewing the situation in other villages, and indeed in towns and cities.

Stages of mental development

Adults are normally capable of mental operations at an advanced abstract and logical level. For educators, one of the most important facets of Piaget's work is the demonstration of the stages which lead to the development of formal operations. These stages are called:

Stage		Age range
I	Sensori-motor	0–2
II	Pre-operational	
	(A) Pre-conceptual	2–4
	(B) Intuitive	4–7
III	Concrete operations	7–11½
IV	Formal operations	11½ +

The main characteristics of the stages are now summarized.

I Sensori-motor stage

Development in this stage of babyhood depends on actions, movements and perceptions through the senses, which become co-ordinated in a relatively stable way. Piaget describes how, without language, the baby begins to build up schemata through intelligent activity. One of the major developments of the sensori-motor stage is constructing the schema of the permanent object, when, for example, the child understands that although a ball has rolled behind a chair, it is still there, and may be searched for at a later time. The child also starts to build up ideas of space, time and causality during this stage. A further important development is the beginning of the understanding of *reversibility* in action as the child discovers that he can not only get from A to B, but also back again from B to A by retracing the route. This is not yet a representation in thought, but is performed in action. It is sensori-motor learning.

II(A) Pre-conceptual stage

This stage is pre-operational because the child is not yet carrying out fully internalized mental activities. He is still linked to perception and to an egocentric outlook, being unable to view things from another's point of view. As language develops, from about 18 months, play can become symbolic, and the child can represent objects in their absence. Thus a cardboard box can become a ship or a house, and, through language, he can begin to invoke objects which are not present perceptually, that is, not in his field of vision. He can reconstruct the past and plan for the immediate future, since he becomes able to think of objects not present, but distant in space. Now imitations and actions become internalized as thought and registered through language. This stage is 'pre-conceptual' because he is not yet able to form concepts by reasoning inductively from particular cases to generalizations. Rather he uses *transductive* reasoning, going from one particular instance to another. Child (1973) gives an example of his 3½-year-old daughter exclaiming, on seeing her mother combing her hair, 'Mummy is combing her hair. She is going shopping.' The reasoning here is that since A occurred with B once, then A must always occur with B.

II(B) Intuitive stage

In this stage, the child is still dependent on superficial perceptions of his environment, and so he forms his ideas impressionistically or intuitively. In attempting explanation, he will be content with one piece of evidence only, basing his conclusions on this. One of the main characteristics of this stage is that the child lacks *conservation*. This is illustrated in Fig. 2.1. In stage i, two balls of clay are rolled, and the child agrees that they are the same weight. In stage ii, one of the balls is rolled into a sausage shape, and when asked which is the heavier, the child may say that the sausage shape, B, is lighter,

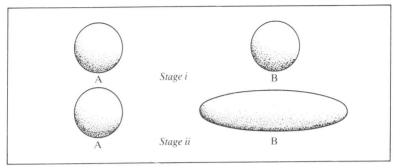

Fig. 2.1 A conservation problem

because it is thinner. He is said to lack the ability to conserve weight, because he centres on only one dimension of the plasticine shapes, and lacks the concept of reversibility, that is, the understanding that the sausage may be rolled back into the ball shape. A child in the intuitive stage of thinking may lack conservation of weight, quantity, volume and number. He is still clearly dependent on what he sees, that is, on perception, rather than what he reasons. This understanding of conservation develops during the next stage, that of concrete operations.

III Concrete operations

The child develops understanding of basic concepts needed for later logical thinking during this stage. These include conservation, inclusion, seriation and reversibility. Much of this development is concerned with analysis and classification, two important skills in concept-building. The concrete operational child can classify objects according to their similarities and differences and can include subclasses within more general classes. He also learns to serialize objects by arranging them according to size or progressive weight. He is organizing his perception and understanding of the world in a way which will help him to internalize his experiences and thus later be capable of manipulating them as thoughts in an abstract and logical manner.

One of the most important characteristics for teachers to understand about the stage of concrete operations is the nature of the inconsistencies the child displays, up to adolescence, when attempting explanations. He remains unable to look at a problem as a whole and take all factors into account. As McNaughton (1966) points out, the concrete-operational child finds it difficult to move away from the concrete relationships he observes, in order to consider possible explanations and set up hypotheses which may be tested to see how far they are compatible with the observed concrete situation.

An example of this was observed when a class of able 12-year-old boys in a London school was presented with the problem in Fig. 2.2. They had examined case studies of hydroelectric and irrigation schemes and were now required to select the best location for such a scheme in the area shown on the map, from points A to D. When asked to give reasons for their choice, it was clear that many of these

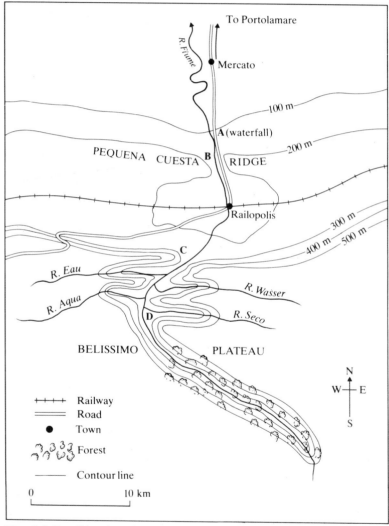

Fig. 2.2 Possible sites for a dam on the River Fiume in Unaria – a hypothetical case study. (From an idea for a geography lesson devised by N. J. Graves)

boys made their decision on the basis of one, or sometimes two factors only. They were not able to weigh all the complex variables together, so as to come to a balanced conclusion.

The concrete-operational thinker still has problems in reasoning about relationships in propositions. When faced with a problem such as 'Birmingham is smaller than London, Birmingham is larger than Southampton, which is the largest of the three?' the child is up against the difficulties of seriation, not with concrete objects within his experience, but with verbal statements. Piaget claims that the problem is rarely solved before the age of 12.

IV Formal operations, or propositional operations

Rapid mental development becomes possible as the child acquires the crucial skills of the concrete-operational stage, and, no longer hamstrung by an egocentric outlook, is able to survey mentally many possibilities from various points of view. Beard (1969) succinctly summarizes the capacities of the teenaged formal thinker, and the following list is based on her summary, some items being directly quoted.

The student having reached the stage of formal operations can:

(a) accept assumptions for the sake of argument;

(b) make a succession of hypotheses which he is able to express in propositions and to test against reality;

(c) begin to look for general properties which enable him to give exhaustive definitions, to state general laws and to see common meanings in proverbs or other verbal material;

(d) go beyond the tangible, finite and familiar in spatial concepts, to conceive the infinitely small and to invent imaginary systems;

(e) become conscious of his own thinking, reflecting on it to provide logical justifications for judgements he makes;

(f) deal with a wide variety of complex relations such as proportionality or correlation.

For the teacher, the main impact of this list must be that if these are the operations which develop in children from the age of about 11½ years, then before they have reached this stage, there are obvious limitations on the forms of mental activity of which they are capable. It is important for the teacher to realize that there will be great variability between children of the same chronological age where their mental development is concerned. A concrete-operational child, for instance, may be advanced where conservation is concerned, but less advanced in his understanding of seriation. It is also clear that some people reach full development in formal operations very late, and some not at all in certain facets of propositional thought. The theory needs to be accepted as a *framework* for the understanding of the development of thinking, rather than as a rigid prescription.

Naturally an important and widely discussed theory such as that of Piaget and his associates, does not escape critical appraisal. Critics of the theory (see Brown and Desforges 1979) have quarrelled with the clinical experimental method, questioned the age ranges assigned to the stages, and disagreed with some of the details of the findings. It has been claimed that Piaget takes too little account of the complexities of language development, yet language was the major source of data for him. Some have suggested that inadequate consideration has been given to individual differences between children, and the varying nature of their experiences. Recently too, it has been claimed that Piaget attributed too much structure and system to the child's thought. For some, the very idea of stages is brought into question when considering the variability of individual development.

Despite these criticisms, the many replications and further experiments based on Piaget's work are testimony to its seminal quality, and there is no doubt that very significant implications for teaching and learning arise from his work.

Although most of the research so far has been undertaken in developed countries, and commonly with socially advantaged children, the evidence points to the fact that the theory applies to children of different social and ethnic backgrounds (see for example, Sigel and Hooper 1968). The need for further work in a wide variety of cultures is obvious. Brown and Desforges (1979) conclude their critical assessment of Piaget with the statement that 'it is fitting that a theory should provide us with a step on which we can reach new levels of understanding. We feel that the time has come to take that step.'

Implications for the teaching of geography

This summary of the stages in the development of thinking has been essential if we are to begin to appreciate the significance of the findings for the teaching of geography. Those who were previously unfamiliar with the theory will still have an incomplete understanding of it, since they have been faced by what, for them, are unfamiliar concepts, and conceptual learning is a slow process. Readers are strongly advised to consult more complete descriptions such as those provided in a good general psychology textbook (e.g. Child 1973), or in a book specifically dealing with Piaget (e.g. Beard 1969), or in a book on cognitive development (e.g. Turner 1975 or Donaldson 1978).

Some suggestions as to the implications of the theory for the teaching and learning of geography now follow:

(a) From the early years of the century, James Fairgrieve (1926) was recommending that in the teaching of geography we should move from the known to the unknown, from the particular to the general and from the concrete to the abstract. This was based on intuition and experience, but the work of Piaget and his associates and replicators has more than justified these basic teaching principles, making it clear that concrete activity precedes propositional thinking. Even experienced adults know the value they attribute to a concrete example when faced with a difficult abstract idea in a book or a lecture.

With younger children, up to the age of about 14, it remains important to follow Fairgrieve's tenets for much of their learning. Sometimes, however, the route may be varied in an effort to lead them on to more advanced thinking skills. Thus, while the normal route for younger children will be to move towards generalizations from the study of specific examples, they may also test out their generalizations by examination of particular cases. For example, a class might produce a diagram showing model locations of villages based on a series of case studies. They could then go on to test the models by further case studies in a contrasting environment.

(b) The question of whether learning geography can help to accelerate children through the stages of cognitive development is clearly of great importance. Much attention has been given to this problem of possible acceleration through training, and the evidence is far from clear. McNaughton (1966) is hopeful that training may be possible and advantageous, suggesting that the writing of Piaget, Inhelder and others shows evidence of the advantages for mental growth of planned manipulation of the learning environment. He indicates the importance, for instance, of Inhelder's work showing how children profited from regular study sessions to improve their reasoning skills. He also stresses the advantages of questioning children about the nature of relationships between the concrete details of what they are studying.

Halford (1972) finds scant evidence that any training procedure has so far changed the operations of child thought. His review of various studies indicates that almost any method works sometimes, and no method works for all children. Almy (1967) stresses the importance of readiness, reporting that attempts to train for specific tasks seem likely to be effective only where the children show 'some uncertainty or readiness' to move to a further stage.

Perhaps we may conclude that the evidence suggests that accelerated development is possible, but that so far prescriptions for teaching techniques designed to achieve this are difficult to recommend. What is clear is that direct teaching of concepts may not be effective, since incomplete understanding may result.

(c) It is likely, then, that the best function of the teacher is to ensure that the children are given thorough support in each stage of development through the learning activities upon which they are engaged. In the pre-conceptual stage, for instance, a varied and

stimulating environment should be provided in the classroom, together with visits outside, because if self-initiated activity is important in mental development, the teacher must provide the child with an environment conducive to active, if controlled learning.

(d) In the concrete-operational years, about 7 to 12, we need to put the child in a position to work on real-life concrete cases in building up his understanding of the world. McNaughton (1966) claims that it is the quality of the experience which counts in determining the stage of a child's mathematical understanding, and so it follows that we need to consider the quality of the experience in our geography teaching, providing, during this stage, sound and varied concrete experiences from which later abstractions can develop. Thus in geography, we shall emphasize case studies based on real-life examples, fieldwork dealing with study at first hand, and games and simulations which involve children in manipulating, in a concrete fashion, notions which they will later internalize for propositional thinking. We shall stress oral work, talking in small groups, in games and simulations; talking about concrete resources, and questioning about relationships, in recognition that language is an important aid to internalization.

Written work will be planned so as to help children use language constructively in their thinking. Language helps us to structure our thinking, and in writing we sometimes need to be precise about our thoughts, and consider how they may effectively be communicated. We shall therefore provide varied opportunities for writing, giving the children a sense of different categories of audience.

The case for an inquiry approach to learning is obvious. To engage children in active exploration of their environment, the teacher will provide them with resources for study, involving them in open or guided inquiry. Thus again, he offers them the opportunity to deal with concrete materials in an active manner. This takes account of Piaget's basic notion of the child as an open, active, self-regulating system.

(e) There are clear implications for curriculum planning, which should ensure that the curriculum, in terms of key concepts and skills, takes note of the critical periods for mental growth. The work of Rhys, for example, shows how the ability to solve problems about spatial matters in areas remote from the child's personal first-hand experience, is fully developed only with the onset of formal operations. He faced children aged 9 to 16 years with five problems in geography and, in analysing their answers, recognized four major response levels, as in Table 2.2 (Rhys 1966 and 1972).

The children in this experiment had not achieved true formal operations until the age of about 15, and we can see that attempts to engage them in work of too abstract a nature would have been of little value earlier in their geographical studies. At the same time it would seem to be important to give children some indication of the problems they will later be able to cope with. They must be stretched to some extent at each stage, so that there is the challenge of problems as yet unsolved, tasks as yet not fully approachable. The sample for Rhys's study was limited, but it is obvious that similar studies in a variety of cultural, ethnic and social settings would be invaluable (see Peel 1971 for further consideration of this question of adolescent thinking).

Table 2.2 Major response levels for children faced with problems of a geographical nature about spatially remote areas. (*Source:* Rhys 1966, 1972)

Response level	Age	Mental age	Principal features
I	11.0 and below	12.0 and below	Not reality orientated
II	12.0–12.6	13.0–13.6	Reality orientated; single piece of evidence used
III	*c.* 13.6	14.0–14.6	Several pieces of evidence combined; able to relate cause and effect
IV	14.6 and above	15.6 and above	Comprehensive judgement based upon hypothetico-deductive reasoning

Curriculum designers should take note of those abilities (pp.41–43) which develop with the growth of logical thinking. It would seem appropriate to provide opportunities for accurate and thorough descriptive work in the concrete-operational stage, leading on to problem-solving in the later stages. In this way, students would be well equipped to move towards model-building and hypothesis testing in their adolescent or teenage years, following the research methods for modern geography.

Moral judgement and moral development

As a conclusion to this section on the development of children's thinking, we need to turn to consider questions of moral judgement on the part of the child. With the increasing commitment of many geographers to the application of their findings to questions of social and spatial inequality, as well as to environmental problems, there is a greater readiness on the part of many teachers to involve their students in the study of issues which are clearly far from value-free.

Such issues may well be of considerable significance for the education of young people, and an open approach is required if value-loaded questions are to be considered in the classroom and the field.

It could be argued that students should understand the part played by attitudes and values in decision-making about the use of space or the management of an environment. Decisions about the routing of an urban motorway, for example, may be influenced by the values held by certain groups in society. Students should consider the views of the various factions in such a contentious issue, in order to appreciate that in such cases, political power may be a significant locational factor.

At the same time, it could be argued, students, particularly in the older age group (twelve years and over), should be encouraged to think rationally about value-laden issues, and to come to their own conclusions as to what view they would be prepared to support themselves. They will inevitably become involved in questions of morals and ethics if they are encouraged to do this.

It is important, therefore, for teachers to appreciate that children of differing ages will show differences in their moral judgements. Piaget (1932) was interested in explaining how children come to make judgements about what they ought to do, or what ought to happen in certain circumstances. How do they learn to distinguish between good and bad, right and wrong, just and unjust? He was not able to propose definite sequential stages for this kind of learning and expression, but he did suggest that there were two different general moral dispositions, one found in the intuitive stage, and the other largely in the ten- to twelve-year-old, in the stage of late concrete operations.

In the intuitive stage, children focus their attention on observable consequences of actions, and are often willing to accept the absolute rules of outside authority. The consequences of an action are more important than the intentions behind it. In the late concrete-operational stage, they come to accept rules relative to particular events, and subject to change by mutual agreement. They are now able to consider the nature of intentions behind an action and the consequence of such action.

Lawrence Kohlberg began his longitudinal and cross-cultural studies of moral development in 1955, and in 1975, he discussed his 'Definition of Moral Stages' in an article entitled 'The cognitive-developmental approach to moral education' (Kohlberg 1975). Early work by Dewey and Piaget was developed and refined on a cross-cultural basis by Kohlberg who proposes in this article, three basic levels of moral development, elaborated into six stages as shown in Table 2.3. Each stage is an organized system of thought, and individuals are consistent in their level of moral judgement. They pass through the stages in sequence, and when an individual has reached a particular stage, he comprehends the lower stages within it. Kohlberg suggests that a person in the concrete-operational stage of thinking, in Piaget's terms, is limited to the pre-conventional level of moral development (Stages 1 and 2) while to achieve level III of moral development, a person's thinking must be fully formal operational.

Table 2.3 Kohlberg's definition of moral stages

1. Preconventional level

At this level, the child is responsive to cultural rules and labels of good and bad, right or wrong, but interprets these labels either in terms of the physical or the hedonistic consequences of action (punishment, reward, exchange of favors) or in terms of the physical power of those who enunciate the rules and labels. The level is divided into the following two stages:

Stage 1: *The punishment-and-obedience orientation.* The physical consequences of action determine its goodness or badness, regardless of the human meaning or value of these consequences. Avoidance of punishment and unquestioning deference to power are valued in their own right, not in terms of respect for an underlying moral order supported by punishment and authority (the latter being Stage 4).

Stage 2: *The instrumental–relativist orientation.* Right action consists of that which instrumentally satisfies one's own needs and occasionally the needs of others. Human relations are viewed in terms like those of the market place. Elements of fairness, of reciprocity, and of equal sharing are present, but they are always interpreted in a physical, pragmatic way. Reciprocity is a matter of 'you scratch my back and I'll scratch yours', not of loyalty, gratitude, or justice.

II. Conventional level

At this level, maintaining the expectations of the individual's family, group, or nation is perceived as valuable in its own right, regardless of immediate and obvious consequences. The attitude is not only one of *conformity* to personal expectations and social order, but of loyalty to it, of actively *maintaining*, supporting, and justifying the order, and of identifying with the persons or group involved in it. At this level, there are the following two stages:

Stage 3: *The interpersonal concordance or 'good boy–nice girl' orientation.* Good behavior is that which pleases or helps others and is approved by them. There is much conformity to stereotypical images of what is majority or 'natural' behavior. Behavior is frequently judged by intention – 'he means well' becomes important for the first time. One earns approval by being 'nice'.

Stage 4: *The 'law and order' orientation.* There is orientation toward authority, fixed rules, and the maintenance of the social order. Right behavior consists of doing one's duty, showing respect for authority, and maintaining the given social order for its own sake.

III. Postconventional, autonomous or principled level

At this level, there is a clear effort to define moral values and principles that have validity and application apart from the authority of the groups or persons holding these principles and apart from the individual's own identification with these groups. This level also has two stages:

Stage 5: *The social-contract, legalistic orientation*, generally with utilitarian overtones. Right action tends to be defined in terms of general individual rights and standards which have been critically examined and agreed upon by the whole society. There is a clear awareness of the relativism of personal values and opinions and a corresponding emphasis upon procedural rules for reaching consensus. Aside from what is constitutionally and democratically agreed upon, the right is a matter of personal 'values' and 'opinion'. The result is an emphasis upon the 'legal point of view', but with an emphasis upon the possibility of changing law in terms of rational considerations of social utility (rather than freezing it in terms of Stage 4 'law and order'). Outside the legal realm, free agreement and contract is the binding element of obligation. This is the 'official' morality of the American government and constitution.

Stage 6: *The universal–ethical–principle orientation.* Right is defined by the decision of conscience in accord with self-chosen *ethical principles* appealing to logical comprehensiveness, universality, and consistency. These principles are abstract and ethical (the Golden Rule, the categorical imperative); they are not concrete moral rules like the Ten Commandments. At heart, these are universal principles of *justice*, of the *reciprocity* and *equality* of human *rights*, and of respect for the dignity of human beings as *individual persons* ('From Is to Ought', pp. 164–5).

Reprinted from *The Journal of Philosophy*, 25 October 1973.

The implication is that in geography due consideration must be given to stages of moral development when we involve students in questions concerning attitudes and values. The stance currently being adopted by many teachers is one which encourages students to explore their own attitudes and values based on the consideration of issues raised within their geographical studies. There may be much to be gained from considering specific issues relevant to the immediate problems of the students themselves, and then working outwards towards the understanding of other people's needs. Once again it is a question of working from the specific to the general, at least in the early stages of learning. Role play can also be an effective means of learning where moral development is concerned, as it enables teachers to present students with the opportunity to see the other person's point of view through the roles adopted. Quite realistic tensions and pressures may be experienced in role-play activity.

Concepts and learning

Throughout the preceding section on the development of children's thinking, concepts and concept attainment have frequently been mentioned. In the introduction it was suggested that geographical curricula are being constructed along conceptual lines. It seems important at this stage to look further into the question of the nature of concepts, their value as the 'structural steel of thinking', and how we can encourage effective conceptual learning in geography.

The nature of concepts

If we are to become efficient at organizing children's learning so as to facilitate their understanding of concepts, then we need to be clear as to what we mean by a concept. Humans have the capacity to organize their experiences by categorizing them so that a whole fund of varied experiences can be subsumed under one concept that is named. In this way, we can make sense of our bewildering and multifarious environment, classifying our experiences and slotting them into our growing conceptual filing system. For Edith West (1971), 'Conceptualizing is the process of categorizing', and so we could say that a concept is an abstraction from events, situations, objects or ideas of the attributes which they have in common. Concepts result from the classification of these attributes, and they are given names, thus enabling us to put them into a system for recall and for use in communicating with others.

If, for example, we imagine the degree of categorizing and classification which goes into a young child's efforts to differentiate the concept of 'cat' from that of 'dog', we can see the sorts of operations employed in concept learning. The child is involved in recognizing those features of cats which can be classed as common to all cats: what psychologists call the *intensive features* of the concept. He also needs to categorize those characteristics which discriminate between cats and dogs, the *extensive features*, discriminating between concepts. He must go on to realize that cats and dogs are subsidiary classes of the inclusive class 'animals', and so on. Learning the name of the concept and being able to apply it correctly in communicating with others is an integral part of this learning process.

We can see that similar activities of analysis, classification, discrimination, synthesis and name-learning must be involved in learning concepts commonly used by geographers. What is involved, for example, in the young school-child's learning of concepts such as river, stream, lake, or of the discrimination needed to differentiate between mountain, hill, ridge and so on? The work of Milburn (1969) shows that in Britain, at least, writers of textbooks tend to assume a too advanced level of conceptual understanding in schoolchildren. Many terms commonly used in books for 11-year-olds were little understood by the children in his test population. These terms, the labels for concepts, included 'basin, bay, beach, canal, cape, cave, fog, lake, mist, mouth, pass, ridge, town, tributary, valley and waterfall'.

Classification of concepts

It will be seen that all the concepts in this list are concrete in nature, and we must assume that abstract concepts would create even more difficulty. The question therefore arises as to whether we can classify concepts in order of difficulty. We have already seen that some concepts are concrete, or in Gagné's terms, 'concepts by observation', since we can learn them by observing and contrasting concrete examples. Other concepts are less related to the concrete, and are called 'concepts by definition' by Gagné (1966). Some examples are:

Concepts by observation	*Concepts by definition*
kiss	love
weather	climate
port	hinterland

We can differentiate a port from other types of urban settlement by observation, but we can understand the concept of hinterland only by defining its attributes. It is not directly observable in its totality, although its representation may be observed when delineated on a map.

Another way of classifying concepts would be to attempt to organize them into a hierarchy with the most general, an organizing concept or key idea, at the top of the pyramid, and more specific objectives lower in the hierarchy, as shown in Fig. 2.3. It is

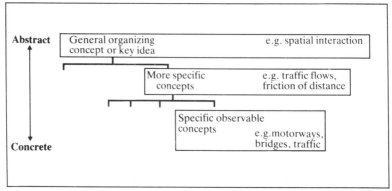

Fig. 2.3 A hierarchy of concepts

interesting to speculate on the value of such a hierarchy in curriculum construction, the theory being that specific, observable concepts will be learned first, in order that higher-level concepts may later be understood. A more detailed example of a hierarchy of concepts is given in Fig. 2.4.

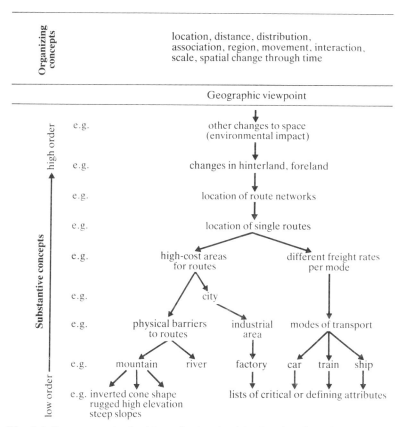

Fig. 2.4 Some aspects of a hierarchy involved in the planning of a transport network. (From a working paper of the Secondary Geographical Education Project of the Geography Teachers Association of Victoria, Australia, April 1975)

The chart reproduced in Table 2.4 sets out some criteria which might be used in considering the difficulty of concepts. This, too, could be of considerable value in curriculum design. The idea is, quite simply, that 'easy' concepts would occur early in a curriculum, 'more difficult' concepts later and 'very difficult' concepts towards the end. In the first row, for instance, we can see that concepts which the child has experienced directly, such as time and cost relationships

Table 2.4 Difficulty of concepts (these criteria must be considered together, not separately). (*Source:* From West 1971)

Criteria of difficulty	Scale of difficulty *Easy*		
Distance from child's experience	Within direct experience		
Distance from observed referents	Referents are phenomena which can be perceived through senses		
	Physical objects	Relationships Specified Defined operationally	Processes
Scope of concepts	Narrow scope		
	Few concepts subsumed under it		Relates few concepts
Certainty of presence of defining attributes	Always present		
Open-endedness of concepts	Closed and so reliable		
Way in which attributes of concept are related	Conjunctive (joint presence of several attributes)		

involved in his journey to school, are easier to understand than concepts which he has probably only experienced vicariously, such as time–cost of supersonic flight. In the second row, it is clear that concepts which are experienced in a concrete way, directly through the senses, are 'easier' than those based on idealized referents, or models. Perhaps the most constructive way to use the table would be to look down the columns, and so summarize 'easy' concepts, for example, as those which have distinct attributes present at all times, are of narrow scope, lack open-endedness and are experienced at first hand, through the senses. Examples of such concepts would include those listed as specific observable concepts in Fig. 2.3, while an example of a 'very difficult' concept would be 'spatial interaction', the

More difficult	*Very difficult*	
Within vicarious experience	Unrelated to past direct or vicarious experience	
Referents are idealized types which do not exist in actuality	Referents are phenomena which must be inferred from observations of other phenomena (constructs)	
	Predispositions Configurations Processes	
Broader scope	Very broad scope	
	Many concepts subsumed under it	Relates many concepts
	Tendency	
Not completely closed; somewhat unreliable	Open-ended; vague boundaries; unreliable	
Disjunctive (presence of one or another attribute)	Relational	
	Specified relationship (ratio, product, verbal)	One attribute affects another
		All attributes interact
	Comparative	

central organizing concept of Fig. 2.3. The concept 'spatial interaction' is not *directly* related to past experience, is very broad in scope, subsumes many concepts under it, is open-ended and so on through the criteria of a 'very difficult' concept in Table 2.4.

Value of concepts

This brief summary of the characteristics of concepts may be concluded by reflecting on their immense value in our thinking. Our ability to conceptualize helps us to make sense of our environment by relating new experiences to past learning. If we did not have this facility, we should have to relearn every experience as a new one. Concepts help to reduce the complexity of the environment, and since we name concepts and verbalize about them, we are able to work in the realm of the abstract as well as the concrete. Concepts become linked in language to help us to propose principles, and principles enable us to suggest explanations and make predictions. A simple example would be to state the principle that large settlements tend to be more widely spaced than smaller, lower-order settlements. Think of the conceptual understanding involved even in such a simple, apparently self-obvious statement. Consider the previous learning which has enabled the writer to state it and the reader to comprehend it.

Learning concepts

This brings us on to consider what is involved in the learning or acquisition of concepts. We have already considered Piaget's notion of new experiences being assimilated to past learning, which may itself be modified to accommodate to the new. His ideas clearly suggest the importance of active exploration of the environment so as to obtain such experiences. In the foregoing discussion of the nature of concepts, operations such as analysis, discrimination and classification have been suggested as of vital importance in concept acquisition.

The work of Vygotsky (1962) has considerable implications for the teaching of children. He was interested in examining the relationship between language and thought, and used a set of twenty-two wooden blocks of varying shape, height, colour and size to investigate the stages in children's acquisition of concepts. He found that 'the ascent to concept formation is made in three basic phases'. These are:

(a) The vague syncretic stage, where the children grouped the blocks in a random (syncretic) way, rather than in any reasoned manner.

(b) Thinking in complexes, when the child has 'primitive' or pseudo-concepts, based on superficial similarities between the blocks.

(c) The potential concept stage, when the child can cope with one of the attributes of the blocks to form groupings. When he can handle all the attributes, he has reached maturity in concept attainment.

These three stages coincide closely with Piaget's developmental theory, and there are clear implications for teaching which are picked out by educational psychologists such as Child (1973) and by geographers in education such as Milburn (1969) and Lunnon (1969). The work highlights the difficulties faced by young children in problems or tasks involving classification. The danger of creating pseudo-concepts through drill learning is obvious, and, as Lunnon and Milburn have shown, children may often use the verbal labels attached to concepts without having any real understanding of what is involved in the concept itself. The general point is that we need to pay more attention to the conceptual level at which we pitch our work with children.

Jerome Bruner has been influential in the recognition of the importance of concepts in learning and thinking. He has emphasized the value of helping learners to understand the conceptual structure of the subject, suggesting that this structure is so basic that some level of understanding may be achieved at any stage. '. . . any subject can be taught effectively in some intellectually honest form to any child at any stage of development' (Bruner 1960). This implies that concrete, low-order concepts of the subject would be considered early on in a course, or with younger children, moving to more difficult, abstract ideas at later stages. Like Piaget and Vygotsky, Bruner proposes developmental stages in the growth of cognition in the child (Bruner 1967). He is concerned to describe how the child represents the world, and suggests that children move from an active stage of representation (enactive) through the use of images (iconic) to the use of a symbolic mode. The child moves from 'doing' through 'sensing' to 'symbolizing' (Turner 1975). Graves (1980) points out that although teenaged students may have passed through all three stages, they may still use enactive or iconic modes when appropriate. In field-sketching or map-drawing, we are using an enactive mode of representation, while when we have to understand some abstract idea through the symbolic mode, say for example the idea of the rank–size rule, we may welcome a concrete example, using the iconic mode, to aid our understanding.

Gagné (1970) classifies learning into eight types and suggests that we probably use very simple types such as signal learning, stimulus–response learning, chaining, verbal association and discrimination learning before concept-learning becomes possible. Concept-learning enables us to go on to rule-learning and problem-solving. Graves (1980) has suggested geographical examples of each of these types of learning, and his work has been used as the basis of Table 2.5 to help set out the meaning of the eight types. The table shows how previous

Table 2.5 Examples of Gagné's eight types of learning

Learning type	Example from geography (based on Graves 1980)	Comment
1. Signal learning	Pupil has pleasurable reaction to atlas map (or some other resource)	A diffuse emotional reaction, often the result of conditioning. Favourable reactions aid motivation

table continues overleaf

Table 2.5 (cont.)

2. Stimulus–response learning	Teacher questions class orally about picture or map projected on screen. He is trying to check that their perception matches his own by questioning about specific points	Questions are stimuli, pupil answers are responses. Teacher reinforces correct responses
3. Chaining	Child links a series of stimulus–responses together to arrive at the idea that early settlers preferred certain types of settlement site	Occurs when two or more previously learned stimulus–responses are linked. One response may become the stimulus for the next response
4. Verbal association	Associations of terms are built up, e.g. 'dormitory town', or 'urban hierarchy'. (Leads to more complex associations, e.g. 'large urban centres may have dormitory towns dependent upon them'. See type 7)	Very common form of learning, a subvariety of chaining. Enables humans to exploit their versatility through the use of language. Words label perceptions.
5. Discrimination learning	Learner discriminates between different architectural types which characterize various urban zones	Basic to concept learning since it helps build classifications. Involves discrimination between similar stimuli which represent the attributes of objects, events and ideas
6. Concept-learning	The concept of 'suburban house types' is acquired	Stimuli are classified in terms of abstracted properties. Involves the learning types 1 to 5. Experience is classified according to these selected abstracted properties
7. Rule-learning	Pupils learn (not by rote learning only) that 'detached houses tend to be found in the areas of a suburb where incomes are high'	A rule is a chain of two or more concepts which expresses a relationship

Table 2.5 (cont.)

8. Problem-solving	Pupils try to find out how to define spatially areas of high income in a city which they are studying	Involves using concepts and rules to help tackle new situations which pose questions for considera-tion

learning of the types included in 1 to 5 is necessary for concept-learning, and how concepts are applied in rule-learning and problem-solving. The reader is recommended to follow this up in Gagné's own writing (Gagné 1970). Gagné has usefully applied the findings of theories of learning to the question of children in school, asking what conditions are necessary for effective learning to take place.

Spatial conceptualization

If there is one particular area of conceptual understanding of special applicability to the study of geography, it is probably that of spatial conceptualization, since in geography we are essentially concerned with spatial location, spatial distribution and spatial relations. Eliot (1970) discusses the nature of spatial ability, suggesting that there are three dominant elements. The first is the ability to perceive spatial patterns accurately and to be able to compare them with one another. The second is concerned with orientation, being the ability to 'remain unconfused by the varying orientations in which a spatial pattern may be presented'. The third ability, spatial visualization, is the ability to manipulate objects in the imagination, and involves such operations as perceiving, recognizing, distinguishing and relating arrangements of objects in space.

These abilities develop with the cognitive growth of the child, as it has been traced by Piaget and others. The child's spatial ability grows from his knowledge of his immediate static perceptual space to his understanding of transformable conceptual space. He is first limited by his perceptions to what he can see or grasp, but he reaches a true conceptual understanding of space when he is freed from the tyranny of perception, and has internalized a system of reversible mental operations. To achieve this, he has to abandon his egocentric view of space, seeing things from his own point of view only, and recognize the possibility of other viewpoints which he can 'see' in his imagination. This enables him to develop mental understanding of relationships such as up, down, right, left, over, under, above, before, behind, and to be capable of comparing mentally length, size of areas, volume and projective relationships. These abilities make it possible for him to conserve dimensions, distances and systems of co-ordinates (Almy 1967). If, as Almy suggests, these are the spatial abilities possessed by adults, we clearly need, as teachers, to have some understanding of the potential which children at various ages may have for developing such abilities.

Again it is Piaget who provides the basic model for the developmental stages in spatial understanding. Catling (1973) notes that Piaget's findings have received general confirmation, including cross-cultural studies. What follows is an attempt to sketch the main features of the development of spatial conceptualization, based on Piaget's outline, but including detail from other sources. The pattern of development takes the child through the understanding of three types of spatial relations: topological, projective and Euclidean. The child in the sensori-motor stage is said to move in a 'space of action' (Hart and Moore 1973). The earliest learning is perceptual, through sight and touch, which enables the 0- to 2-year-old to become aware of his own local practical spatial world. His spatial viewpoint is totally egocentric. From about the age of 2, the child can begin to evolve from perceptual understanding to mental spatial representation, or conceptualization.

In the pre-operational stage, about 2 to 7 years, the understanding of topological relations begins to form. The child develops ideas of proximity, separation and order of objects in space, and of enclosure and continuity. His viewpoint is still egocentric, in that he finds it difficult to imagine scenes of models from any viewpoint other than his own. It is his own small world that matters to him. Gradually the egocentric orientation gives way to a fixed system of reference, based on the home, certain landmarks and familiar places, all discrete and unconnected. The child may begin to develop understanding of how co-ordinates work through the recognition of the 'vertical' and the 'horizontal'.

By the age of about 7 years, and the beginning of concrete operations, projective understanding begins to develop as his ability to deal with relationships in space increases. He becomes more aware of configuration and location, and can map or place objects in better approximation of the right order. He remains egocentric, in that areas that matter to himself are given priority, and he still has difficulty in imagining arrangements from other viewpoints. Maps dealing with routes or with home areas are more easily drawn and understood than those presenting a general picture of a remote area; that is, remote from the child's experience.

From around 9 years or later, Euclidean understanding develops and leads on to full spatial conceptualization, when the child, through the application of a system of co-ordinates, can understand spatial relationships. He can, for example, place objects in a drawing so that they are related to each other in terms of size, proportion and distance and so that they are correctly located in relation to the frame of the picture. See Fig. 2.5 which illustrates the development of

Stage	Map style	Comments
Topological	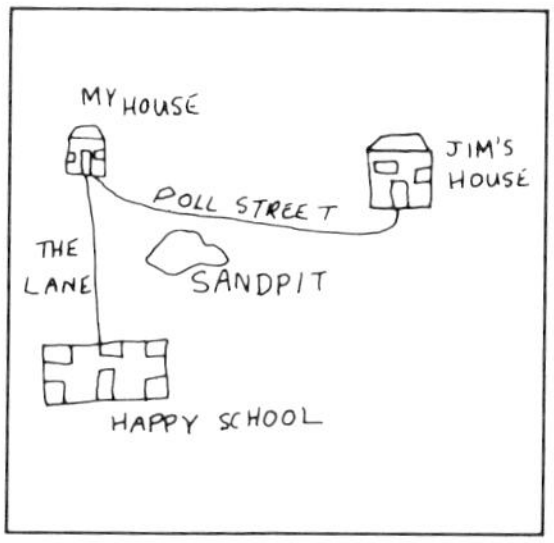	Highly egocentric; known places connected to home; solely iconic; direction, orientation, distance, scale non-existent; unco-ordinated 'map'
Projective I	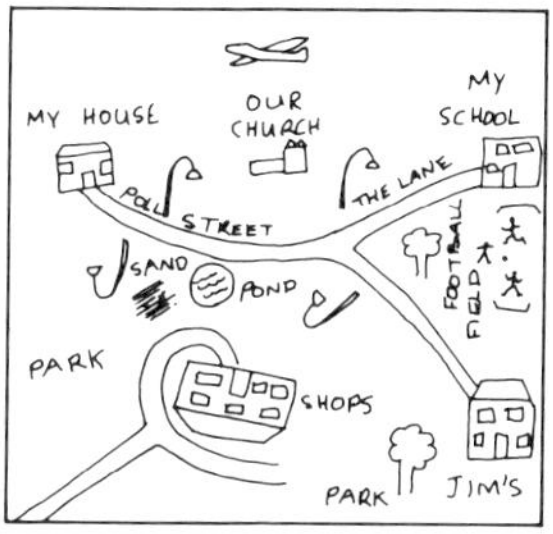	Still essentially egocentric; partial co-ordination, and connection of known places; direction more accurate, but scale and distance inaccurate; road in plan form, but buildings iconic; little development of perspective
Projective II	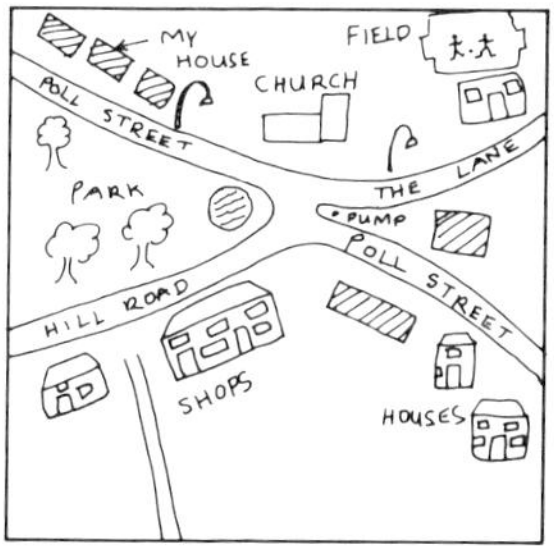	More detailed and differentiated; better co-ordination; continuity of routes; some buildings in plan form; direction, orientation, distance and scale improved; better perspective
Euclidean	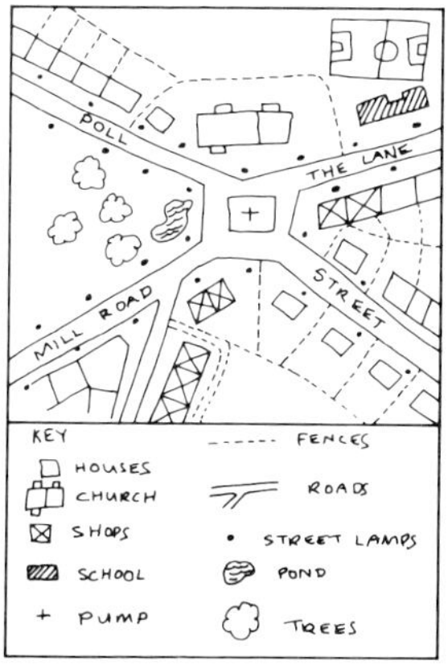	Abstractly co-ordinated and hierarchically integrated map; accurate and detailed; direction, orientation, distance, shape, size, scale roughly accurate; map in plan form; no symbols highly iconic, so key necessary

Fig. 2.5 A developmental sequence of cognitive map representation. How children's mental mapping develops. (From Catling 1978)

children's spatial ability through map drawing. As Eliot (1970) states, the child has now developed a cognitive organization, a system of mental operations, which permits him to 'maintain the relative position of parts of a figure, of figures relative to one another, or the whole display relative to different points of view'. He has become aware of the relationships which link objects to other viewpoints or orientations, and has therefore discovered perspective and different viewpoints. As formal operations develop, the student becomes able to consider theoretical space, mentally abstracted from concrete particulars. Understanding of the concept of infinity enables him to cope with concepts of distance, length, area and volume in mental operations. Table 2.6 is an attempt to summarize the main elements of spatial cognitive development.

Table 2.6 Summary of spatial cognitive development. (*Source:* Based on Hart and Moore 1973). The growth of children's understanding about space

Age (notional)	Levels of organization of spatial cognition	Types of spatial relations
Notes	Spatial understanding is related to the stages of cognitive development as proposed by Piaget	Stages in understanding the way things are placed and related in space
11½	Formal operational	
7–11½	Concrete operational	
2–7	Pre-operational	
0–2	Sensori-motor	

Types of spatial relations column shows ascending arrows labelled: topological → projective → Euclidean

Implications for teaching and learning geography

In this section we have briefly reviewed the nature of concepts and discussed some ideas on the learning or acquisition of concepts. The question of spatial conceptualization has been considered. What are the implications of this work for the teaching and learning of geography? (See also Chs. 3 and 4.)

(a) Understanding of the nature of concepts and of the way in which conceptual learning takes place has clear implications for curriculum planning. If conceptual understanding is necessary for effective learning and problem-solving, then this suggests that our aim in teaching a subject will be to help children gain an understanding of those concepts which are fundamental to the field of study. For many teachers this will involve a careful structuring of the geography

Modes of representation	Systems of reference	Types of topographical representation
Ways in which ideas about spatial matters are represented by the child (after Bruner 1967)	Types of reference the child employs to act as 'known' points to which his spatial understanding is linked	Characteristics of types of drawn map which the child produces from his own mental maps

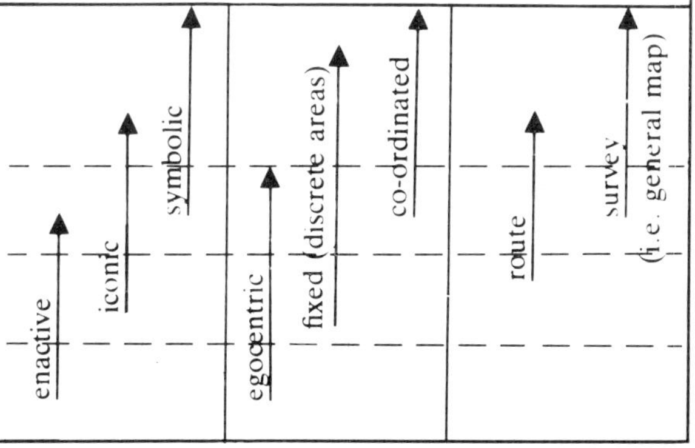

Diagram (ascending arrows within each column):

Modes of representation: enactive → iconic → symbolic

Systems of reference: egocentric → fixed (discrete areas) → co-ordinated

Types of topographical representation: route → survey (i.e. general map)

programme. After completing a study of the understanding of certain concepts in geography by 5- to 12-year-old children, Lunnon (1969) suggested the following format for construction of the curriculum:
  (i)   identify the key concepts;
  (ii) structure them;
  (iii) express them in operational terms in the light of the experience and existing mental schema of the pupils;
  (iv) indicate the level of intricacy at which the concepts are to be developed at a particular age level.
He stressed the need for children to gain increasing experience with examples of the concepts, stating that exemplars should crop up upon a continuum of increasing meaningfulness, and that a sequential 'spiral curriculum' is therefore required. Readers may recognize the influence of Bruner's work in this formulation.

(b) The teacher's role is to be seen more as a provider of appropriate experiences for conceptual learning than as a source of factual information. Inductive teaching approaches are to be adopted, since children do not fully understand a concept by learning a dictionary definition of it. Teachers will therefore need to provide opportunities for classifying, discriminating, naming and comparing based on exemplars and non-exemplars of the concepts in question.

(c) Gagné's work suggests the importance of the early stages in learning concepts. It would seem to be useful to consider the nature of the stimuli involved in stimulus–response learning, for example. Are they appropriate stimuli for the age and ability of the children, or are they too complex and too abstract, as may be the case with some maps or written passages? The importance of suitable reinforcement of responses must also be stressed. Learning must be rewarding if constructive motivation is to develop.

(d) The importance of spoken language is currently receiving greater attention. Since we name concepts and commonly express our rules and problems in language, it follows that spoken as well as written language can be a powerful learning tool. When children are constructively engaged in discussion in small groups, language can aid their thinking, and ideas may be sparked off in a very creative manner. Opportunities for such talk occur in games, simulations and various problem-solving activities. The social interaction resulting from such group work is also to be valued.

Written language, as we have already seen (p. 30) could be used more as a constructive aid to learning rather than mainly as a method of reporting back for assessment purposes. Recent research has suggested that more expressive writing may result from a reconsideration of the purpose of the writing and the audience for whom it is intended. There are obvious constraints when the writing is produced for assessment by the teacher as evaluator, while expressive work may aid learning (Martin *et al* 1976).

(e) The development of spatial abilities and spatial conceptualization might be seen as of particular concern to the teacher of
geography. Much more effort could be made to engage young
children in such activities as simple orientation games, manipulation
of models from different viewpoints, including the plan view,
construction of their own mental maps and exercises involving the
translation of three-dimensional models into two-dimensional maps.
Much work remains to be done in this field, involving conscious
efforts on the part of teachers to aid the development of children's
spatial learning.

Considerable attention has been given to the implications of
Piaget's theory and of the nature of concepts and their acquisition,
because it is felt that much can be done to improve the quality of the
contribution which geography can make to a person's education if the
relationship between theory and practice can be strengthened. There
is evidence that more could be done to 'engage the ability of the
pupils to think abstractly and logically about their physical, economic, social and political environments, and to develop their skill at
organising enquiries about the geography of a country in a structural
manner' (Slater 1970).

Perception and geography learning

The suggestion that we need to consider the nature of the stimuli
offered to children leads us finally to the problem of perception.
What difficulties do children face in the perception of data such as
those provided by the secondary sources of maps, diagrams and
pictures?

Perception of the environment at first hand

The growth of academic interest in environmental perception will be
well known to readers. As early as 1970, Saarinen was able to
produce a stimulating overview of work in this field (Saarinen 1970).
In 1980, Graves summarized the main areas of interest as: 'perception and environmental quality, hazard perception, urban images,
perception from certain routes, perception of barriers, micro-areas
and personal space, perception of far places and lastly preferential
perception'. For the behavioural geographer, the way men see the
world, and in particular their own immediate environment, is an
important area of research, since perception may guide cognition and
so feed into decision-making.

At school level, too, interest is developing in the way children see their world. The importance of the child's level of understanding and his past learning has already been stressed. It follows, then, that we need to begin with the child's own images of the environment in question, if we are to develop effective learning experiences (Hart 1979).

For this reason, teachers are trying to find out what children's perceptions of their environment are like, and what factors guide or limit their perception. This can be attempted by involving children in analysis of maps or pictures of the area being studied, simply finding out which features stand out for them and why. A second approach is to ask them to draw maps from memory, or cognitive maps, of local areas, or of journeys familiar to them. It seems particularly important for children to be encouraged to talk about the places which have significance for them, and for teachers to be ready to listen and learn.

Research based on analysis of children's representations of their cognitive maps suggests that a series of stages of cognitive mapping ability may be recognized, (Catling 1976) (see also Fig. 2.5). In the first stage, the sensori-motor stage, drawing abilities are not developed and earliest efforts are scribbles. The second stage, that of egocentric spatial perception (Topological in Fig. 2.5) sees the depiction of features drawn as pictures, with little understanding of the way elements of the landscape are related to each other in location. Home is a focal point, routes dominate the map and only those features which have significance in the experience of the child are depicted. At the stage of objective spatial cognition (Projective I in Fig. 2.5), a child's 'picture map' may be strongly egocentric, but relationships are more clearly expressed and places are connected. Some parts of the map are co-ordinated, but features of personal significance may take on exaggerated size.

In the stage of abstract spatial reasoning (Projective II and Euclidean in Fig. 2.5), (often reached by secondary school age, around 11–12 years), the child realizes that the vertical viewpoint is essential. Relationships are co-ordinated over the map, and distances are more proportional. Some elements may still be shown pictorially in the early stages, and written information may be included while the child is still learning to use conventional forms and symbols. As the child progresses through this stage, he or she becomes more aware of the selective and purposeful nature of maps. The links between the development of cognitive mapping ability and spatial conceptualization are clear (see pp. 46–47).

The study of children's representations of their mental maps can reveal much useful information. As teachers we can learn a good deal about our students' environmental experiences and perceptions through study and discussion of their drawings of their cognitive maps.

There is enough evidence here to suggest that teachers may well benefit in their work from carrying out small-scale investigations of the environmental perception of the children in their own classes. This will provide a very constructive base line for future work, since it will present the teacher with some knowledge of the children's perceptual abilities as well as their previous learning and present cognition. It may also lead to better understanding of what influences the environmental perception of children, and what are the limitations or constraints which affect their perception, not only of their home area, but also of spatially remote areas which they have not experienced at first hand.

Perception of secondary sources

This brings us on to consider the problem of working from secondary sources in the geography classroom. What difficulties do children face in their perception of complex visual sources such as maps, diagrams and pictures? Texts on the psychology of perception show how perception may be influenced by a variety of factors such as past learning experiences, level of conceptual understanding, motivation and so on. They also indicate particular perceptual difficulties which may arise due to the nature of the material being studied. It is obvious that in maps, pictures and diagrams, geographers have visual materials, which, because of their complexity, may give rise to perceptual problems in their interpretation. Satterly (1964) recognized perceptual as well as conceptual difficulties in working with maps. Among the perceptual problems, he included those of differentiating between similar symbols, and the problem of discriminating between the confusion of lines which may be included on topographical maps. He saw this as a problem of perceiving embedded shapes, where contour lines, for example, compete with field boundaries or other lines on the maps for clear definition.

Satterly tested a group of children with batteries of tests to assess their mapwork performance and a number of psychological variables concerned both with their level of attainment of spatial conceptualization and their perceptual ability. His conclusions showed that perceptual reasoning may be a major factor underlying success in certain aspects of mapwork. In particular, he suggested that the best single predictor of mapwork skill is perception of embedded shapes.

This single example of research into the problems of map interpretation indicates the sort of difficulty which we need to be aware of in presenting pupils with complex visual data for study. It should be striking enough to suggest that further reading into the matter could well be beneficial for teachers working with all age levels from young children to adults. Articles by Heamon (1973) and Dale (1971) are significant here.

Implications of perception studies for teaching

(*a*) Early training is needed to help improve the perceptual skills which build into spatial conceptualization and may play an important part in map study. Suggestions made by Satterly include the idea that young children could be involved in analysing shapes, so that they become more conscious of spatial relationships. A range of different shapes might be presented to the children, for example, so that they can compare and contrast them orally. They might cut out the shapes in white, and stick them on a black background. Then they will cut out further shapes to fill in the black spaces. Children could be engaged in exercises in understanding spatial relationships along the lines of Piaget's well-known three mountains experiments (see Brearley and Hitchfield 1966). They could observe and discuss the model, try to recognize pictures of the model from different viewpoints, produce maps and diagrams of it and so on. Models of homes or villages might be used as well. This might lead on first to the study of large-scale maps of areas familiar to the children, and then to the use of printed large-scale maps and plans. The importance of engaging children in talk about spatial relationships in the course of this work needs to be emphasized.

(*b*) The importance of the teaching of skills for effective photograph interpretation must be stressed. Children should be encouraged to appreciate scale, for example, and avoid the temptation of concentrating on shape rather than size of objects. They would thus be trained to search the whole picture rather than concentrate on the centre of the scene or on the most striking feature. An effort should be made to help them consider explanations of features rather than be content with description only. Practice in sketching and labelling may well help in this work. Young children tend, as Long has shown (1953, 1961), to project themselves into the picture, and this sort of phantasy can be used as a creative stimulus from time to time. In areas where photographs are an unfamiliar resource, their value as teaching material may well be enhanced by discussion work, and by an analytical investigation of the content of the picture. In this way, perceptual difficulties may be resolved. Large-scale vertical aerial photographs of the local area can provide a useful introduction to working with maps.

(*c*) Investigations into children's use of atlases also suggest that training in the reading of atlas maps would be beneficial. In his early work, Sandford (1966), involved 340 children aged 11 to 18 in an undirected examination of an atlas map of Asia. They were asked to 'Write down what the map tells you about Asia.' Analysis of the children's responses revealed that they were up against very real perceptual and conceptual difficulties when faced with such a task. This study showed clearly that we may tend to assume that our

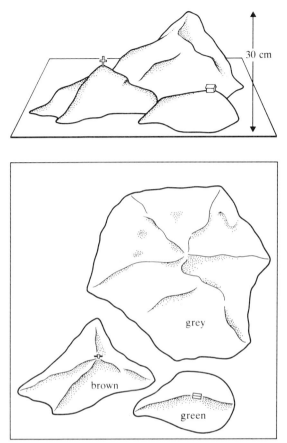

Fig. 2.6 Model for the three mountains experiment. (From Brearley and Hitchfield 1966)

students are more advanced in their facility for using maps and in their conceptual understanding of them than is in fact the case.

Sandford proceeded to devise a course to improve the atlas mapwork of 11–12-year-old children in an English school. He found that their perception, techniques and interpretations improved having completed the course, but their conceptual understanding of the reality behind the atlas map was not so much improved. This may indicate more about the nature of conceptual development than it does about the effectiveness of the course.

The general implications of these studies of perceptual problems is that we probably need to pay more attention in school geography to the nature and quality of our pupils' perceptions. We should question them as to what they perceive, and encourage them to discuss their perceptions and to raise questions about difficulties. We need to recognize the sorts of difficulties which may arise from particular examples of resources for learning, and check on the accuracy of the children's perceptions. Accurate perception is of considerable importance in effective conceptual learning.

Conclusion

In this chapter we have tried to raise some questions concerned with children's mental development and their learning in geography. Some of the research findings may be limited in their applicability because they are based on small-scale research. There is a need for further investigations. In particular, cross-cultural studies are required, replicating some of the research with groups of a variety of age and ability, and concentrating specifically on the skills and concepts involved in geographical study. The implications of the research findings also require further investigation. The present position is that, in general, implications are suggested, but practical programmes of work need to be designed, implemented and evaluated in a continuing effort for curriculum development.

CHAPTER 3

Approaches to teaching and learning strategies

BENOIT ROBERT

The trouble with education, as with medicine and other fields of study whose roots are partly in the arts and the sciences, is that the best teaching methods are in fact the most difficult; it is difficult to use the Socratic method without having first acquired some of Socrates' qualities, as for example, a respect for a child's developing intelligence. (Piaget 1929)

Introduction

This chapter will be essentially concerned first, with discussing various teaching methods in relation to the learning in geography; secondly, with suggesting a typology of space which will be followed by illustrations of two methodological approaches to the teaching of spatial problems in: (a) a developing country; and (b) little humanized landscapes like those of the Canadian Northlands; thirdly, a geographical game will be described; and fourthly, introductory programmed learning units on map reading will be illustrated.

Although other, equally valuable, teaching strategies could have been chosen to illustrate the theme of this chapter, those in fact chosen have the merit of demonstrating not only the broad categories of teaching strategies but also the present preoccupations of geographers and of Unesco. Teachers need to have at their disposal a number of teaching methods in order to choose those appropriate to the topics being taught and to liven up teaching by the use of a variety of approaches. Thus it is important that a student learns to classify and subdivide global space on the basis of given criteria. It is one way of becoming aware of the complexity of the planet. The examples chosen to illustrate this process also enable the student to become aware of the problems of the Third World, whose population constitutes a majority in the human race. The study of the Canadian Northlands, a 'fragile environment', is used to illustrate the great ecological and environmental concerns of our epoch in view of technological development in the exploitation of natural resources.

The use of games and simulations has developed considerably in education and consequently merits consideration here, especially as it is a teaching strategy which is applicable in many different circumstances. Lastly, it was felt that the skill of learning to read large-scale maps and particularly contour maps was worth illustrating by means of a programmed learning approach, since this is an area of skill learning suitable for individualized learning techniques.

Methods of teaching and learning

Teaching methods may be divided into two broad groups: expository methods and inquiry or discovery methods. Expository methods may themselves be subdivided into two types: the lecture method and the programmed learning method. Inquiry methods may take the form of open inquiry–discovery methods or of guided inquiry–discovery methods (Hyman 1974).

Expository methods are essentially deductive methods in which facts, concepts, relationships, and generalizations are described by the teacher or printed in a textbook with a view to students understanding and assimilating them. Thus the ideas or facts are exposed (hence expository methods) by the teacher, or in a traditional textbook or in a 'programmed learning' sequence, and it is up to the student to learn them. On the other hand, inquiry methods are basically inductive methods moving from a given case to a generalization, from a hypothesis to a principle, from a problem to a solution, hence such a method is often associated with a problem-solving approach. The student begins with a problem or a set of facts, and will try to compare these facts with others in order to arrive at a hypothesis which may help to explain a discrepancy between the facts. While he is doing this he will pick up ideas and concepts and may eventually arrive at a principle, a generalization or even a law. The following is an example of the problem-solving approach and its results from the *Harvard* Cognition Project (Bruner 1960). Some 12-year-old pupils were asked to decide on the location of large hypothetical towns in the north of the Middle West of the United States, using a map without place names, but with an indication of the relief and natural resources. After group discussions, the pupils put forward certain plausible hypotheses about where a large town might be sited, namely:

(a) at the meeting point of three of the Great Lakes;
(b) near the Mesabi range;
(c) near the area of rich soils in Iowa.

Such a simulation made it necessary for the pupils to discover the nature of the positive factors which influence the location of a large town. Thus they realized that a town does not exist for its own sake, but that its development is linked to its hinterland, to the transport network, and the industrial, commercial and financial services which it can provide for its surrounding region.

In applying inquiry methods, the teacher acts like a guide or a counsellor; he becomes a 'resource' for the students. The dissemination of inquiry methods into most schools is not an easy matter. Such methods require many resources including a great deal of documentary evidence. They take up much of the teacher's time in their preparation and organization and are demanding in terms of the teacher's capacity and involvement. On the other hand, expository methods require the teacher to act as a master of his subject. Although such methods are usually labelled as 'traditional', they are by no means easy to put into operation. A stimulating lecture is usually the result of long experience as well as of erudition. In practice teachers choose one or the other (or an infinite number of variants) according to what they propose to teach, whom they are teaching, the school environment and of course their own predilections.

Student teachers often wonder what is the ideal or the best method of teaching geography. It is true that some research work has tended to indicate that the learning of certain ideas by programmed learning methods is more efficient than by more traditional methods, but other research work has failed to confirm such a finding. Similarly the problem-solving approach seems to be one which motivates students to a greater degree than expository methods. But none of the research studies are conclusive and the debate on teaching method continues. The teacher with experience will argue that the best method is the one which gives the best result with the students, whatever its label. Thus, though the use of a simulation exercise may succeed in motivating some students on certain occasions, a good lecture may be just as motivating in other circumstances. There is no such thing as 'the best teaching method', even if some methods seem to give better results in certain specified situations; the results of any method are a function of the teacher's motivation and of the effort he has put into the preparation of his teaching, as well, of course, as the attitude of his pupils. Some teachers who are eminently successful using expository methods might fail disastrously if they attempted to put into practice inquiry methods without undertaking adequate preparation and changing their attitude to the teaching/learning process.

Geography is a subject eminently suited to the use of a variety of teaching methods. Teachers should experiment from time to time with different types of teaching techniques, such as the use of games, simulations and programmed learning.

Teaching and learning strategies

Although geography can be thought of as contributing to a student's understanding of the spatial aspects of various problems, it can also play a vital role in developing in children and students certain concepts, in increasing their powers of critical thought and in making them aware of the multiplicity of causes to any situation.

As we saw in Chapter 2 several psychologists have developed an interest in the evolution of the conceptual understanding of children, of whom the best known are Piaget, Bruner and Gagné. Only in the last 15 years have their models of children's mental development been applied to an understanding of the process of learning geography. Now, although geography (as we saw in Ch. 1) has certain values which it attempts to contribute to a student's total education, the teacher must be capable of harmonizing such values with the exigencies set by our knowledge of the student's mental development (e.g. the different conceptions of spatial relationships held by children at different ages). Geographical values cannot be learned by students if the teacher ignores all the progress which cognitive psychology has made in the last 20 years.

To meet this point, Hilda Taba elaborated a model of teaching and learning the purpose of which is to enable the development of inductive mental processes. This is contained in the Taba Social Studies Curriculum (Taba 1967) in which a teacher's guide indicates methods of procedure. Taba's model is essentially based on the idea that the content of various subjects serves merely as a resource for the learning of certain ideas, concepts and modes of thinking.

Starting from a series of questions, prepared by the teacher, the student could pass through the three stages of:
1. concept formation;
2. inferring and generalizing;
3. applying principles in new situations (see Joyce and Weil 1972).

In order to develop concepts the pupil must begin to analyse his experiences and group them. From these categories of experiences which we can define as concepts (see Ch. 2), he will begin to make inferences and generalizations. The teacher may stimulate the pupils to make comparisons by posing such questions as, 'What do you notice, what did you see, what did you find? What differences are there between x and y? What does this suggest to you?'

The same teaching strategy may be used to lead them into the stage of applying principles. Using appropriate questions the teacher may create a situation where the student feels the necessity of applying his previously learned principles. For example: 'In such a circumstance what do you think will happen? Why do you think it will happen the way you describe and not any other way?'

Taba's inductive teaching model incorporates the Socratic dialogue.

The teacher must beware of giving ready-made answers; rather will he create a situation in which the student himself will develop his own concepts, arrive at a generalization and eventually apply his generalization or principle. It is possible to use Taba's model at all stages of education. For example, for children of 10–11 years, the supermarket may be an interesting resource (Taba 1967). In order to function properly a supermarket must be well located, offer appropriate goods and services and have suitable equipment. From a 'field trip' to the supermarket or from the evidence of photographs and maps, the teacher can, by posing precise questions, get the children not only to describe what they see but to understand the relationships between what they see. As a result of these 'learning experiences' the children will begin to understand the functions not only of the particular supermarket which they are observing but of all supermarkets. They will also begin to understand some of the general principles which govern supermarket location.

Taba's teaching–learning model makes the teacher more conscious of his methods and of the tendency for curricula to become more and more content-weighty as time goes by; it will tempt him to rethink his teaching style and strategies and experiment with new curricula. In fact most recent efforts to renovate geographical education have been directed towards ways of improving the learning of children and students. This does not imply that content is to be neglected, on the contrary, but content is made dependent on having precise objectives. The experience of the American High School Geography Project illustrates this tendency.

The High School Geography Project covers six themes of which five are in the realm of systematic geography and the sixth is in that of regional geography (Gunn 1972). The six themes may be taught during one academic year to students aged 14–16. The structure of the High School Geography Project is indicated on Figs 3.1 and 3.2 (a), (b) and (c).

A typology of space

Introduction

This section will be divided into three parts, each consisting of a suggested teaching unit. First a teaching unit to establish that there may be ways of categorizing various types of areas on the earth. Then following on from this, two types of areas will be studied: areas in developing countries and the poorly developed areas in countries with industrial economies, illustrated by reference to the Canadian Northlands. Two teaching–learning methods will be used: guided inquiry–discovery methods in the case of developing countries and

Geography in an urban age

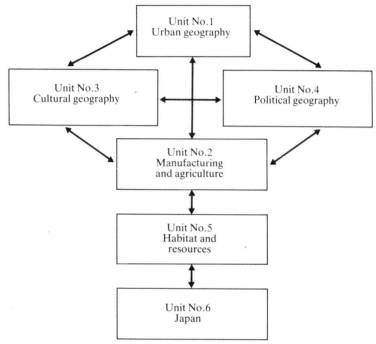

Fig. 3.1 The structure of the American High School Geography Project

Fig. 3.2(a) Procedures followed in the preparation of each HSGP unit

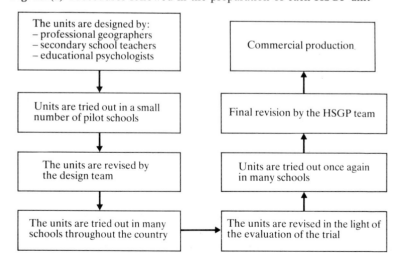

Fig. 3.2(b) Procedure for teaching one sub-unit

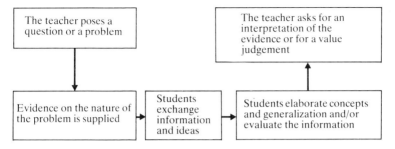

Fig. 3.2(c) Example of procedures followed in the activity of deciding on the location of the METFAB factory

Question
What factors influence the location of a factory?

Problem
In which of the twenty-five largest towns in the USA would you set up a new metal fabricating factory?

Evidence is provided on the raw materials needed, the labour force, transport required, the financial structure of the firm, etc.

Role-playing simulation set up with students acting as members of a board of directors having to make decisions on locations based on the evidence.

Conclusion
The students learn the kinds of factors which influence industrial location discussions.

the expository method in the case of the study of the Canadian Northlands.

The division of earth space

This teaching unit was designed for students aged 15–16 years. Its objectives are the following:
(a) to make students discover the broad division of the globe;

(b) to enable students to understand and seek relationships between different types of maps and other data;

(c) to enable students to formulate criteria for classifying spaces;

(d) to make students construct a synthetic map of various types of spaces;

(e) to enable students to make comparisons between the criteria for classifying space used by professional geographers and their own criteria.

The teacher using a series of small-scale maps can lead the students to discover different types of areas. These maps should be those of world climates, world population distribution, world production of agricultural and industrial goods, world distribution of Gross National Product per capita. Before being able to discover various types of areas, students will need to be able to understand what the maps represent. Then they will need to select criteria for dividing the world into regions. Some may use economic criteria and others will use landscape criteria. Eventually they will list and describe their regional divisions as well as the criteria used. Inevitably this typology of space will be embryonic and unsophisticated. But certain features will be noticeable in such a regional division: empty areas, industrialized areas and so on.

Subsequently the students will compare their own divisions with those established by geographers. The teacher could use Dolfus's (1970) division of earth space into:

(a) occupied but little-organized space;

(b) space organized by traditional pre-industrial societies;

(c) technologically developed industrialized areas.

It is important that students realize that such a typology of space may be modified by using different criteria. Students may then undertake to map world areas based on Dolfus's scheme. They will need to ask themselves whether a country forms part of area (a) or (b), or (c) etc. Such an exercise develops in students the ability to visualize the world in regions and the idea that such regions are complex and of great variety. The map which they draw represents their crowning efforts, the synthesis following the previous analysis, comparisons between different criteria; it also enables them to interpret evidence and to exercise their ability to see the relationships between different phenomena.

In using Dolfus's or any other scheme for dividing up earth space, the teacher must sensitize students to the contingencies attendant upon such divisions: they are, like all classifications, dependent on the purpose for which they are made. They are in no sense absolute. They are a means whereby the complexity of earth space may be reduced by selecting certain characteristics and showing how the variations in these over the earth surface may lead to a subdivision of that surface.

(a) The nature of developing areas

The following teaching unit is devised for students in the 15–17 age range, and contains references to certain concepts which will need explicating if the whole unit is to be meaningful. For example, the statement that 'the per capita Gross Domestic Product in Bangladesh is equivalent of $US 70.00', is meaningless to most students unless it is compared with similar figures for developed countries. The reality behind those figures may be made accessible to the student by the description of daily life in Bangladesh. Figure 3.3 does much to illustrate the gulf which exists between rich and poor nations. The students may be asked to draw similar diagrams using the figures given in Table 3.1 using various threshold figures for very low-income, moderately low-income, moderate-income and high-income countries. They might be asked to spell out what each category of country might provide in the way of public health services and social security services. They might also be asked how far there was a correlation between high income and quality of life, however defined. Such questions and exercises might lead to a growing awareness among students of the responsibilities of the rich nations towards the poorer nations.

A general aim of such a teaching unit would be to sensitize students to the grave problems of imbalance in development within the Third World. Specific objectives would be:

1. the location of Third World countries;
2. the comparisons of the main components of underdevelopment;
3. the discussion of Lacoste's (1976) fourteen characteristics of underdevelopment (see p. 67–68);
4. the writing of a case study on one or more problems of the Third World.

At the end of such a teaching unit, students should be capable of localising and describing the main problems of the Third World, of analysing the main factors responsible for underdevelopment and of reaching their own conclusions about the main processes involved.

Using selected statistical tables and graphs, the student will note the large number of countries whose Gross Domestic Product per capita (Table 3.1) is less than $ US 1 000 per year. By juxtaposing on one graph Gross Domestic Product per capita and total population in each country, Figure 3.3 shows clearly the contrast between rich and poor countries. The teacher may then describe, explain and compare the evolution of the economies of the industrial and Third World countries by analysing the historical sequence portrayed in Fig. 3.4.

The limits of the Third World as given by Lacoste (1976) (Fig. 3.5) illustrate the difficulty of such a categorization, since several countries have some characteristics of developing countries and others of developed countries. Tables 3.2(a), 3.2(b) and 3.2(c) show changes in world population, in birth-rates and in death-rates.

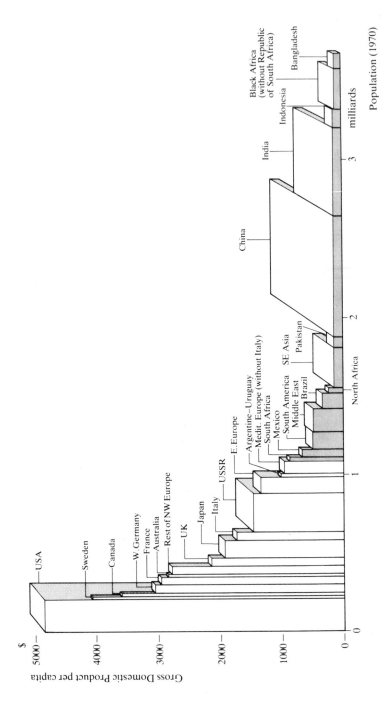

Fig. 3.3 Population in relation to per capita Gross Domestic Product. (*Source:* Lacoste 1976)

Table 3.1 *Per capita* Gross Domestic Product (US $) of world nations. (*Source:* International Bank for Reconstruction and Development; *United Nations Statistical Yearbook*; and Lacoste 1976)

	1970	1977		1970	1977
A. United States	4760	8665	**B.** Israel	1960	4079
Kuwait	4000	11307	Austria	2010	6377
Arab Emirates	3000	–	Puerto Rico	1410	3304
Sweden	4040	9474	Italy	1760	3040
Switzerland	3320	9570	Czechoslovakia	2230	–
Canada	3700	8583	USSR	1790	–
New Zealand	2700	4251	Japan	1920	5002
Luxemburg	2420	7717	Ireland	1360	2943
Australia	2820	7239	Venezuela	930	2794
			Hungary	1600	–
Denmark	3190	9041	Argentine Rep.	1160	1920
Libya	1860	7422	Poland	1400	–
Iceland	1850	8715	Cyprus	970	1629
France	3100	7172	Greece	1090	2824
Norway	2860	8809	Romania	930	–
FRG	2930	8406	Uruguay	820	1319
Belgium	2720	8058	Spain	1020	3152
UK	2270	4377	Trinidad	890	–
Finland	2390	6365	Bulgaria	760	–
Qatar	1500	11300	Singapore	800	2594
Netherlands	2430	7683	Hong Kong	850	2381
GDR	2490	–	Rep. of S. Africa	760	1436
Brunei	950	1378	Chile	720	865
C. Yugoslavia	650	1294	**D.** Egypt	210	485
Panama	730	1250	Sri Lanka	910	244
Lebanon	580	603	S. Korea	250	950
Mexico	670	1150	Sierra Leone	190	214
Jamaica	550	1478	New Guinea	300	–
Costa Rica	560	1481	Mauritania	140	292
Mongolia	460	–	Thailand	200	412
Portugal	660	1560	Congo	220	574
Surinam	–	1191	Kampuchea	130	–
Nicaragua	430	967	South Vietnam	200	–
Cuba	530	–	Cameroon	130	427
Guatemala	360	869	Cent. Afr. Rep.	140	218
Peru	450	646	Indonesia	80	320
Albania	600	–	Mozambique	240	295
Colombia	340	568	Sudan	120	298
Guyana	340	562	Togo	140	269

table continues overleaf

Table 3.1 (cont.)

	1970	1977		1970	1977
C. Malayasia	380	781	**D.** Uganda	130	266
Turkey	310	999	India	110	141
S. Salvador	300	–	North VietNam	100	–
Iraq	320	1 226	Kenya	150	309
Dominican Rep.	350	897	Madagascar Rep.	130	232
Iran	380	1 999	Pakistan	100	200
Gabon	320	5 677	Yemen	80	–
Brazil	420	1 482	China	160	–
Saudi Arabia	440	6 155	Dahomey	90	–
Taiwan	390	–	Guinea	120	164
Ghana	310	498	Niger	90	130
Algeria	300	954	Nigeria	120	399
Ivory Coast	310	1 251	Tanzania	100	212
Honduras	280	506	Afghanistan	80	153
Jordan	250	697	Chad	80	158
Liberia	240	389	Haiti	110	250
Senegal	230	331	Laos	120	69
Zimbabwe	280	530	Nepal	80	106
Paraguay	260	745	Burma	80	120
Tunisia	250	821	Zaïre	90	148
Ecuador	290	814	Ethiopia	80	97
N. Korea	330	–	Mali	70	89
Syria	290	839	Bangladesh	70	93
Zambia	400	523	Burundi	60	73
Angola	300	434	Malawi	80	140
Morocco	230	453	Somalia	70	155
Bolivia	180	445	Upper Volta	60	91
Philippines	210	412	Rwanda	60	155

	Average GDP US $		Population (millions)	
Africa	250	(1972)	391	(74)
Latin America	670	(72)	315	(74)
Asia (except Japan)	365	(72)	2 097	(74)
North America (except Mexico)	6 550	(74)	235	(74)
Europe	3 820	(73)	470	(74)

While Tables 3.1 and 3.2(c) can be used to illustrate the extent of the Third World, groups of students could be used (three to five students per group) to find out the various characteristics of developing countries from statistics, graphs and maps. Having discovered these characteristics, they could compare them with

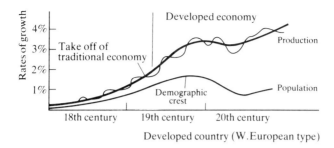

Fig. 3.4 The relationship between population and production in developing and developed economies. (*Source:* Lacoste 1976)

Table 3.2(a) World population (millions). (*Source:* Lacoste 1976; and *United Nations Statistical Yearbook*)

	1900	1950	1977
World	1 650	2 501	4 070
Europe	296	392	521
USSR	134	180	259
North America	82	166	240
Japan	44	84	113
Asia (including Middle East)	881	1 368	2 124
Africa	133	219	426
Latin America	63	164	342

Lacoste's list which follows:
1. inadequate diet for the inhabitants;
2. illiteracy; mass epidemics; high infant mortality;
3. wasted or neglected resources;
4. a high proportion of labour employed in agriculture and with a low productivity per man;
5. a low proportion of the population in urban areas; a small middle class;

Table 3.2(b) Birth-rates (in 0/000) for selected areas. (*Source:* Lacoste 1976)

	1950–54	1970–74	1990–95
Africa	47	47	41
South Asia	47	43	30
East Asia (without Japan)	37	31	21
Latin America	41	37	33
Europe	20	18	17
USSR	26	18	18
North America	25	20	19
Japan	24	19	15

Table 3.2(c) Death-rates (in 0/000) for selected areas. (*Source:* Lacoste 1976)

	1950–54	1970–74	1990–95 (*provisional*)
Africa	26	19	10
South Asia	27	15	9
East Asia (without Japan)	20	12	9
Latin America	15	9	6
Europe	11	10	10
USSR	9	8	9
North America	9	9	9
Japan	9	7	9

6. limited industrialization;
7. an inflated and parasitic tertiary sector of the economy;
8. a low per capita Gross Domestic Product;
9. high unemployment and underemployment; use of child labour;
10. an economy and society highly dependent on foreign capital or aid;
11. great social inequalities;
12. a weakly structured economy and society;
13. a high rate of population growth;
14. an awareness of the situation by the intelligentsia and an attempt to change it.

Though these criteria may be used to delimit the Third World, they may not apply to all countries normally considered part of it. Several socialist states claim to have solved the problem of unemployment and even claim to be short of labour. Again rapidly increasing population, though clearly a problem in many Third World nations,

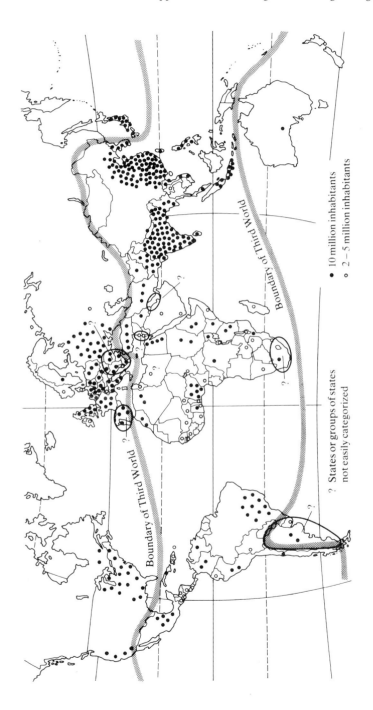

Fig. 3.5 Suggested boundaries of the Third World. (*Source:* Lacoste 1976)

seems either to be under control or great efforts are being made to slow down demographic growth. In general, the fourteen characteristic features of the Third World are valid, with some countries having undertaken measures to eliminate one or more of these features.

Given the complexity of such a teaching unit, the teacher needs to be a guide as well as a resource. The questions he poses must lead the students to discover the fundamental aspects of underdevelopment. Students will not only be asked to gather information, produce maps and graphs, but they should be asked to interpret these in a critical fashion. Group discussions may help students to become aware of many different points of view.

(b) Poorly organized areas

A case study of the Canadian North

The conquest of the northern lands by the white man is a recent phenomenon. Only in the twentieth century have many efforts been made to explore and understand this area. Nevertheless, man's ability to survive in these cold lands is not yet certain in spite of modern technology. The Inuit people, however, can teach other men how they have successfully adapted to such an environment. Since the Second World War, and particularly since the energy crisis of the 1970s, industrial man has begun to examine the possibilities of exploiting the North's considerable resources (petroleum, iron, copper and asbestos). As a result, modern technology is beginning to transform this area which for centuries has kept a precarious equilibrium. These changes are drastically modifying the northern lands; it seems as though the southerner's perceptions of it are far from the objective reality (Wonders 1971; Mowat 1976; Wonders and Mills 1976; Dosman 1976).

Teachers working under the aegis of the Canada Studies Foundation, have developed teaching materials on the Canadian North, which have already been submitted to trials with 16–18-year-old students in Quebec Province (Robert 1975). The teaching unit consists of three parts:
(a) a brochure giving a general statement of what the North is really like;
(b) a teacher's guide;
(c) suggestions for evaluating the unit.

The teaching style used was to personify the Canadian North and therefore to pose questions through analogies, as though the area was a human being. Thus the content is divided into six activities based on the following questions:
1. Northern lands, where are you?

2. Northern lands, what are you like?
3. Northern lands, how used you to live?
4. Northern lands, how are you developing?
5. Northern lands, how can we get to you?
6. Northern lands, what is your future?

Each part of the unit consists of the following six elements:
(a) a brief introduction to the theme;
(b) a description of the main activities to be undertaken;
(c) teaching resources (or suggestions for such resources);
(d) a statement of the educational objectives to be reached and suggestions for evaluating these;
(e) a teaching strategy;
(f) additional suggestions for the teacher.

Ideally, such a teaching unit is best taught to a group of 20–30 students aged 16 to 18 in a room equipped for projecting slides and containing the usual geography room equipment. It would have additional purpose if it could be taught in winter (in non-tropical lands!) and if it were possible to invite people who have actually lived in the northern lands to talk to the students. Table 3.3 (p. 72) indicates the ways in which the various themes may dovetail into one another and into the associated main ideas and learning activities. As an example, the second and fourth activities in the learning sequence are shown below. These require the school to be able to show slides and films and to possess certain documentary resources.

Activity II

Northern lands, what are you like?

A. INTRODUCTION

This activity puts the student in contact with the natural elements of the Canadian North: the relief, climate, the sea, the flora and fauna. The text, 'Northern lands, what are you like?' describes each of these elements and helps to debunk ideas such that the northern lands are the sterile habitat of the polar bear. The concept of 'habitability' relates to current efforts to develop the area and to the challenge offered by this realm of cold.

Not more than 2 hours need to be devoted to this theme.

B. MAIN PARTS OF THE ACTIVITY

According to circumstances, this activity may be divided into two parts:
1. The showing of a film to bring reality to the subject.
2. The basic activity is teacher-directed, in which the aim is to obtain an understanding of the nature of the northern lands' ecosystem.

Table 3.3 Summary table of teaching sequences

Themes	No. of hours in class	Main activities
1. Where are you?	3	1. Reading and analysing a text 2. Teacher–student interaction (questions, explanations)
2. What are you like?	2	1. Lecture illustrated by maps and slides 2. Film
3. How used you to live?	5	1. Reading and annotating a text 2. Film 3. Construction of an igloo
4. How are you developing?	4	1. Film 2. Group discussion of the film
5. How can we get to you?	2	Choice to be made by students and/or teachers
6. What is your future?	3	1. Critical reading of two texts 2. Forum with experts

C. RESOURCES
1. Provided for:
   (a) the student:
   Text: Northern lands, what are you like?
   Illustrated by 8 photographs, 8 maps and 1 drawing;
   Selective bibliography;
   List of films.
   (b) the teacher:

Main ideas	Suggested homework
Stages in the settlement of the North Criteria for defining zones in the North Characteristics of the main zones in the Canadian North	Devising or solving a crossword puzzle Drawing a map Essays
The elements of the material environment; land, water, climate The biotic environment: flora and fauna	Vocabulary construction Cartographical location Devising or solving a hidden word puzzle Visual display Visit to a zoo Essays
Characteristics of the traditional life of Eskimos	Commentary based on photographs Essays
Man's activities in the Arctic lands Impact of technology Problems of adaptation and exploitation	Reading of source material Audio-visual display Mapping Essays
Trade and communications at present in the Canadian North New methods of transport used in the area	Reading of source material Visual display Devising a tourist trail research Essays
Rationalization of resource exploitation Environmental conservation New ways of life to be thought out	

29 slides, of which 11 are in the text given to the students.
Exercise and research or discussion topics.
2. Equipment required but not provided with the activity:
Film – *The Canadian Tundra* or *The Canadian Far North – flora and fauna*,
Projectors – 35 mm and 16 mm, and screen;
Episcope;
Wall map of the Canadian North.

D. EDUCATIONAL OBJECTIVES AND EVALUATION PROCEDURES

At the end of the activity the student should:

1. In terms of content:
    (a) be capable of knowing some of the main place names and geographical terms relating to the physical environment of the Canadian North;
    (b) understand the spatial organization of the continent and maritime physical environment of the Canadian North;
    (c) have discovered the physical factors which limit human settlement in the Canadian North;
    (d) be capable of appreciating the richness of the North's flora and fauna.
2. In terms of general skill and abilities:
    (a) understand better the concept of physical environment;
    (b) have better developed his powers of observation, his spatial conceptualization and his ability to describe areas verbally.

Evaluation may be based on the homework (see G below).

E. GUIDELINES

As this topic involves the learning of precise notions relating to physical geography, it was thought best to use direct instruction rather than the use of inquiry methods which might have given disappointing results. With the help of the books suggested in the bibliography and a specialized text on physical geography, the teacher should be able to make the theme clear to students. With the teaching resources available, it should be possible for students to learn the ideas of distance, of the extent of the northern lands and their location, and to begin to interpret the interrelationships in the natural environment.

The film *The Canadian Tundra* or *The Canadian Far North – flora and fauna* should help in the acquisition of the stated objectives by providing additional information and motivation.

The homework should help to develop the basic notions acquired in class.

F. ADVANTAGE OF THIS TEACHING STRATEGY

By using such a procedure:

1. information is economically transmitted;
2. the subject-matter can be readily analysed;
3. the learning process may be controlled;
4. the student's attention can be focused on the subject.

G. SUGGESTIONS FOR HOMEWORK

1. Draw up a list of geographical terms relevant to the Canadian North.
2. Locate on a map the main locations in the Canadian North (see

Fig. 3.6, p. 80).
3. Make a visual display on the flora and fauna of the Canadian North.
4. Write an essay on a subject relevant to the theme – such as:
   (a) Discuss Hamelin's contention that 'In Canada though not everything is in the North, everything comes from the North.'
   (b) The climatic influence of the North on the rest of Canada.
   (c) Elaborate on the following passage: 'The tundra seems, to the "civilized" man, a place of solitude. The early explorers called it, "the sterile land". This sterility is but an illusion for the Indians and the Inuits, for whom the tundra is their habitat, it is a source of life, of satisfaction and happiness, similar to that that all men feel about their native land.'
   (d) What makes for ecological equilibrium in the Far North?
   (e) Describe the main characteristics of the areas over which roam the polar bear, the caribou and the lemming.

Activity IV

Northern lands, how are you developing?
A. INTRODUCTION
This theme is concerned with man's life in the cold regions of the northern hemisphere, and with the techniques which allow him to live in all latitudes. It shows the new ecological context resulting from the introduction of new technology into the North, the problems of adaptation and exploitation and the unequal developments of the North.
   The time taken for this activity should not be more than 3 hours.

B. MAIN PARTS OF THE ACTIVITY
These are:
1. Viewing the film *Man and Cold*.
2. Discussion in groups of the film's content and implications.

C. RESOURCES
1. Provided for:
   (a) *the student*:
      Text: *Canada's Northern Policy: retrospect and prospect*, illustrated by 3 photographs;
      Text: *The Canadian North-west, some geographical perspectives*, illustrated by 11 photographs and 1 map;
      Map of the *Nordic World*;
      Selective bibliography.
   (b) *the teacher*:
      30 slides of which 12 are photographs in the texts;
      Suggestions for discussion topics.

2. Required but not provided:
   Projector – 16 mm and screen;
   Film – *Man and Cold*

D. EDUCATIONAL OBJECTIVES AND EVALUATION PROCEDURES

At the end of the activity the student should:

1. In terms of content:
   (a) have a knowledge of the main development occurring in the cold areas of the northern hemisphere;
   (b) be aware of the disparities between regions and nations in economic development and by comparison be capable of assessing the degree of development in the Canadian North;
   (c) be able to point to precise examples illustrating the way development has occurred in the Canadian North;
   (d) understand the nature of the struggle between technology and the cold climatic conditions;
   (e) be aware of the new concept of 'habitability' in the North.
2. In terms of general skills and ability:
   (a) be able to observe, compare and be conscious of relativities;
   (b) understand man's ingenuity in organizing his environment.

E. GUIDELINES

Given the time and teaching materials available for this activity, it is not possible to deal in detail with the development of the Canadian North. We suggest the use of the film *Man and Cold* which in 2 hours covers most of the ground.

This method will enable the student to understand the Canadian North and compare it with other northern lands. He will also become aware of the techniques used to develop cold lands and of the ways such techniques are being disseminated.

The student wishing to develop an in-depth understanding of the Canadian North should consult the references where he will find some useful works.

To complement the documentation, two texts are appended indicating the various policies applied to the Canadian North up to 1969. These documents can be used as the basis for a talk, a discussion or some other activity. We strongly recommend that students undertaking this activity should read them at home.

The second part of the activity is a discussion of the film by the students in small groups.

As the film is the main basis of this activity, the teacher should be familiar with it and have made an analysis of its difficulties, its intellectual level, the kind of vocabulary used and so on. He will, as a result, be able to suggest points for discussion and lines of inquiry, which will help the student to attain the educational objectives postulated. For example, the film makes possible a comparison between the levels of development in the Canadian and Scandinavian North.

F. ADVANTAGES OF THE PROCEDURE
1. Student motivation will be greater.
2. Points of view are exchanged by the students and their capacity for self-expression is developed.
3. Learning takes place in small groups.
4. There is a stimulus to the learning of analytical techniques through the confrontation of criticisms made by different observers of the film.

G. SUGGESTIONS FOR HOMEWORK
1. Undertake research on one region of the Canadian North in a directory, encyclopedia or specialized journal.
2. Devise thematic maps on economic aspects of the Canadian North.
3. Write essays on one of the following subjects:
   (a) Describe the problems of cultural adaptations that the native people have as a result of the expansion of Canadian industrial civilization into the North.
   (b) Discuss the following statement: 'The conquest of the Canadian North is making possible a fundamental change in traditional urban life and the advent of a new habitat which necessitate a total rethinking of a way of life.'
   (c) The Mackenzie Basin is a favoured region in the development of the Canadian North. Do you agree?
   (d) 'The Canadian North is the extension of an economic area basically foreign to Canada.' Discuss.
   (e) 'The challenge of the Canadian North is timely: it makes possible a development which is unavoidable and at the same time provides an opportunity for the Canadian to excel.' Discuss.
   (f) With precise examples, describe the problems of constructing buildings and means of communication in the Canadian North.

Games in geography: railroad-builders, a simulation game

It may be as well to begin by getting ideas clear about the nature of games and simulations as teaching strategies. Simulations are an attempt to reproduce under classroom conditions a situation which would normally have existed in very different circumstances. An example of a simulation is role-playing: students may be allocated various roles in a planning-decision situation in which the objective is to arrive at a decision as to whether a road should or should not be built through a particular area; students may play the roles of contractor, developer, planning consultant, local surveyor, local politicians and so on. A simulation can be structured into an operation game, in so far as a set of rigid rules and constraints limit the action which may or may not take place. More often than not operational games have an element of chance built into them to indicate that what happens in real life is often affected by chance happenings. A pure game such as chess is not a simulation since it does nothing to simulate a real situation, though it may have a spin-off in the spatial logic it may develop. Most games in geography are simulation games.

Games have been used in geographical education for a long time. Teachers either invented their own games or used existing ones. They were seen essentially as a means of diversifying teaching techniques and increasing student motivation. Some teachers, of course, felt that games were too frivolous to be used for the serious purpose of educating a younger generation.

Experiments with gaming techniques in the classroom have resulted in the development of games which not only motivate students but also have important cognitive objectives within the field of geographical education. For example, in the High School Geography Project, the METFAB simulation is concerned with problems of industrial location and the PORTSVILLE simulation attempts to show how a coastal town may develop and assume a certain structure. In the relevant journals (*Journal of Geography, Geography, Teaching Geography, Classroom Geographer*, etc.) several articles may be found describing geographical games and simulations suitable for different age levels. Books have even been published on geographical and other games such as those of Walford (1969) and Tansey and Unwin (1969). Thus, in general, games may be used as a useful complement to other teaching methods rather than as a replacement of these.

The following game is an adaptation of Walford's game 'Railway Pioneers' to Canadian conditions. It shows that the basic model developed by Walford may be used with due changes in detail for other areas in the world (Robert 1974).

Objectives
This game may be used with students of 14–16 years of age. The teachers need to know it well as they will be responsible for applying its various rules.
1. To identify the physical constraints (relief, rivers, climate, distances) on railway construction.
2. To discover the technical construction problems met by the railway engineers.

3. To find out which chance factors have a positive or negative influence on railway construction.
4. To develop co-operative behaviour among the students.
5. To make students analyse problems met and take appropriate decisions.

Materials required
Provided:
1. Six relief maps of Canada (Fig. 3.6) and a grid (Fig. 3.7) on which are printed:
   (a) physical constraints as figures (2 to 8);
   (b) town locations;
   (c) control stations (in red);
   (d) chance points (in blue);
2. Six transparencies on which the student will draw his railway routes.
3. Six dice.
4. Ten control point cards.
5. Sixteen chance cards.
6. Six company cards showing their:
   (a) registration;
   (b) capital;
   (c) headquarters;
   (d) contract.
7. Report forms.
8. A master transparency for the teacher.
9. A transparency showing the whole game.

Not provided but recommended:
1. A wall map of the relief of Canada.
2. A map showing Canadian railways to enable a comparison with reality at the end of the game.
3. For each group, a relief map of Canada.
4. Felt pens of different colours (washable).

Aims of the game
Each group of students forms a railway company of the nineteenth and early twentieth century, whose aim is to build a railway from one end of Canada to the other, bearing in mind the departure and proposed arrival points. Each group must take note during the game of the different factors likely to influence railway-building such as the relief, the need to cross rivers, to pass through towns, the exigencies imposed at the control points and the chance factors.

The groups
For the purposes of the game the Grand-Trunk and Inter-colonial

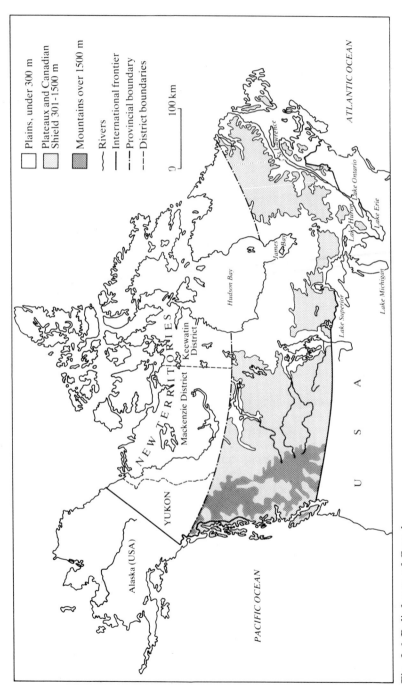

Fig. 3.6 Relief map of Canada

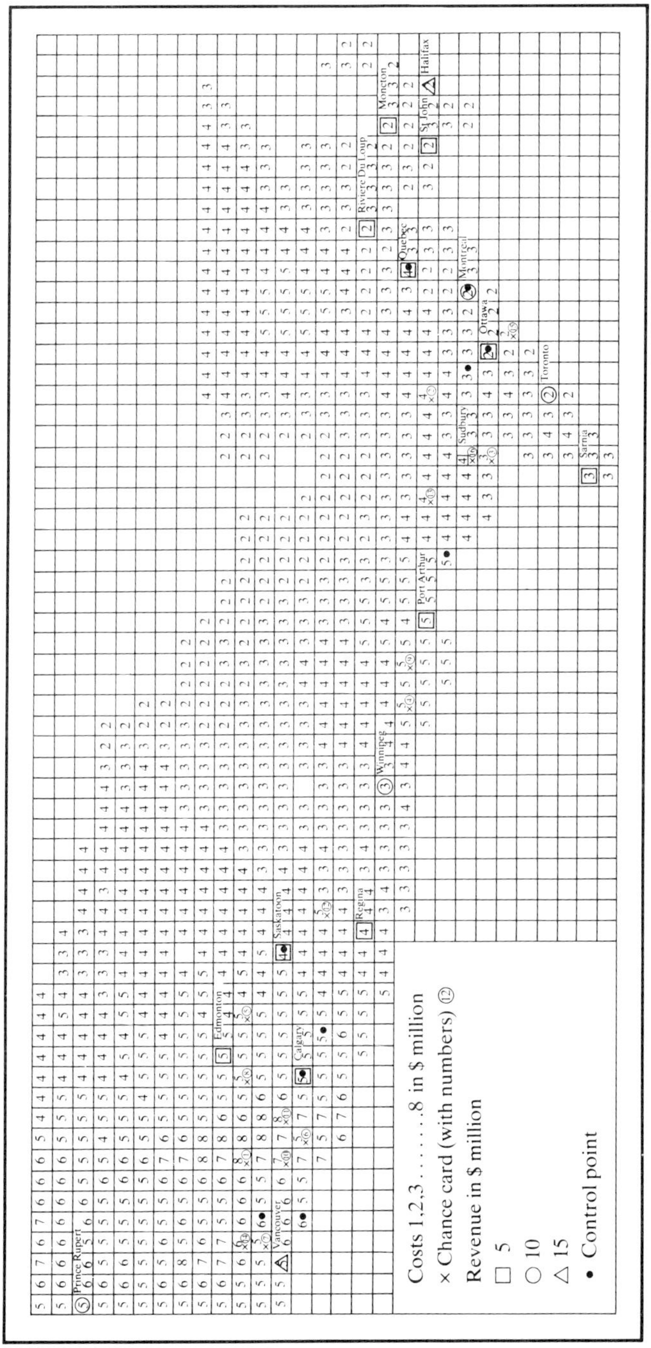

Fig. 3.7 Grid for the railway game

companies were eliminated, thereby leaving three main transconti-
nental companies:
The Canadian Pacific;
The Canadian Northern;
The National Transcontinental Grand Trunk Pacific (N.T.G.T.P.).
If necessary, it is possible to divide each company into two halves, an
eastern half starting from Quebec and a western half starting from
Winnipeg, but each building railways westwards.

Names of groups
Once the student groups have been formed, they may choose the
company that they wish to be. The easiest way is to let the chairman
of each company pick up a name card lying face down from the
teacher's desk.

Starting the game
The order in which the companies start building the railway may be
determined by throwing a die. Movement along the map is also
determined by the dice.

Rules and terminology
Companies and their capital:
1. Canadian Northern Railway Company (west section).
   Capital $45 million.
2. Canadian Northern Railway Company (east section).
   Capital $40 million.
3. N.T.G.T.P. (east section).
   Capital $40 million.
4. N.T.G.T.P. (west section)
   Capital (fictional) $35 million.
5. Canadian Pacific Railway (east section)
   Capital $40 million.
6. Canadian Pacific Railway (west section).
   Capital $25 million.

Costs imposed by physical constraints
These are marked as ranging from 2 to 8 on the map (Fig. 3.7). Each
unit stands for $million. Thus a figure of 5 means $5 million in costs
incurred by a company crossing that particular territory.

Towns
Squares, circles and triangles on the map indicate the location of
towns in Canada. According to the symbol used, these towns
represent revenues for the railway companies which reach them.

Squares $5 million   Circles $10 million   Triangles $15 million

These revenues are not cumulative – they are once-for-all revenues accruing to companies reaching the town first. If subsequently another company reaches the town, it will have to share its revenue with the first company according to a percentage fixed by the first company. For example Sarnia yields $5 million. The Canadian Pacific then received $5 million for being the first to reach Sarnia. If subsequently the Canadian Northern reached Sarnia then, although it also receives $5 million, the Canadian Pacific may insist on sharing this on a fifty/fifty basis, thereby leaving only $2.5 million for the Canadian Northern. If eventually the National Transcontinental reaches Sarnia it may be forced to give $2 million to the Canadian Pacific, $1.5 million to the Canadian Northern and only keep $1.5 million for itself. The share here is on a forty/thirty/thirty basis.

These are given by way of example; in practice the first company to reach the town may impose its own rates on subsequent companies to reach the town.

Rivers
From time to time companies will have to construct bridges over rivers. Unless otherwise indicated, this will cost the company $2 million in each case.

Control points
The dots on the map indicate control points where construction must stop, even if the dice play would allow a company to continue beyond the control point.

The referee (teacher) will indicate at the control points whether each group may continue or will need to retrace its steps. Precise directives will be given in each case by the referee. If the company is allowed to continue building it will travel on the number of steps allowed by its dice throw.

Chance cards
The crosses indicate that chance cards must be taken up if a company stops at this spot. These cards indicate whether the company gains or loses money. A small number by the cross will indicate to the referee which chance card is appropriate.

Report forms
These consist of balance sheets of revenues and expenses. All such items must be entered on the sheet. Further, after moving through ten squares, each company must buy up more rolling-stock to enable it to proceed to the next stage. To keep a count of the need to buy such rolling-stock, each company is required to keep a tally of the cumulative number of squares through which it has passed from the

beginning. With one die, it is not possible to begin buying more rolling-stock until just before the third throw.

Capital
This is the money each company starts with at the beginning of each game.

Net capital
This is the money each company has at the end of each stage and consists of the initial capital plus or minus any revenues and/or expenses incurred during that stage.

Balance
This is the revenue minus the expenses at each stage of the railway construction.

Total costs per stage
This is the total of all costs incurred at each stage.

Automatic revenue
At the end of each stage each company will receive $2.5 million if it has covered three squares or less, and $5 million if it has covered four squares or more. *N.B.* If you lose your turn or are subject to 'demolition' you cannot receive this automatic revenue. You will then transfer the automatic revenue which you received two turns ago but which you did not use.

Deficit
A group cannot play if:
1. it is in deficit before playing;
2. by throwing the dice it spends more capital than it has. It can then only play up to its capital resources and wait for more revenue before playing.

   In order to become solvent again, a company may miss several turns. It will receive automatic revenue and may start playing again as soon as its capital is sufficient to allow it to continue constructing the railway.

End of game
This occurs as soon as a company has attained its terminus, or at any appropriate time determined by the teacher–referee.

Control points cards
1. QUEBEC CONTROL POINT
Several companies will need to cross Quebec Bridge. The first company to do so must disburse $15 million for the construction costs

and miss one turn (construction time). Companies subsequently using the bridge must also lose one turn and must negotiate with the first company for crossing rights.

2. MONTREAL CONTROL POINT

As for the Quebec Bridge, but the first company to build the Victoria Bridge must pay $7 million and lose a turn. Other companies also lose a turn and negotiate crossing dues.

3. OTTAWA RIVER CONTROL POINT

This territory is not to be used by any of the companies. All companies having gone in that direction must rip up their tracks at half cost back a sufficient number of squares to allow them to set off in another direction. This demolition of track must be noted on the report forms under the heading 'Control point'.

4. GOUIN RESERVOIR (ABITIBI, P.Q.) CONTROL POINT

This area is prohibited for the Canadian Pacific and Canadian Northern companies. These companies, if they reach this control point must tear up their tracks back four squares at half cost. Note the demolition on the report form under the heading 'Control point'.

5. LAKE SUPERIOR CONTROL POINT

This is forbidden for the N.T.G.T.P. Railway Company. The track must be torn up for four squares back at half cost. A new direction must be chosen at the next turn. Report the demolition on the report form under the heading 'Control point'.

6. SASKATOON CONTROL POINT

Not allowed to the Canadian Pacific and N.T.G.T.P. companies. No revenues to be derived from this town, and track to be demolished at half cost back to a point permitting a new direction to be taken. Note on report form under the heading 'Control point' and cancel revenues attributed to town.

7. SOUTH SASKATCHEWAN CONTROL POINT

Prohibited to all companies. Tear up track back two squares at half cost. Take a new direction at the next turn. Note demolition costs on report form under heading 'Control point'.

8. CALGARY CONTROL POINT

This town is monopolized by the Canadian Pacific Company, and any other company building tracks to it must forfeit the town's revenues and tear up its tracks at half cost for a distance sufficient to allow it to change direction. Note the demolition on the report form under the heading 'Control point'.

9. FRAZER RIVER CONTROL POINT

Forbidden to the Canadian Pacific who must demolish their tracks back four squares if they reach the river (at half cost). They may choose another direction at the next turn. Note the costs on the report form under the heading 'Control point'.

10. PACIFIC COAST CONTROL POINT

This is forbidden to all companies, and all must retrace their steps by five squares at half cost if they reach this point and find a new direction. Note the demolition costs on the report form under 'Control point'.

Rolling-stock purchases

Each time a company has crossed ten squares it must invest in new rolling-stock. The cost is $100 000 for each ten squares up to a maximum of fifty.

Locomotive	$12 000
Goods truck	$ 725
Passenger coach	$ 1 000
Flat truck	$ 575

Chance cards

1. AVALANCHE

As a result of intensive blasting operations in the Rocky Mountains, the Canadian Northern workmen have provoked an avalanche causing ten lives to be lost and very serious damage. Costs are $2 million inclusive of damages to the bereaved families.

2. GOVERNMENT GRANTS

As it is building in an area which is sparsely inhabited and developed, the N.T.G.T.P. is being given financial help by the government. As a result the next turn will cost half the costs indicated on the map.

3. GOOD WEATHER

The area to the south of Sudbury is enjoying a long period of good weather, thereby facilitating railway construction. The companies operating in this section gain $2 million in revenue.

4. LOUIS RIEL

The Louis Riel rising involving the half-castes in 1885, will enable (irony of fate) the Canadian Pacific Railway Company to complete its current works by obtaining a government loan and through its shares being quoted on the British stock-market. It therefore gains $3 million in capital.

5. SETTLEMENT IN THE WEST
The growth in the population of the prairies at the beginning of the century, and the development of wheat farming encouraged by the Canadian Northern Company's low freight charges compared with the Canadian Pacific's have favoured the former company which now receives $1 million additional revenue.

6. INDIANS IN THE WEST
The religious authorities and numerous half-breeds in the West have encouraged the Cree Indians to sign a treaty allowing the Canadian Pacific to continue constructing its railway through their territory. This saves many kilometres of detour. The Canadian Pacific Company therefore benefits and is given an additional throw of the dice.

7. CHINESE LABOURERS
The arrival of numerous Chinese labourers on the Pacific coast enables labour to be hired in British Columbia. The Canadian Northern and N.T.G.T.P. benefit from this and their costs are halved for their next turn.

8. CROSSING DESERT
The territory around Edmonton is part of the Second Northern Reserve and belongs to the Canadian Pacific Company. Thus the Canadian Northern and N.T.G.T.P. companies must pay dues to the Canadian Pacific even if they are the first to reach Edmonton. These dues amount to $2 million.

9. MARSHLANDS
All companies operating to the north-west of Lake Superior between Port Arthur and Lake of the Woods have great difficulties with the marshy conditions. As a result the costs per square for the next turn are increased by $1 million.

10. FOOD SHORTAGES
The manager of the N.T.G.T.P. Company has forgotten to send an order for the workers' food. As a result the men have to be rationed and the number of hours of work is reduced. Miss one turn.

11. FINANCIAL PLOT
The N.T.G.T.P. has intrigued with London bankers (Baring Bros), and as a result the Canadian Pacific finds it impossible to sell its shares in Britain. The Canadian Pacific misses one turn.

12. SNOWSTORM
An early snowstorm (25 September) makes work impossible in

Saskatchewan between the Assiniboine and Saskatchewan rivers. The companies involved must miss one turn.

13. ALL'S WELL
Work continues without interruption.

14. FLOODS
Owing to the rise of floodwaters in the Columbia River caused by the melting snows in the Western Cordillera, all companies operating in the area miss one turn and must pay $1 million to repair damage to tracks.

15. FLOODS
The waters of the Ottawa River have suddenly risen and the work teams in the area must wait for the fall in the river before continuing their work and repairing damage. Miss one turn and spend $500 000 in repairs.

16. GROWTH IN SUDBURY
The mining centre at Sudbury develops quickly, thereby bringing extra revenues to the companies operating through these towns. Throw a die to find out how much your company benefits: 1 on the die equals $1 million in revenue.

Individualized learning

Individualized learning refers to those methods which enable students to learn individually and which do not depend on teacher-to-pupil interaction. It is particularly suited to the learning of certain skills, concepts and principles which form a well-organized sequence and hierarchy. There are various ways in which individualized learning may be organized, but the most common and the most researched is that known as 'programmed learning'. Essentially a 'programme' is a series of stimulus–response sequences in which the question (stimulus) asks for an answer (the response) which the learner can immediately check for accuracy. Since the programme is arranged in very small 'steps', the response of the learner is usually accurate; this reinforces his learning and motivation and enables him to continue with the programme. Although some programmes are of the 'branching' type which allow fast learners to take 'large steps' in the sequence, most programmes are of the 'linear' type with short step sequences.

Programmed learning is useful as a means of giving remedial learning to students who have missed work and can make up this learning on their own, or simply as a variation on other teaching strategies. What evidence there is, indicates that as a teaching technique it is as effective as other techniques within a limited range of objectives. Clearly, it is a method which cannot be used over long periods of time with a class, otherwise boredom sets in. Neither is it a method suitable for open-ended situations or where expressive objectives are sought in human geography. It is suitable for such a skill as elementary map-reading. It is important to bear in mind that all teaching programmes need to be validated with a particular target population in mind, and that this means trying out the programme and modifying it until it works adequately.

Learning to read a medium-scale map (1/25 000, 1/50 000) presents certain difficulties for young students, e.g. those between 11 and 12 years of age. The main difficulty is the one facing all map-readers, namely how to convert the symbols on the map into a mental representation of the reality which they stand for. Most topographical maps show relief, drainage and such man-made features as towns, villages, buildings and means of communications, as well as the relevant names. There is therefore a problem of learning the symbols and the scale on which various features are represented. In most cases relief is shown with the aid of contour lines and spot heights. But maps give a plan or bird's-eye view of the world, whereas our daily experience of spatial reality is an elevation or side view. It is therefore necessary for the student to be able to carry out the mental operations required to transform a plan to a more normal ground viewpoint and vice versa. Further problems of vertical exaggeration will arise if students attempt to draw cross-sections, the exaggeration varying according to the extent of vertical relief on the ground.

Thus, in general, learning to read maps is not an easy process, and a skill not fully mastered will result in difficulties for the learner attempting to progress further. What follows is a programmed lesson with the title 'Simple land forms' (Okunrotifa 1974). These among others were tried out in Nigerian schools and constitute an introduction to certain aspects of map-reading. They were designed to be used by pupils aged 11 to 13, but are here given by way of samples.

SIMPLE LANDFORMS

Frame 1

You have known about hills and mountains.

Both of them are high land areas
rising above the surrounding lands.

Unlike hills, mountains often rise
above 300 metres.

Which is higher: a mountain
or a hill? _____

FIGURE 1 shows a hill over
90 metres.

Now, draw the contour lines
representing the hill.

FIGURE 1

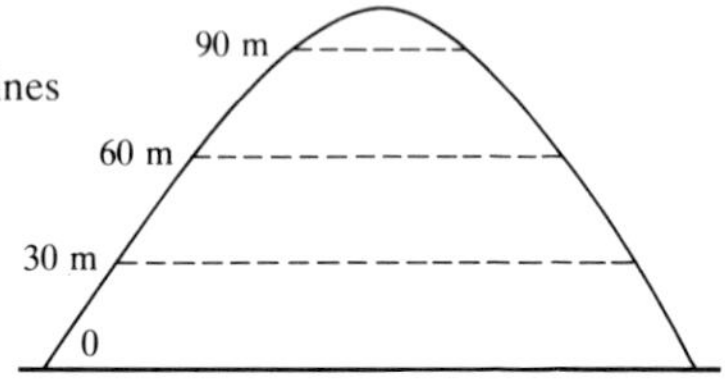

90 m
60 m
30 m
0

ANSWER

mountain

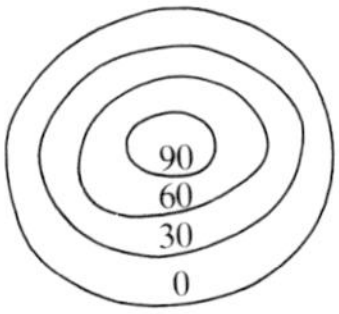

90
60
30
0

Frame 2

You have drawn contours showing a hill.
FIGURE 2 shows the contours representing a RIDGE.
A RIDGE is a LONG NARROW AREA OF HIGH LAND.

FIGURE 2

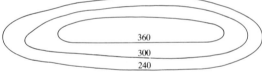

360
300
240

FIGURE 2 is a ————— and ————— highland
The ridge is over ——————————————— metres.

ANSWER

long, narrow

360

FIGURE 3 **Frame 3**

FIGURE 3 shows a —————
because it appears to be ·
a ————— ————— area
of high land.

150
180
210

ANSWER

ridge

Long narrow

FIGURE 4

FIGURE 4 also shows
a _____

It is a ____ and ____
highland

FIGURE 4

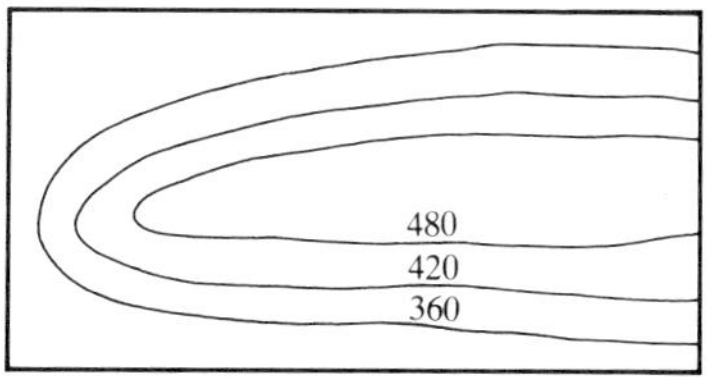

480
420
360

ANSWER

ridge

long narrow

A plateau is a HIGH LAND WHICH HAS A FLAT OR A
NEARLY FLAT SURFACE.

Which of the following: FIGURE 5, FIGURE 6, shows a hill?
Which of them shows a plateau?_____ (FIGURE 5/FIGURE 6)

FIGURE 5   FIGURE 6

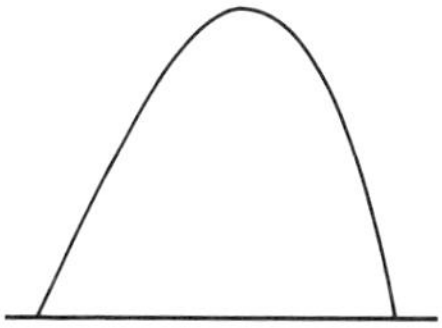

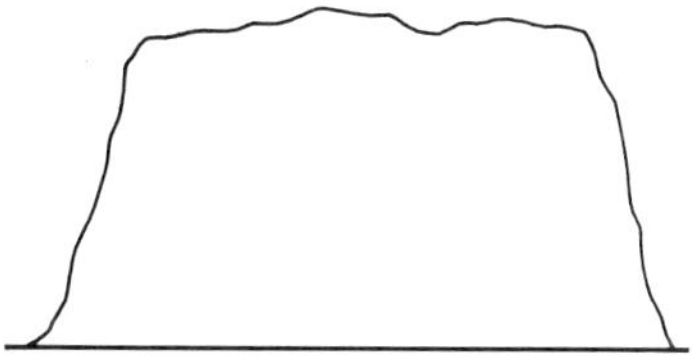

ANSWER

FIGURE 5 = HILL

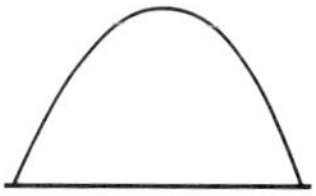

FIGURE 6 = PLATEAU

FIGURE 7A shows a plateau over 120 metres.
FIGURE 7B shows the contours representing the plateau.
A plateau is a high land which has a ____ or a nearly ____
surface, but a ridge is a ____ ____ area of high land.

FIGURE 7A: PLATEAU   FIGURE 7B: PLATEAU

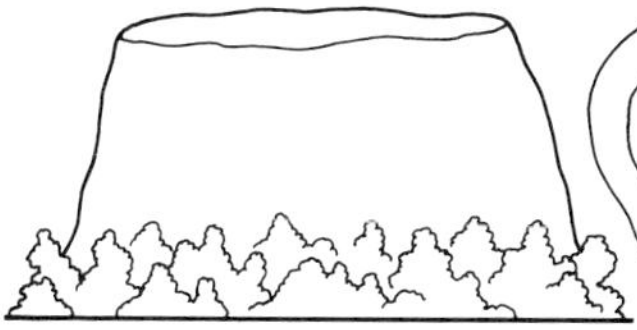

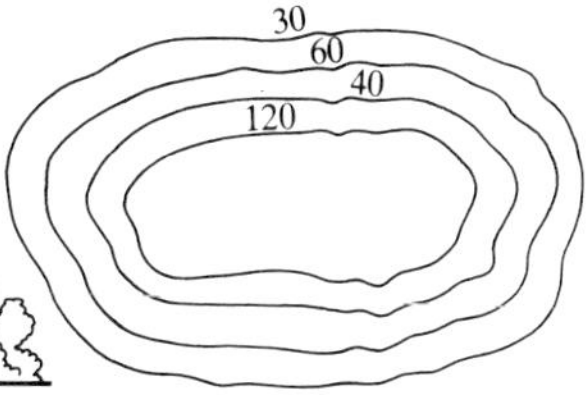

30
60
40
120

ANSWER

flat   flat

long, narrow

1. Which of the following contours: A and B below shows a plateau? _____

2. Which of the contours: A and B shows a ridge? _____

3. A high land which has a flat or a nearly flat surface is a _____

FIGURE 8

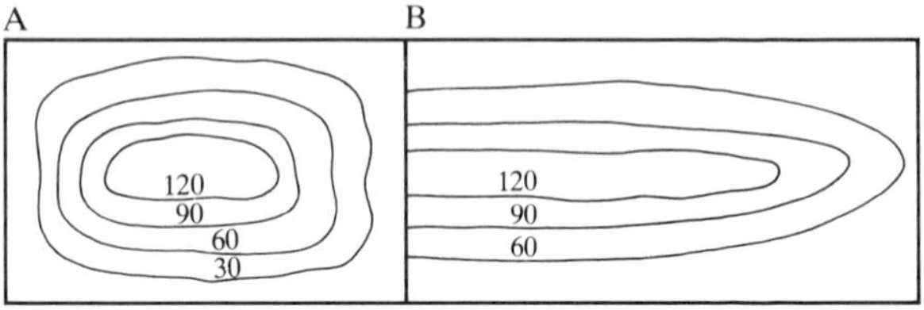

A   B

ANSWER

1. A

2. B

3. plateau

FIGURE 9 shows a _____

The highland has an almost _____ surface

FIGURE 9

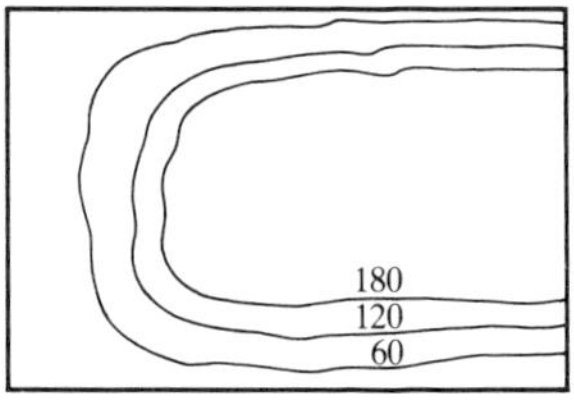

ANSWER

plateau

flat

FIGURE 10   FIGURE 11

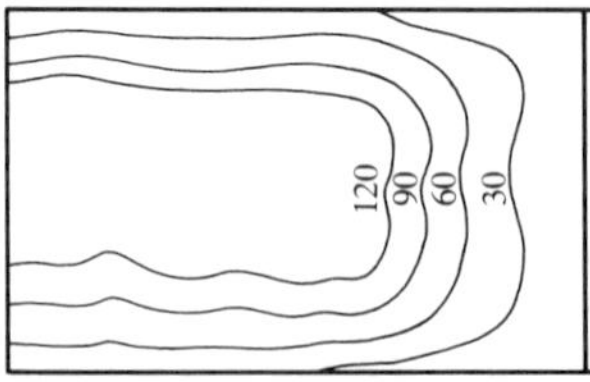

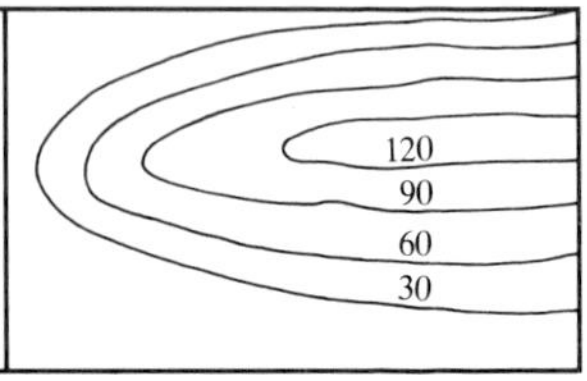

A ridge is a _____ and _____ area of high land but a plateau is a high land with a _____ surface

FIGURE 10 is a _____ FIGURE 11 is a _____

ANSWER

Frame 10

A ridge and a plateau are 2 different high lands. Now, let us learn about another type of high land.

long, narrow

flat

FIGURE 12

plateau

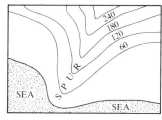

ridge

In FIGURE 12, a high land extends towards a lowland.

Such a HIGH LAND WHICH EXTENDS TOWARDS A LOWLAND
is called a _____

ANSWER

Frame 11

spur

A spur is a high land which extends towards a ——————.

ANSWER

Frame 12

FIGURE 13 shows a high land which extends towards a lowland. Such a high land is called a _____.

FIGURE 13

lowland

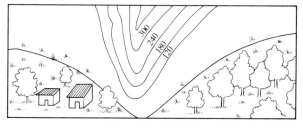

ANSWER   Frame 13

The contours representing
a spur look like letter
"V" V-shaped contours
may represent a _____.

FIGURE 14

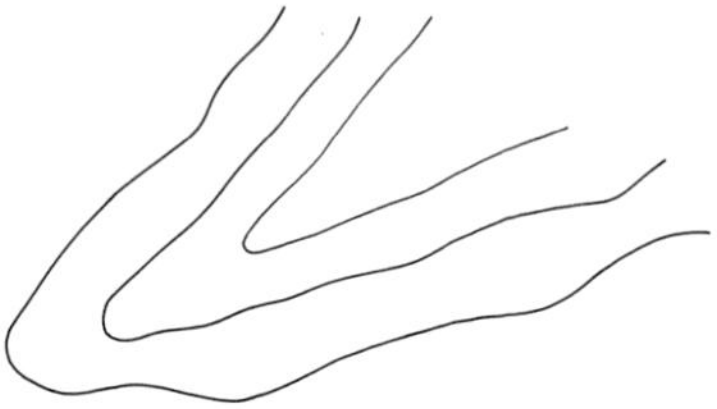

spur

ANSWER   Frame 14

spur

1. A long narrow area of high land is a _____.
2. A high land which has flat or an almost flat
    surface is a _____.
3. A spur is a high land which _____ to a _____.
4. The contours representing a spur look like
    letter _____.

ANSWER   Frame 15

1. ridge   LOWLAND areas may be FLAT or nearly FLAT.

2. plateau   On a contour map, a flat lowland is shown
                  as an area with few IF ANY, contour lines
3. extends   at all.
   lowland
                  There may be _____ (very few/very many)
4. V   contour lines on the map of a flat lowland
                  area.

ANSWER

very few

Frame 16

FIGURE 15

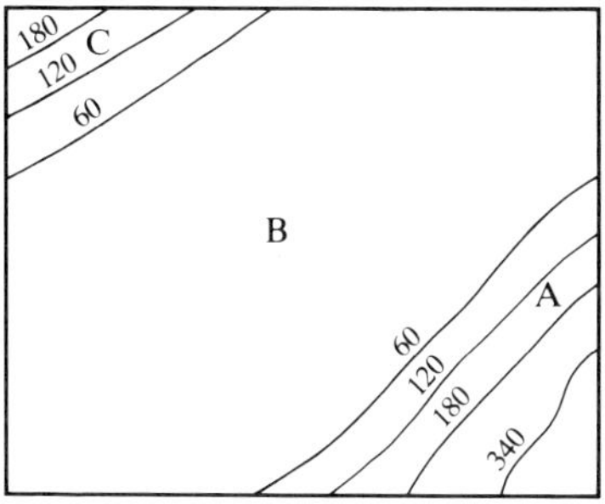

Look at FIGURE 15
Which of the points
A, B, C, lies on a flat
lowland?_____

ANSWER

B

Frame 17

FIGURE 16 has a _____ (very flat/nearly flat) lowland.
FIGURE 17 has a _____ (very flat/nearly flat) lowland.

FIGURE 16   FIGURE 17

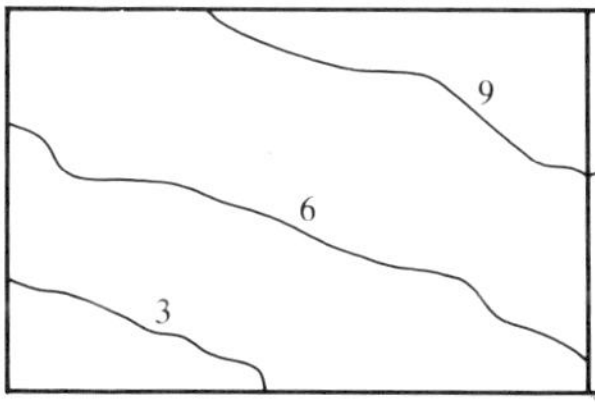

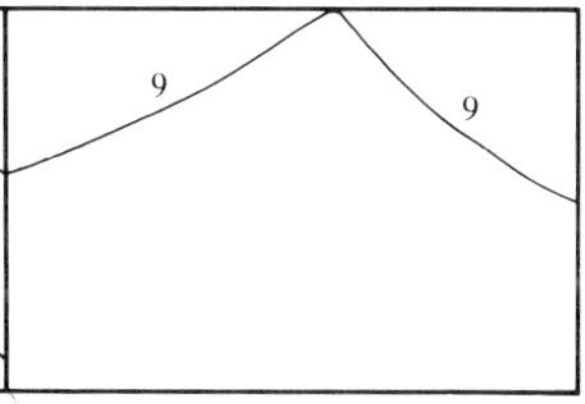

ANSWER

FIGURE 16
nearly flat

FIGURE 17
very flat

Frame 18

You know that a valley is a low area of ground
usually cut by a river or stream between areas of higher ground.

FIGURE 18

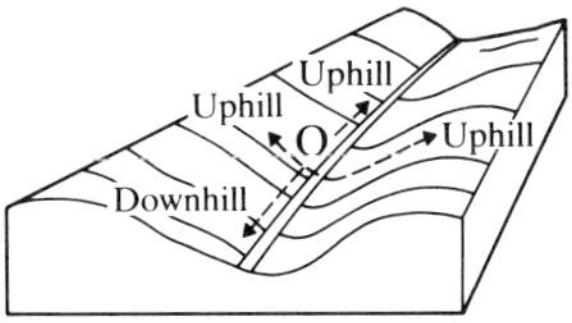

In
FIGURE 18, O lies in a _____.

ANSWER

valley

Frame 19

In FIGURE 19, which of the following: A, B, C, lies in a valley _____

How many hills surround the valley? _____

The Vertical Interval (V.I.) of the contour is _____ metres

FIGURE 19

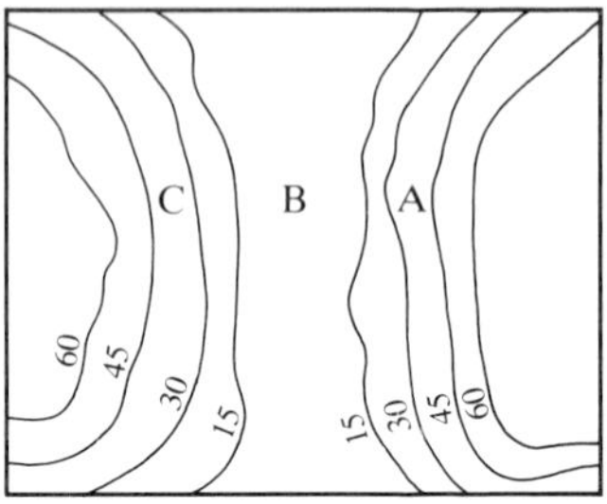

ANSWER

B

Two

15 metres

Frame 20

FIGURE 20

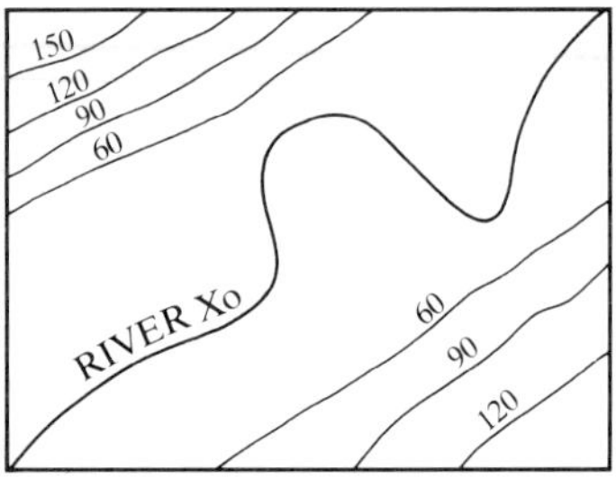

Scale 1 centimetre to 20 kilometres

The river Xo flows through a _____.

The scale of the diagram shows that the bottom of the valley is _____ (narrow/wide).

ANSWER

valley

wide

Frame 21

Like spurs, the common contours representing valleys are V-shaped.

In FIGURE 21, the contour lines are _____ shaped and they represent a valley.

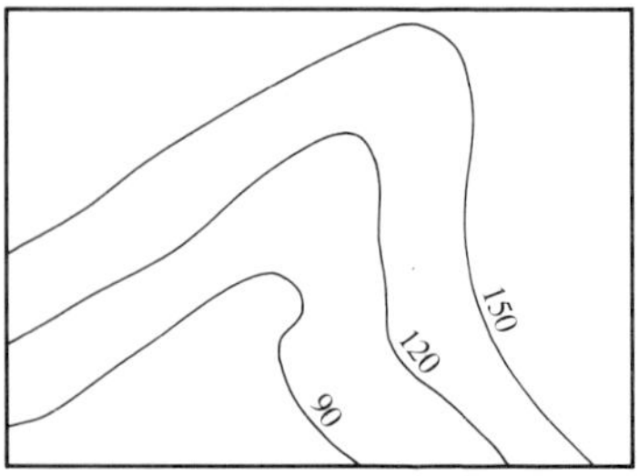

ANSWER

V

FIGURE 22 shows a river valley   Frame 22

FIGURE 22

A river flows from a
height of _____
metres above
sea-level in the
valley.

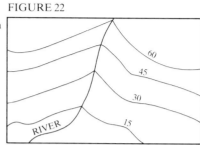

ANSWER

60

Frame 23

V-shaped contour lines may
represent a _____ or a _____ .

ANSWER

When the arms of V-shaped
contour lines are close, the
valleys are NARROW but
when the arms are wide the
valleys are WIDE.

FIGURE 23 is a _____
(wide/narrow) valley

FIGURE 24 is a _____
(wide/narrow) valley

valley, spur

Frame 24

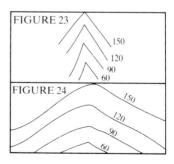

ANSWER

Frame 25

In FIGURE 25 the highest contour lines: 150 m, 120 m are outside and the lowest contour lines: 90 m, 60 m, are inside.

narrow

For a valley, the highest V-shaped contour lines are usually _____ (inside/outside).

wide

FIGURE 25

Frame 26

ANSWER

outside

FIGURE 26   FIGURE 27

Study FIGURE 26 and FIGURE 27. You may think that both FIGURES are almost alike but if you study them closely you will see that in FIGURE 26, the highest contours are outside and in FIGURE 27, the LOWEST contours are _____

ANSWER

Frame 27

FIGURE 28   FIGURE 29

outside

When the highest V-shaped contour lines are outside it is a valley. But when the lowest V-shaped contour lines are outside it is a SPUR.

FIGURE _____ is a valley. FIGURE _____ is a spur.

ANSWER

FIGURE 29 =
valley

FIGURE 28 =
spur

Frame 28

1. You have known that a spur is a high land which extends towards a _____ .
2. You have also known that V-shaped contours may either be a _____ or a _____ .
3. When the highest V-shaped contours are outside, it is a _____ .
4. When the lowest V-shaped contours are outside, it is a _____ .

ANSWER

lowland

valley, spur

valley

spur

Frame 29

When the _____ V-shaped contours are outside, it is a valley and when the _____ V-shaped contours are outside it is a spur.

ANSWER

highest

lowest

Frame 30

FIGURE 30 shows a _____ (spur/valley).

You know this because the _____ V-shaped contours are outside.

FIGURE 30

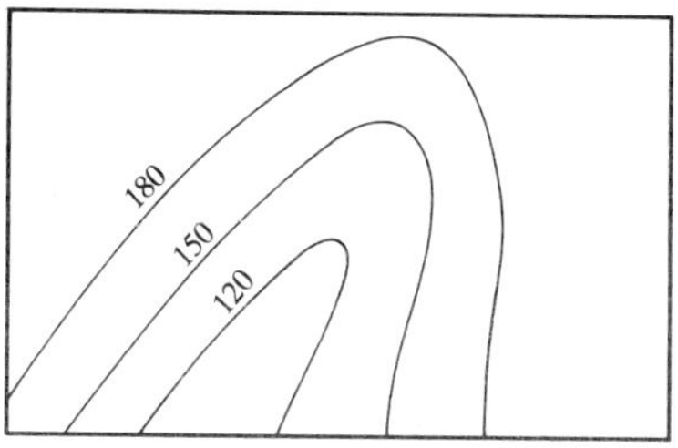

180
150
120

ANSWER   Frame 31

FIGURE 31 shows a _____
(valley/spur).

valley

You know this because the
_____ V-shaped contours
are outside.

A high land extending
towards a low land is
a_____ .

highest

FIGURE 31

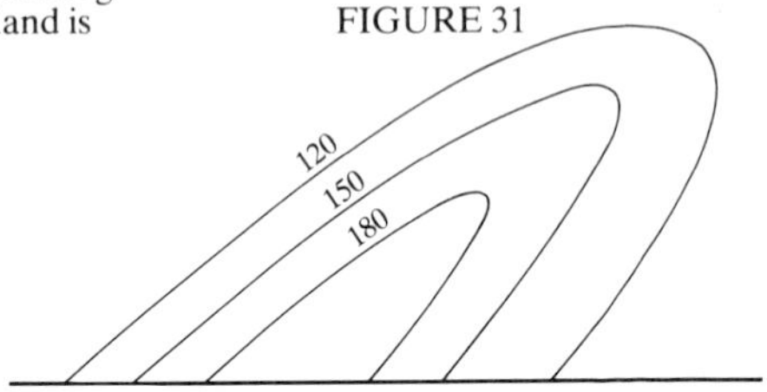

120
150
180

ANSWER   Frame 32

Which is a valley? _____ (FIGURE 32/FIGURE 33)

spur

Which is a spur? _____ (FIGURE 32/FIGURE 33)

FIGURE 32   FIGURE 33

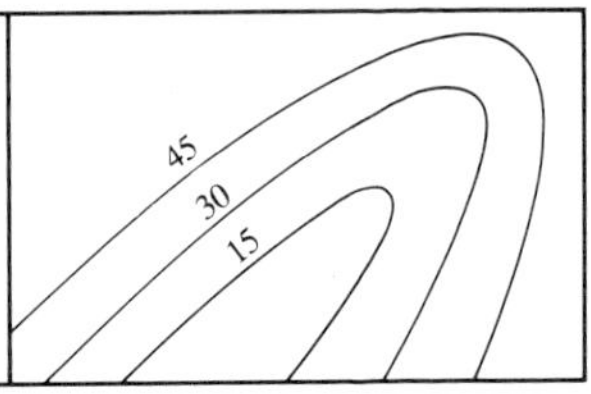

lowest

spur

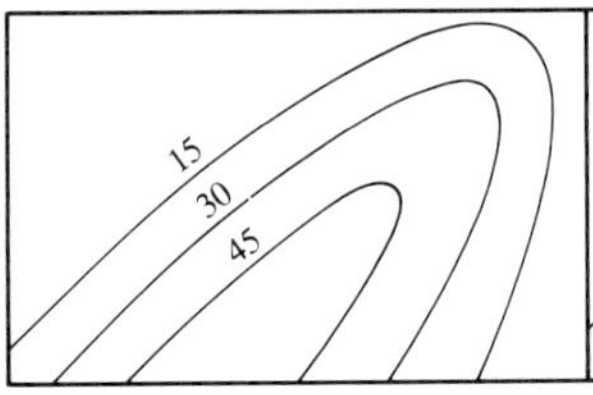

15
30
45

45
30
15

ANSWER   Frame 33

FIGURE 33 =
valley

You have known that:

1. A plateau is a high land which may
   have a _____ surface.

FIGURE 32 =
spur

2. A ridge is a _____ _____ area of high land.

3. A spur is a high land which _____ towards a _____ .

ANSWER

1. flat

2. long, narrow

3. extends lowland

Frame 34

You also know that:

1. V-shaped contours may either be a _____ or a _____ .

2. When the <u>highest</u> V-shaped contours are outside, it is a _____ .

3. When the <u>lowest</u> V-shaped contours are outside, it is a _____ .

4. Draw, in your answer papers, the contours for a valley and a spur.

ANSWER
1. valley
   or
   spur

2. valley

3. spur

4. compare your drawings with those in frame 32

Any piece of land that is not level has what we call SLOPE.

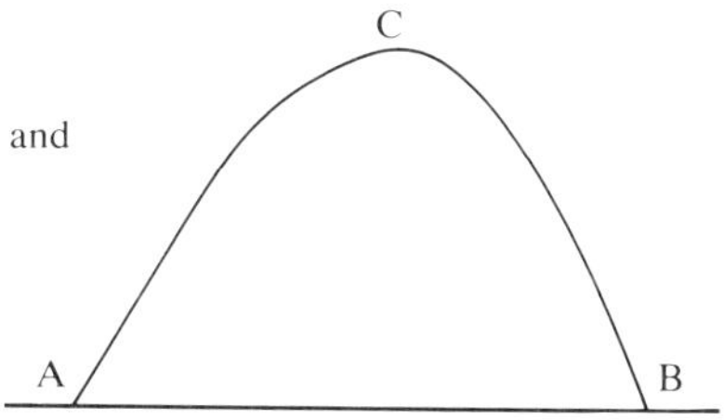

IN FIGURE 34, AC and BC are _____ of a hill.

Frame 35

FIGURE 34

ANSWER

slopes

AC and BC are 2 slopes of the hill in FIGURE 35. The slope of AC is NOT broken: it is an even slope.

The slope of BC is <u>broken:</u> it is an <u>UNEVEN</u> slope

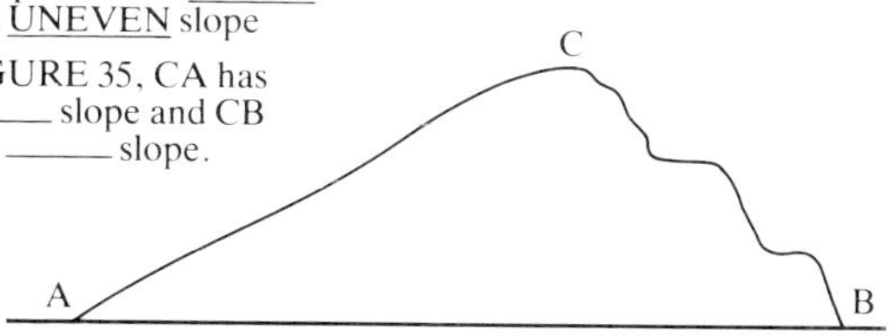

In FIGURE 35, CA has an _____ slope and CB has an _____ slope.

Frame 36

FIGURE 35

ANSWER

even

uneven

Frame 37

The contour lines in FIGURE 36 are evenly spaced. This means that they are almost at equal distances apart: AB = BC. The contour lines therefore show an EVEN slope.

FIGURE 36

A slope is even when the contour lines are _____ spaced or are almost at _____ distances apart.

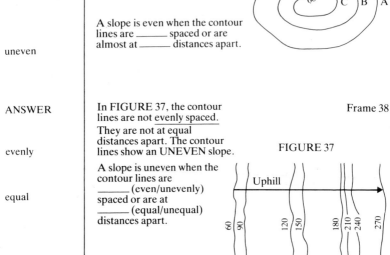

ANSWER

evenly

equal

Frame 38

In FIGURE 37, the contour lines are not evenly spaced. They are not at equal distances apart. The contour lines show an UNEVEN slope.

FIGURE 37

A slope is uneven when the contour lines are _____ (even/unevenly) spaced or are at _____ (equal/unequal) distances apart.

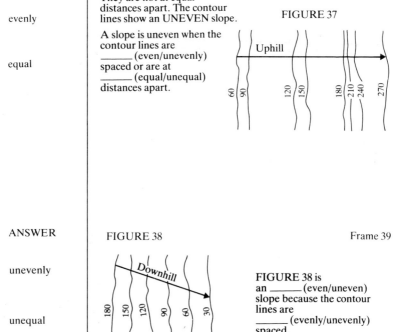

ANSWER

unevenly

unequal

Frame 39

FIGURE 38

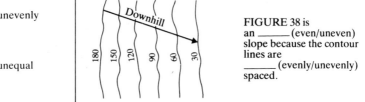

FIGURE 38 is an _____ (even/uneven) slope because the contour lines are _____ (evenly/unevenly) spaced.

ANSWER

even

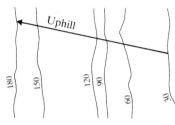

FIGURE 39

FIGURE 39 is an
_____ (even/uneven)
slope because the contour
lines are _____ spaced

Frame 40

evenly

ANSWER

uneven

When contour lines are almost equal
distances apart, they show an _____ slope
but when they are not at equal distances
apart they show an _____ slope.

Frame 41

unevenly

ANSWER

even

uneven

When land rises very quickly so that it
is difficult to ride a bicycle up it, we
say that the slope is STEEP.

Land that rises slowly has a
gentle slope.

In FIGURE 40,
AB is a _____ slope
BC is a _____ slope

Frame 42

FIGURE 40

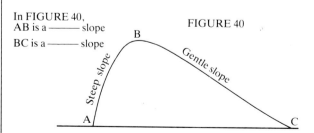

ANSWER

steep

gentle

Frame 43

Study carefully the 2 FIGURES as you read this:

FIGURE 42 shows the contours representing FIGURE 41

Along AB where there is a steep slope, the contour lines are close together but along BC where there is a ______ slope, the contour lines are farther apart.

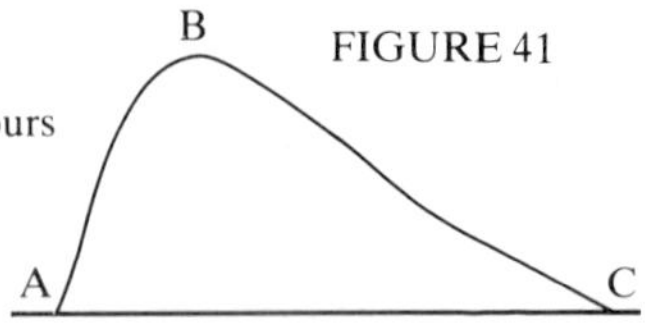
B
A
C

FIGURE 41

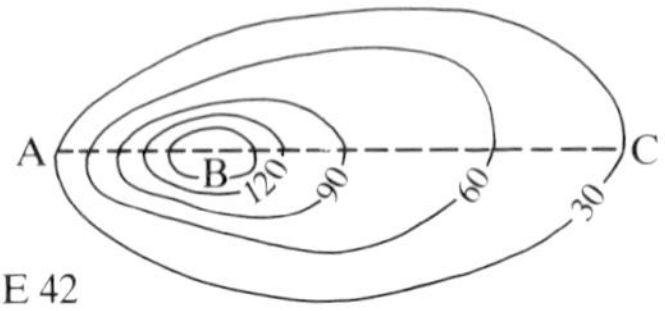
A
B
C
120
90
60
30

FIGURE 42

ANSWER

gentle

Frame 44

When the contour lines are close together, the slope of land is STEEP.
But the slope of the land is GENTLE when the contour lines are ______ ______

In FIGURE 43:

Slope CB is ______

Slope AB is ______

FIGURE 43

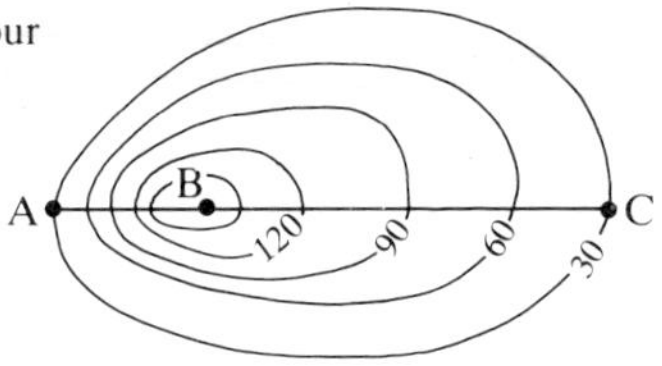
A
B
C
120
90
60
30

ANSWER

far apart

gentle

steep

Frame 45

FIGURE 44

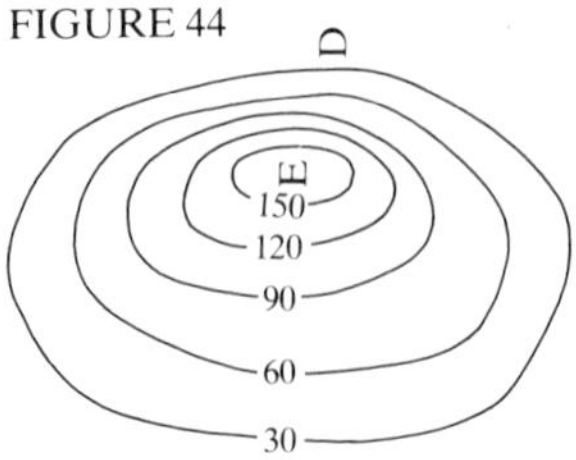
D
E
150
120
90
60
30

In FIGURE 44, ED is a ______ slope.

You know this because the contour lines along ED are

______ ______ (farther apart/closer together)

ANSWER	FIGURE 45	Frame 46

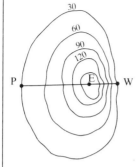

steep

closer together

Along EW the contour lines
are ——————— together than
along PE.

EW has a ——————— slope
and PE has a ——————— slope.

ANSWER		Frame 47

closer

steep

gentle

The closer together the contour lines, the s ———
the slope. The farther apart the contour lines,
the g ——————— the slope.

ANSWER	FIGURE 46	Frame 48

steeper

gentler

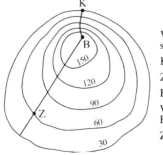

What is the height, above
sea-level, of the following:

K = ——————— metres
Z = ——————— metres
B = ——————— metres

Which is going to be an
EASIER SLOPE to climb:

ZB or KB? ———————

ANSWER

K = 30 metres

Z = 60 metres

B = 158 metres

ZB

Frame 49

Look at Frame 48, FIGURE 46, ZB will be an easier slope to climb because it is less s_____ .

KB is a _____ slope.

ANSWER

steep

steep

Frame 50

Look at the highland in FIGURE 47

The main slope in the west is AKB and the main slope in the east is _____ .

FIGURE 47

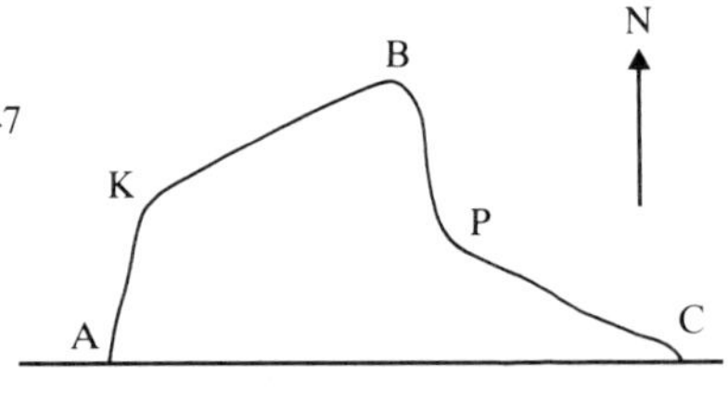

ANSWER

CPC or BPC

Frame 51

Let us study slope AKB,
AK is a steep slope
but KB is a gentle slope.

A slope which rises steeply at the bottom and gently at the top is called a CONVEX slope.
AKB is a _____ slope.

FIGURE 47

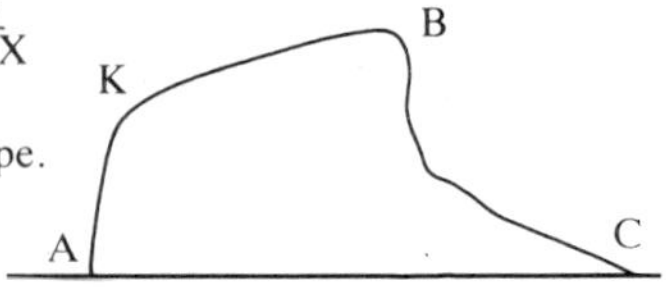

ANSWER

Frame 52

A convex slope rises
steeply at the bottom
and _____ at the top.

convex

AK rises _____ .

KB rises _____ .

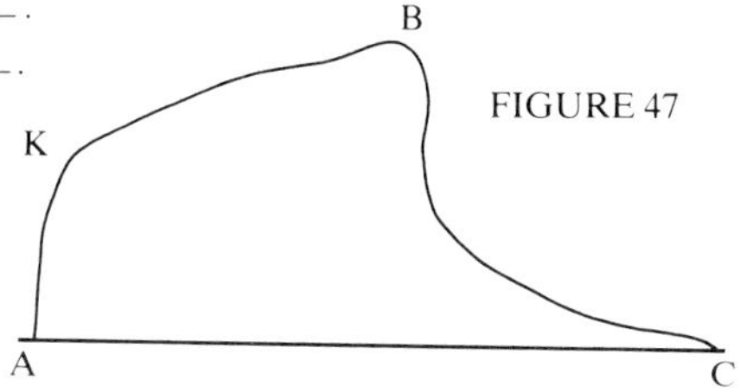

FIGURE 47

ANSWER

Frame 53

Let us study slope CPB

In slope CPB, CP is a gentle
slope but PB is a steep slope.

gently

A slope which rises gently at
the bottom and steeply at the
top is called a CONCAVE
slope.

steeply

gently

CPB is a _____ slope.

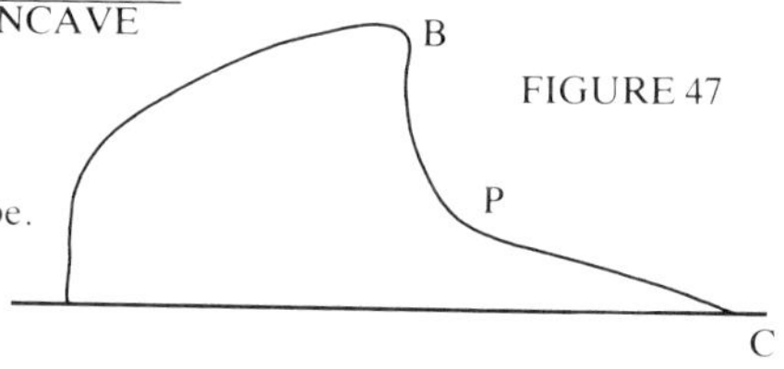

FIGURE 47

ANSWER

Frame 54

A concave slope rises
gently at the bottom
and _____ at the top.

concave

CP rises _____ .

PB rises _____ .

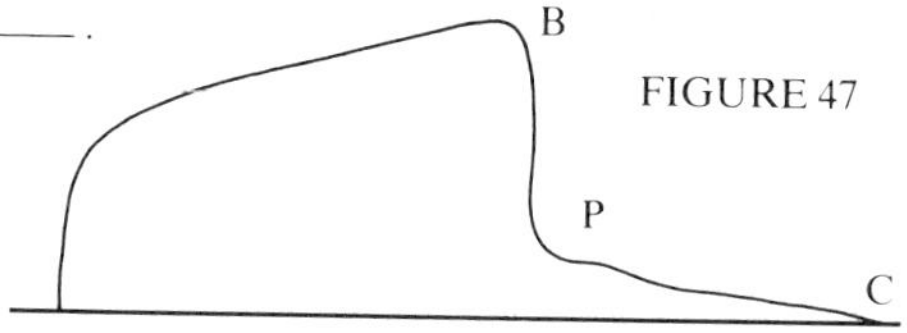

FIGURE 47

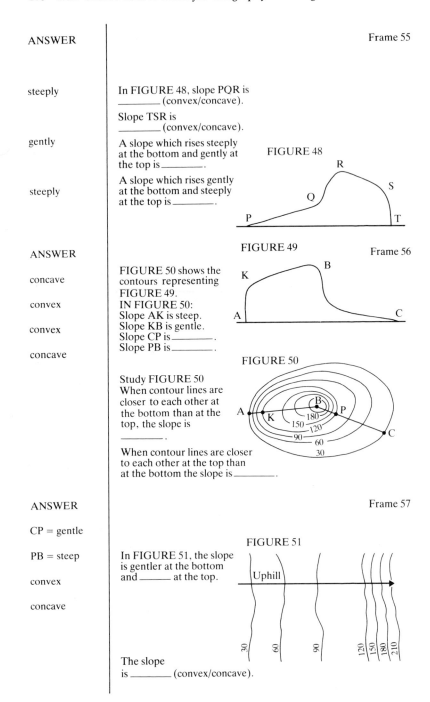

ANSWER

steeply

gently

steeply

Frame 55

In FIGURE 48, slope PQR is
_____ (convex/concave).

Slope TSR is
_____ (convex/concave).

A slope which rises steeply
at the bottom and gently at
the top is _____.

A slope which rises gently
at the bottom and steeply
at the top is _____.

FIGURE 48

FIGURE 49

ANSWER

concave

convex

convex

concave

Frame 56

FIGURE 50 shows the
contours representing
FIGURE 49.
IN FIGURE 50:
Slope AK is steep.
Slope KB is gentle.
Slope CP is _____.
Slope PB is _____.

Study FIGURE 50
When contour lines are
closer to each other at
the bottom than at the
top, the slope is

_____.

When contour lines are closer
to each other at the top than
at the bottom the slope is _____.

FIGURE 50

ANSWER

CP = gentle

PB = steep

convex

concave

Frame 57

FIGURE 51

In FIGURE 51, the slope
is gentler at the bottom
and _____ at the top.

Uphill

The slope
is _____ (convex/concave).

ANSWER

steeper

concave

Frame 58

FIGURE 52

Uphill
30
60
90
120
150
180
210

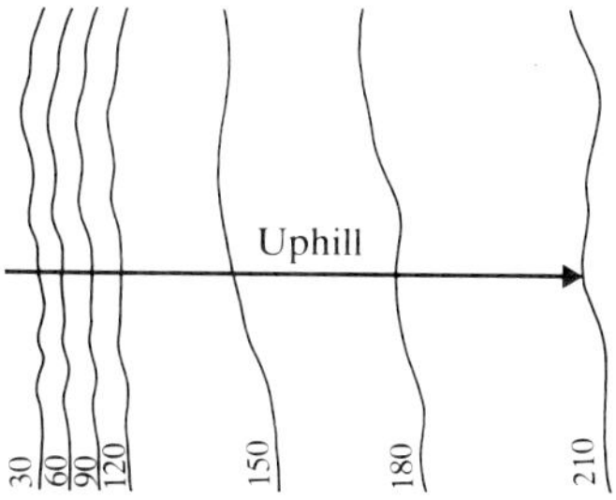

IN FIGURE 52, the slope is ________ at the bottom and ________ at the top.

The slope is ________ (convex/concave).

ANSWER

steeper

gentler

convex

Frame 59

FIGURE 53

Uphill
30
60
90
120

FIGURE 54

Uphill
30
60
90
120
150

FIGURE 55

Uphill
30
60
90
120
150

1. Which of the FIGURES shows a convex slope? FIGURE ________
2. Which of the FIGURES shows an even slope? FIGURE ________
3. Which of the FIGURES shows a concave slope? FIGURE ________

ANSWER

Figure 55 = Convex

Figure 53 = Even

Figure 54 = Concave

Frame 60

1. A high land extending into a lowland is a ________.
2. A high land with a flat surface is a ________.
3. A long, narrow area of high land is a ________.
4. FIGURE 56 shows a ________.

FIGURE 56

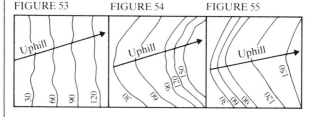

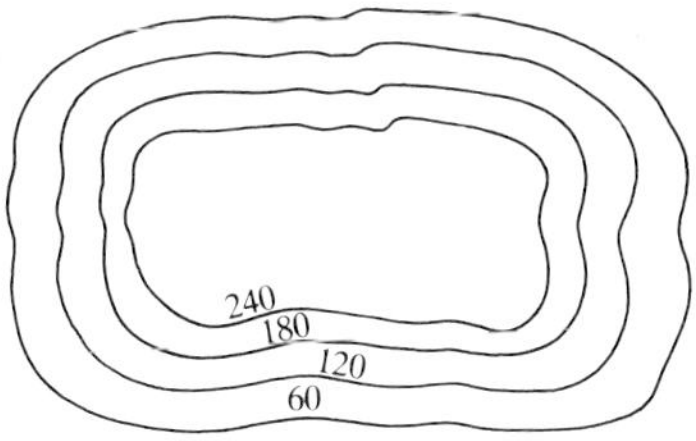

240
180
120
60

ANSWER

1. spur
2. plateau
3. ridge
4. plateau

Frame 61

FIGURE 57 FIGURE 58

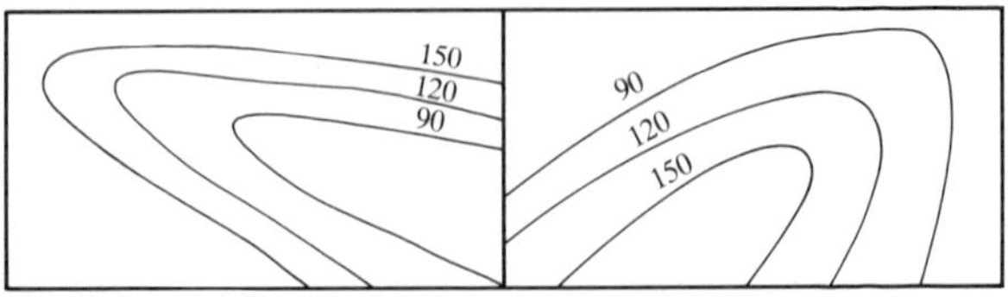

1. Which of the FIGURES is a spur? FIGURE ______
2. Which of the FIGURES is a valley? FIGURE ______

ANSWER

1. FIGURE 58
2. FIGURE 57

Frame 62

1. A high land which extends towards a lowland is a ______.
2. FIGURE 59 shows a ______.

FIGURE 59

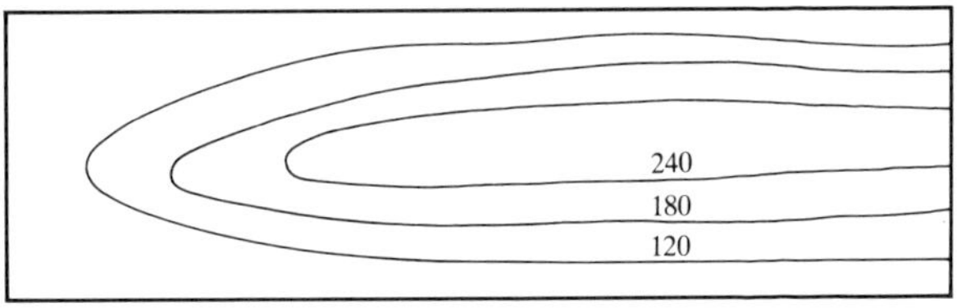

ANSWER

1. spur
2. ridge

Frame 63

1. The closer together the contour lines the s ______ the slope.
   The farther apart the contour lines the g ______ the slope.
2. A slope that is steep at the bottom, and becoming less steep high up is ______.
3. A slope that is steep at the top, and becoming less steep lower down is ______

ANSWER

1. steeper
   gentler

2. convex

3. concave

Frame 64

FIGURE 60

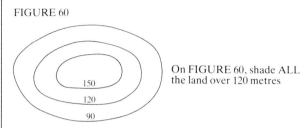

On FIGURE 60, shade ALL
the land over 120 metres

ANSWER

FIGURE 60

Frame 65

The Vertical Interval (V.I.) of
the contours in FIGURE 60
is _____ _____ .

ANSWER

30 metres

Frame 66

How high are each of the dots marked on FIGURE 61?

FIGURE 61

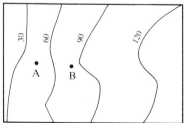

Dot   Height
A _____ metres, approx.
B _____ metres, approx.

ANSWER

A = 45
B = 85
   (more or less)

Frame 67

In FIGURE 62, would you be walking <u>uphill</u> or <u>downhill</u> from A to B? ———

The height of P is ——— metres.

ANSWER

uphill

P = 170
   (more or less)

Frame 68

THE END

Conclusion

The purpose of this chapter has been, first, to indicate certain strategies appropriate to the teaching of geography. Secondly, I have shown that it is possible to begin with a model of spatial division and then decide on what strategies to use. Thus one can begin by considering content or by considering methods, but ultimately both must be present in a harmonious form.

Often, however, methods of teaching and the content of what is taught have been seen as opposing contenders for the teacher's attention. Some have argued that in order to teach well, one needs to be essentially a good geographer. Others have argued equally strongly that the content is of no great importance granted that the teaching methods are pedagogically sound. These two extreme positions are still debated in teacher training institutions and schools. Our purpose has been to demonstrate that geography as a school subject enables the teacher to use a variety of teaching strategies in which the content and method form an integral whole in the reality of classroom practice.

Teaching and learning techniques, whether they are new or traditional, will be effective as long as the teacher is motivated to make them work. For example, using the materials of the High School Geography Project requires, on the part of the teacher, even if he is a trained geographer, a willingness to study the materials in detail in the light of his knowledge of the classes he is teaching. He will need to adapt some of the materials and perhaps reject certain ideas as inappropriate for the group he has in mind. The same is true for any other curriculum development project. Any innovation in geographical education (or any other subject for that matter) requires a good deal of work and energy on the part of the teacher. But this should be no excuse for teaching by one method only and practising a dull routine. On the contrary, it is essential to be constantly rethinking one's teaching methods and renovating the content used.

What kind of geography do we wish to teach? Is it to be an idiographic study characterized by the explanatory descriptions of landscape, or a nomothetic study concentrating on generalizations, theories and relationships concerning the spatial aspects of society? On what kinds of paradigms of geography should we base our teaching? Should we use a 'spatial organization paradigm', in which theoretical models and mathematical techniques are widely used, or should we use an 'ecosystem paradigm' which links up some of the traditional concerns of geography with the environmental problems of today (Graves 1980)?

CHAPTER 4

Real problem-solving

CLYDE F. KOHN

In the field of teaching and learning, as indicated in the introduction to this book, change and the development of new ideas are proceeding at a rapid pace. New programmes of study and new teaching strategies are finding their way not only into the lower schools but into colleges and universities as well. Teachers and school administrators are being challenged at all levels of instruction to make education more meaningful to the individual, more relevant to our times, and more intellectually challenging. Units of instruction are being developed that influence change in the cognitive, affective and manipulative abilities and behaviour of the learner. Attention is being given to the development of value systems and to psychological factors which influence learning in general, as well as learning in specific disciplines such as geography. This chapter will deal with an important new style of teaching geography which deserves careful consideration and evaluation by teachers throughout the world, in areas where resources available for teaching and learning are scarce, as well as in those parts of the world where they are plentiful and where systems of education are well developed. The approach has, as its goal, the development and implementation of *real* problem-solving as a means for furthering geographic education. Implicit in this goal is the challenge to the teacher: 'Does solving problems that are real to students enrich teaching and learning in geography, and if so, in what ways and to what degree?' This approach is the essence of a project funded by the National Science Foundation (USA) and known as the Unified Science and Mathematics for Elementary Schools (USMES). The author is a member of the project's planning committee. (The project may be reached at the education Development Center, 55 Chapel Street, Newton, Massachusetts 02158, USA.)

Characteristics of the real problem-solving approach

The problem-solving approach to learning in general, and to learning in a specified discipline such as geography, is by no means a new idea.

It has been with us throughout the twentieth century. Traditionally, problem-solving as an approach to learning has been concerned with problems for which solutions have already been found by professionals in a given discipline through individual or group research. For example, 'How can farmers in the Middle West of the United States adjust to problems of insufficient rainfall during a given year or over a period of years?' is a vital problem to Middle Western farmers and to professional agronomists who have researched that problem. It is not an immediate 'real' problem, however, to school-children, albeit an important one to be studied in a geography class. It might become a problem if there ever became a shortage of food due to inclement weather conditions or high prices. But the problem would be a different one for the student. It might be, 'How can I help my parents increase our family food supply?'

Two essential characteristics distinguish *real problems* from *discipline-orientated* or *academic problems*. First, real problems arise from areas of concern to the students which produce tensions that can be resolved only by solving the problem in a satisfying manner; and, secondly, they involve the choice of a course of action from among two or more possible solutions. In other words a real problem is one that confronts an individual or group of individuals for which an acceptable course of action requires the gathering of accurate and reliable information, becoming acquainted with the accumulated knowledge in the area of concern, analysing all available information relevant to the problem, identifying satisfactory outcomes from among several possible solutions dependent on one's value systems and putting the accepted solution into action. Even then, there will be honest and sincere differences of opinion because individuals and groups have different value systems, and hence draw different conclusions from the same data and analytical methods, and even from the several proposed solutions.

The real problem-solving approach when used as a basis for selecting and organizing curriculum materials and learning experiences is in reality the application of reflective thinking to social problems or situations that confront a specific learner or group of learners. In this thinking process, five phases are commonly recognized:

1. Feeling confused or perplexed, or sensing being blocked in one's action.
2. Intellectualizing the confusion, perplexity or blockage into a problem to be solved; that is, recognizing the problem, or challenge as it may be called.
3. Formulating one hypothesis after another as leads in searching for factual material which will resolve the doubt, settle or dispose of the perplexity or blockage according to the value system of the problem-solvers.

4. Deciding which offers the best possible solution from among several.
5. Evaluating the solution by overt action, and accepting the conclusions if the action results agree with those rationally deduced, or reject the results if they do not.

Reflecting on these five phases, it is obvious that problems which have already been solved, or which have ceased to be troublesome, do not produce a social tension and are not, therefore, real problems. It is just as obvious that problems selected for class consideration must be contemporary and real for the learner, and that they must be problems for which courses of action can be immediate, direct and overt. Many of the solutions may require action by the community in which the learners live.

Although more lengthy examples of real problems will be presented later, perhaps an example will help at this time to clarify the meaning of a real problem. All individuals are thrust, from time to time, into new social groups or situations. Coming to school for the first time is one such occasion; so, too, is coming to college, or moving from one locality to another, or shifting from one school to another within the same town or city. Feelings of confusion or perplexity are aroused, and the individual must intellectualize the confusion or perplexity into a problem to be solved. Elementary, secondary or college students can be challenged to find a solution to this real problem: 'How can we help new students when they enter our school for the first time?' It should be kept in mind that different solutions to such a problem may, and probably will, emerge depending on one's cultural setting. Children throughout the world find it difficult to adjust to new social groups. How to meet the challenge of doing so is a real problem for them. Note that real problems most often begin with, 'How can we (or I) . . .'

Rationale for the real problem-solving approach

What is the rationale for introducing the real problem-solving approach into the teaching of geography? At least three reasons may be advanced.

First, it is becoming increasingly clear that problem-solving abilities are essential for citizens of all nations, be they highly developed or developing. Although many have written on this subject, the broad purpose is perhaps best summed up by John W. Gardner in his book, *No Easy Victories* (Gardner 1969). He states that nations have the capacity to create new problems as rapidly as their old ones are solved. Individuals or groups are called upon, constantly, to improvize solutions to problems they won't recognize until tomorrow. This need not be so.

Throughout the world, the only formal mechanism available for educating future citizens in the skills of problem-solving is the school. It follows, therefore, that problem-solving should be a significant proportion of the school programme. Unfortunately, realization of this goal calls for a revamping of much of our educational system, and for the production of a different product. Almost seven decades ago, John Dewey (1916) wrote:

'If there is special need of educational reconstruction at the present time ... it is because of the thoroughgoing change in social life accompanying the advance of science, the industrial revolution, and the development of democracy. Such practical changes cannot take place without demanding an educational re-formation to meet them, and without leading men to ask what ideas and ideals are implicit in these social changes, and what revisions they require of the ideas and ideals which are inherited from older and unlike cultures.'

This statement is as true today as it was in 1916.

A second reason for incorporating the solution of real problems in our teaching–learning experiences in geography is related to the student. The approach is functional in that it is built upon the needs and interests of students and is designed to help them adjust to life situations. In a real problem-solving situation, as a student or a group of students develop a solution, they are required to examine their individual values as well as the values of others. In turn, value systems affect their sensitivity to other problems. Students who have developed an awareness of their values as they optimize a solution are on better ground to support what they conclude. They are aware of the extent to which the solution is based on subjective rather than objective data.

Finally, one of the more significant results of learning through the real problem-solving approach is the impact it has on the learning process itself. The approach furnishes a natural objective – the solution of a problem. Students see purpose in their activities and the necessity for reaching and implementing a decision; thus, interest is heightened and intrinsic motivation provided. The approach also permits pupils to share in determining problems to be studied, and in designing activities and procedures to be used in studying them. Moreover, because problem-solving is based upon the process of reflective thinking, students become involved in gathering facts, attaining skills, clarifying value systems and choosing from alternative solutions. Finally, the approach encourages students to do further research and to develop better work habits and study skills.

Criteria for judging the suitability of real problems

In order that teachers may wisely lead their students in the selection of suitable problems for study in the classroom, some criteria are helpful in judging the suitability of the problems to be selected for consideration. References have already been made to some of these. For example, problems should be selected with the needs and interests of a particular group of students in mind. What may be a problem for one group may not be for another; or what may be a problem for one time or place may not be a year later or in another locale. This calls for flexibility in programme planning. Secondly, students should have a part in the selection of problems for which they are to find solutions, and in the development of activities and procedures to be used in solving them. This criterion is based on the premise that a problem is not a problem to students if they do not perceive it as such. Thirdly, a problem selected for consideration should involve the choice of a course of action from among two or more possible solutions, thereby calling decision-making techniques into play.

To these three criteria, another half-dozen may be added. Four, the problem selected should be sufficiently common and recurrent to justify consideration by the whole class or a major portion of it. Problems which concern only an individual or a very small group of students do not meet this criterion. Likewise, problems which are of only immediate and of passing interest are also of doubtful value, although such interests may be capitalized on to stimulate a broader interest. The problem of, 'How can we arrange our desks to hold a committee meeting?' may be an immediate problem for a class, but it would not meet the criterion proposed for a class challenge. However, the fact that there is a blockage to better interaction between students might lead to a broader problem, 'How can our classroom be better managed to meet our needs?' These two challenges would certainly meet the criteria of commonality and recurrence.

Five, problems should be significant enough to warrant class contribution. The most important problems are those which facilitate the development of an understanding of issues of major concern to the largest number of people. 'How can we develop and incorporate non-polluting habits into our day-to-day living?' is a problem significant enough to warrant consideration. Or, 'How can the recreational facilities for young children in our neighbourhood be improved?' also meets this criterion.

Six, problems need to be suited to the maturity of the students. However, this is often not so much a criterion for selecting a problem as of treating the problem and materials used in studying it. In fact, as illustrated, the same problem may be studied profitably by the same group of students at different grade levels. In general, those which are associated with one's family, school and immediate neighbourhood are better suited to young children, but not always, whereas those which relate to a larger community (state, nation, world) are more complex and are better suited to adolescents and young college-age groups. The high price or shortage of gasoline (petrol), for example, becomes a real problem to the teenager who drives an automobile, whereas it is not to a younger child. Intermediate-grade students might become involved in designing a better school playground, whereas college-age students are more directly concerned about renewing a part of the larger community.

Seven, problems selected should be ones for which adequate and suitable materials are readily available. Many difficulties are encountered due to permitting classes to tackle problems for which there are not adequate library or community resources, or for which data cannot be collected. This leads to superficial teaching and to empty verbalizations. It prevents critical thinking based on sound research and dependable knowledge. Thus, before permitting a problem to be selected for class work, the teacher needs to survey the resources of the school and community to make sure that adequate materials will be available to students. Caution must be exercised, however, in applying this criterion, for to adhere too strictly to it may deny students opportunities to find out for themselves that some problems are much more difficult to solve than others.

Eight, problems which students consider as real are commonly not within the domain of a single discipline. Rather, skills, concepts and processes from a variety of disciplines are involved in solving real problems. But this is not a new problem in geographic education. Geography teachers are fully aware that to explain spatial behaviour, or to understand and analyse the location of some event or the distribution over space of like phenomena, students must call upon knowledge generated in other disciplines – the earth sciences, economics, sociology, anthropology, political science, to name just a few. As a result, the real problem-solving approach does not often fit very well into a single discipline. There is a necessity for rearranging class schedules, sometimes drastically, if real problem-solving experiences are to be provided. This is likely to be truer at the upper levels of instruction than in the lower grades.

Nine, problems to be solved should be selected in the light of previous educational accomplishments of the students. It is important for teachers to analyse previous experiences in order to note gaps in the students' backgrounds; furnish leads and clues for the selection of future problems; and guard against unnecessary duplication of problems studied in previous years. It should be kept in mind, however, that if not handled with care, too much planning can lead to a contrived and artificial setting. Problems should arise naturally and spontaneously, based upon student needs or experiences. Teachers must be alert to possibilities as they occur. To force an issue, in order to fill some gap, warps the process.

Real problems of a geographical nature

Although real problem-solving requires the application of skills, concepts and processes from many disciplines, there are real problems that are essentially geographical in nature. These can be initiated in geography classes and developed as units of study in geography. They grow out of the traditions in geography which William Pattison (1964) has so clearly defined: (1) the earth science tradition; (2) man–land tradition; (3) the area studies tradition; (4) the spatial tradition. Before identifying real problems in each of these traditions, their unique contributions to the study of geography might well be outlined.

At one time in the history of geography its content was highly weighted in favour of topics now included in the study of earth science. It was to geography that other scholars and the lay public looked for information about landforms, the waters of the earth, the atmosphere surrounding the earth and the association between the earth and the sun. When one studied geography, one expected, in addition to learning where places were, to become informed about the natural environment in which man lived, and how this environment differed from place to place. This tradition still lives on, but earth science today is increasingly taught by teachers trained in science education rather than in geography.

Traditionally, geographers have been given to exploring man–environment problems. This concern with man–land relationships still persists, and is in fact increasing as a result of man's concern over the deterioration of the environment and the growing scarcity of natural resources. Currently, much research in geography is concerned with man's perception of, attitudes towards and his effects upon, natural conditions. In like manner, there has been in recent years an increase in the scheduling of courses involved with man–natural environmental interactions.

The third tradition in geography, sometimes referred to as the regional tradition, is concerned with characterizing particular places, be they nation-states, world regions or social areas within cities. This tradition reached its apogee in the late 1930s and during the decade of the 1940s. Geographers looked upon themselves as synthesizers of knowledge about particular areas, and felt called upon to interpret the personality of these areas, or regions, as their responsibility. The demand for such intelligence cannot be disputed. Man has always been interested in the world beyond his immediate vision. Explorers, discoverers, statesmen and general laymen have been interested in the nature of places, their unique characteristics and attributes. Regional courses and research have long been a hallmark of scholarship in our discipline. Today we have geographers who are not only interested in advanced nations but in what is often referred to as

Third World areas. They possess the techniques and methodologies for observing, measuring and analysing the distribution and covariance of natural and cultural phenomena within specific parts of the earth's surface so that they might employ empirical methods of inquiry to the development of holistic, integrative descriptions of these areas.

Turning next to the fourth tradition as a basis for defining real problems for study in geography classes, namely the spatial tradition, we find that it is of great interest within the profession at this time. It contrasts sharply in terms of goals, techniques and methodologies with the study of regions. As indicated above, regional studies assumed a holistic, integrative approach, focusing on the qualities of particular places and events at particular times, or on changes in these qualities over time. Conclusions drawn from any one specific regional study can be applied only with great care to areas or events differing in their natural or cultural characteristics. Only in a limited number of situations do such studies become suitable building blocks for the understanding of other specific places.

In contrast, the spatial approach attempts to discover how economic, social and political processes are spatially organized, or how outcomes generated by these processes are evidenced at given times and in particular places. This new model for geographical research and instruction was inaugurated in the mid-1950s. It was new both in substance and in methods of investigation. It may be characterized as a more abstract, theoretical approach to geographic research and instruction, involving analytical methods of inquiry and leading to the application of theory to the solution of societal problems. It also leads to the development of generalizations that are held to be logically valid about the spatial aspects of a small set of closely defined events embedded in a wide range of natural and cultural settings. Generalizations may take the form of tested hypotheses, models or theories, and the research is judged on its scientific fit and validity. The aim is to produce knowledge that has predictive value and is useful in understanding reality. Adoption of the analytical approach has helped geography become a more nomothetic, or law-giving science.

The spatial approach has proved especially helpful in recent years to those geographers who have become interested in the solution of 'welfare' problems. Many geographic theories and models have been helpful in solving problems such as the delivery of health care or the organization of space to provide better education, as well as in the study of problems such as poverty, unemployment, social disorganization and social injustices arising from maldistribution of many political, economic and social facilities.

It is from these four traditions in our discipline – the earth science tradition, the man–environment tradition, the regional tradition, and the spatial interaction tradition – that we can draw problems to challenge learners at all levels of instruction and in all parts of the world. These problems should be real to the learner and drawn from tensions which he or she feels.

Predicting the weather: an example of a real problem drawn from the earth science tradition (a USMES teaching unit)

Introducing the problem

The first responsibility of a teacher using the real problem-solving approach is to recognize when a particular problem, or challenge, arises. For example, learning how to predict the weather in order to plan some event, or to be properly dressed for it, is a problem for many children in almost all natural and cultural settings. Most children have been disappointed at one time or another by 'bad' weather – a picnic cancelled because of rain, a family outing postponed because of fog and so forth. 'Bad' weather becomes a problem to them. Under such conditions it is natural that the class will ask, 'How can we predict weather so that we might plan when to have our class picnic (or some other event)?' This is known as the direct approach.

A less direct way of introducing the problem of predicting weather may arise during the solution of another real problem. For example, were students trying to solve a traffic problem, they might discover that weather is one of the factors that needs to be considered. This may lead them to the study of weather prediction.

Or, a third way may arise during a class discussion of some other topic in geography. For example, children involved in the study of the geography of their own or some other community may become interested in an investigation of local weather conditions and their prediction.

The real problem may be stated as follows: 'How can I predict the weather for . . . (this afternoon, tomorrow, next weekend)?'

Suggested class activities

To start off, the teacher might pose the simple question, 'What difference does the weather make to you?' There is sure to be a lively discussion which might include different types of weather, and what help it would be to know ahead of time what the weather will be like.

Following this discussion, the class might be taken outside to observe the weather conditions at a particular time. Several such observations may be made.

Back in the classroom, the students might discuss the things they think make the weather. These might be recorded on the chalkboard or a piece of paper as hypotheses. After such a brainstorming session, the class may decide to work in small groups to investigate certain factors they think are important – the cloud types, temperature, precipitation, pressure, wind speed or direction. The flow chart (Fig. 4.1) suggests some of the activities that might take place.

Motivated by their own experiences and curiosity, some groups may want to construct simple weather instruments; these may be calibrated using local weather data. A few children may decide to check on the records of past weather and the factors present at the time.

Data collected may be presented in several ways, as for example, line graphs. A wind-direction group may make a circular scatter graph. Other scatter graphs may be constructed to compare the data of two groups. Histograms may be plotted to show the number of days it rained or was sunny with certain changes of pressure.

Predictions should be correlated with observations as early as possible in the unit. This might be brought about by the simple question, 'What do you think the weather will be for the game (or some other event) today?' A record should be kept to help correlate weather conditions at one time with actual weather conditions that follow. The class may decide to issue short-range local weather predictions for the school or community. Some competition may be worked out with more professional local weather forecasters!

As the children collect the data and make their observations and predictions, they may see the need for more data or different types of data. Other activities may include the comparison of the students' measurements with the weather forecaster's measurements, or the introduction of another factor such as high- and low-pressure areas on which to base their predictions. Class discussions and informal discussions with other students may determine possible improvements to their predictions and information necessary for documentation.

Action based on solution to problem

Hopefully, the unit might culminate in some action. The students might set up a weather station in school and post day-to-day weather predictions. Or, they may write up predictions for the school newspaper.

General comments on problem

The problem of predicting weather has been tried out successfully, in the USA, at grade levels from two (7–8-year-olds) to eight (13–14-

Challenge: 'How can I (we) predict the weather for ....
(this afternoon, tomorrow, next weekend)?'

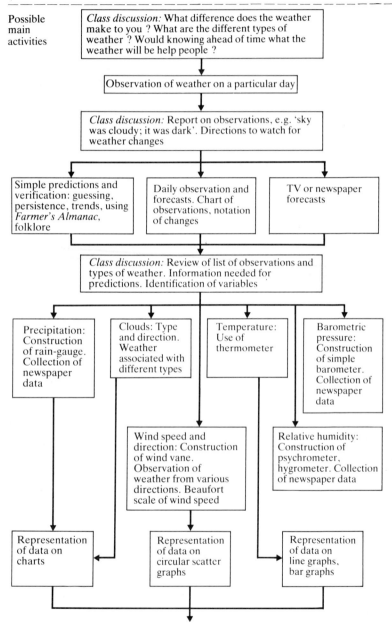

Possible
main
activities

Class discussion: What difference does the weather
make to you ? What are the different types of
weather ? Would knowing ahead of time what the
weather will be help people ?

Observation of weather on a particular day

Class discussion: Report on observations, e.g. 'sky
was cloudy; it was dark'. Directions to watch for
weather changes

Simple predictions and
verification: guessing,
persistence, trends, using
Farmer's Almanac,
folklore

Daily observation and
forecasts. Chart of
observations, notation
of changes

TV or newspaper
forecasts

Class discussion: Review of list of observations and
types of weather. Information needed for
predictions. Identification of variables

Precipitation:
Construction
of rain-gauge.
Collection of
newspaper
data

Clouds: Type
and direction.
Weather
associated with
different types

Temperature:
Use of
thermometer

Barometric
pressure:
Construction
of simple
barometer.
Collection of
newspaper
data

Wind speed and
direction: Construction
of wind vane.
Observation of
weather from various
directions. Beaufort
scale of wind speed

Relative humidity:
Construction of
psychrometer.
hygrometer. Collection
of newspaper data

Representation
of data on
charts

Representation
of data on
circular scatter
graphs

Representation
of data on
line graphs,
bar graphs

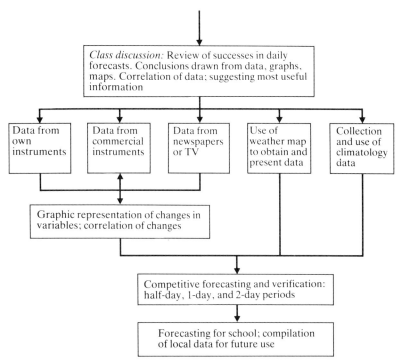

Fig. 4.1 Flow chart for weather predicting

year-olds). It is a problem that might also be developed with high school students (14–18-year-olds).

From logs submitted by teachers who have developed these challenges, a rather lengthy list of activities may be compiled. These include the following:

A. Introduction of challenge

1. Discussion of weather including students' personal experiences with it.
2. Observing of weather conditions using only the five senses.

B. Organizing into groups and discussion of tasks

C. Construction activities associated with weather instruments

1. Wind-measuring instruments.
2. Thermometer.
3. Coffee can barometer.

4. Mineral-oil barometer.
5. Hair hygrometer.
6. Comb nephoscope.
7. Sling psychrometer.
8. Balances to measure relative humidity.
9. Mini weather station.

D. Data collection and representation activities

1. Listening to TV and radio weather reports for data on weather variables.
2. Instrument readings – rain-gauge, thermometer, sling psychrometer, hair hygrometer, balance to measure relative humidity, and weather balloons.
3. Weather maps.
4. Construction of charts, bar, line and scatter graphs and peg-board graph (used in discussion of correlation).
5. Calculating averages.

E. Prediction activities

1. Discussion of application of data to weather prediction.
2. Comparison of weather bureau prediction and 'actual' weather.
3. Short-term prediction.
4. Long-term prediction.

The problem may be extended by having students compile monthly charts of measurements of the different variables in weather predicting, i.e. precipitation, cloud cover, humidity, wind speed, barometric pressure. In this way they could observe weather conditions at various times of year, and predict weather in different seasons.

Finally, as suggested in the list of activities, learning how to predict weather will lead students to examine local weather maps that appear in daily newspapers. From time to time throughout the year the teacher might call the attention of the class to particularly interesting weather phenomena, and have the class discuss reasons for them.

The wise use of energy: an example of a real problem drawn from the man–environment tradition

Introducing the problem

Societies throughout the world are facing problems growing out of their relations to the natural environment – problems related to the growing scarcity of energy sources, the depletion of natural resources, waste disposal, air and water pollution, the ample supply of food and the despoliation of one's living environment.

Among these, the energy crisis which currently confronts a large part of the world provides almost endless possibilities for students, of all ages, to learn about themselves, their nation and the world at large. By studying aspects of the energy crisis, students can see where humanity has been, where it is now and where it might be going. The problem to be solved may be stated as follows: 'How can I (or the people of my country) use energy more wisely?' It should be borne in mind, however, that the precise nature of the energy crisis may change from year to year, consequently what follows may need to be adapted to new circumstances (see Fig. 4.2).

Suggested class activities

The specific learning experiences used in solving this problem will depend, of course, on the age levels and backgrounds of the students. A series of instructional modules have been developed by the Primary Environmental Education Project at the University of Georgia (USA) appropriate for 6-, 7-, and 8-year-olds, under the co-direction of Everett T. Keach, Jr, and Elmer D. Williams. The purpose of this project was to develop and field test nine instructional modules designed as supplementary material for a primary-level social studies programme. The nine modules are as follows:

Module 1A: Support for Man's Activities – A Look at the Land
Module 1B: Support for Man's Activities – Water
Module 1C: Support for Man's Activities – Air
Module 2A: Solid Waste Disposal
Module 2B: Water Pollution
Module 2C: Interdependence in the Environment
Module 3A: Interdependence in the Environment
Module 3B: Management of Water Resources
Module 3C: Protecting Our Air Resources

For students aged 13–18, the challenge may focus on the energy needs of either the local community or the nation as a whole. The older students who drive automobiles will undoubtedly be most interested in the shortage of motor fuel.

The class might be asked to discuss the principal uses of energy in their community or nation. Four such uses are commonly recognized: transportation, industrial, commercial and residential. The challenge may be carried out by investigating the kinds and amounts of energy consumed by each of these four principal users. Students will discover that these are: (1) energy from fossil fuels (coal, petroleum and natural gas); (2) energy from the sun (solar power, fuel wood, food, direct wind and water power and hydroelectric power); (3) nuclear energy.

At this point, the class may form committees to investigate each of

Possible activities in solving the problem:
how can I (or the people of my country) use energy more wisely ?

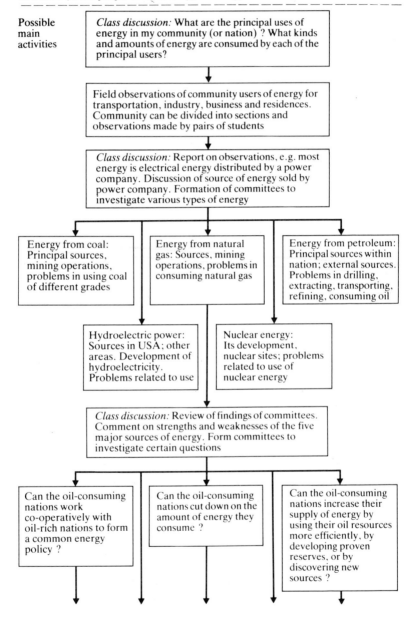

Possible
main
activities

Class discussion: What are the principal uses of energy in my community (or nation) ? What kinds and amounts of energy are consumed by each of the principal users?

Field observations of community users of energy for transportation, industry, business and residences. Community can be divided into sections and observations made by pairs of students

Class discussion: Report on observations, e.g. most energy is electrical energy distributed by a power company. Discussion of source of energy sold by power company. Formation of committees to investigate various types of energy

Energy from coal: Principal sources, mining operations, problems in using coal of different grades

Energy from natural gas: Sources, mining operations, problems in consuming natural gas

Energy from petroleum: Principal sources within nation; external sources. Problems in drilling, extracting, transporting, refining, consuming oil

Hydroelectric power: Sources in USA; other areas. Development of hydroelectricity. Problems related to use

Nuclear energy: Its development, nuclear sites; problems related to use of nuclear energy

Class discussion: Review of findings of committees. Comment on strengths and weaknesses of the five major sources of energy. Form committees to investigate certain questions

Can the oil-consuming nations work co-operatively with oil-rich nations to form a common energy policy ?

Can the oil-consuming nations cut down on the amount of energy they consume ?

Can the oil-consuming nations increase their supply of energy by using their oil resources more efficiently, by developing proven reserves, or by discovering new sources ?

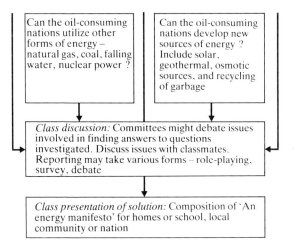

Fig. 4.2 Possible activities in solving the problem: how can I (or the people of my country) use energy more wisely?

these types of energy, its long-term strengths and weaknesses as an energy source and its effect on the local community or nation. Special attention might be given by the committees to the location of energy sources, as for example, the sources of fossil fuels in their nation and the world. The reports might include how deposits of coal, petroleum or natural gas were formed and describe present mining techniques. Following presentation of the reports, the class might discuss such questions as, 'What are the benefits to mankind derived from nuclear power generation?' or 'What harm might result from nuclear power generation, including problems of nuclear waste disposal?'

Solving the problem

As students proceed with their analyses, they will discover that in talking about the energy crisis, most people have in mind problems concerning the production and consumption of petroleum and petroleum products, especially motor fuel and fuel oil. These are the fossil fuels that supply much of the energy needs of both the industrial and Third World nations of the world. All of these nations, except the USSR, Nigeria, Indonesia and Venezuela, currently consume more oil than they produce. They depend upon oil-rich nations, many of which are located in the Middle East, to satisfy their needs. Many of the subsequent class activities might focus, therefore, on such questions as:
1. Can the oil-consuming nations work co-operatively with the oil-rich nations to form a common energy policy?

2. Can the oil-consuming nations cut down on the amount of energy they consume?
3. Can the oil-consuming nations increase their supply of energy by using oil resources more efficiently, by developing proven reserves or by discovering new sources?
4. Can oil-consuming nations utilize other forms of energy – natural gas, coal, falling water, nuclear power?
5. Can oil-consuming nations develop new sources of energy?

Committees might be appointed to work on each of these questions. A variety of activities might be undertaken by each of these groups. For example, the committee assigned to study ways in which oil-consuming nations might work co-operatively with oil-rich nations to form a common energy policy might do some role-playing. Each committee member might represent a particular country including two or more highly industrialized nations, at least two oil-rich nations, and two or more nations from the Third World that do not have adequate supplies of petroleum. Nations which might be represented are Saudi Arabia, Libya, Great Britain, France, the United States, Japan, the USSR, Ghana and India. These representatives might meet at a conference to draw up a plan for working together co-operatively. The rest of the class might serve the representatives as 'resource personnel', supplying members with data to support their stands. They will need to consult newspapers, journals, magazines, reference books and people available in their community. If a stalemate arises in the conference, several outcomes are possible. For example, the industrial nations might not agree among themselves and each might then seek unilateral agreements with the oil-rich nations. Or, the industrial nations might quarrel among themselves and leave the conference. Or, the oil-rich nations might join with the Soviet Union to confront the industrial nations with an ultimatum. How the representatives work will depend on their attitudes, knowledge of the situation and willingness to compromise.

The committee studying the possibility of using less energy might conduct a survey on what their classmates would be willing to do to cut down on the amount of energy they consume. The questionnaire would include equipment used in the home, at school, to transport goods and people. The results of this survey might be discussed with the class as a whole.

The committee charged with studying the substitution of other forms of energy (coal, falling water, nuclear power, natural gas) for petroleum might debate such issues as: 'Industrial nations should use more of their coal resources to meet the energy challenge', or 'The industrial nations should solve the energy shortage by developing more nuclear power plants'.

The committee assigned to investigate new sources of energy might direct their attention to the development of solar power, energy from the rocks beneath the surface of the earth (geothermal energy), more use of wind power or the use of osmotic power developed where rivers flow into the oceans. Yet another source of energy the committee might investigate is the recycling of solid waste materials, or garbage.

As a concluding activity, the class might write, 'An energy manifesto', designed for their homes or school, local community or their nation.

The social characteristics of my community: an example of a real problem drawn from the regional tradition

Introducing the problem

Learning in geography has long focused on describing and interpreting the nature of areas, and the differences that exist from place to place – commonly referred to as the study of regional geography. Young people, it has been found, are as curious as adults about the world in which they live – the local community, state, region, nation or places in foreign lands.

Most regional studies in geography customarily emphasize the natural setting of areas and their economic development or land-use. Quite often their social characteristics are overlooked or only briefly alluded to, despite the fact that social well-being is a matter of real concern. Therefore, the problem to be studied might be phrased as follows:

'How can I improve the social characteristics of (my country, or some other part of the earth's surface)?'

Social well-being in an area is generally defined in terms of selected social indicators. Seven of these are commonly accepted as appropriate criteria: the economic well-being of a place (its wealth, per capita income, and employment status); its health conditions (both physical and mental); its provision of education; the living environment (housing conditions, air and water pollution, resource base); the degree of social organization or disorganization; the degree of participation or alienation of individuals or groups; the quantity and quality of recreational facilities (see Fig. 4.3).

Suggested class activities

The problem may be introduced by having students discuss what they consider to be the 'best' kind of community in which to live. The discussion may take the form of 'brainstorming', with each student

Challenge: 'How can I find out about the social characteristics of — — — — — — (my community, country, or some other part of the Earth's surface)?'

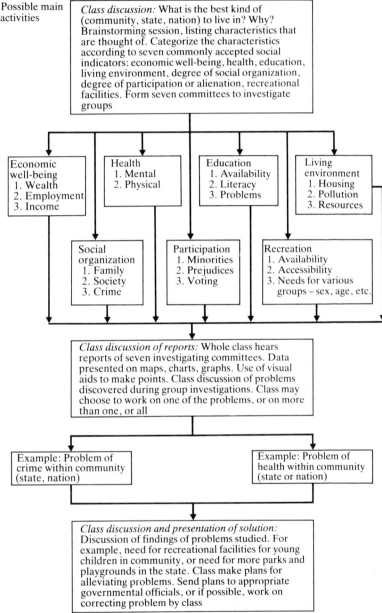

Possible main activities

Class discussion: What is the best kind of (community, state, nation) to live in? Why? Brainstorming session, listing characteristics that are thought of. Categorize the characteristics according to seven commonly accepted social indicators: economic well-being, health, education, living environment, degree of social organization, degree of participation or alienation, recreational facilities. Form seven committees to investigate groups

Economic well-being
1. Wealth
2. Employment
3. Income

Health
1. Mental
2. Physical

Education
1. Availability
2. Literacy
3. Problems

Living environment
1. Housing
2. Pollution
3. Resources

Social organization
1. Family
2. Society
3. Crime

Participation
1. Minorities
2. Prejudices
3. Voting

Recreation
1. Availability
2. Accessibility
3. Needs for various groups – sex, age, etc.

Class discussion of reports: Whole class hears reports of seven investigating committees. Data presented on maps, charts, graphs. Use of visual aids to make points. Class discussion of problems discovered during group investigations. Class may choose to work on one of the problems, or on more than one, or all

Example: Problem of crime within community (state, nation)

Example: Problem of health within community (state or nation)

Class discussion and presentation of solution: Discussion of findings of problems studied. For example, need for recreational facilities for young children in community, or need for more parks and playgrounds in the state. Class make plans for alleviating problems. Send plans to appropriate governmental officials, or if possible, work on correcting problem by class

Fig. 4.3 Flow chart for discovering social characteristics of ... (my community, country, or some other part of the earth's surface)

listing characteristics that come to mind without discussing them at length. As traits are mentioned, they might be recorded on the chalkboard or a large sheet of paper. After the list has been compiled, the class might be led to group the items in terms of the seven indicators listed above.

Committees may now be formed to study each of the several indicators as they pertain to the place or area selected for study. If it is their own community, data might be gathered by fieldwork. For example, schools might be located on maps, and if possible the home location of each student in the several schools might be indicated. If the problem is being explored by a class in a large city, the 'community' may be defined as part of the total city.

The committee studying alienation and participation might undertake to examine voting behaviour in the community. What percentage of the eligible voters in their community exercise their voting privileges? What parts of the community, or precincts, exhibit the greatest turn-out of voters? The least? The committee might seek reasons for the differences.

Perhaps another committee might find out more about crime (a form of social disorganization). Maps showing the location of different types of crime within the community might be compiled. Reasons for the distributions might be hypothesized.

Still another committee might study the recreational facilities available to the citizens of the local community (the state, nation or some other part of the earth). Again, the play areas and facilities might be mapped to see how accessible they are to all citizens of the community. Recreational facilities for various age groups might be investigated – the elderly, families, teenagers or very young children.

Growing out of these investigations of the seven social indicators of a community's well-being, the class might become aware of problems that need to be solved. For example, some parts of the community may not have recreational areas readily accessible to young children. Or, robberies may be high in some parts of the community. How can they be stopped? Or, it may be discovered that the community, or certain areas within it, do not receive adequate health care. Doctors, nurses or health care centres may be scarce. What might be done to correct the situation?

Action based on solution of the problems

As committees present their findings to the class, students may be permitted to discuss the reports. Solutions to the problems presented by the committees might be advanced. Action programmes might be discussed. For example, the class might draw up a plan for improved recreational facilities to present to their local governmental representatives. Or, discussion of areas of high crime rates – thefts, homicides and so forth – might lead to a community campaign to lessen the number of crimes. The class might draw up a list of things that families or the community officials might do.

Instead of working on all seven aspects of social well-being, the class may decide to select one of the social indicators and put their full effort behind a programme for improving that particular social condition.

Were larger areas selected for study – a state, the nation or another nation in the world – the basic geographic unit of measure would need to be discussed. For one's state, data could be collected on a county basis. For the nation, state or provincial data would be suitable. The geographic scale becomes important in determining the type of data to collect, the presentation of the data and the conclusions reached.

It should be kept in mind that the smaller the geographic scale (that is, the larger the unit area), the less likely it becomes for action programmes to be initiated as a result of the solutions advanced. The chances of 'improving' social conditions of a nation are less than correcting some social condition at the neighbourhood or community level. On the other hand, nationwide movements do get started at community levels!

Getting there: an example of a real problem drawn from the spatial tradition

Introducing the problem

Young and older people alike are often faced with the problem of getting from one place to another. Thus, students of all ages may respond enthusiastically to this challenge as they discuss problems they face in getting around their community. Through a study of 'getting there' learners can be introduced to such concepts as nodes, networks, transportation flows, public and private means of transporting goods and people and a host of other important concepts related to the study of geography. A similar problem is considered in relation to the Moscow underground in Chapter 7, p. 229.

In some classes student investigations may focus on getting from their homes to school and back, whereas other classes may investigate ways of getting to and returning from recreational, educational and cultural facilities within the community. Once students realize that a problem of getting from one place to another really exists either for themselves or for others in the community, they may decide to work in small groups on different aspects of the problem. The real problem may be stated as follows: 'How can I (we) get most safely, (rapidly, cheaply) from _____ to _____'.

It may be noted that in the upper grades, the problem may be in getting from one locality to another, or from rural to urban centres and so forth (see Fig. 4.4).

Suggested class activities

The flow chart in Fig. 4.4 suggests some of the activities that may take place in class. (This is one of the prototype problems developed in the USMES project.)

The class may wish to survey other students for their opinions on the problem and its possible solutions. The tallying and graphing of their survey data will help them decide which tasks should be undertaken first and what data they need to collect.

Some 12-year-old students worked on this problem by finding ways to use public transportation for field trips. They chose possible sites for these excursions and investigated routes, costs and schedules of public transportation. Several classes in the school found this information useful, and so it was put into a booklet for distribution.

In another school students worked on the problem of findings ways to get from their area into town and return. One of their proposed solutions was the construction of bicycle paths. When initial information had been gathered on possible routes and costs, the students called the local government office to determine what had to be done next. The commissioner agreed to meet with the class and discuss their proposal. Following a presentation by the students, the commissioner listed what had to be done if the students were serious about their bicycle path proposal.

The students in the class then acted upon the commissioner's suggestions. The class scheduled a presentation to the full panel of commissioners. To this meeting they brought petitions in support of a bicycle path, and maps of their proposed routes. In addition, they presented background information on their activities and answered any questions raised by the panel of commissioners. The commissioners seemed impressed with their presentation and ordered the county engineer to conduct a feasibility study of the bike path.

Activities involved in collecting and presenting data provide opportunities for fieldwork, making surveys, compiling maps and charts, taking photographs and writing reports. Stimulating questions for which answers might be sought include:

Do you have trouble getting around the community? Why?

Are routes and places clearly marked?

Are directions available for getting to important places?

How do you get around in your community?

Possible activities in solving the problem:
how can I (we) get most safely, rapidly, cheaply from one place to another in my
community ?

Possible main activities

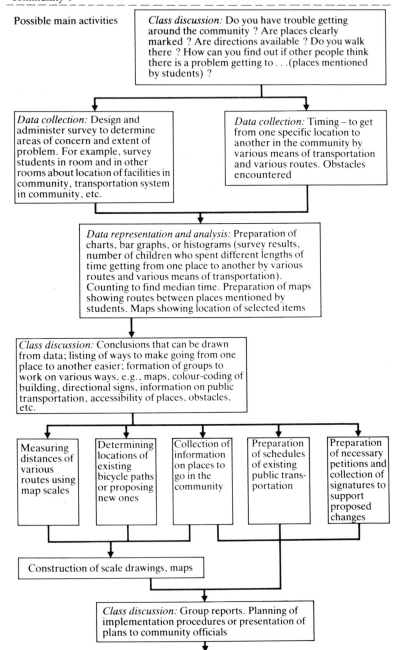

Class discussion: Do you have trouble getting around the community ? Are places clearly marked ? Are directions available ? Do you walk there ? How can you find out if other people think there is a problem getting to . . .(places mentioned by students) ?

Data collection: Design and administer survey to determine areas of concern and extent of problem. For example, survey students in room and in other rooms about location of facilities in community, transportation system in community, etc.

Data collection: Timing – to get from one specific location to another in the community by various means of transportation and various routes. Obstacles encountered

Data representation and analysis: Preparation of charts, bar graphs, or histograms (survey results, number of children who spent different lengths of time getting from one place to another by various routes and various means of transportation). Counting to find median time. Preparation of maps showing routes between places mentioned by students. Maps showing location of selected items

Class discussion: Conclusions that can be drawn from data; listing of ways to make going from one place to another easier; formation of groups to work on various ways, e.g., maps, colour-coding of building, directional signs, information on public transportation, accessibility of places, obstacles, etc.

Measuring distances of various routes using map scales

Determining locations of existing bicycle paths or proposing new ones

Collection of information on places to go in the community

Preparation of schedules of existing public transportation

Preparation of necessary petitions and collection of signatures to support proposed changes

Construction of scale drawings, maps

Class discussion: Group reports. Planning of implementation procedures or presentation of plans to community officials

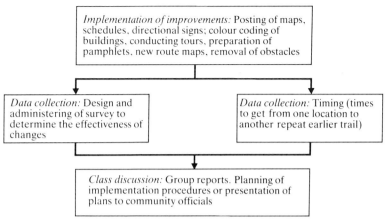

Fig. 4.4 Possible activities in solving the problem: how can I (we) get most safely, rapidly, cheaply from one place to another in my community?

How do you feel when you get lost?
How could you find out whether others have trouble getting around the community?
Can you make it easier for yourself and others to get around in the community?
Why do you travel from _____ to _____? Are there obstacles in your way?

As students become involved in this problem, opportunities will arise for the teacher to test students' *perception* of distances and the relative location of places, and to help students develop more accurate notions about these spatial characteristics of a community. In this way students will come to develop better mental maps of familiar areas, and eventually conceive distances, directions and relative locations better when using maps of unfamiliar areas and places.

Action based on solution to problem

Depending on the aspect of the problem which a class has elected to explore, several solutions might evolve. For example, one class of students aged 14–16 years investigated the problem of getting to and from school by bus. This is a challenge that confronts students in most large cities, in rural areas where regional community schools are in existence and in medium-sized cities as well. Solutions included the better location of pick-up sites, the need for dry and heated pick-up sites during the winter season, the development of rules and regulations governing students riding on buses, the need for small buses to pick up fewer students living at long distances from school and larger buses to pick up students living nearer the school. By having a mixture of different-size buses, it was proposed that the smaller buses could become 'express' buses once they had picked up students living furthest from the school. The students riding these buses would not have to spend so much time getting to and from school.

Note has already been made that one class requested its county commissioner to study the problem of developing a bicycle path so that students could ride bicycles more safely to and from school.

Another class discovered that the flow of traffic could be modified by introducing one-way streets near their school, and thereby make it easier for students to walk to and from their classes. Still another class proposed changes in bus routes and bus schedules to meet certain needs for getting around their community.

Growing out of these studies, students gain an understanding of concepts such as accessibility of places relative to each other and of intervening obstacles to travel (see Ch. 3). They also become more aware of why they travel from one place to another. They might discover that their needs could be satisfied by travelling to alternative places providing intervening obstacles were removed, or public transportation routes or schedules changed.

In this day of shortages and high costs of petrol, it is important that students, their parents and fellow citizens find new solutions to the problem of 'getting around' their community or in travelling from their community to another.

The teacher in relation to real problem-solving

The implementation of real problem-solving teaching strategies as set forth in the four examples presented in this chapter, raises a very important question – one which in itself is a 'real' problem. 'How can teachers be prepared to handle this type of instruction?'

From the four challenges presented, it can be deduced that teachers need to handle both directed and discovery learning situations. In their role in managing real problem-solving, teachers will be called upon to serve as co-ordinators and collaborators rather than as directors or authoritative answer-givers. In their preparation, they will need experiences that will provide the understanding and abilities to enable them to:

1. Be alert to the 'real' problems confronting their students and to introduce problems to be solved in a meaningful way.
2. Act as a co-ordinator and collaborator. Assist, not direct, individuals or groups of students as they investigate different aspects of the problem.

3. Permit the students to become involved in the problem and in carrying out in-depth investigations, by asking questions which stimulate thoughtfulness.
4. Be patient in letting students make mistakes in finding their own way. Offer assistance or point out sources of help for specific information only when a student reaches the point of frustration in the approach to the problem.
5. Make any necessary arrangement for fieldwork, interviews with peers or community resources and for collecting data.
6. Provide frequent opportunities for group reports and student exchanges of ideas in class discussions. Permit students to examine procedures critically, improve or set new directions in their investigations.
7. End the class's general participation in studying problems when student interest or the overall accomplishments of the class in finding and implementing solutions to the problem indicate a lack of further interest.
8. If motivated, permit some students to continue work on a voluntary basis on one problem while the rest of the class begins to identify possible approaches to another problem. (USMES)

Summary

Some of the basic ideas which shape the theory of real problem-solving instruction might be noted in closing. For example, several developments in the behavioural sciences have to do with the solution of problems. Among these are cybernetics, general systems theory, information theory, pattern recognition theory, decision theory and game theory. General systems theory involves a goal, purpose or function that is served, and the components that are interacting to achieve these objectives. Thus, given a problem, an attempt is made to reproduce or simulate in a schematic and simplified way the problem situation, retaining those variables and conditions which are relevant to the problem and overlooking all other details.

Viewing man as an information-processing system has prompted learning theorists to ask different kinds of questions about how people solve problems, make decisions and think creatively. The model of man as an information-processing system, focuses attention, therefore, on processes, and requires a rigorous identification of the stages through which man moves in this cognition of the environment.

In addition to theories drawn from the behavioural sciences, those interested in helping students learn how to solve problems base their work on theories of learning. Among recent theories of this nature, several give promise of shaping the curriculum and teaching

strategies of the future. For example, Piaget and his colleagues have
identified four stages of intellectual maturation through which they
believe children pass as they grow towards maturity (see Ch. 2). His
work serves as a guide for the selection of examples or exercises used
to help the student learn problem-solving procedures.

But all the theorizing that has been done is for naught unless some
linkage is developed between theory and practice. The question
arises: 'Is classroom instruction making use of advances in theory?'
Unfortunately, many modern theories related to problem-solving
have been unnoted and untested by practitioners in the classroom.
The most dramatic changes are probably reflected in the wider use
now given to the case-study approach and to the active interest in
games and simulation. Still other teaching strategies rely heavily on
the idea that the learner generates his own knowledge and that this
process of knowledge-generation occurs as the result of the learner's
encounter with a baffling or unresolved – that is, problematic –
question or situation. This is the approach that has been discussed in
this chapter.

CHAPTER 5

Gathering information

P. OLATUNDE OKUNROTIFA

The traditional picture of the process of teaching geography has the teacher transmitting knowledge and map skills to students. Such a teacher selects the content and delivers it to the students by having them read, listen to or examine materials he has selected. He asks questions which test their recall of the factual data. Sometimes he has students perform selected activities, often followed by more fact-orientated questions. Such teaching does not provide the student with opportunities to practise the varied skills employed by modern geographers.

In recent decades geographical methodology has witnessed considerable changes and improvements. The methods of approach in geographical study are today increasingly being marked by emphasis on concepts, models, hypotheses and theories, while the land area, country, region or part of the earth (the field) is being used mainly, or exclusively in certain cases, as a laboratory or testing-ground for such hypotheses or theories. Scientific problem-solving approaches which can be tried and reproduced elsewhere, with similar or stated varying conditions and premises, now mark the science of geography. These approaches require the teacher to move from the role of dispensing data to helping the student find the data for himself. He encourages the student to do his own thinking and to arrive at his own conclusions. The teacher seeks to foster student independence rather than maintaining student dependence. He guides the students in using the tools and developing the skills necessary for the investigation at hand. One of the several methods of inquiry currently advocated involves broadly the steps shown in Fig. 5.1. According to this approach a problem of study is stated. Then a hypothesis (or tentative solution) is put forward, which will need investigation and testing. It is then decided what types and what amount of information are needed to test the hypothesis, as well as where and how to collect the required data. The data are then collected either in the field or in the laboratory, from maps or other sources. These data are then processed, the results considered and tested for significance, and the hypothesis accepted, modified or rejected on the basis of the result achieved. The scientific approach delineated and illustrated is mainly

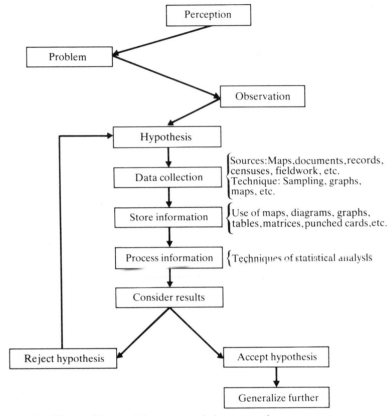

Fig. 5.1 The problem-solving approach in geography

applicable to experimental or testing purposes in geographical
studies, the description being built into the phases of experimentation, interpretation and reporting of the results. Thus, it is organized
around a chosen initial idea (or hypothesis), or a tentative set of
possible explanations for a given problem being studied.

Whether the geographer should adopt only techniques which are
scientific, in the sense understood by the physicist, is debatable. The
definition of a problem for investigation and the methods appropriate
to it depend in the widest sense on the individual's view of the aims of
geographical study. Whatever his general approach, in any particular
investigation, the student must be capable of collecting data relevant
to an objective which he has himself defined. He must be able to
decide:

1. how and where to obtain information;
2. how to prepare materials collected for processing;
3. what methods of analysis to employ;

4. how to draw conclusions from the processed data.

It is the first of these which is the main concern of this chapter. However, it must be stressed that the collection of data cannot be divorced from the other processes. The student must plan the three subsequent stages before deciding the precise nature of the data he should collect.

Identifying the problem for study

As can be seen from the model in Fig. 5.1, the identification of the problem for study forms an important point of departure in any problem-solving approach in geography.

Geographical problems are of various types. There are those concerned with spatial patterns, shape and networks. For fieldwork, these constitute the 'how' questions aimed at the quantification of the areal or spatial variations in structural patterns. Examples of questions which could emanate from such problems are: 'How do settlements grade in terms of sizes, functions or services provided, in their hierarchy? How do slopes differ with distance along valley sides? How do drainage densities vary between areas?' There are also problems concerned mainly with the processes operating within and between phenomena. Such problems mainly raise 'why' questions aimed at quantifying the relationship or processes that make for variations in form – 'Why do contrasting areas of a city, village, country etc. differ in their density of population, house types and housing conditions? Why does one rural area attract migrants from another rural area? Why do river sediments vary along a river valley?' There are also problems dealing with investigation of the dynamic nature of phenomena, arising from an input or outflow of energy. Questions emanating from such problems may include: 'By how much and at what rate does agricultural land-use change? At what rate do agents or processes of slope reduction, or of deforestation, for example, bring about change?'

The identification of these problems may be done from maps, particularly during mapwork exercises; through the observation of the characteristics and relationships of phenomena during field excursions; or by reading already published literature. It could also be suggested by experience acquired through other ways. Though these sources can be quite useful, a major source of problems for investigation in schools could be such themes as:

1. urban growth processes (or any other aspects of the processes) say, in Bombay, India;
2. aspects of the morphology and/or erosion processes on the plateau of Bolivia in South America;
3. cultural landscapes and patterns of human spatial organizations in the Yoruba land of Nigeria.

From such themes could be derived various models, concepts and/ or hypotheses that could be specifically investigated. For example, deriving from the first example of the themes suggested above, any of the urban growth models (concentric, sector or multi-nuclei) or of urban land-use segregation, or of population zonation and spatial density differentials in cities, among others, may be specifically investigated, as required.

The identification of a problem should be a major step in the development of many geography lessons, even if all the questions posed and the tentative answers suggested may not eventually be investigated in the field. None the less, the themes of many geography lessons or the treatment of such themes should lend themselves to the posing of problems for investigation. For example, a treatment of the spatial aspects of agriculture in some countries or locality should include, among other things, the idea of the distance (and costs) factor from settlements or market centres in relation to:
1. location of different crop types;
2. varying intensity of land-use at each point or distance;
3. variations in farm sizes;
4. variations in the number of visits which farmers make to their farm plots at different locations and, thence, in the amount of labour, extent of attention or demand made on the plots in each zone.

An example of a problem which can be posed in connection with the above could be: 'How does the extent of attention which a farmer gives to his plots at different locations vary with distance from his settlement? Or what effects has distance on the extent of attention which a farmer gives to his various holdings?' Such a treatment holds some advantages for students. First, they can immediately appreciate the relevance of fieldwork to classroom lessons. Second, they can learn to obtain information from relevant literature or references on the problem or theme.

Planning for data collection

Having identified the problem for study, the students should be led to suggest tentative answers to the questions or problem for study, making sure that each aspect of the tentative answer is precise enough to facilitate the collection of data in the field. At this stage, it should be decided whether the data needed are measurements to be made by the students; data to be collected by questionnaire; or from documentary sources such as census data, vital registrations, agricultural surveys, household surveys, industrial surveys or other published or unpublished records.

In the case where the data are to come from measurements by the students, it will be decided whether these will involve counting, weighing, pacing, estimating, measuring with instruments and so on, or combinations of these. The instruments required for the measurements will then be provided. Where questionnaires are to be used the nature of the questions and how they are to be delivered will also need to be agreed upon during the preparatory stage.

It is often helpful to decide beforehand where to go for the measurements, what rules to observe and to whom to address the questions. In other words, the sample frame should be decided upon. Simple sampling techniques, some of which are discussed in the sections below, should at this juncture be introduced or revised as appropriate. In order to enable statistical analysis and tests to be carried out, or mathematical models to be constructed, and in order to make such exercises useful, appropriate sampling procedures should be aimed at, especially in higher classes.

The students should practise how to record the results of their measurements in their field notebooks, or how to administer the questions, and tick, underline, encircle or otherwise record the answers given by the respondents. Preparations for the correct use of a field notebook will include especially the technique of tabulation and the construction of simple tables based on the variables and relationships to be investigated. Before the actual fieldwork the nature of the tables should be agreed upon, and the notebook prepared (ruled, numbered, headings indicated if possible) in advance for recording the data in the field. If this part of the preparation is satisfactorily handled, much of the work will have been done.

In addition to all these preparations there should, of course, be some search for or review of relevant literature on the theme, concept or project being undertaken. There would also be the search for relevant background information on the locality, region or other unit area where fieldwork is to be conducted. Inevitably, with school students, the teacher will need to give a strong lead.

Sampling

To undertake a successful field survey, it is essential to know the nature of the total population. A population refers to all the units of a group, e.g. the population of cocoa trees in West Africa or the population of motor cars in Great Britain. One of the main problems that we meet in the course of geographical study is that of 'data explosion'; there are just too many isolated pieces of information concerned with spatial distributions for it to be possible even to start to analyse them all. Hence, quite often, it may be impossible, difficult or impractical to measure or count an entire population when investigating a problem. For instance, suppose a city council wants to introduce a new measure for collecting additional taxes from the inhabitants of a city. The council might decide to determine what the reactions of the inhabitants would be to this new measure. In such a case, it is impractical and even unnecessary to ask the opinion of every inhabitant in the city. The commonest practice is to select a small percentage of the inhabitants and ask whether or not they favour the new measure. Such a small percentage is called a *sample* and the technique which we use to choose the limited body of data is that of *sampling*. The *total population* from which samples are selected is called the *sampling frame*.

Why sample?

The decision to sample or not will naturally be guided by certain criteria. Some of these are:
(a) The obvious possibility of reduced cost in studying a sample instead of the larger collection is a cardinal point. More and more often, geographers are measuring features studied and recording observations in an accurate numerical form. Such measurements can be a laborious, time-consuming business, and measuring every item may result either in an excessive waste of time on data collection or may produce a very limited study. Sampling is thus an invaluable way of streamlining the data collection process.
(b) The practicality of proposed methods of collection is an important criterion. It may be that the number of individuals in the parent population, e.g. sand grains on a large beach, is so great that measuring all of them would be impossible from a practical point of view. If we carry out sampling correctly, a limited selection of sand grains will be sufficient for making a generalization about all the sand grains on that beach. In other circumstances, however, measurement of the whole population is possible, but sampling represents a more efficient use of our energy while still allowing us to make reliable statements about the whole population.
(c) Greater speed in surveys must necessarily result from using a sample.
(d) A few well-trained recorders can more usefully spend their time collecting detailed and accurate information from a few members of the population.
(e) Finally, there may be no choice for the investigator but to use a sample if the population is infinite.
　From the foregoing, sampling appears quite advantageous in the sense that it ensures detailed study of the few items selected from the population. It also saves time, minimizes costs and tends to give more accurate results owing to its greater attention to detailed examination.

Sampling methods

To draw legitimate inferences about populations from samples, one must be certain that the sample really represents the population. If a sample is drawn from a population in a biased fashion so that it is not typical of the population, it would be impossible to generalize to the population from the sample. One method of avoiding biased selection is to assign *randomly* members of the population to the sample. In random sampling, each member of the population has the same chance (or probability) of being included in the sample. In a population of N members, for instance, the probability of selecting any member into the sample is $1/N$. The assumption here is that all members of the population are randomly distributed.

A simple but time-consuming method of drawing a sample randomly is to assign numbers to the entire population, then enter the numbers on discs and place all discs in a container, to be drawn out one at a time. When the desired proportion of discs have been drawn from the container, the subjects whose numbers coincide with these discs can be considered a randomly selected sample.

A more efficient method of randomly sampling from a population is to employ a table of random numbers. Tables of random numbers are so called because there is no bias in the sequence of digits. They consist of rows and columns of numbers arranged at random so that they can be entered at any point and used by reading in any direction, right or left, up or down. Complete sets of random-number tables are published in various books on statistics.

Table 5.1 Excerpt from a table of random numbers

9	3	0	0	9		0	9	4	9	0		4	3	6	4	0
5	5	2	4	1		1	8	9	3	2		5	8	4	7	4
6	9	5	3	8		2	9	6	6	1		7	7	7	3	8

To illustrate the use of a table of random numbers, imagine that we wished to select 50 factories at random from a parent population of 225 factories. Each of the factories should be assigned a number from 001 to 225. The necessity of inserting the zero before all the single and two-digit numbers arises from the fact that 225 is a three-digit number and the number of digits for all subjects must be the same when using a random numbers table. Then, taking each column at once and starting from the extreme right-hand column of Table 5.1 and working downwards, the first number 48 (048) would be included, as would the sixth, number 21 (021), and so on until 50 factories have thus been randomly identified. Irrelevant numbers such as 473, 647 and 387 are simply discarded. If the same numbers are encountered twice before 50 factories have been selected, simply ignore those numbers which have already been selected.

In addition to random sampling methods, there are other ways of securing a representative sample of the population. If a population exhibits spatial clusters as illustrated in Fig. 5.2.(a) and 5.2(b), then it will be more appropriate to adopt the *stratified sampling* techniques to choose samples from it. The population is partitioned into segments in order to make sampling realistic and meaningful. For instance, for a survey of cassava consumers in Ibadan, Nigeria, the city may be partitioned into three strata on the basis of social status: high-class area, I; middle-class area, II; and low-class area, III. Probably, because of the social status of the people in area I, their diet is most diversified – they eat less cassava while the people in area III largely feed on cassava. Thus, the distribution partitioned in Fig. 5.2. Samples from each stratum may be selected at random. The sampling fraction, that is, the percentage of the items selected for study in each stratum, may be uniform or vary from one stratum to another depending on the expediency of the situation.

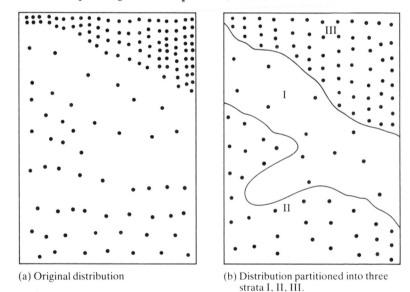

(a) Original distribution

(b) Distribution partitioned into three strata I, II, III.

Fig. 5.2 A hypothetical distribution of cassava consumers. (a) Original distribution; (b) distribution partitioned into three strata I, II, III

Lastly, if the items of a population are distributed at regular intervals, the *systematic sampling* method may be adopted. For instance, in a study of a sample from a list of 225 factories, the first factory of the sample can be selected at random while others are chosen at regular intervals, e.g. every fifth or every tenth factory.

Thus, we should reach the target of 50 far more quickly than by working through random-number tables. However, care must be taken to avoid such regular intervals that will lead to the selection of items which exhibit some sort of bias, e.g. if the list of factories is in order of size, then choosing every fifth factory on the list may lead to a bias in favour of small or large factories.

Size of sample

To complete the sample frame, it should be agreed upon how many people should be questioned, or how many measurements are to be made. Students should be brought to realize that where possible a total enumeration of all the population (the total number of objects being investigated) is the ideal. But since this is not often possible, particularly with the types of objects that geographers study, the percentage of the total population to be included in the sample should be decided upon, where the total population is finite and known. If, however, the population is infinite or the total is unknown, the fieldwork should aim at a large sample. A sample of thirty or more measurements is usually regarded as large and, all being well, can be relied upon far more than a small sample. Where small samples are inevitable, some specialized statistical techniques are usually required.

Obtaining the information

In any study, an investigator may have a choice of collecting the relevant data himself or of relying entirely on existing data already collected by someone else. The existing data may be in published or unpublished form. Sometimes the investigator may collect data to supplement what already exists. There are several situations when no available relevant data exist and the investigator must collect his own data. Some familiarity with the range of possible sources of information and with ways of tapping them is essential before any plan of inquiry is finalized. Geography makes use of field observation and measurement, interviews and questionnaires, information published in maps, documents and statistical tables. Any one exercise may well involve a combination of these sources. In whatever way data are obtained, one needs to bear in mind that there are accurate and inaccurate data. The main criteria for judging the merits of collected data or of the methods of collection include:

(*a*) the cost of collecting the data;
(*b*) the time spent in collecting the data;
(*c*) the accuracy of the observations;

(d) practicability of proposed methods of collection;
(e) representativeness of the samples if a sampling is done;
(f) the ability to assess and to minimize the various errors and biases which lead to uncertainty in the conclusions.

For an investigator who uses other people's data, it is still essential that he knows how the data were collected. Such knowledge and the above criteria should enable him to decide on the reliability of the data and their suitability for the problem under study.

Field observation

Acquiring information through fieldwork involves training in making observations over a period of time, and depicting the distribution of the phenomena observed in the field. Both procedures could be applied to the study of such variables as weather, vegetation, geomorphological processes (like river flow, load deposition, slope action), traffic flow, migration flow or journeys to work or to shops, spatial or structural growth of settlements and so on.

Probably the most common way of carrying out these procedures is to observe weather conditions and to keep a record of climatic statistics. Since many schools and colleges have a small weather station, it is not difficult to organize the students for such work. Even without a weather station to use, it is always possible to take daily notes of the weather. This is something which everyone can do and is, moreover, something in which everyone has some interest. Table 5.2, for instance, illustrates some data which young geography pupils can collect as a result of their observation of weather.

There are other kinds of continuous records which can be kept. It is instructive, for example, to undertake a brief traffic census. This involves observing and recording the number and type of vehicles which pass a fixed point over a period of a few hours, or during a short regular time – say half an hour – on every day for a week. Another exercise which is easy to arrange consists of observing land-use or the character of vegetation along a suitable stretch of road. By taking observation at appropriate intervals throughout the year, it will be possible to record how the height, colour and general appearance of plants and crops change with the different seasons.

Additionally, as a way of sharpening students' powers of observation, it might be useful to provide them, during field excursions, with copies of route profiles of such excursions. An excursion route profile is a tabulation of geographical features for different sections of a route. In the example below (Table 5.3), the starting point of an excursion is settlement Y_0, the destination settlement Y_n, and Y_1, Y_2 ... are intermediate locations on the route. Geographical features over the distance Y_0 to Y_1 and Y_1 to Y_2 ... etc. are respectively

Month _____

		Temperature				Hygrometer		Humidity %	Rain (mm)	Pressure (mm)	Wind		Visibility	Sky	Cloud
		Temp. °C	Max. temp. °C	Min. temp. °C	Diurnal range (max-min)	Dry bulb °C	Wet bulb °C				Speed	Direction			
1	10a.m.														
2	10a.m.														
3	10a.m.														
4	10a.m.														
5	10a.m.														
6	10a.m.														
7	10a.m.														
8	10a.m.														
9	10a.m.														
10	10a.m.														
11	10a.m.														
30	10a.m.														
31	10a.m.														
Monthly total or average															

SUMMARY 1. Mean monthly temperature _____ 4. Prevailing wind _____
2. Monthly range of temperature _____ 5. Monthly rainfall _____
3. Relative humidity _____

Master's signature _____

Table 5.2 Weather observation

Table 5.3 An excursion route profile: a student's example

Features	Sections of a route			
	Y_0 to Y_1	Y_1 to Y_2	$\longrightarrow$	Y_{n-1} to Y_n
Settlements (number, size, type)	Ten; Hamlet, Villages, Dispersed	One; Town Nucleated		Seven; Villages, Linear type
Traffic flow (number of vehicles in opposite direction)	3: 2 lorries 1 car	7: 4 cars 3 lorries		4: 3 lorries 1 car
Land-use type	Settlement; Cultivated land; Forest	Settlement; Industry; Grassland		Settlement; Water and Marsh Forest and woodland
Soil types	Clay soils	Red soils		Sandy-loamy soils
Forest types (dominant trees or grass species)	Rain-forest – mahogany, iroko, obeche	Baobab, Palms		Palms, Acacias
Drainage characteristics (valleys, speed of flow)	Upper course of the R. Kobe – steep-sided fast-flowing	Lower course of the R. Kobe – very wide valleys, rather sluggish flowing		Quick succession of narrow valleys with streams
Major landforms	Undulating	Hill ridge		Inselberg landscapes

Y_0	Y_1	Y_2	Y_{n-1}	Y_n

entered into the columns of the table. Students should record the major or striking features they observe during the journey. In addition, they should write down the questions that such features evoke in their minds. It is also important for students to make relevant sketches and diagrams of the features, especially the patterns and networks, that they observe. These will include things like road networks, village plans, settlement rings, gap or springline settlements, drainage networks, interlocking spurs, gullies and vegetation canopies.

Finally, it is pertinent to emphasize that fieldwork is not just a matter of observation and taking of records. These are merely a minor aspect of field exercise. Fieldwork stimulates thinking and 'indeed the soul of the work is gained only when the thinking that is inspired by observation is logical, searching, and critical' (Davis 1954). It is mainly by these means that a sound disciplinary value is added to fieldwork and that it becomes essentially scientific. The point being emphasized here is that observation is a part of science only when it is associated with some rigorous thinking, arguments and inferences. Field observation will, at first, suggest comparatively few ideas which are important or original enough to be worth pursuing further. Further ideas will be generated by manipulation and analysis of the data originally obtained in the field, or by examination of appropriate secondary sources, some of which are considered later in this section.

Field sketching

Field sketching is a valuable way of collecting data in the field. Although it is both more profitable and more pleasurable to those with a natural gift for sketching it has much to commend it to those less gifted. It provides a collection of illustrations and enormously increases the powers of observation. Instead of a comparatively hasty visual survey of a piece of country which gives neither an accurate nor a lasting mental picture, field sketching results in a permanent record and encourages an exact appreciation of line, angle and form, the value of which can hardly be overemphasized in relation to geographical method. It forces the student to be selective in his observations.

A careful examination of photographs is one of the most practical ways of collecting data in geography. The use of this method is considered in Chapter 7. As compared with photography, field sketching has both advantages and disadvantages. Both have their place in regional investigation and description. Photography is accurate and a photograph has a range of tone and a suggestion of depth which the field sketch can rarely rival. Detail is shown in a photograph which is omitted from a sketch, and which is available for later reference to correct and supplement the memory and the field drawing. Similarly, the field sketch has much in its favour. It is financially within the range of every student. For a small sum of money can be bought the materials for a large number of sketches, whereas photography is a constant expense. Conditions of light and atmosphere, though important, are much less limiting in relation to field sketching than to photography. Another comparable advantage is that distant features of which the outline can be traced by the eye can more easily be sketched than photographed, and some degree of exaggeration may justifiably be introduced. Conversely, it is often desirable to omit some details and to select only certain features for illustrating a geographical description. Therefore, in a field sketch, landforms can be shown in outline and trees or houses which would obscure this line may be omitted. Similarly, other lines than those which would be most emphatic on a photograph may be emphasized in the drawing. Also, one is sure of field sketch, but there is no absolute certainty of a picture from an undeveloped plate or film in the camera.

In drawing a field sketch, the following might prove useful:

(a) A single line should suffice to show the outline of a hill and shading should be confined to showing the angle and character of slopes.

(b) Coloured pencils may be used if they can add anything to the drawing. Distributions can often be shown quickly in colour.

(c) Keep the sketch as neat and as simple as possible. The complicated panorama with countless minute annotations is of little real value if it fails to show immediately the main essentials of a view (see Fig. 5.3).

(d) It is advisable not to combine physical characteristics with features of human geography unless the object of the sketch is to show a relationship between the two. If, for instance, data are to be collected for examining the effect of the physical environment on human activities, then field patterns, farms, etc. should be included. It might be found simpler, however, to draw two sketches – one showing the physical characteristics accurately labelled and the second showing the same features unlabelled, but including the land-use features required.

Field measurement

At the secondary-school level, students should be able to make use of simple measurements to aid on-the-spot descriptions. For example, local relief and valley depths can be determined; slopes can be measured; frequency or density of occurrence of tree species or economic crops can be counted; density of houses, roads or traffic can also be calculated; while sizes of farms, fallow lands and wasteland can be measured. To describe an area as one of small, medium or large farms, for instance, requires some measurements and estimations of the farm sizes and proportions belonging to each range of sizes, however roughly done.

Fig. 5.3 Rapid shading for effect in 3B pencil. Looking down the Idanre Hills in Ondo State, Nigeria

There are several types of field measurements in geography, all of which are quite valid, especially for routine teaching projects in secondary schools, although with varying degrees of accuracy and thus usefulness, particularly for serious geographical studies. These can be grouped broadly under the following categories:
1. Pacing, use of palm, arm, or other parts or senses of the human body, where the appropriate scales and measurement transformations of such parts of the body are fairly correctly established.
2. Measurements using instruments, and reading off the values or data from such instruments.
3. Computations and estimations, especially simple computations and rough estimations of linear, areal and voluminal dimensions of features for analysis purposes.
4. Counting – of the frequency of occurrence of the features or variables in question, in time and place.
  Each of these or a combination of them can be used, as appropriate or practicable, for the actual measurements in the field.
  The *repeated measurements* and the value of the *mean* (average) result of the several repeated measurements is another aspect of field

measurement which is of great importance in scientific fieldwork. It helps to establish the extent or margin of errors involved in the measurements. Moreover, it renders the results data more reliable as the error margins are known and could be taken care of during further calculations. As much as possible in the field, accurate recording of the measurements should be insisted upon and ensured.

Questionnaires

Having selected samples, we need to focus attention on the questionnaire which is a technical document comprising all questions necessary to lead to the required information.

A geography teacher wishing to compare two varieties of a crop will do so by observing them in the field. Various studies about landuse, site and situation of a town or village and communications are often conducted through direct observation in the field. Increasingly, however, as geographers concern themselves with patterns of social interaction and with the motives governing human decision-making, more than just the observable patterns in society must be measured. In these circumstances, in order to study social and economic processes, we need to obtain information directly from members of the public. With a farm study, the geographer has often recognized the value of enlarging on observed information by asking the farmer concerned details about how regularly fields are grazed, how frequently fences are repaired, what implements are used by farmers and where they are kept. The number and kind of shops in a town can be recorded from observation, but it is more difficult to discover the extent of the area served by those shops. It is true that some useful information on this problem could be obtained either by examining bus services from published timetables or by asking shopkeepers for details of the area served by deliveries. However, if we put a series of questions to a sample of the public concerning their shopping journeys, we will have direct evidence of the area served by the town's shops. Thus, by questioning the public, geographers can gain information which can help their investigations in ways that field measurement or secondary sources could not.

To design a good questionnaire, one must understand the basic research problem and its component parts. For instance, the research problem concerning migration from Sokoto Emirate to south-western Nigeria could be subdivided into: (a) the characteristics of the origin; (b) the characteristics of destination; (c) the characteristics of the migrants; (d) why and how they migrate. On the basis of these subdivisions we can deal with the basic details of the individual questions under each section.

Having selected the topics to be included in a survey, we must formulate questions to cover each topic. The *number*, *order* and *type* of questions constitute the main elements of the design of a questionnaire. There are two main categories of questions. The first asks for specific information from a respondent, e.g. what is your age? Have you been to Chicago? A subset of the factual questions are the classificatory questions which relate to age, sex, religion, ethnic origin, education, to enable us to classify people into different categories. On the other hand, opinion questions seek to find out the opinion or the attitude of the respondent to certain events or phenomena. There are also open-ended and pre-coded questions to which the possible alternative answers have been previously decided by the questioner, e.g. 'Which of the following correctly indicates how you travel from your town to Rio de Janeiro?'

_____*(a)* by air
_____*(b)* by rail
_____*(c)* by car
_____*(d)* by sea

We now give some guidelines for the design of a good questionnaire. The guidelines, meant for the investigator or the questionnaire drafter, are to ensure the minimization of the possible shortcomings of the data that may arise from the two principal agents, the respondent and the interviewer, involved in the data collection process.

(a) Simplicity and clarity

Simple, clear and unambiguous questions are more likely to have more meaningful responses than complicated and ambiguous questions. For example, a study in which one of the topics of interest is the marital status of the respondent could have a question like 'Married or single?' The question is not clear and is ambiguous. Divorcees and widowers are left out. An alternative way of asking the question is 'Are you married, unmarried, widowed, divorced or separated?' Vague expressions such as, 'in general', 'on the whole', should be avoided. Furthermore, double-barrelled questions like 'Is wind erosion active in Timbuktu because the area is dry?' should be avoided.

(b) Number of questions

The number of questions naturally depends on the number of topics or variables being investigated. Ideally, they should be as few as possible. Too many questions resulting in a lengthy and sometimes voluminous questionnaire may discourage a respondent from giving the type of co-operation that he might have given with fewer questions. Repetition of questions should be avoided.

(c) Arrangement and order of the questions

A well-arranged and well-ordered sequence of questions showing a logical and continuous flow of thought could be very helpful to a respondent. This is all the more so with a lengthy questionnaire.

(d) Open-ended and closed-ended questions

Questions leading to a limited number of definite and readily tabulated answers are to be preferred to those that call for many possible answers which cannot easily be classified. The former type is called *closed-ended* while the latter is called *open-ended*. A question framed in such a way as to demand only the three alternative answers 'Yes', 'No', and 'Don't know' is an example of closed-ended question.

(e) Other points

Other types of questions to be avoided are those that provoke some strong feelings in the respondent and those of a rather personal and confidential type. Where the nature of the study makes such questions unavoidable, some prefatory and explanatory notes seeking the respondent's co-operation and assuring him some secrecy in the use to be made of the information can be very helpful in softening an otherwise unyielding respondent. One way of ensuring secrecy is to use code numbers for each respondent instead of his name. This approach is all the more necessary if the questionnaires are sent by mail.

Before interviewing a person, one must try to enlist his/her interest and co-operation in one's project. This means one must be as polite as possible and not flare up even in the face of disappointment, or provocation.

It is advisable to have notes explaining and clarifying difficult and easily misunderstood points and terms in questionnaires. For instance, in a study involving farmers, a farmer could be defined in various ways – an adult male taxpayer engaged in farming, full-time or part-time, or an adult male who has the right to the produce of a farm and who need not physically work on the farm. Such notes are meant to ensure that all the respondents interpret questions the same way. Where interviewers are used, the notes form a set of instructions for them.

The use of questionnaires in gathering information in geography is fraught with various problems. The respondent, for instance, can spoil the investigator's master plan through deliberately distorted answer, non-response, unnecessary enthusiasm to give answers that will please the interviewer or the investigator. Additionally, the enumerator's carelessness in recording the response or in making measurements where necessary, over-projecting or under-projecting his personality during interviews and general failure to keep to instructions are obvious problems. Where mail questionnaires are used to obtain information, this source of bias will not arise. However, a disadvantage of mail questionnaires is that the percentage of non-responses can sometimes be high. By applying the guidelines suggested above some solutions might be obtained to these problems. The lesson to be learnt from such problems is not that questionnaire surveys should be avoided, but rather that one should use them sparingly, and in order to collect information not available in other ways.

Sources of existing data

In the preceding paragraphs we have considered some methods by which geographers can gather information. In gathering information for a particular investigation, the geographer should not be familiar only with the methods by which primary data may be generated. A great deal of valuable information is also available in unpublished and published forms. In the section below, some brief mention will be made about these sources of data.

Unpublished sources

Data in their original form exist in the files, log-books, and various registration forms of many government and non-government departments. To be able to make effective use of these sources without too much vain and wasteful search effort, some familiarization with the subject-matter and the organizational set-up of the departments is advantageous. In more advanced countries where such events as births, deaths and marriages are compulsorily registered, there is usually a central place like the Registrar-General's Office in Britain where original information on any of these events can be obtained.

The task of obtaining such information in some other places could be tremendous. In Nigeria, for example, one may have to search through the files of all such institutions as the ministries, law courts, churches, mosques and hospitals to be able to get anything near the required data.

The original essays and dissertations written by geography students are often valuable but unpublished sources of data. These materials are available in school or university libraries. The geography departments of educational institutions also keep copies of such materials.

Published sources

Published data are naturally more readily accessible than unpublished ones. Listed below are the main sources of published data.

(a) Statistical abstracts, bulletins and reports issued by government departments, especially their statistical units. The bulk of most of these publications is generally made up of tables derived from data collected by the department itself or by some other agencies. Examples of such materials are the *Statistics of Education in Nigeria*, Lagos, Federal Ministry of Information, which provides statistical data on education, *Annual Abstract of Statistics*, HMSO, also includes economic and social statistics for the United Kingdom under such headings as employment, population, fuel, production, distribution and transport. Other sources are *Annual Statistical Abstract of the United States*, US Department of Commerce, Bureau of the Census, and *Monthly Summary of Australian Conditions*, National Bank of Australasia, 6–8 Tokenhouse Yard, London EC2. Details from the latest national censuses and tables on such matters as the populations of large cities and the patterns of international migration are obtained from the United Nations *Demographic Yearbook*, the United Nations *Statistical Yearbook* and the UNESCO *Statistical Yearbook*. Statistical information concerning international passenger movements often found in shipping and airline timetables and in Cook's continental rail timetables can also be included in this category.

(b) Miscellaneous reports of government and non-government agencies. These are not reports specially made up of tables. The tables that feature in such reports are normally incidental and used mainly to summarize the activities of the agency over the period covered by the report. Examples of such reports are Federal Ministry of Education, *Investment in Education: The Report of the Commission on Post-School Certificate and Higher Education in Nigeria*, Lagos, Government Printer, 1960, Federal Republic of Nigeria; *Second National Development Plan, 1970–74*, Lagos, Federal Ministry of Education, 1970; and Ghana: *Seven-Year Development Plan 1963/64 – 1969/70*, Accra, Office of the Planning Commission, 1964.

Most nations will provide information and statistical data upon request by the teacher or departmental head. Such requests should be sent on official school letterhead and be directed to Information Centre, Statistics Division, Government Printing Service (or whatever title is appropriate) in the capital of the country concerned. Information may also be obtained by writing directly to the Ambassador of a particular nation at the official delegation address in your own national capital. Requests for information should be made well ahead of requirements, since the processing of requests may take a minimum of 6 months in some instances.

(c) Published maps are invaluable sources of information on patterns in the physical and human landscapes. To some extent the *Oxford Economic Atlases* provide such information on the world, United States and Canada, USSR and Eastern Europe, the Middle East and North Africa, Western Europe and Africa. The publications of the Ordnance Survey, Geological Survey, Soil Survey and Land Utilisation Survey and Directorate of Overseas Surveys, with their details of spatial patterns, form an invaluable guide for many studies within the British Isles. From an Ordnance Survey 1:25 000 or 1:50 000 map, geographers can measure the slope characteristics of an area with a fair degree of accuracy, but we should not also expect the same map to provide a full explanation of those characteristics. However, published maps do constitute a very convenient source of quantifiable data, dealing with anything from stream networks to settlement patterns.

(d) Standard textbooks also contain statistical data to a limited extent, dealing with topics ranging from the mean monthly temperature and precipitation tables (found in most books on climatology) to the statistics of commodity production by value or volume (found commonly in economic geography textbooks). Other general reference books such as *Statesmen's Yearbook* and *Whitaker's Almanack* also include some statistical tables. For global patterns, the *Production Yearbook* is published annually by the Food and Agricultural Organization of the United Nations with national tables of crops, livestock and size of holding. In most of these sources, tables are usually included as supporting information to illustrate the author's argument. The student undertaking an independent investigation will probably need to refer to a publication where information is tabulated for its own sake.

(e) Research reports and learned journals. There is a great variety of such materials in geography. Examples are *Research Papers*, School of Geography, University of Oxford, *The Nigerian Geographical Journal, The Professional Geographer, Revue de géographie alpine, l'Espace géographique, New Zealand Geographer, New Zealand Journal of Geography*, and the *Transactions of the Institute of British Geographers*. As in *(d)* above, these are not tables reporting sources. They are usually devoted to reports of specific research investigations.

(f) Magazines and daily newspapers. Examples of such materials are *Le Monde, The Times, New York Times, Daily News* (Tanzania), and *Nigeria Magazine*. Though we cannot make a hasty generalization about the authenticity of data from these sources, some fairly reliable data, especially of a geographical character, do occasionally appear on the pages of some of them. As a rule, a great deal of caution is required in using data based on these sources. Being news-orientated publications with a varying degree of commercialism, they

can hardly be expected to be objective and to eschew propaganda.

In making use of these published materials, there may be an unfortunate gap between the information obtained by field investigation and that published in official sources. This is partly because there is a need to protect the confidentiality of the industrialist, or a farmer who provides information, and so the information when published, normally refers to relatively large areas. Details of, say, an industry's income or a farmer's income are generally not made available. It is in this situation, where published sources are unsatisfactory, that investigators may be able to unearth data by questioning individuals and local organizations.

(g) Literature. Although novels, short stories and travel books are not sources of objective data in the accepted sense of the term, they may be used as useful evidence to reinforce information of a more objective type, or they may be used as ways of stimulating interest in a problem or situation. The process of glacial erosion may be made real by a mountaineer's account of his attempts to cross a glacier; a hurricane is made vivid by the personal recollections of someone who was caught in one; the problems of farmers subjected to a drought may come to life through a literary extract from such a novel as John Steinbeck's *The Grapes of Wrath*. Teachers may find it useful to store a number of such passages to read or give out to a class at an appropriate time.

Some exercises on data collection

In this section it is proposed to describe some exercises on village and market surveys which could be undertaken in secondary schools. The main purpose is to illustrate some procedures of getting pupils involved in data collection.

I. The absence of a published large-scale base map (1:10 000 or larger), as is often the case in schools in many developing nations, need not discourage fieldwork involving, say, village surveys. At the secondary-school level, pupils should be able to construct their own sketch maps on the basis of compass bearings and pacings. With the aid of the sketch maps and the following set of instructions, a village survey could be organized.

Objective
To collect data for the study of the form and functions of a village in Nigeria.

Organization
Students will be divided into pairs. Each pair will be given a specific part of the village to survey.

Equipment
Students will need field notebooks and pencils. Compasses may be provided. Separate notebooks will be required for a fair copy of the results of the work and for explanatory script.

Method
1. Measurement will be by pacing and compass bearing.
2. The main road may serve as the base line.
3. The position of every building is to be plotted, with its dimensions and orientation.
4. The use of buildings is to be noted:
   (a) Number all sites on the map and compile a corresponding annotated list in your field notebook.
   (b) Typical building functions: dwelling-house, shop (what sort?), workshop (product?), mosque, council offices, hut, mill, etc.
   (c) Note that some buildings may have more than one use: e.g. the verandah of a dwelling-house may be used for a market stall (what is sold there?)
   (d) Note that multi-storey buildings should have uses recorded for each floor.
   (e) Some buildings may be incomplete and unoccupied or new and unoccupied. Note this and estimate the intended building use. Similarly for deserted/ruined structures try to deduce former use. Remember to note the state of repair.
   (f) There are structures which, though significant, are not strictly buildings, slaughter pens, etc. Do not forget to record these.
   (g) Note also surfaced paths, streams, major rubbish tips, latrines, etc.
5. Buildings materials to be noted:
   (a) Walls: sun-dried bricks, mud, cement blocks, etc. often faced with cement or mud plaster.
   (b) Roofs: thatch, corrugated iron, etc.
   (c) Verandah: mud, concrete, etc.
6. Remember that taking photographs or making drawings is a good way of recording information.
7. Most of these exercises can be done by observation, but there is nothing to stop you asking questions as well.
   Each pair of students should be able to produce a map of part of the village, with all sites numbered and an annotated key attached. These maps may then be joined together and a total village coverage obtained.

II. Periodic markets are important foci of economic activity in village communities in Nigeria. They are both the initial bulking points for the supply of local agricultural produce to urban areas and the ultimate retail outlets in the chain of distribution of everyday household necessities to rural inhabitants. The following paragraphs describe the exercises on data collection concerning marketing activities in and around villages already studied by pupils.

Objective

The objective is to collect data concerning the nature and role of rural periodic markets in villages already studied. There are three distinct exercises. It is intended that in each market studied the three exercises should be carried out simultaneously, students being divided into three groups for this purpose. At the end of the study, students should be able to relate information about the market to that of its hinterland and the village where it is located. We can formulate the hypothesis that there is a significant relationship between a market, its hinterland and the village in which it is located.

Exercise I

This exercise is to assemble general information about the market in relation to its hinterland and to the village where it is located. The specific tasks are to:

(a) Make a sketch map of the village and the position of the market site. The location of other retail functions such as permanent shops and small daily markets should be indicated.

(b) Count the number of houses in the village.

(c) Gather relevant information concerning the market itself. For example, when the market was founded, its periodicity, whether it is served by a lorry park, the number of stalls, if any, stall rent and the person who collects the rents.

(d) Estimate the number of vehicles arriving at the market. A record should be kept of the number and time of lorry arrivals and departures. Lorry type should be noted, using the following classifications: large truck, large passenger lorry, small passenger lorry, others. This job can be done on a shift basis but it requires that there should always be one person 'on duty'.

(e) Interview lorry drivers in order to obtain the following information:
   (i)   Place of origin (i.e. town left that morning).
   (ii) Time of departure
   (iii) Route – i.e. via such and such places.
   (iv) Approximate cost of journey per passenger.
   (v)   Approximate cost of journey for standard items of freight (i.e. per 100 yam tubers, per sack of gari, per tin (i.e. per 4 gallons) of palm oil).
   (vi) Whether or not this market is the final destination or just a point of call on the way to some other place.

(f) Record the number of passengers and the type and amount of produce being off-loaded from each lorry.

Exercise II

This exercise is concerned with the collection of information relating to the kinds of business being transacted in the market. The following tasks are suggested to be carried out.

(a) Make a sketch map of the market-place, showing the patterns of alignment of the stalls, the number of stalls, selling pitches, etc. Indicate the distribution of the main categories of articles being sold (follow the classification of goods suggested in section *(b)* below).

(b) Count the number of traders selling goods in each of the following categories:

    (i)   foodstuffs (specify main types);
    (ii)   edible oils (specify) and salt;
    (iii)   local soap;
    (iv)   hardware (bowls, plates, knives, spoons etc.).
    (v)   tools (hoes, cutlasses etc.);
    (vi)   fuels, matches and candles;
    (vii)   soap powders, toiletries, medicines;
    (viii) kola, sweets, cigarettes;
    (ix)   charms and native medicines;
    (x)   cloth and clothing;
    (xi)   books, pencils, pens, stationery;
    (xii) others.

(c) Visit each trader in turn and record the commodity being sold and the amount available for sale. The results should be listed in your field notebooks as follows:

Trader 1. Pepper, six piles. Okro, six piles, etc.
Trader 2. Yams, sixty.
Trader 3. Gari, one large bowl.
Trader 4. Margarine, six small tins. Bread, twenty loaves.
Trader 5. Palm oil, three kerosine tins.

Exercise III

This third exercise involves interviews with both people who are buying and people who are selling things in the market. A basic concern is with where they come from, because it is hoped that in this way we shall be able to work out the sphere of influence of each market studied. The suggested questionnaire is given overleaf.

THE QUESTIONNAIRE

Name or Number (1, 2, 3, etc.) ....
Age (which you may have to guess)...
Sex ....   Occupation ....

What have you come to do in this market?
....   *(a)* shopping for household
....   *(b)* shopping for personal requirements
....   *(c)* to sell goods
....   *(d)* to sell and buy

No.	Commodities Bought	Cost	No.	Commodities Sold	Cost
1			1		
2			2		
3			3		
•			•		
•			•		
•			•		
10			15		

(The following questions would be suitable for professional traders and those who are buying for personal or family requirements except *(f)* and *(h)* for the latter group.)

(a) Where is your home town?
(b) Where do you live at present?
(c) From which place do you come to this market?
(d) What is your mode of transport?
(e) How long does it take you?
(f) If selling, where do you buy the goods for sale?
(g) If buying, where do you intend to sell the produce that you purchase?
(h) Where was the last market you attended?
(i) When?
(j) For what purpose?

Before using the above questionnaire, it is necessary to call students' attention to the fact that they are likely to come across a fairly diverse group of people in data collection for the study of a rural market. Some will be at the market because they are professional traders who are selling produce or buying it to resell it in a city like Ibadan. Others will be there to purchase household or personal requirements. A further group of people, such as wives of farmers, may be selling a small amount of produce in order to make the money for the week's household shopping, which they will then buy in the market when their own goods are sold. Strictly speaking, separate interview schedules are needed for each of these different groups of people, but since the questions students will want to ask are fairly simple and few in number it is easier to provide, with the aid of the questionnaire above, a general guide to the questions students should ask rather than a series of schedules on which they would fill in the answers to questions.

Collating the data

Before any detailed analysis begins, one of the things to do with the raw data is to check through the field record books and question-naires for any mistakes, inconsistencies and incompleteness. In some cases, it may not be possible to carry out these corrections, and a visit to the field may then be necessary. It should, however, be realized that it is not very often that a revisit is possible. For example, a road traffic survey conducted to find out the amount and frequency of daily traffic between two towns cannot be expected to be reproducible. There is no way of going back to check whether or not the number of vehicles reported for any particular hour is correct.

With open-ended questions the responses have to be classified into relatively small numbers of groups. The process of classifying answers and of sometimes identifying them by number and letter is called *coding*. When closed-ended questions are used, it is possible to code all the possible answers before the answers are actually received. This is called *pre-coding*. For instance, the question, 'How do geography pupils respond to the teaching of statistical techniques?' is an open-ended item on a questionnaire recently given to geography teachers. Such an open-ended question generated different responses which the investigator coded into three categories:
(a) negative responses from pupils;
(b) positive responses;
(c) neutral responses.

This is one type of coding normally carried out *after* obtaining responses.

The following are closed-ended items on the same questionnaire:

Educational qualifications of geography teachers

Indicate with a tick which of the following qualifications you possess:

Higher degree

University degree with teaching qualification

University degree

Teachers' diploma in geography

In these figures it is possible to *code* (items) *before*, that is, pre-code, obtained responses. The figure 1 may be assigned to higher degree, 2 to university degree with teaching qualification, 3 to university degree, etc. etc.

Whatever is done, coding or pre-coding, a check through the answers for proper classification, numbering and lettering is still called for at this stage. This whole process of checking through questionnaires and notebooks is sometimes called *collating*.

Pilot study

In order to obtain information about the feasibility of procedures for study and also about how well each phase of the main study will work, investigators often conduct a preliminary study before the main study is conducted. In other words, investigators do not always take a straight plunge at the main study as this might result in wasteful use of resources without necessarily obtaining the best results. Such a preliminary study, called a *pilot study*, is normally carried out on a much smaller scale than the envisaged one. It could be helpful in investigating costs, discovering organizational difficulties and in establishing routines to be followed in the main study. A pilot study could also lead to new ideas not already formulated in the problem and could throw some light on the kind of variation to be expected among the units of the population. A knowledge of such variation is often essential in determining the sample size of any subsequent study if sampling is to be done.

The collected data will eventually have to be used in drawing conclusions and writing reports about the population from which it came. But how does one go about drawing conclusions from a whole mass of notebooks and questionnaires which may run into thousands and which may contain no more than 'yes', 'no', and such like information. As these raw data become more meaningful when put in numerical form, our first task then is to attempt to quantify these masses of qualitative data. Basically our task consists of organizing the data by finding out the number of responses in the various categories classified. It is from these numbers that are formed many tables and diagrams used in describing and analysing the relevant population. The tabular and diagrammatic presentation of data and their analysis constitute the main content of the next chapter.

CHAPTER 6

Processing information

P. OLATUNDE OKUNROTIFA

It is unfortunate that most people are afraid of statistics. The reader who habitually takes fright at the mere mention of mathematical terms and symbols should be reassured immediately. Elementary statistics are easy to understand. No specific mathematical skill is necessary to understand what statistics is all about. In fact, no mathematical ability beyond a competence in the basic procedures of arithmetic (addition, multiplication, division and subtraction) is presupposed in this chapter.

The word 'statistics' originally meant numerical data systematically collected about phenomena. (The use of such data was tied to the needs of national states; thus the term.) These phenomena may relate to population or economic information which is vital to a country or to business enterprises. For example, we talk about population statistics, employment statistics, trade statistics and so on. Government and other agencies usually employ statisticians whose main duty is to design efficient ways of collecting and summarizing these types of data.

Statistics has become a scientific method for collecting, organizing, presenting and analysing numerical data so as to enable us to draw valid conclusions and make reasonable decisions based on available information. That part of statistics concerned with collecting and summarizing data is called *descriptive statistics*. That part concerned with drawing conclusions about the data is called *statistical inference*. The descriptive part of statistics, therefore, constitutes a sort of preliminary step into inferential statistics and is well suited as introductory material at the secondary-school level.

The nature of statistical data: population, sample, variables

In statistics, population refers to a collection of numbers which exist in fact or conceptually. The geographer is often interested in the number of items because the best way to deal with the problems associated with the items depends partly on their number. A population may refer to a countable or uncountable set of items. For example, the geographer may be interested in problems relating to the total number of people in Argentina, the total number of inhabitants of a city or village, the total number of students in a college or the total number of voters in an election. These are countable numbers representing a *finite* population. On the other hand, the geographer may also be interested in studying sand grains on a large beach or trees in a country. In practice, these are uncountable phenomena representing an *infinite* population.

Statistical methods are usually applied to data obtained from a finite or an infinite population. As indicated in Chapter 5, quite often, it may be impossible to measure or count an entire population when investigating a problem and so a small percentage of the total population, or a sample, is used. To be useful a sample needs to be representative of the total population. This will make it possible to draw dependable conclusions about the entire population from an analysis of data collected on the sample. Inferential statistical methods, therefore, may be described as methods for drawing conclusions about populations from samples. The opinion of an unknown population is inferred from the opinion of an observed sample. Statistical inference is based on *induction*, that is, we argue from the specific to the general or from the sample to the population. Statistical inference is quite distinct from *descriptive statistics* which is the process for collecting and summarizing numerical data.

The numerical data collected for a sample are usually in the form of *variables* which are attributes capable of assuming different numerical values. There are two types of variables – *continuous* variables and *discrete* variables. The former can assume any value in some range of values. For instance, in measuring distances, it is possible for any kilometre value and parts (fractions) of a kilometre to be recorded, e.g. 4.485 km, 5.612 km, etc. In other words, continuous variables are such that there are no clear-cut or sharp breaks between the possible values. Discrete variables can only be measured in terms of whole numbers (integers) and not in fractions. For example, the number of livestock, buildings, motor accidents during a day or the number of children in a family can assume any of the values 0, 1, 2, 3, 4, 5, etc. – but not 0.8, 1.47 or 8.67.

Statistical techniques used in the analysis of numerical data depend to a large extent upon the character of the data themselves. This chapter does not attempt to provide a comprehensive account of all the techniques that are available for this purpose. The few methods described have been included because they are both effective and relatively simple, and thus widely used.

Descriptive statistics: organizing and summarizing data

In Chapter 5, some methods of gathering information in geography were considered. The information gathered by those methods was *raw* data – 'raw' because nothing was done to extract any meaning from the numbers. For instance, in Table 6.1 with as many as twenty-five scores it is very difficult to get the 'feel' of the data merely by inspecting columns and rows of figures. With a little effort we can discover that the lowest score is 15, and that the highest is 30. But it is difficult to see how the scores are distributed between these two numbers. Are they spread evenly between 15 and 30? Are the scores 'bunched' in the middle, around 18, or what? Obviously we cannot tell this by looking at the haphazard arrangement of scores in Table 6.1. We need a more readily comprehensible format for the data. We have already discussed the primary purpose of statistical methods – to make an inference for an entire population from a sample. In order to make such an inference, we need the preliminary step of describing the sample. Descriptive statistics provide the methods for performing this preliminary function of simplifying and summarizing measurements about the sample. Descriptive statistical methods fall into two main categories: graphical methods and numerical methods.

Table 6.1 Percentage of land cultivated in twenty-five randomly selected villages in Ekiti District, Nigeria

25	27	23	29	25
28	22	25	22	23
30	24	17	24	28
24	21	23	17	19
23	19	26	20	15

Graphical methods

The graphical method attempts to present in pictorial form the set of measurements (data) taken from a sample so as to give the reader an adequate visual description of these measurements. The common graphical method utilizes a *frequency histogram* or *frequency distribution* that shows how the data are distributed over the axis of measurements. Frequency distribution is an arrangement of numerical data according to size and magnitude.

To construct a frequency histogram for the data in Table 6.1 above, the following steps are necessary (see Fig. 6.1).
1. The *range* of the data is determined. This is the difference between the highest and lowest figures in the set of data.

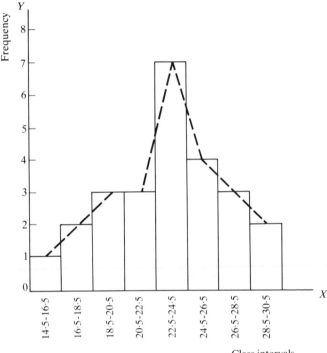

Class intervals

Fig. 6.1 Frequency histogram and polygon

2. Using the range as a guide, the data are divided into a number of convenient-sized groups. These groups are defined by *class intervals*. The size of the class interval depends upon the number of values to be included in the distribution. The range is divided by the number of class intervals desired and the resulting size is rounded off. By starting with 14.5 and ending by 30.5, we want to guarantee that none of the measurements falls on a boundary point.

3. The groups are then placed in a column with the lowest class interval at the top and the rest of the class intervals following according to size.

4. The data are scored. Each figure is checked once next to the class interval into which it falls.

5. We then proceed to tally the given scores and record the class frequency (Table 6.2, columns 2 and 3 respectively). In column 3, we note 1 is the frequency, i.e. the total number of villages, cultivating between 14.5 per cent and 16.5 per cent of their land, and 7 is the frequency of villages cultivating between 22.5 per cent and 24.5 per cent of their land. The information in this column is called a *frequency distribution*.

Table 6.2 Tabulation of data (in Table 6.1) for a histogram

1 Class interval	2 Tally	3 Frequency (f)	4 Relative frequency $\frac{(f)}{n}$
14.5–16.5	I	1	1/25
16.5–18.5	II	2	2/25
18.5–20.5	III	3	3/25
20.5–22.5	III	3	3/25
22.5–24.5	IHI II	7	7/25
24.5–26.5	IIII	4	4/25
26.5–28.5	III	3	3/25
28.5–30.5	II	2	2/25
		25	

6. The frequency distribution is then graphed as in Fig. 6.1. The frequency values are put on the vertical axis (the ordinate) and the class intervals on the horizontal axis (the abscissa). The resultant graph is called a *frequency histogram*. A joining together of the class mid-point values at the top of the column yields a *frequency polygon*.

The *relative frequency distribution* in column 4 (Table 6.2) gives us the proportion (fraction) of the total number of villages (twenty-five) which fall into any of the class intervals. For instance, 1/25 or 4 per cent or the total number of villages cultivate 16.5 per cent of their land or less. The histograms of the relative frequency distribution can also be drawn in the same way as that of frequency distribution (Fig. 6.2). The reader will note that both Figs 6.1 and 6.2 are identical except for the vertical scale where percentages are recorded in Fig. 6.2 instead of numbers as in Fig. 6.1.

A histogram provides a simple visual impression of the shape of a distribution. In the case of the histogram of cultivated land in twenty-five villages, there are obviously a greater number of values around the middle range. It is quite possible in another sample of villages to obtain a histogram where there are a greater number of values towards the lower or upper end of the range. Asymmetrical distributions of this sort are said to be *skewed*. There are two types: the right (positively) skewed distribution and the left (negatively) skewed distribution. The former is caused by the extremes in the higher values distorting the distribution towards the right (i.e. the values fall off gradually to the right of the highest point), and the latter is caused by extremes in the lower values which distort the distribution towards the left (i.e. the values fall off gradually to the

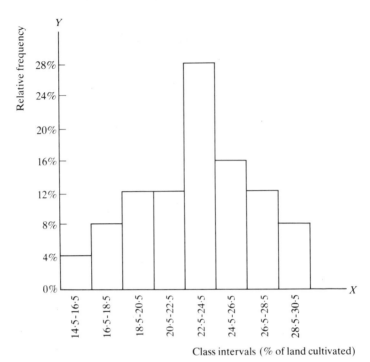

Fig. 6.2 Relative frequency histogram

left of the highest point) (see Figs 6.3 and 6.4). Many distributions such as those in Figs 6.1 and 6.2 are more or less symmetrical in shape. A non-skewed distribution which is bell-shaped is referred to as a *normal distribution*.

Although quite useful for illustrating a distribution, the histogram does not help greatly in describing it. There are, however, a number of indices that can be calculated fairly easily, and which provide more

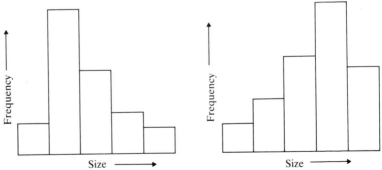

Fig. 6.3 Histogram with a positive skew **Fig. 6.4** Histogram with a negative s

objective descriptions of the two main properties of a distribution, namely, *central tendency* and *dispersion*. These are considered in the sections below.

The numerical descriptive measures

The graphical methods described in the previous section were simply ways of reorganizing the data with little or no loss of information. The major advantage of using graphical methods is the *visual* representation of the data. The graphical method is unsuitable for making inferences about the data. Therefore, we now turn to numerical descriptive measures. Here we seek a set of numbers or indices that characterizes the frequency distribution of our measures and at the same time will be useful in making inferences about the population. There are two highly useful sets of measures: the first refers to the central point of the distribution and the second to the spread of the distribution.

Numerical measures of central tendency

There are several ways by which the centre of a distribution can be measured. The most important kinds, discussed here, are the arithmetic mean, the median and the mode. Each has advantages and disadvantages depending on the data and the intended purpose.

The arithmetic mean
This is the most commonly used of all measures of central tendency. The index is often simply referred to as the mean, and it is the one that we most frequently imply when we take an average. It is calculated by summing all the individual values of the variable, and then dividing this total by the number of values summed. Expressed mathematically,

$$\bar{X} = \frac{\Sigma X}{N}$$

where $\bar{X}$ is the mean value of the distribution, ΣX (spoken as 'sigma X') the sum of all values of X (the variable) and N the total number of values in the distribution. Thus, in the case of our data on percentage of land cultivated (Table 6.1) the mean percentage is given by

$$\bar{X} = \frac{579}{25} = 23.16 \text{ per cent}$$

When there is a considerable number of items in our data set, it is generally too laborious to compute the arithmetic mean by the method outlined above. For instance, if the arithmetic mean is to be applied to data containing 30 000 items, correct addition of the huge mass of numbers in this manner is almost impossible without error. A more convenient and efficient method is to group the data into the form of frequency distribution, and then compute the arithmetic mean for the distribution. The arithmetic mean may be computed from the distribution in Table 6.2 by assuming that the cases are distributed evenly between the limits of the group. This would result in an average value for all values in the class interval equal to the mid-point of the group. Thus, the total value for each group may be obtained by multiplying the mid-point of the group by the number of cases in the group (see Table 6.3).

For the distribution in Table 6.3, the mid-point of the first class interval (15) is multiplied by the frequency for that group (1) in order to obtain the total value for all cases in the class interval. The products (Table 6.3, column 4) are then added to obtain the total value of all cases in the frequency distribution. This sum is divided by the number of cases (N) to obtain the arithmetic mean. The general formula for calculating the arithmetic mean from grouped data is

$$\bar{X} = \frac{(f \times \text{M.P.})}{N}$$
$$= \frac{569}{25} = 22.76 \text{ per cent}$$

Table 6.3 Computation of arithmetic mean from grouped data

1 **Class interval**	2 **Mid-point (M.P.)**	3 **No. of villages frequency (f)**	4 **Frequency × Mid-point ($f \times$ M.P.)**
14.5–16.5	15	1	15
16.5–18.5	17	2	34
18.5–20.5	19	3	57
20.5–22.5	21	3	63
22.5–24.5	23	7	161
24.5–26.5	25	4	100
26.5–28.5	27	3	81
28.5–30.5	29	2	58
		25	569

The result is only approximate since we are in effect assuming that the mean of all the values within a particular class is equal to the mid-value of that class, which is rarely the case and is not so in this example.

Even though the arithmetic mean is easily understood and relatively simple to compute, its major disadvantage is that its value may be greatly distorted by extreme values and therefore it may not be typical of a distribution.

The median
If a set of values is arranged from the smallest to the largest, the median is the value of the middle item. Thus, it is defined as that value above and below which an equal number of actual values are found. If the number of values in the distribution is odd, then the middle value in the ranked list is taken as the median. Thus, in our data in Table 6.1, the thirteenth value in the order, 23, is the median. If, on the other hand, there is an even number of items, the median (or middle value) is taken as the arithmetic mean of the two central items. Thus the median for 8, 8, 9, 10, 13, 14 is $\frac{(9 + 10)}{2} = 9.5$.

The fact that the median is not affected by the size of the extreme values makes it useful for certain purposes. The median provides important information, especially about a distribution in which a relatively small number of values are extreme in one direction or the other. For instance, consider the distribution of the incomes of 6 000 citizens in an oil-producing area in Nigeria. Virtually all of these citizens earn less than 15 000 naira per year. However, a few of them, the managers and engineers, earn as much as nearly all the others combined. The median of this distribution of incomes gives a better picture of the economic level of the area than does the mean, because the median is not influenced by the vastness of the incomes of a few. The median is therefore often a more revealing measure than the mean, especially when both are obtained from a distribution that contains a relatively small number of values at one extreme.

The mode
The mode is the value which occurs with the greatest frequency in a set of data – that is, the most frequent or most common value. In a frequency distribution curve, the mode will correspond with the value of the maximum point (ordinate). For example, the set of data in the second column of Table 6.4, has a mode of 20. A set of data may also not have a mode. The set of data in the first column of Table 6.4, for instance has no mode. On the other hand, it is possible to have a set of data where we have more than one mode. An example of this is shown in Fig. 6.5 where the modes are 23 and 25. That distribution is 'bimodal'.

Measures of spread (deviations)

A measure of central tendency does not adequately describe geographic data. It tells us something about a frequency distribution but

178   *New Unesco Source Book for Geography Teaching*

Table 6.4 Crude birth- and death-rates in some tropical African countries, 1969. (*Source: United Nations Demographic Yearbook*, 1970, New York, 1971)

	Crude birth-rates/1 000	Crude death-rates/1 000
Central African Republic	48	30
People's Republic of the Congo	43	20
Gambia	39	21
Ghana	47	24
Kenya	50	20
Togo	55	29
Uganda	42	20
Zambia	51	19

we are usually also interested in knowing how the values are distributed around the central one. It is, therefore, necessary to consider measures of the spread (variability or dispersion) of the data.

The simplest measure of variability is the *range* which is the difference between the largest and the smallest measurements. Thus, in our data in Table 6.1, the range is $30 - 15 = 15$. The range is a fairly crude measure since it ignores too much of the available information by focusing attention only upon two specific values; further, it is obviously affected by extreme values.

A very important measure of variability is based on the dispersion of the data about the sample mean (mean deviation). Large deviations indicate more variability of the data than do small deviations. Deviations from the mean can be used in different ways. As the sum of all deviations from the mean is zero, therefore we base a measure of spread on the sum of squared deviations from the mean. The average of this sum of the squared deviation from the sample

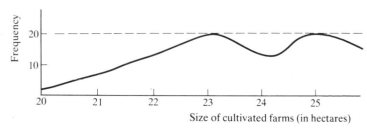

Fig. 6.5 A bimodal distribution of farms

mean is called the *variance*, which is denoted by S^2. Given a set of measurements, X_1, X_2, X_3 ... X_n, the sample variance is

$$S^2 = \frac{\Sigma_{i=1}^{i=N}(X_i - \overline{X})^2}{(N-1)}$$

where S^2 is the sample variance, X_i the ith term (each value separately), $\overline{X}$ the mean and N the number of items in the sample.

Now let us calculate some measures of spread from our data in Table 6.1. We first calculate the difference between each value (ith) in the sample and the mean ($\overline{X}$ = 23.16). The first value is 25, so (25 − 23.16) = 1.84. That value is squared (1.84 × 1.84) to equal 3.39. This is completed for each *case* and the products summed (Table 6.5).

Applying the variance formula above, we get:

$$\frac{\Sigma_{i=1}^{i=N}(X_i - \overline{X})^2}{(N-1)} = 357.47 \quad \text{or} \quad (25-1) = 24$$

$$S^2 = \frac{357.47}{24}$$

$$= 14.89$$

In computing the sample variance (S^2) we arrive at a quantity measured in the square of the original units. Therefore, to find the square root of the sample variance we use $\sqrt{S^2} = S$. The square root of the variance is called the *standard deviation* (S), a statistic which is frequently used in geographic research. In statistical notation σ is used for the population standard deviation and S for the sample standard deviation. The formula for calculating the standard deviation is thus given as

$$S = \sqrt{\frac{\Sigma_{i=1}^{i=N}(X_i - \overline{X})^2}{(N-1)}}$$

Thus, in our data in Table 6.1, the standard deviation is

$$S = \sqrt{14.89}$$
$$= \quad 3.86$$

While the mean (23.16) is an *average* of the measures in a set, the standard deviation (3.86) is a measure of how distant the individual values in a distribution are removed from the mean value. Thus, in our example, 3.86 is a measure of variability of the percentage of land cultivated in Ekiti District in Nigeria (Table 6.1).

Table 6.5 Calculation of the variance and standard deviation

Cultivated Land (X) (%)	$(X - \overline{X})$	$(X - \overline{X})^2$
25	1.84	3.39
28	4.84	23.43
30	6.84	46.79
24	0.84	0.71
23	−0.16	0.03
27	3.84	14.75
22	−1.16	1.35
24	0.84	0.71
21	−2.16	4.67
19	−4.16	17.31
23	−0.16	0.03
25	1.84	3.39
17	−6.16	37.95
23	−0.16	0.03
26	2.84	8.07
29	5.84	34.11
22	−1.16	1.35
24	0.84	0.71
17	−6.16	37.95
20	−3.16	9.99
25	1.84	3.39
23	−0.16	0.03
28	4.84	23.43
19	−4.16	17.31
15	−8.16	66.59
$\Sigma X_i = 579$	$\Sigma (X_i - \overline{X}) = 0$	$\Sigma (X_i - \overline{X})^2 = 357.47$

Recording information on maps and diagrams

In the foregoing sections, we have considered some statistical procedures by which data could be organized and summarized. However to the geographer, a numerical distribution is most meaningful when placed within a spatial context. Each item within the distribution then has two properties, one being its value or quantity, and the other its location which may be either a point or an area. Together, these properties produce the pattern of areal variation which constitutes a spatial distribution. The description of spatial distribution is best achieved, not by attempting to summarize the data statistically, but by illustrating the properties mentioned in the form of a map. Map construction is therefore a basic geographic technique, especially so since visual description is a vital first step in seeking to explain a distribution of this type.

Geographers record information on maps and diagrams by means of symbols which can be grouped into two classes: those which are intended primarily or solely to record the location of phenomena, and those designed to show either quantitative distributions or simply quantity alone.

The symbols of the first category are both varied and numerous. Their use is limited to maps, and they comprise the methods employed for showing such features as vegetation, houses, churches, markets, rivers and all the multiplicity and variety of phenomena which exist together on the earth's surface.

The symbols and methods used for representing quantity on maps and diagrams may be considered in four main groups:

(a) symbols of uniform size which are placed over a map in different numbers to indicate quantity;
(b) symbols which themselves vary in size according to the quantities they represent;
(c) the use of isometric lines;
(d) the use of shading.

In the sections below we will be concerned only with the methods involved in the construction of the quantitative maps mentioned above. Each of these is adaptable to a fairly wide range of data, but inevitably each has its own specialities, and its own strengths and weaknesses.

The use of symbols of uniform size

Of the four groups of quantitative maps indicated above, the simplest is the dot map. Dot maps are widely used in geographical work, and Fig. 6.6 is an example. In this map each dot represents 70 000 persons, and the placing of the dots gives a general picture of the distribution of the Fulanis over the northern states of Nigeria. The scale of dots for such a map needs to be carefully chosen if it is to be effective. Badly chosen scales will result in there being either too few or too many dots to bring out the distribution pattern. A well-chosen scale, on the other hand, will yield a pattern of dots which faithfully reflects the distribution of the feature being shown. The dots must be carefully placed to achieve this result. The data for dot maps are commonly available according to political or administrative units, which are not necessarily 'geographical regions' in terms of the features being mapped. For example, the statistics for Fig. 6.6 were available by 'divisions'. These divisions are simply administrative areas of different shapes and sizes, over which the population of the

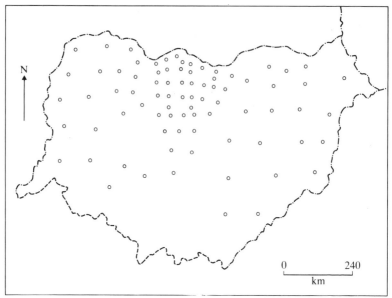

Fig. 6.6 Distribution of Fulanis in Northern Nigeria

Fulanis is by no means evenly spread. Consequently, in making Fig. 6.6 the dots had to be located considering factors such as the absence of settlements on lakes or land reserved for growing trees, the scarcity of villages on steep mountain slopes, etc. Where a lightly settled division was next to a heavily settled one, the distribution of dots in the former was 'weighted' towards the latter in the absence of evidence suggesting a different arrangement. It was also necessary to make sure that the boundaries of the divisions could not be seen on the finished map. This was achieved by placing some dots actually on the boundaries in appropriate cases, thereby preventing the boundary lines from appearing on the finished map as narrow 'dotless' areas.

Representing quantity by single symbols

The use of symbols which themselves vary in size according to the quantity they depict is one of the fundamental ways of representing quantity on maps and diagrams. Some of the most popular and standard ways of doing this are by means of circles, rectangles and lines.

Circles illustrate quantities on maps by using a scale which is related either to the diameter of a circle, or to the area of a circle. In Fig. 6.7, the cattle population in four areas – Kano, Bornu, Sokoto

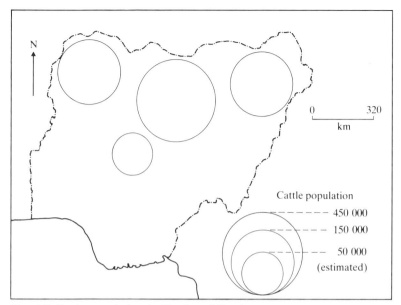

Fig. 6.7 Cattle population in Northern Nigeria

and Bauchi in Nigeria, has been illustrated by means of circles. The diameters of the circles in Fig. 6.7 are directly proportional to the cattle population in the areas.

In addition to representing quantity by circles, it is possible to use rectangles. Rectangular symbols are particularly valuable for showing phenomena which accumulate over a period of time, such as monthly rainfall or the total production of goods in a week, or month or year. When drawn on a map, rectangles normally indicate quantity by variations in their lengths rather than in their widths. This is the case in Fig. 6.8, where narrow rectangles, or 'bar-graphs', have been used to show the amount of hand-presses used in some parts of the palm belt of Nigeria.

Some of the symbols which have just been discussed in relation to maps may also be used in diagrams. A divided circle, for instance, is a good way of showing how a total is made up of individual items. In Fig. 6.9 a single circle has been divided to show the utilization of land in The Netherlands. It simplifies the choice of scale for a diagram like this to express the individual statistics as percentages of the total. One per cent will then be represented by 3.6° of a circle. This is the scale adopted in Fig. 6.9, and measurements with a protractor show that 13 per cent of The Netherlands is under forest, 19 per cent is non-agricultural land, 22 per cent arable and 42 per cent is pasture and 4 per cent is horticulture. Divided circles like this are also called 'pie-graphs'.

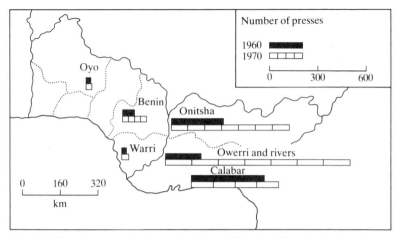

Fig. 6.8 Hand-presses in the palm belt of Nigeria. The simple hand-press gives an oil extraction rate of 65 per cent as compared with 55 per cent by traditional hand methods of extraction. The increasing use of such presses represents a significant development in the palm oil industry.

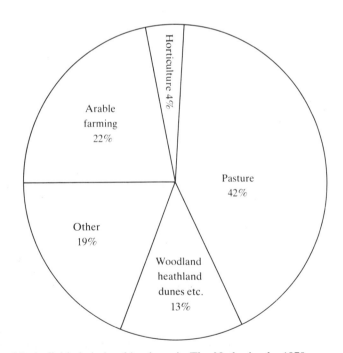

Fig. 6.9 A divided circle of land-use in The Netherlands, 1978

Divided rectangles, like divided circles, may be used for quantitative diagrams. They can be used alone to show the divisions of a given total, or else several can be employed to compare the make-up of different totals. A feature which is particularly well shown by divided rectangles is how the proportions of comparable occupations or products vary from one place to the other. Figure 6.10, for example, shows the varying amounts of motor vehicles produced by different countries. The productions of individual countries are expressed as percentages and are shown on the rectangle accordingly.

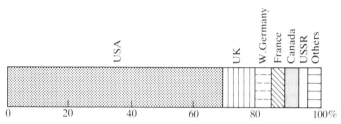

Fig. 6.10 Motor vehicles: chief world producers

Representing quantity by isometric lines

There are two main groups of maps which involve some indication of quantity as well as spatial distribution, known as 'quantitative areal maps'. The first group includes maps where quantities are indicated by lines of equal value, such as contours and isotherms. The second group consists of maps which depict average values per unit of area over some administrative region for which statistics are available, such as density of population per square kilometre, the percentage of land under cultivation and the yield per hectare of arable land.

It must be admitted that there is a considerable amount of confusion concerning the multiplicity of terms which have been coined to denote variants of these cartographical terms. For example, to cover all lines representing constant values on maps, the terms *isopleth, isarithm, isoline, isobase, isogram, isontic line* and *isometric line* have been used at various times.

Isometric lines constitute one of the fundamental ways of representing quantity on maps and diagrams. The word 'isometric' is derived from the Greek *iso*, meaning equal, and *metron*, meaning measurement. Isometric lines, therefore, are lines joining points of equal measurement or value. When such lines are used on maps they are generally called isopleths.

The general principles involved in drawing isopleths are illustrated in Figs 6.11 to 6.14 which relate to temperatures in °C but not to air temperatures. The first step is to establish as many points as possible

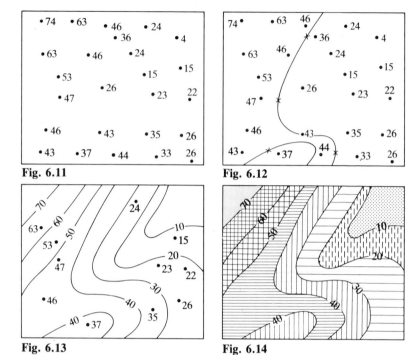

Fig. 6.11

Fig. 6.12

Fig. 6.13   Fig. 6.14

Figs 6.11–6.14 The interpolation of isopleths

for which precise values are given, as in Figs 6.11 and 6.12. These points are then used to interpolate the positions of other points having values of the different isopleths required. In doing this, it is assumed that the value between one point and another changes at a constant rate unless there is evidence to the contrary. Thus, the 25°C isotherm may be assumed to pass midway between two stations with average temperatures of 20°C and 30°C. These isopleth maps can be used to depict climatic distributions (isotherms, isobars, isohyets and isonephs), salinity of the sea (isohalines) and, in fact, any feature where figures are available and can be plotted for a series of particular points.

Representing quantity by shading

It could be quite valuable to combine the use of isopleth lines on maps and diagrams with another fundamental way of showing quantity: the use of shading. Careful shading or tinting will generally improve the clarity and appearance of an isoline map. For instance, it is not difficult to visualize the effect which shading has on the diagram in Fig. 6.14. By shading or colouring areas between the isopleths, a greater visual impact is provided.

As a rule, different colours should not be used for quantitative shading. Colours need to be artistically applied if they are to be pleasing, and a change of colour tends to give the impression of a change of phenomenon. Black and white shading is preferable to shading in any other colour. The principle to follow consists in increasing the depth of shading gradually from the smallest value to the largest. The upper category is often conveniently shown in full black, and the lowest by light, widely spaced dots or perhaps by no shading at all. An increase in the depth of shading can be achieved by techniques such as enlarging the dots, thickening the lines, bringing the lines closer together or crossing the lines.

The statistics which geographers use are mainly available only by countries, or by administrative divisions. Consequently, it is often convenient, or necessary for want of more detailed information, to map data according to such areas of statistical or administrative convenience. When the data are illustrated by shading on this basis, the resulting map is known as a 'choropleth' map. To eliminate the effect of area size on the quantities involved, each total is expressed in standardized form as a ratio to area. Thus, population totals become densities of persons per square kilometre (or some other unit of area), and crop areas are converted into percentages of the total area of farmland. Other types of information normally measured within an areal context can also be represented on a choropleth map. Examples are land value, crop yield or fertilizer input, all of which are commonly measured in units per hectare. Figure 6.15 illustrates how other types of information not necessarily measured within an areal context can also be represented on a choropleth map. The map shows the annual per capita energy consumption of African countries.

Inferential statistics

With the aid of the model in Fig. 5.1, we have illustrated the stages of scientific investigation in geography. First, according to the model, the geographer identifies his problem and then sets up hypotheses (propositions which can either be falsified or attested). The next step in the sequence is the collection of information against which to test the hypotheses. The activities involved in these stages have been discussed in Chapter 5.

So far, this chapter has been devoted to the processing of information. Apart from the organizing and summarizing of data often carried out at this stage, it also involves predictions based upon the data collected. At this stage, a number of hypotheses formulated

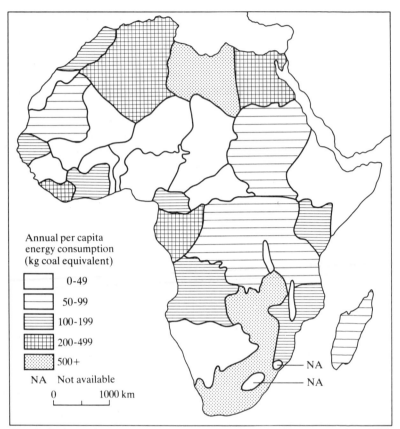

Fig. 6.15 Annual per capita energy consumption of African countries, 1970. (*Source: United Nations Statistical Yearbook*, 1971)

initially may have to be modified or even replaced to reflect the reality of the situation under study. The final stage is that of verification. The main concern at this stage is to ascertain the extent to which the hypotheses are valid. The data assembled have to be carefully processed and analysed before any meaningful conclusions or inferences can be drawn from them. The procedures involved in these last two stages constitute the content of the sections which follow.

Predictions based on data collected and the verification of hypotheses are important aspects of inferential statistics. Such predictions are often associated with two types of variables: independent and dependent variables. An independent variable may be considered as the cause in the cause–effect relationship, e.g. the degree of slope of land. On the other hand the dependent variable refers to the effect in the cause–effect relationship, e.g. the value of land-use. In inferential statistics when comparing the data from two samples we wish to know whether the differences between the samples have been caused by the independent variable. We would not expect the two samples to be absolutely identical – there are bound to be some differences *just by chance*. The problem for inferential statistics is to decide whether the *actual* differences are due to chance, or whether these differences are so large that we can ascribe them, at least in part, to the effects of the independent variable. In this description of statistical inference we are using the word 'chance' as a shorthand for the effects of irrelevant variables that are not perfectly matched across the two groups of samples. We shall continue to use the term in this sense. To sum up, then, we shall be using statistics to infer from the data whether the predicted effect of the independent variable actually occurred in the study. We are making inferences from observable data to discover whether causal relationships between variables exist.

From the foregoing, it is clear that inferential statistics is based not on certainty but essentially on probability. For this reason, it is important to consider briefly some aspects of elementary probability theory which is basic to inferential statistics and which is also of notable significance to sampling.

Probabilities range from absolute impossibility (a probability of 0) to absolute certainty (a probability of 1). For instance, the probability that a given river will flow upstream is 0 as this possibility is ruled out. On the other hand, the probability that all men who are now alive will die is unity. In between these two extremes is a wide range of possibilities. Some probabilities are, however, derived from empirical situations. For example, the probability that a coin tossed once will have its head up is 0.5, since there are two possibilities – a head or a tail – and each event has an equal chance of occurring.

Null and alternate hypotheses

As said earlier, it is necessary to formulate hypotheses before analysing data. An untested assertion of a relationship is usually referred to as a hypothesis. It is something which needs to be tested. We may use statistical tests to compare two (or more) sets of different data to establish a mathematical relationship between them (correlation) or determine two samples as coming from the same population. Thus, if we had two samples of rice yield per hectare from two contrasting areas, Kwara and Oyo States in Nigeria, we could use statistical tests to establish whether the two sets of values of rice yield were sufficiently similar to be likely to form part of the same distribution (or population), or whether they were so different as to be unlikely to form part of one distribution (or population). In other words, we could establish whether observed differences in yield had a high probability of being the result of chance variations, or whether the variations were unlikely to be the result of chance and therefore represented a difference between Kwara and Oyo States.

In order that a statistical test may be used it is necessary first of all to set out the proposition in precise terms. It is customary to do this by the formulation of two hypotheses, written symbolically to H_0 and H_1. H_0 is the *null hypothesis*. It is termed 'null' because it states that the two samples form part of the same population, and there is a high probability that the observed differences are due to chance variations. H_1 is the *alternate hypothesis* and states that the observed differences are so great that they are unlikely to be the result of chance, and the two samples must therefore be regarded as coming from different populations. If we consider our hypotheses for rice yield per hectare in Kwara and Oyo States of Nigeria, H_0 will state that 'there is no significant difference between Kwara and Oyo States in terms of rice yield per hectare'. H_1 will state that 'the observed differences between Kwara and Oyo States are so great that it is unlikely the two sets of values form part of the same population'. Only if the result of the test leads us to reject H_0 and accept H_1, may we confidently begin to look for reasons why this difference should exist.

Significance and rejection levels

The concept of statistical significance refers to the probability of obtaining a difference between a population statistic and a sample statistic, or between two sample statistics.

By conducting a statistical test on the data of a study we shall be able to say *how likely it is that any given difference is due to chance.* If it is very unlikely that the difference could be caused by chance – say the *probability* is 1 in 780 – then we would conclude that the independent variable is responsible for the difference. The difference is then said to be significant. If, on the other hand, the difference between the two groups could easily have arisen by chance, then there is no reason to ascribe it to the effect of the independent variable. The findings are *non-significant.* Naturally we usually hope for significance, since this implies that our prediction is correct.

Now, you may ask, how unlikely must the chance explanation be before we reject it, and regard the result as significant? This is essentially an arbitrary matter – a matter of convention rather than basic principle. Many geography researchers choose a *significance level* of 0.05 or 1/20, or 95 per cent confidence, often called *the 0.05 level of significance*, meaning that the particular result has only a 5 per cent chance of occurring through random variations. Similarly, 99 per cent confidence is referred to as the 0.01 level of significance. That is, the result will happen by chance less than once in a hundred times. Associations of numbers that are likely to occur through chance variations less than five times in a hundred are said to be *statistically significant.*

Generally, in geographical problems the 0.05 level of significance is regarded as sufficiently rigorous. But the actual percentage of confidence (i.e. rigour) that is required for any particular problem can only be decided by the investigator. This degree of confidence is known as the *rejection level* (i.e. the level of significance at which we decide H_0 may safely be rejected), and represented symbolically by α.

Thus, if we decide that the 0.05 level of significance is sufficiently rigorous in the case of our rice yield samples from Kwara and Oyo States of Nigeria (i.e. $\alpha = 0.05$), and if the result of the test shows that there is at least a 95 per cent probability that the values in the two samples are not from the same population, we can reject H_0 and accept the alternate hypothesis, H_1; we now have a sound statistical basis from which to seek reasons for the difference in yield.

Statistical tests

The concepts presented in the foregoing sections are meant to provide readers with some background in the practical aspects of statistical testing that are to follow. A statistical test is simply a device for calculating the likelihood that our results are due to chance fluctuations between samples. Different tests calculate this likelihood in different ways, depending on the design of the study and the nature of the dependent variable.

The steps of the general hypothesis-testing procedure are presented here in formal order. It is important not only to go over them but to conceptualize the total approach, as we may make references to this approach in the sections that follow.

1. The investigator must state the hypothesis that he is about to test, in the form of a null hypothesis (H_0) which states that the two samples are part of the same population and that whatever observed differences are found are due to chance. The alternative hypothesis (H_1) states that the differences between the samples are so great that they are unlikely to be the result of chance.

2. He must pick a significance level based on the considerations already discussed. For instance, he may decide to test his hypothesis at the 5/100 significance level, *usually written as the 0.05 significance level.*

3. He must gather his random sample of observations and compute the sample value of interest to him. The value must then be

located on a significance table and compared against the pre-selected probability level such as the 0.05 level, as suggested above. If the sample value computed is below the significance level on the table, then the value is said to be statistically not significant. If it is above the significance level, the value is said to be statistically significant.

4. *(a)* If there is no statistically significant difference between the samples, they can be assumed to come from the same population and the null hypothesis (H_0) can be accepted.

(b) If there is a statistically significant difference between the samples, they can be assumed to come from different populations and the null hypothesis can be rejected and the alternative hypothesis (H_1) accepted.

In the sections that follow, examples intended as practical illustrations of the way in which statistical techniques can be employed in the classroom within the context of hypothesis-testing are provided. By describing the application of a few commonly used techniques, it is hoped to show how varying degrees of complexity and objectivity can be introduced to suit 16–18-year-old pupils of moderate ability, while dealing with the same basic information. The situations chosen represent only a fairly limited field of geographical study, and it should be emphasized that the statistical methods involved are capable of much wider application, even at school level, than is necessarily implied here.

The t-*test of significance*

Probably the most common use of the *t*-test is to determine whether the difference between two samples is significant. The test is a fairly simple one and it can quite easily be computed by sixth-formers.

The exercise in which the test is used resulted from fieldwork carried out by a group of sixth-formers (i.e. the last year of the secondary-school course) at Ibadan in Kwara and Oyo States of Nigeria. Two samples of farm sizes were obtained from the two states.

With the data in Table 6.6, the students set up the null hypothesis (H_0) that there is no significant difference between the farm sizes in Kwara and Oyo States of Nigeria.

Then they proceeded to calculating the *t*-value as follows:

$$t = \frac{|\bar{X}_1 - \bar{X}_2|}{\sqrt{\dfrac{S_1^2}{N_1} + \dfrac{S_2^2}{N_2}}}$$

where $|\ \ |$ means the positive value ignoring the negative signs.

Table 6.6 Two samples of farm sizes (in hectares)

	Kwara State (N_1)	Oyo State (N_2)
	0.3	0.3
	0.3	0.3
	0.8	0.6
	1.3	0.8
	1.8	1.3
	3.0	1.8
	3.3	1.8
	3.6	4.3
	3.8	7.0
	4.8	9.8
Total	23.0	28.0
Mean ($\overline{X}$)	$\overline{X}_1 = 2.30$	$\overline{X}_2 = 2.80$
Standard deviation	$S_1 = 1.61$	$S_2 = 3.24$
	$S_1^2 = 2.59$	$S_2^2 = 10.50$
	$N^1 = 10$	$N_2 = 10$

Thus in our example:

$$t = \frac{|2.30 - 2.80|}{\sqrt{\dfrac{1.61^2}{10} + \dfrac{3.24^2}{10}}}$$

$$= \frac{0.50}{\sqrt{\dfrac{2.59}{10} + \dfrac{10.50}{10}}}$$

$$= \frac{0.50}{\sqrt{0.26 + 1.05}}$$

$$= \frac{0.50}{\sqrt{1.31}}$$

$$= \frac{0.50}{1.15}$$

$$= 0.44$$

The next step is the computation of the number of degrees of freedom, to determine if the *t*-value of 0.44 is statistically significant. In obtaining the degrees of freedom (df) the following calculation is used:

$\mathrm{df} = (N_1 - 1) + (N_2 - 1) = N_1 + N_2 - 2.$

In this case, the degrees of freedom are $(10 - 1) + (10 - 1) = 18$. The value of $t = 0.44$ is compared with the values which give significance at 18 degrees of freedom in a t-table. Most statistical textbooks and manuals will contain such a table. The t-table will give the values necessary for a certain level of significance (0.05 or 0.01). With 18 degrees of freedom a value of 2.10 is necessary at the 0.05 level of significance and a value of 2.88 at the 0.01 level of significance. Any value less than these, such as 0.44, is probably the result of chance and not the result of some identifiable condition or variable.

Since the calculated t-value of 0.44 is less than the t-values from the table, at such high probability levels the inference is that there is no significant difference between farm sizes in Kwara and Oyo States. This means, in effect, that the two samples can be said to have been drawn from the same parent population. In other words, the factors which affect farm sizes in both states are broadly very similar. (N.B. This test is not applicable if the distributions are skewed.)

Correlation

The areal distribution of phenomena, either on the land or on maps, poses interesting aspects of geographical study. The details of the spatial arrangement of the variables forming the components of the phenomena being studied often give indications of apparent relationships between the variables. More important than the significance of differences between geographical characteristics, is the interrelationship between two or more variables. The interrelationship is described by the word 'correlation'. If families with many children tend to have a higher income than families with few children, we say that there is a *positive correlation* between the two variables of family size and family income. If, however, families with many children tend to have a lower income than families with few children, we would say that a *negative correlation* exists, instead of a positive one. The third possibility, that family size varies regardless of family income would lead us to say that there is a *zero correlation* between family size and family income.

These three classes of correlation (positive, negative and zero) are shown graphically in the four parts of Fig. 6.16. The four graphs in the figure are each called scatter plots.

Scatter diagrams (or scatter plotting) can be widely used in school geography to show how one variable may be related to another. They are frequently constructed, for instance, by younger pupils in the science laboratories of secondary schools to show how an increase in

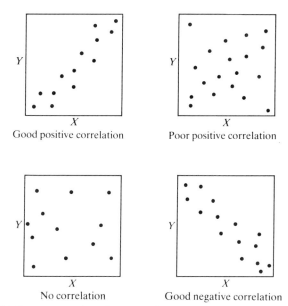

Fig. 6.16 Some examples of scatter diagrams

one variable is accompanied by an increase or decrease in another. In Table 6.7 the altitude above sea-level and the mean annual rainfall for fifteen stations in the Benin Republic of West Africa are recorded.

Figure 6.17 shows the scatter diagram recording altitude and rainfall. The broken line is a roughly drawn line indicating the relationship between rainfall and altitude. To assist in drawing it, one fixed point recording the mean altitude and rainfall can be inserted and the line made to pass through it. On the other hand, a reasonably accurate line can be inserted by eye without calculating the mean and it shows that, in general, an increase in height of 100 m corresponds to an increase in rainfall of about 250 mm.

Scatter plotting is valuable in that it indicates whether or not some sort of relationship (correlation) exists. It can usefully provide an initial indication of the nature and extent of the relationship between two variables, and may help in deciding whether further testing, using more objective methods, is likely to be worthwhile. However, scatter plotting does not give any precise measure of the degree of correlation or of its significance. Methods, within the reach of secondary school pupils, for quantifying such relatonships are examined in the following paragraphs. They have been selected from several methods which provide a measure whereby the degree of relationship can be expressed numerically. For two of them, Spearman rank and Pearson product moment, this measure is known as the

Table 6.7 Altitude and mean annual rainfall for fifteen stations in the Benin Republic

Station	Altitude (m)	Rainfall (mm)
1	22	912
2	44	1 020
3	56	1 260
4	61	860
5	62	1 060
6	140	1 040
7	170	1 130
8	185	1 480
9	225	1 410
10	232	1 410
11	262	1 620
12	275	1 460
13	331	1 670
14	342	1 780
15	351	1 470

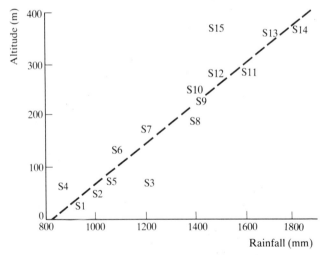

Fig. 6.17 Scatter diagram showing the relationship between altitude and rainfall for various stations in Benin

coefficient of correlation. It is thus possible to compare accurately the degree of correlation obtained when one variable is matched in turn with others, and thus indicate further fruitful lines of investigation of spatial relationships. Furthermore, it is possible to say with a stated level of confidence whether or not the correlation is a chance occurrence.

The Spearman rank correlation coefficient

This test operates at a satisfactory level of precision for many purposes with the result that this technique is of great value especially for obtaining a generalized estimate of correlation. It is easy to learn, and its working should appeal to the common sense of 15-year-old pupils, and also perhaps to able 14-year-olds.

This technique allows the degree of relationship between two variables to be assessed objectively, and expressed in precise numerical form as a correlation coefficient. The test is not concerned with the actual numerical values of either variable, but only with their position in a ranked list. This is called a non-parametric test. For this reason the values of both population density and distance from the city centre of Lagos, Nigeria, are ranked in order, in Table 6.8, from highest to lowest. It should be noted that this test is not so useful if the total number of items to be ranked is small, e.g. less than ten.

Once the data have been ranked, the next step is the calculation of a value D, defined as the difference between each distance rank and its population density rank. In the sixth column the value D^2 is worked out for each case. Once calculated, D and D^2 are tabulated

Table 6.8 Calculation of rank correlation coefficient

A km from city centre	Rank	B Population density	Rank	D	D^2
1	10	312	1	9	81
1.5	9	215	2	7	49
2.5	8	150	3	5	25
3.5	7	120	4	3	9
5.5	6	95	5	1	1
7	5	84	6	−1	1
8	4	70	7	−3	9
11	3	52	8	−5	25
13	2	30	9	−7	49
15	1	15	10	−9	81
					$D^2 = 330$

with the rest of the information, as illustrated in Table 6.8. The D^2 column is then summed, and the total entered at the foot of the column.

For purposes of testing, a hypothesis should be stated: there is no significant relationship between distance from city centre (variable A) and population density (variable B) in Lagos, Nigeria. This, as indicated earlier, is a null hypothesis. If the result is significant then the null hypothesis will be rejected.

The formula for determining the Spearman rank correlation coefficient is:

$$\rho = 1 - \frac{6 \, \Sigma \, D^2}{(n^3 - n)}$$

where D is the difference in ranking, $\Sigma \, D^2$ is the sum of all the values of D^2, and n the number of pairs in the sample. Applying this to the figures for Lagos, it reads:

$$\rho = 1 - \frac{6 \times 330}{1\,000-10}$$

$$= 1 - \frac{1\,980}{990}$$

$$= 1 - 2$$

$$= -1.00$$

The value of ρ (rho) has a possible range of between -1 and $+1$. A value of $+1$ implies perfect positive correlation, and a value of -1 perfect negative correlation. If there is no correlation at all between the two variables, then ρ is equal to zero. In the case of the Lagos exercise, the null hypothesis is totally rejected by the ranking method. Complete *inverse* correlation between density of population and distance from city centre in Lagos is shown – i.e. as distance increases, population density decreases. Using a critical values table for Spearman's rank correlation coefficient, one can determine that with $n = 10$, any value equal to or greater than 0.746 is statistically significant at the 0.01 level. Therefore, the value of -1.00 would occur less than once in 100 by chance, leading us to reject the null hypothesis.

Having rejected the null hypothesis an alternative one is adopted, i.e. that there is significant statistical correlation between distance from city centre and population density in Lagos.

The Pearson product moment correlation coefficient

The correlation coefficient (ρ) obtained by using the ranking technique explained in the paragraphs above is very useful as it is relatively simple to apply. However, as mentioned above, it cannot be used with accuracy with less than ten, or more than thirty cases. Also, as it uses rank order of the variables and not the actual values, some precision is lost. The Pearson product moment coefficient which makes full use of interval data[1] gives a more precise statement. This coefficient, which uses actual values, is called a parametric test. For instance, in the case of the Lagos population data, the product moment coefficient, $r = 0.86$ (see calculations below) compared with $\rho = 1.0$ by ranking method. For the product moment coefficient, interval data only can be used. It is, obviously, the more precise, taking into account the size of the interval between values.

The formula for the Pearson product moment coefficient of correlation (called r) which is considered simplest to apply is

$$r = \frac{\Sigma(X - \overline{X})(Y - \overline{Y})}{\sqrt{[\Sigma(X - \overline{X})^2][\Sigma(Y - \overline{Y})^2]}}$$

when $\overline{X}$ is the mean of the X column, and $\overline{Y}$ the mean of the Y column.

Alternatively, $(X - \overline{X})$ may be written x, and $(Y - \overline{Y})$ may be written y, that is:

$$r = \frac{\Sigma xy}{\sqrt{(\Sigma x^2)(\Sigma y^2)}}$$

The following steps for the calculation are applied to the Lagos population data (see Table 6.9).
1. Add up column 1 and divide by the number of cases (ten) to give the mean of the X-values ($\overline{X} = 6.8$).
2. Do the same for the Y-values in column 2 ($\overline{Y} = 114.3$).
3. Complete column 3 by subtracting $\overline{X}$ from each value of X. Some values will be minus quantities. Check to see that the column total is 0.
4. Do the same for the Y-values (i.e. subtract $\overline{Y}$ from each value of Y).
5. Multiply numbers in column 3 by numbers in column 4 and enter the results in column 5.
6. Square each number in column 3 and enter it in column 6.
7. Square each number in column 4 and enter it in column 7.
8. Sum numbers in column 5 to give $(X - \overline{X})(Y - \overline{Y})$ or xy $= (-3485.40)$ noting the signs carefully.

---

[1]The *interval* scale is that in which the actual amount of difference, or interval, between one observation and another is known and taken into account. For example, if area A has 12 hectares, area B has 8 hectares, area C, 4 hectares, the interval between A and B is 4, and that between B and C is 4.

9. Add up numbers in column 6 to give $\Sigma (X \times \bar{X})^2$ or $\Sigma x^2 = (217.60)$.
10. Add up numbers in column 7 to give $\Sigma (Y \times \bar{Y})^2$ or $\Sigma y^2 = (74634.10)$.

The figures necessary to calculate the correlation coefficient are now available and these could be substituted in the formula for the Pearson product moment coefficient of correlation given above.

Table 6.9 Population density in Lagos

1	2	3	4	5	6	7
X	Y	$(X - \bar{X})$ x	$(Y - \bar{Y})$ y	xy	x^2	y^2
1.0	312	−5.8	+197.7	−1 146.66	33.64	39 085.29
1.5	215	−5.3	+100.7	− 533.71	28.09	10 140.49
2.5	150	−4.3	+ 35.7	− 153.51	18.49	1 274.49
3.5	120	−3.3	+ 5.7	− 18.81	10.89	32.49
5.5	95	−1.3	− 19.3	+ 25.09	1.69	372.49
7.0	84	+0.2	− 30.3	− 6.06	0.04	918.09
8.0	70	+1.2	− 44.3	− 53.16	1.44	1 962.49
11.0	52	+4.2	− 62.3	− 261.66	17.64	3 881.29
13.0	30	+6.2	− 84.3	− 522.66	38.44	7 106.49
15.0	15	+8.2	− 99.3	− 814.26	67.24	9 860.49
68.0	1 143			−3 485.40	217.60	74 634.10

$$\bar{X} = \frac{68.0}{10} = 6.8 \qquad \bar{Y} = \frac{1\,143}{10} = 114.3$$

Where X = kilometres from city centre, and Y = persons per residential hectare.

$$r = \frac{\Sigma xy}{\sqrt{(\Sigma x^2)\,(\Sigma y^2)}} = \frac{-3\,485.40}{\sqrt{217.60 \times 74\,634.10}}$$

$$= \frac{-3\,485.40}{\sqrt{16\,240\,380.16}} = \frac{-3\,485.40}{4\,029.94} = -0.86$$

Determining the statistical significance of r is a relatively simple matter, since tables of values that r must equal or exceed at given levels of significance are available in the appendices of most statistical texts. The significance of the coefficient, −0.86, with an n of 10 is determined by entering the table where the number 8 $(n-2)$ appears under the column 'degrees of freedom'. Reading across to the right, it can be seen that an r of −0.86 is large enough to be significant at the 0.01 level of significance.

As has been seen, considerably more computation is involved to arrive at a product moment coefficient than with the ranking method. Unless a calculator is available, this can be a very lengthy process.

With regard to all correlation techniques, it must be emphasized that a statistically significant relationship does not necessarily mean that the variables are directly causally related. The tests simply show whether or not there is a correlation which is unlikely to have occurred by chance, and indicate its strength. If the correlation is significant, then the next step is to find out what explanation can be found for this. There may or may not be a causal relationship between the two variables correlated. This needs to be investigated.

The chi-square test

This section is concerned with the use of the chi-square test (chi-square is written symbolically as χ^2). The test is applicable when dealing with data which have been categorized according to particular attributes, for example, land utilization data, or classified on a numerical basis. In essence the test is used to match appropriately categorized or classified values, referred to as the observed data, against a similarly arranged but theoretical set of values, referred to as the expected data. The object is to determine whether differences between the two are the result of chance occurrence, or whether there might be some other explanation of the observed phenomenon. Chi-square is a non-parametric statistic since it is not based upon the properties of the normal curve, nor of the standard deviation, and does not require measurement on an interval scale.

For the remaining part of this section an illustration of the use of the test is presented. Let us suppose that we are concerned with the reactions of the Hausas, Ibos and Yorubas to a newly proposed tax measure in Nigeria. We wish to test the hypothesis that each of the ethnic groups holds the same attitude towards the tax measure. Members of the three groups are asked to indicate whether their reactions are favourable, indifferent, or unfavourable. Incidentally, the variable reaction to the tax measure might be viewed by some as continuous, but so long as we are assigning its values to distinct categories, we may use the chi-square test.

Suppose that data are collected for a sample of 100 Hausas, 200 Ibos and 100 Yorubas, and that the values obtained (not underlined) are given in Table 6.10. The *expected frequency* for any cell has been found by multiplying its corresponding row total by its corresponding column total and dividing the product by the grand total for the sample. The grand total for our sample is 400. Thus, in effect, the expected frequency for cell number (5) in Table 6.10 is $\dfrac{90 \times 200}{400} =$

45. Note that we have computed each frequency by this procedure and each is underlined in Table 6.10. It corresponds to the distribution of attitudes on an equal chance basis.

Table 6.10 A 3×3 contingency table

	Favourable	Indifferent	Unfavourable	Totals
Hausa	80 52.5 [1]	10 22.5 [2]	10 25 [3]	100
Ibo	55 105 [4]	70 45 [5]	75 50 [6]	200
Yoruba	75 52.5 [7]	10 22.5 [8]	15 25 [9]	100
Totals	210	90	100	400

Table 6.11 Computation of chi-square for a 3×3 table

(1) Cell	(2) Observed frequency	(3) Expected frequency	(4) Difference	(5) Square	(6) $\dfrac{(O-E)^2}{E}$
	O	E	$O-E$	$(O-E)^2$	
1	80	52.5	27.5	756.25	14.40
2	10	22.5	−12.5	156.25	6.94
3	10	25	−15	225	9.00
4	55	105	−50	2 500	23.81
5	70	45	25	625	13.89
6	75	50	25	625	12.50
7	75	52.5	22.5	506.25	9.64
8	10	22.5	−12.5	156.25	6.94
9	15	25	−10	100	4.00
					$\Sigma = 101.12 = \chi^2$

The sum of the quotients in column (6) in Table 6.11 is called the *chi-square* statistic. Note that the procedure for computing the chi-square value of 101.12 has been described, but it has not been justified here. The proof that it is a meaningful procedure is beyond the scope of this book. For those who are interested in the proof, see Further Reading at the end of this book. Stated symbolically, we have

$$\chi^2 = \Sigma \frac{(O-E)^2}{E}$$

where O is the observed frequency and E the expected frequency for the same cell.

Before we can use our obtained value of chi-square and the

probability table to test our hypothesis, we must determine the number of *degrees of freedom* involved. We will state a general rule concerning the number of degrees of freedom to be used in similar problems of any degree of complexity. The number of degrees of freedom is equal to the number of cells remaining in the chi-square table after the last row and the last column are eliminated. Symbolically we have:

$$df = (N_1 - 1)(N_2 - 1)$$

where there are N_1 rows and N_2 columns.

We now know that our obtained value of 101.12, is based upon four degrees of freedom $(3 - 1)(3 - 1) = 2 \times 2 = 4$. The cut-off point given in the probability table is 9.49 for the 0.05 level. Since our obtained chi-square value (101.12) is much larger than the appropriate value in the table, we reject the hypothesis that the sample came from a population in which attitude towards taxes was independent of ethnic groups.

Statistical techniques described in foregoing paragraphs have two distinct merits over other methods. First, they sharpen the student's awareness of his environment by presenting to him in concrete, quantitative forms information about its characteristics and variability. Secondly, the art of statistical methods teaches the student the art of orderly classification and arrangement of data with a view to rational interpretation, the drawing of logical inferences and the development of generalizations.

Reporting of findings

This chapter and the previous one have dealt mainly with ways of collecting and using data in geography. Such data provide material from which to prepare geographical reports suitable for publication, or at least for being read by others. Preparing these reports will often go hand-in-hand with the construction and comparison of simple scatter diagrams, line graphs, histograms, distributional maps, photographs, flow diagrams, regression lines and so on. These often demonstrate geographical facts and relationships more clearly than any written account, and range from illustrations the aim of which is simply to present the essential facts of a situation, to those designed to show what spatial relationships exist between different phenomena, and how much relationships vary from place to place.

In reporting findings in geographical studies, students need to learn to organize their ideas. Spewing a disordered jumble of raw facts or data into a report form not only fails to convey information to the reader but usually indicates that the author has not grasped the significance of his materials for interpretation. Meaning cannot be easily derived from chaotic masses of isolated items. Data must be grouped and ordered into logical patterns before they can convey clear messages. Only through some intellectual effort coupled with some literary competence can the student organize facts so that they deliver the precise ideas he has in mind.

In describing procedures employed in geographical studies, the student needs to be trained in giving accurate and detailed description of how the work is done, as well as all the information that the reader needs to judge the validity, adequacy and suitability of the methods and instruments employed. However, the kinds of procedural information presented will depend on the nature of the study.

The presentation and analysis of the data constitute a vital part of any geographical study. Because of the wide variety of studies and kinds of data that exist, no specific directions can be given for organizing this section of the report. The analysis of data may consist of photographs, maps, diagrams, tables, figures and paragraphs of discussion that point out important aspects of the data. Raw data may be recorded in the most convenient form for collecting, but in the body of the report data relevant to each hypothesis must be classified in ways that reveal the pertinent information required to accept or reject the hypothesis. As already shown in this chapter, the data are subjected to specific statistical treatments and the values that are obtained, rather than the data, are reported in the study. When this procedure is followed, the treatment to which the data are subjected is clearly specified.

In the analysis of data, the student points out the important facts that the collected evidence reveals and notes their relationships. He does not repeat all the detailed information that is in the photographs, maps, diagrams, tables and graphs, but rather interprets what the facts mean – their causes and effects and whether they confirm or reject the hypothesis. Extracting the meaning from the data is one of the most difficult phases of an investigation. However, the level of interpretation and judgement of the results achieved will vary with the problem, and according to the particular purpose of each study. In every case, however, interpretation and judgement should be based on sound (statistical or other) grounds. The results achieved and interpretations made should necessarily be compared with the situations in other parts of the world where similar problems have been investigated, and/or with results achieved in previous studies by the class. After drafting an explanation, the student needs to examine the data for exceptions, try to account for them and restate his explanation if necessary. Any uncontrolled factors that may have affected the results, and their possible implications, are discussed. At this stage the abstractions or hypotheses should be returned to and looked at for rejection, modification or acceptance as the case may be, and for making further generalizations where appropriate. Also, additional issues or problems requiring further investigation raised by the study, or ramifications of the original questions not answered by it, should be recognized.

In some cases a final report of the findings would require the citing and tabulating of the relevant references and bibliographies. Therefore students should learn to present this often vital information in the accepted or currently adopted conventional systems. The use of index cards should also be taught and encouraged.

In the summary, the student briefly reviews the procedures, findings and the evolution of the problem. The important points in the study are brought together in the summary, but not all the evidence upon which they are based is repeated. The conclusions are stated precisely and related directly to the hypotheses that are tested. The conclusions announce whether the findings of the study confirm or reject the hypotheses. Careful qualifications are included that stipulate the precise condition or limits to which the conclusions apply. If the conclusions modify an existing theory, this fact is discussed. If the investigation raised any questions that suggest areas of further research, this information is presented tersely.

CHAPTER 7

Studying relationships and building models through the analysis of maps and photographic evidence

FRANCES A. SLATER and BRIAN SPICER

Introduction

This chapter is not concerned with explicating the techniques and specific skills of map-reading, aerial photograph interpretation and the comprehension of diagrams. Sources to guide us in these tasks are numerous and several are listed in the reference section at the end of this book. Rather, we seek to show by example how the information contained on maps, photographs and diagrams can be used by teachers to lead students to an understanding of concepts, to the describing and explaining of spatial patterns and the derivation of generalizations, models and even theories.

A second disclaimer is necessary. The suggested exercises which accompany the commentary, materials and resources are not always tied to specific ages or methods of class organization. We appreciate that teachers work in a variety of educational systems and must often follow guidelines set down in national or locally derived curricula. We leave it to individual teachers to judge if, when and where the suggestions are used. We are confident that you will experiment. experiment.

Harvey (1972) provides a view of the similarities between maps and theories. His view is emphasized here since it provides the operational rationale of the chapter. Maps and theories help us find our way around for they are both selective ways of representing a varied and complex reality. It is all too easy to get lost in too much richness of detail. Harvey postulates four analogous functions for maps and theories. First, both perform the task of storing information; second, both describe very generally the appearance of particular instances of reality; third, both have a capacity to tell us what will happen if we go into an area and so we are able to cope with applied problems such as navigating (using a map) or predicting (using a theory); and fourth, they give us the means for thinking about more complex relationships. We may examine maps in order to search out higher-order patterns or generalizations or use a map or theory as a touchstone for examining the intricate variety of an area.

While the main body of the chapter is concerned with showing how more readily available and traditional maps and photographs of settlement patterns may be used to build conceptual understanding and to analyse general relationships, we preface that discussion with some comments on the significance of maps and photographs derived through the application of recent technical (remote sensing) and conceptual (the application of the concept of perception) advances. Computer mapping is also referred to in a later section dealing with patterns in cities.

A new window on our planet – satellite photography

Remote sensing and satellites: mapping techniques of the future

'Remote sensing' is the term used to describe the techniques of obtaining information about the spatial, chemical or physical properties of a distant object or area without making contact with it. The most common remote-sensing techniques are imaging survey methods such as aerial photography, thermal sensing or side-look radar mapping. These methods allow very rapid cover of large areas to produce maps of 100 per cent reliability and are effective even in poor weather conditions.

The index mosaic (Landsat imagery) of the south-east Mediterranean (Fig. 7.1) gives a clear picture of the areal extent of each scene, the strip-like coverage available and how these are joined to create the mosaic. Note the Nile Delta, the vegetation/desert boundary at the Israeli frontier in the Negev, the geological rift in which the Dead Sea lies and the Suez Canal. The advantages for cartographers in building maps from such data are obvious and it is being shown that many existing maps believed to be extremely accurate need to be modified as the images from the Landsat satellites become available. The efficiency of the map as a storage device is thus being increased.

One of the most exciting developments in the remote-sensing field has been the mounting of sensors in orbiting satellites, since this gives the potential of viewing the whole world at a variety of scales, and most importantly, can give repetitive coverage of any area to allow mapping of dynamic changes such as seasonal variations. Increasingly, these are providing the data for generating predictions to form the basis for future planning and decision-making.

The work started with the meteorological satellites in the 1960s. For example the Nimbus series showed global weather patterns, and now continues with the NOAA[1] series. The Apollo and Gemini manned satellites prior to NASA's[2] moon landings showed the potential of high-definition imagery obtained from orbital altitudes in

GAZA / SINAI / JORDAN

Fig. 7.1 Index mosaic of the south-east Mediterranean area produced from Landsat imagery. (*Source:* Nigel Press)

earth resources work. The main development in this field, however, has been the Landsat (formerly ERTS) series launched by NASA for the United States Geological Survey. Landsat 1 and 2 are in polar orbits, synchronous with the sun at a height of 912 km. The satellites repeat their ground track every 18 days, and produce imagery in strips covering 185 km width on the ground in four spectral bands (green, red, red/infra-red and infra red) by a scanning technique. The signals are transmitted to ground receiving stations as electromagnetic signals which can be recorded as a digital record on magnetic tapes and then converted into photographic images similar to television pictures. The digital form of the record is very important since this gives the powerful capability of digital image processing to produce enhanced images and by using spectral discrimination techniques to obtain thematic maps which concentrate on one element of the earth's surface, e.g. vegetation. Knowledge of the luxuriance or otherwise of, for example, prairie grass can give a grazier advance information on which to base his grazing plans.

[1]NOAA = National Oceanic and Atmospheric Administration.
[2]NASA = National Aeronautics and Space Administration.

In the photographs (Fig. 7.2 (a)–(d)) the darker areas show the extent of seasonal flooding from the Logone River draining Lake Chad. Three different seasons are illustrated and provide essential information for the planning of new transport and communication links in the area.

The present Landsats are restricted by ambient weather conditions, the limited spectral response of the sensors and the lack of ground receiving stations. Additionally, the stereo effect commonly found with aerial photography is not readily obtainable, but this is not a great disadvantage except in the fields of geology and geomorphology. In the future we can expect to see all-weather sensors such as radars in operation, and other parts of the spectrum will also be used to produce more information about surface conditions and areas; undoubtedly a global network of receiving stations and relay satellites will be established and utilized by decision-makers in resource exploitation, weather forecasting and land-use management, for example.

The small scale of available satellite imagery is at present a disadvantage for some survey purposes, but an example of future capabilities has been given by the S190B high-resolution mapping camera carried on board the Skylab manned space laboratory. This camera has produced excellent quality photographic images of much of the earth's surface and demonstrated that photogrammetric quality imagery with stereo coverage at scales of at least 1:50 000 and probably larger will be readily obtainable in the future and could become the mainstay of all future survey mapping.

Figure 7.3 shows an area of western Brazil photographed by the S190B camera. Note the road networks, small settlements, agricultural field patterns and smoke from bush fires (probably jungle clearances). Such photographs can also provide farmers with information about the availability of pasture, and information on the health of vegetation in particular regions. In the United States and Canada this technique has already been widely employed to modify the perception of pastoralists and farmers so that the wisest possible land-management decisions are made.

Man's perception of his planet – spatial imagery

Increasingly, geographers along with other social scientists have come to recognize that the objective application of economic principles may not be a sufficient basis for explaining much of the decision-making that precedes man's use of the space in which he exists. There has been a realization that man's decision-making may be less closely linked to objective realities than to his perception of the world.

Much of the research work which has taken place to date has been

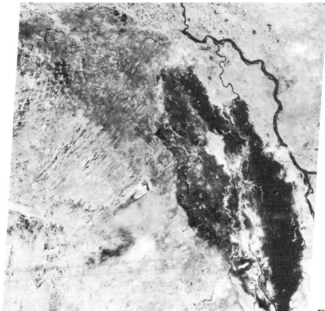

Fig. 7.2(a)

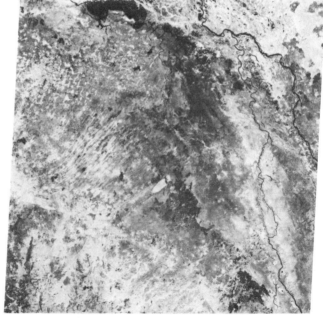

Fig. 7.2(b)

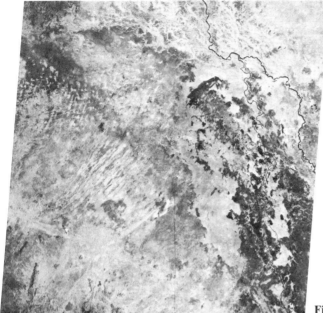

Fig. 7.2(c)

Fig. 7.2(d)

Figs 7.2(a), (b), (c) (d) Seasonal flooding south-east of Lake Chad, Nigeria. (*Source:* Nigel Press)

Fig. 7.3 Skylab S190B scene of the Campo Grande area, western Brazil

concerned with two main aspects – (a) perception of the city, and (b) regional imagery.

(a) Perception of the city

How do people perceive cities?

How do people see cities? How do they relate different parts of the city to each other? How do they function in relation to the city? How do people perceive themselves in relation to the urban environment? What do they see as their role in creating and maintaining the city in which they live?

The seminal work of Lynch (1960) on the image of the city was the first systematic investigation in this area.

Lynch's aim was to gain a working understanding of the visual quality and what he termed the 'legibility' of the American city. The images he studied took the form of graphic maps reproduced by subjects from memory. The information yielded by these maps was later supplemented by data gained through personal interview with the subjects.

Lynch's procedure was to compare the information obtained through map and interview with the objective physical reality of the three cities being studied. This method of analysis necessarily involved subjective judgements but, nevertheless, it enabled Lynch to define and describe five major elements which were judged to give both structure and meaning to the images of the residents of these three cities. These elements Lynch named and defined as follows:

1. Paths
These are the pathways or channels along which the individual habitually or potentially moves. They may be streets, freeways, railway lines, rivers, footpaths. For many people such paths are the predominant element in their image and hence provide a structure for the organization of, and orientation to, the image.

2. Edges
Edges are the boundaries between areas, between the known and the unknown, between the familiar and the unfamiliar. They may be shores, walls, a major road access or even an edge of development. For the individual the importance of edges is that they enable physical delimitation of areas, e.g. of the central business district or the wider metropolis.

3. Districts
A district is an area which for a particular individual has a common identifying and relevant characteristic. For example, an individual may regard and describe a particular area as 'an industrial district – ugly and polluted'. In fact, the district may have both residential and commercial components of significance, but the individual's perception is dominated by what he perceived to be the undesirable hallmarks of industrialization.

4. Nodes
These are points of intensity in, and of focus to, the image. While they may be junction points such as a major road, or railway junction, they may also be points of concentration such as a supermarket or an airport.

5. Landmarks
As the term suggests, landmarks are physical reference points which

exist in the physical environment. If a particular building or feature is to serve as a landmark to the individual it must be able to be readily singled out by the individual and it must have functional significance for him or her. For example, a tavern alongside a busy road may not only have great 'legibility' (i.e. great impact) but it may also serve as a guide-point to the motorist traversing the suburban network. Figure 7.4 shows examples of each of these five elements derived from Lynch's work in Boston.

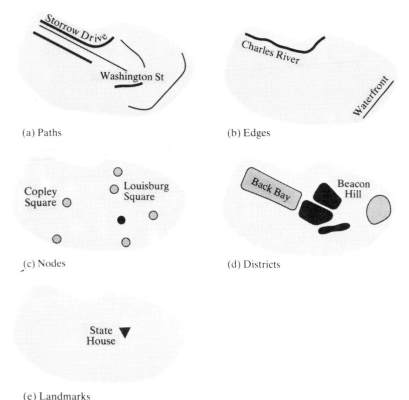

(a) Paths

(b) Edges

(c) Nodes

(d) Districts

(e) Landmarks

Fig. 7.4 Mental maps of Boston: the five main elements in the image of Boston as seen by interviewees. (*Source:* Lynch 1960)

Since Lynch's pioneering work, however, other researchers have used his procedures in a variety of ways in studies which have sought further understanding of man's perception of, and relationship to, his environment. More recently, Lynch (1977) co-ordinated an international team to look at the way small groups of young adolescents use and value their spatial environment. Their techniques including cognitive mapping (see Chapter 2) and time budgets are educationally valuable and compatible with a humanistic trend in geographical education encouraging children to explore their own real or imagined datascapes. Indeed, the international range of research in this area is considerable and teachers all over the world may find it useful to construct a unit of work around the themes of images of cities and regional images. Hence the work of several researchers in addition to Lynch is reviewed. The purpose of the review is to erect signposts for teachers interested in following through the work. Students should be guided to an understanding that modes of spatial organization are not necessarily specific to a particular culture.

De Jonge (1962) followed Lynch's work in the United States with a study of residents of Amsterdam, Rotterdam and The Hague with special emphasis on their image (as represented by 'a rough map of the area such as you imagine it for yourself').

De Jonge's map data were also reinforced by interviews which were directed towards finding out what was most relevant to the subjects (e.g. 'What are, in your opinion, the most striking elements and buildings in this area?'. 'Are there any places here or elsewhere where you find orientation very difficult?'). Again, these questions could be put to students (aged 14–17 years) and the data processed over six or seven geography periods. Drawing up a model featuring the most frequently occurring buildings and most striking elements should conclude the exercise and the class encouraged to make general statements applicable to their town or city.

Gulick (1963) also used Lynch's technique to study the city images of residents of Tripoli (Lebanon). The maps produced (Fig. 7.5) were similar in style to those drawn by Lynch's respondents and suggested that the urban image is a product *both* of visual and of socio-economic associations.

In a later study, Appleyard (1970) in a study of Ciudad Guyana, a new city in eastern Venezuela, examined inhabitants' maps of their local areas and of the whole city to explore further the several ways in which people structure cities, and to see whether different groups in the population would structure the same city in different ways. His subjective sorting of maps led him to the view that the maps predominantly used sequential elements (roads) or spatial elements (buildings, landmarks, districts) as a structural device, although the most accomplished maps used both elements. Figure 7.6 shows examples of these elements as they appeared in particular types of maps.

At approximately the same time as Appleyard was working at Berkeley, Ladd was engaged in similar work at Harvard using neighbourhood maps as a basis for developing an understanding of areas subjectively defined as neighbourhood by urban adolescent Negroes.

The 60 boys in Ladd's study were from low socio-economic status

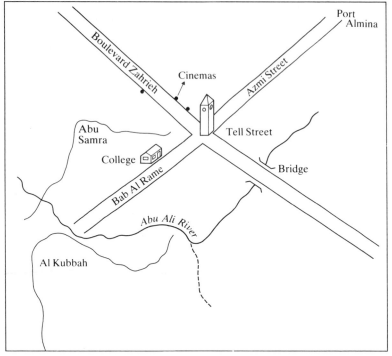

Fig. 7.5 Image of Tripoli. The Tell as hub with a rare instance of specifying a school building. (*Source:* Gulick 1963)

backgrounds, attended the same post-primary school and ranged in age from 12 to 17 years. These boys were asked to give a verbal description and also to draw a map of their neighbourhood.

As well as recording the presence of particular elements (e.g. number of streets and the actual size of the area shown on the maps) Ladd attempted to classify the maps into a number of types on the basis of the subjective sorting of the maps. This also involved the development of a number of descriptive categories (e.g. drawing is pictorial) which took into account both form and content elements as criteria in assessing the drawings.

Figures 7.7(a), (b), (c) and (d) show examples of the types of maps produced by the boys in Ladd's study.

(b) Regional imagery

Group I (*n* = 9) Drawing is pictorial. The subject represents houses, other buildings and elements which might be part of a street scene. (Example given in Fig. 7.7 (a).)

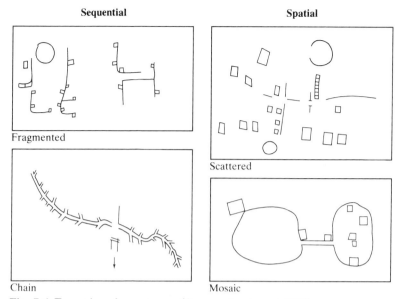

Fig. 7.6 Examples of map types. (*Source:* Appleyard 1970)

Group II ($n = 13$) Drawing is schematic. It contains lines or areas which are not clearly connected to each other. It is poorly organized. (Example given in Fig. 7.7 (b).)

Group III ($n = 12$) Drawing resembles a map. It seems well organized, that is, the connections between areas are clear. It could be used for orientation to the area. (Example given in Fig. 7.7 (c).)

Group IV ($n = 9$) Drawing resembles a map with other identifiable landmarks which would make the area recognizable. Connections between areas are clear. Could be used for orientation to the area. (Example given in Fig. 7.7 (d).)

Gould and White are two geographers who have attempted to establish the mental maps held for wider spatial areas than the city (see Fig. 7.8). In their survey, cross-sections of young people (aged 16 to 18 years) from schools in Britain were used to determine the perceived views of the country. The students were asked to rank the counties of England, Wales and Scotland in terms of their locational preferences – from the county where they would most like to live and work to the one where they would least like to live and work.

The results were analysed and maps showing the perceived surface of desirability produced for each school. Although the maps for each school differed, there were several distinctive common elements. First, each map showed a high rating for areas immediately adjacent

(a)

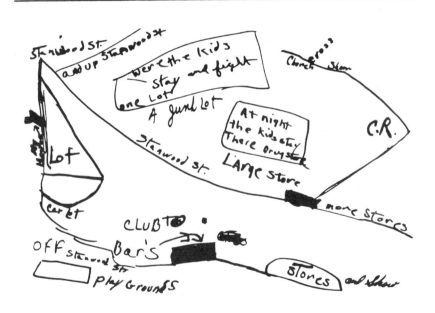

(b)

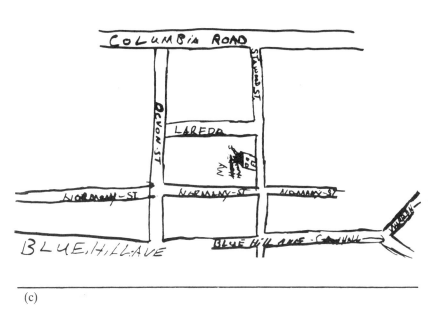

(c)

(d)

Figs 7.7(a), (b), (c), (d) Examples of maps of Groups I–IV. (*Source:* Ladd 1970)

to the school; secondly, the southern counties were perceived as being generally more desirable than Scotland and the North. However, this perception was at its strongest in southern schools; thirdly, the attitude to London showed a marked dichotomy with students divided between those strongly attracted and those repelled. This kind of regional research has also been undertaken in other countries including Nigeria and the USA. The two maps (Figs 7.9 and 7.10) show the impact of maturity on the perception of young people in Nigeria.

The results achieved to date raise many questions. How persistent are these mental images in space and time? Do they correctly evaluate the spatial area within which our locational decisions – such as the decision to migrate, the decision as to where to live and work, etc. – are made? Is it possible to extend the method to include the spatial concepts of governments, industry and other groups?

Student activities

The study of mental or cognitive maps of spatial imagery is an activity which has only recently begun to find its way into the geography of the classroom. Yet, it is not unthinkable that secondary students should be able to tackle the Lynchian type of study (see Lynch 1960, Appendix B) and derive the major elements from their own observations.

Teachers could ask students

1. To make a list of the first ten things they think of when their town is named.
2. To draw, from memory, a map showing their neighbourhood (or city) for the benefit of a person who has not visited it previously. Groups of students may then be asked to examine the maps so produced and to define –
   (a) common edges and nodes;
   (b) common landmarks;
   (c) common pathways;
   (d) common districts;
   and to measure the size of the neighbourhood shown. Comparisons could then be made between the size of neighbourhood portrayed by different groups of students, e.g. Is there any difference in the size of neighbourhood portrayed by boys and the neighbourhood by girls? Can your students suggest why such differences might occur? In many cultures such differences occur because boys are given far more freedom to travel and roam around their local district than are girls. Adults, of course, tend to

Fig. 7.8 Regional images. Contrasts in the images of Britain held by senior pupils at four schools in different locations; the most desirable areas of the country are in a darker shade. (*Source:* Gould and White 1974)

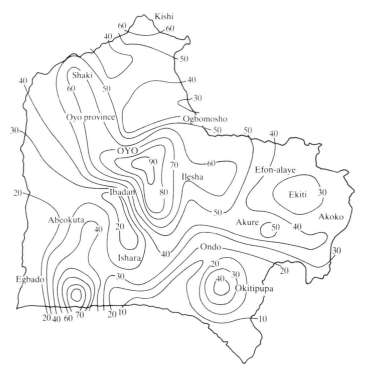

Fig. 7.9 Oyo: mental map of 13-year-olds. The isolines show places of equal preference – the higher the value the more preferred the place or area. (*Source:* Gould and White 1974)

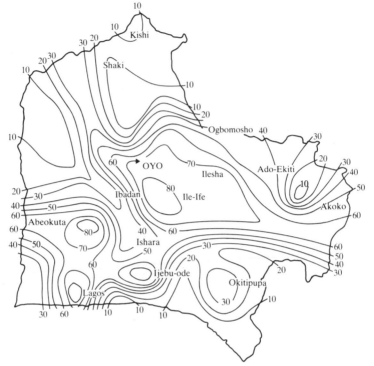

Fig. 7.10 Oyo: mental map of 23-year-olds. (*Source:* Gould and White 1974)

be aware of a much greater area than do young children and adolescents. People living in rural areas may draw maps of larger areas than do people living in urban areas.

3. Similar studies of the mental maps of adults could be made with each student asking one adult to prepare such a map. Subsequent discussion can be held on a number of aspects, e.g.

   (a) the general significance of the map produced;
   (b) the significance of such maps to planners and government;
   (c) the possible impact of an urban development project which would involve the elimination of some of the key elements of the common image, and the possible creation of new edges, nodes, paths, districts and landmarks.

4. An interesting class lesson, or series of lessons, would be to attempt to sort and classify the town, neighbourhood or regional maps of students from one school or from a number of schools. The maps could be compared with each other and with those contained in this chapter and elsewhere in this book (Ch. 2), and the differences described and discussed. The outcome could well be to accelerate one facet of mental development through

exposing the students to the various types of maps and at the very least to make students aware of their varying perception and methods of representation.

5. Students could be asked to consider, for example, the impact of the building of a motorway through their neighbourhood or city on their perception and action space, *or* to study a set of spatial images produced by people resident in their neighbourhood or city and suggest a site for a new motorway. It is important to contrast economic solutions with perhaps more costly schemes which have a less devastating personal impact.

From mental maps to cartographic reality – settlement patterns and functions in man's environment

A topographical map (sheet 100 of the UK Ordnance Survey, 1/50 000) showing part of the Vale of Pickering in Yorkshire, England, displays a multiplicity of features – roads, rivers, gentle slopes and steeper ones, churches, old earthworks and long barrows (prehistoric burial mounds), small villages, woods and isolated farmhouses. The objective is to select one or two features and to examine them for patterns and relationships. Let us take settlement and communication and attempt to reach general understandings based on relationships between these two categories.

The largest town on the map – by area – is Malton and Norton located broadly between the four grid references: 775 721; 790 727; 800 710; 790 710. With a class it is probably helpful to construct a grid – on the blackboard or on an overhead transparency – and shade in Malton and Norton. If the size of the map is reduced to a quarter so that one square on the grid equals four of the map squares a conveniently sized working map is produced (Fig. 7.11). It is the *size* of the light-grey blockings which indicate Malton and Norton's importance. It has the most buildings. In addition, Malton and Norton also has a greater number of lines of communication running through it than any other settlement. A relationship between the size of a settlement and its accessibility is established. Is there a recurring pattern in this relationship?

Let us then look at villages which cover approximately one-eighth to one-quarter of a grid square – the next biggest settlements on the map. Decisions on which villages fit into such a category are best made using tracing paper on which a grid square has been drawn and divided into eighths. Villages within this size category in our judgement are – Rillington, 854 742; Barton-le-street 722 742; Amotherby, 750 735; Swinton, 758 735; Scagglethorpe, 835 725; Welburn, 720 680; Low Hutton, 762 676; Settrington, 839 702; and Westow, 754 653 – nine villages in all. These can be marked on the

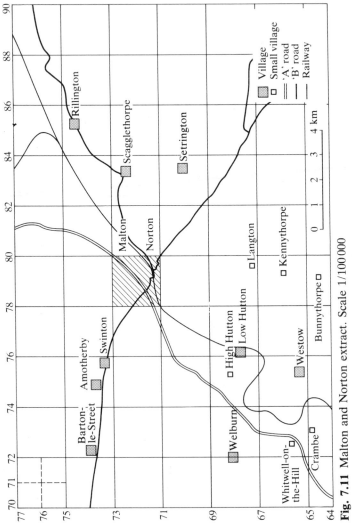

Fig. 7.11 Malton and Norton extract. Scale 1/100 000

working map or overhead transparency by a block of 0.5 cm square. What connections do these villages have with Malton and Norton? What kinds of roads join these villages and the largest settlement? Five of the villages are on 'A' or 'B' roads meeting in Malton and Norton. Low Hutton was once connected by rail (the station has been closed but we can assume that it had some influence on the growth of Low Hutton). Today two narrow metalled roads join it to the A64. The other three villages are located on either wider or narrower metalled roads, Settrington and Westow being at the junction of three roads. Two-thirds of the villages are on routes leading directly to Malton and Norton and the settlements are, on average, about 3 km from their nearest neighbour.

Two sizes of settlement and their connections have been examined. If the investigation now narrows, for the sake of expediency, to the south-west quarter of the map even smaller villages are found. Six small villages less than one-eighth of a grid square in area, and generally closer to one-sixteenth in area, can be identified: Whitwell-on-the-Hill, 723 658; Crambe, 733 649; High Hutton, 754 685; Langton, 797 672; Kennythorpe, 789 660; and Burythorpe, 792 649.

If six small villages can be identified in one-quarter of the map one could estimate that over the whole map there are 24 (6×4) smaller villages, though in reality this is a slight overestimate. These smaller villages without exception are served by the narrow metalled roads, and distances between the smaller villages average about 2 km.

The smallest settlements, the farms and hamlets, occur widely and exceed eighty in number. The farmhouses are normally connected by tracks to the metalled roads. Several general questions and statements may now be suggested, summarized thus:
1. What relationship seems to exist between the size of settlements and their number? *The larger the settlement, the fewer they are.*
2. What relationship exists between the size of settlements and the distance between them and their neighbours? *The larger they are, the further apart they are.*
3. What relationship exists between the size of settlements and the number and types of communication running through them? *The larger they are, the greater the number of links and types of connection with other places.*
4. What pattern is there to the kind and number of links between settlements of the same size and of different sizes? *The smaller settlements are usually linked to one another by narrow roads which in turn join wider roads leading to larger settlements. Settlements are linked to one another and then to the next largest size of settlements* (Doggett 1975).

Analysis of settlement and communication patterns establishes several of the principles of central place theory – without necessarily using the term or introducing the associated geometry.

This exercise originally used with a class of 12–13-year-old English children and carried through to the stage where they articulated the general statements, suggests that indeed anything can be taught to any child at any stage of development in some intellectually honest form, and it is a positive example of the high levels of thinking which may be achieved when Bruner's more open philosophy of courteous translation replaces the more rigid interpretation of mental development derived from Piaget (Bruner 1960). The results of selecting two features on the map and examining relationships engaged the students in a process of building towards a 'theory' or recurring patterns of relationships. That exceptions will always exist is expected. Towns and roads are built as the result of human decisions and these are not subject to deterministic laws. The many clues of long historical habitation of the area on the Malton and Norton sheet must tempt the geography teacher to call in his historical colleague and indulge in some team teaching as a way of reflecting upon complicated relationships which are linked to the generalizations established.

Another line of investigation is to test the general statements in other areas of the world. Consider one instance. Figure 7.12 shows the distribution pattern of settlement in central Iowa, USA, where three sizes are specified together with two grades of highway.

A count of the number of settlements in each category, converted to a percentage and plotted on Fig. 7.13, shows that the relationship between size and number of settlements has a similar hierarchical pattern to the Malton and Norton map. And from the road network it is clear that larger settlements are more often at a convergence of routes than smaller places.

Emphasis has thus far been placed on the analysis of settlement and communication patterns. A number of numerical techniques to measure the relative accessibility of places within a road network have become common in geography, and the application of one of these can reinforce further the general idea of the importance of Malton and Norton as a central place, the central place in the hierarchy. Malton and Norton has so far been considered on the basis of the number of lines of communication leading into it, the apparently most accessible town. Through the use of a concept borrowed from graph theory, the relative accessibility of a town (node) can be expressed as a number to be compared with other numbers. The network of 'A' and 'B' roads and the rail links can be simplified as in Fig. 7.14. The relative accessibility of settlements can now be calculated. The distance between pairs of settlements is expressed as the number of links along the shortest path connecting them. Thus the distance between Barton-le-street and Malton and Norton is three links. A link is defined as the connection between two settlements. The information is best set out in a connectivity matrix,

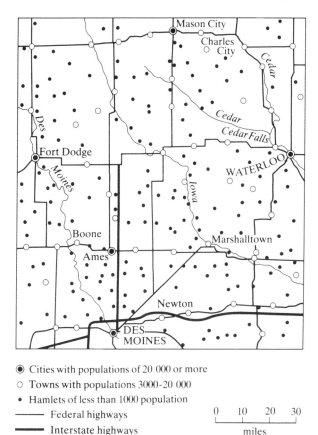

● Cities with populations of 20 000 or more
○ Towns with populations 3000-20 000
• Hamlets of less than 1000 population
——— Federal highways
▬▬▬ Interstate highways

0   10   20   30
miles

Fig. 7.12 Settlement and communications in central Iowa, USA

i.e. a table which tells us whether the places are or are not connected in some way. The row sum (see Table 7.1) for each node provides a measure of its relative accessibility. Malton and Norton with a total of ten is in fact the most accessible place. Barton-le-street the least.

Figure 7.14 is a version of selected features (particular communication lines and settlements) of the map extract. It is a kind of 'transformation' of the reality which the conventional map symbolizes. Figure 7.14 is known as a topological map. What similarities and differences exist between it and the map?

Similarities which apply to the example given here include the maintenance of the same number of nodes, or settlements, the equivalent linking of the nodes and the preservation of their order or relation to one another and the same number of linkages (edges). The most obvious difference involves scale. The distance between settlements *is not* in a ratio to that on the ground distance, and

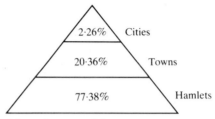

Fig. 7.13 Settlement hierarchy pyramid

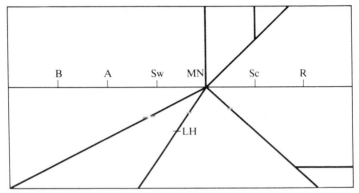

Fig. 7.14 Topological map of the Malton and Norton area

Table 7.1 Accessibility matrix of the Malton and Norton area

From	To	B	A	Sw	MN	Sc	R	LH	Row sum
B		0	1	2	3	4	5	4	19
A		1	0	1	2	3	4	3	14
Sw		2	1	0	1	2	3	2	11
MN		3	2	1	0	1	2	1	10
Sc		4	3	2	1	0	1	2	13
R		5	4	3	2	1	0	3	18
LH		4	3	2	1	2	3	0	15

direction is not preserved either. The topological transformation which maps countries of the world according to population totals rather than area has long been used in geography. This brief example and discussion provides no more than a cursory introduction to more recent extensions of the idea – extensions which are often related to ways of measuring not only the accessibility of places within networks but also the directness, density and connectivity of networks (Kansky 1963; Dalton, R. *et al* 1973).

In addition, topological maps are being used to show the changing relationships between places if time or cost of travel is used as a measure of distance rather than mileage distance. Figure 7.15 is a further illustration of a topological map and may be used in class in the following way: A tourist from Irkutsk arrives in Moscow and stays with friends near the Taganskaya Station. He wishes to visit a number of places via the Metro and asks his hosts for advice.

(a) 'Where can I obtain a good view of Moscow?'
'Travel to the Leninskie Gory Station. You could also visit the university as well.'

(b) 'I wish to see the Exhibition of Economic Achievement in the USSR.'
'Take the Kaluzhsko-Rizhskaya to Prospekt Mira.'

(c) 'Besides the GUM store in Red Square, where else could I do some shopping after visiting Lenin's Mausoleum?'
'To view the Mausoleum take the Metro to Dzerzhinskaya and for shopping get out at Kalininskaya.'

(d) 'We are having dinner this evening with our friends, the Ivanovs. Where shall I meet you?'

Fig. 7.15 The V.I. Lenin Moscow Metro. (*Source:* Intourist 1976)

'I shall be waiting at 19.00 hours at the entrance to the Dinamo Station.'

Have your class plan a route for the tourist. It is interesting to note that since a standard charge is made for any journey, long or short, on the Moscow Underground, the cost distance between any one station and all others is the same, though the time distance inevitably varies.

With care it should be possible to construct topological maps of the route networks of any country and develop exercises on accessibility, connectivity or directness. Interesting questions such as – 'Is the capital of a nation always the most centrally placed settlement within the network?' – may be attempted. If the capital is not always centrally placed where would links need to be built in order to achieve this (if it was desired)? Are some places more central with regard to the rail network than to the road or airline networks? Where do rivers and canals need to be included in such network analysis? Sea routes, electricity transmission lines and pipelines also contribute to the pattern of networks round the globe and can be analysed in the same way as in the example of Malton and Norton.

Settlement functions

The Vale of Pickering map extract shows that settlements of varying sizes and importance are a characteristic pattern of our environment. There are many reasons why settlements develop, grow and sometimes disappear from a particular location.

In this section it is intended to show how photographs as well as sketch maps may be used as resources to facilitate hypothesis formulation and to develop concepts of location, site, function, basic and non-basic activities, renewable and non-renewable resources and to establish the general idea that settlements develop in response to resource use. It is important to realize that relative location (i.e. where an object or activity is located in relation to the locations of other objects or activities) is judged to be a resource, albeit a somewhat more abstract one than coal or gold, and as such relative location explains the siting of many settlements. Note that a centrally placed location implies situations relatively close to other objects or activities; marginal locations are those far from such objects or activities, inaccessible to them or at the margins.

A good way to begin a study of cities is to consider their locations. Have the students consider the location of their own settlement and the following questions. Is it the middle of a mountain system? In a desert? Is there a river nearby? The chances are that the answer to the first two questions is 'no', but to the third, 'yes'. Settlements do grow in mountains and deserts, but most often they have been sited on plains, in valleys, along rivers or beside oceans.

Early settlers to a country usually occupied land where they had a chance of making a living. They were attracted to sites having resources that could be used as food, fuel and building material, and sites having forests or coal or water that could supply fuel and be harnessed for power were favoured.

Settlers had to be able to obtain food easily so they were attracted to sites near fertile soil or they settled near places where food could be brought in with little difficulty either overland or by water. The possibility of developing easy transport connections with other areas was important.

Sometimes people modified a site by draining swamps, filling in tidal lands, dredging rivers, levelling hills and building flood walls. By building canals, highways and railroads, improved connections with other places were developed. After a discussion on the location of settlements to bring out some of the points above, have the class examine the sketch maps in Fig. 7.16 and answer the question, 'Where is settlement most likely to develop in the year indicated?'

With reference to the sketch labelled 1800, in Fig. 7.16, a student might suggest A as a readily defensible site or a route centre; B might be considered too exposed and too close to poorly drained land; and although C is isolated it might be suggested that one of the inlets could provide a good harbour, but a counter suggestion could be that there would be little room for future expansion (if, indeed, first settlers orient their thinking to the future); and D, in 1800, might be considered inaccessible. These other hypotheses would represent feasible reasons for choosing among A, B, C and D as a place for settlement. The obvious necessity for further information, if a firm conclusion is to be reached, might lead the class to study the history of their own settlement or a number of settlements in their country or over the world. Any additional information which a teacher invents about the sites will eventually tip the balance in favour of one, and such a strategy could be built into the lesson.

In the second sketch, labelled 1830, at first glance site A appears to offer a harbour in a period when ships were the major means of long-distance transport and communication in the New World, but again adjacent swamp land might be perceived as a negative factor. Site B in the second sketch in Fig. 7.16 is relatively close to the forests, presumably exploitable, but it is isolated from coastal shipping. Not only location but relative location is realized to be significant and, in the Brunerian sense, the concept of location is given added depth and meaning. Site B, for instance, would require road links with the coast and might therefore develop only at a later stage. Site C may offer a sheltered harbour while D is in an exposed location and one which is furthest from the forests if these are to provide an economic base for settlement. Students might, however, suggest D as a readily defensible site.

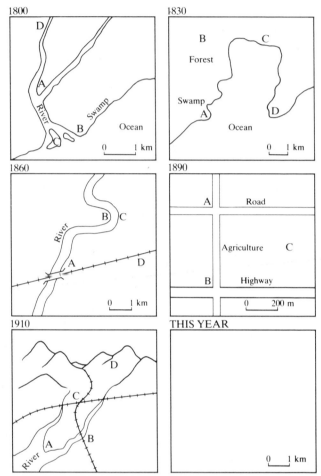

Fig. 7.16 Settlement sites. Select the letter representing the site at which a settlement is more likely to develop in the year indicated. (*Source:* Getis and Getis 1966)

In using the same question, listing the hypotheses put forward for all sites in all sketches and considering them altogether, the class is being guided towards formulating generalizations about the variables influencing the decision to settle in one place rather than another. If the class then goes on within the context of Fig. 7.16 to link the level of transport technology with other variables, it may be considered that a principle between two or more variables has been established. The list of hypotheses derived from this exercise could be compared with the variables known to be decisive in influencing the choice of site in real towns and cities. A final list to be produced by the students of the most frequently occurring reasons in the decision to select a site would evaluate their understanding of the objective of the lessons and the effectiveness of this strategy for introducing settlements.

Some of the reasons suggested for the location of settlements provide clues about how people in the settlements earn their living in order to provide for some of their basic needs such as food, clothing, shelter and recreation. A class might be directed to look at the photographs in Figs 7.17 and 7.18–7.25 and apply the following questions to each one. 'What is most likely to provide the livelihood or main occupations of the people living there?' Essentially we are asking what is the function of a settlement? What makes it tick? What keeps it 'alive'?

Fig. 7.17 Settlement A: 'What is most likely to provide the livelihood of the people living here?'

The photograph, Fig. 7.17, is basically a clearing in a man-made forest. It would be reasonable to hypothesize that many people in the settlement earn their living by felling, milling and processing timber. Will everyone be directly involved in this occupation though? What other jobs may people have? Let us digress momentarily. Although we cannot be sure from the photograph, there are likely to be grocery stores, clothing shops, banks, hardware stores, a school and a doctor. These shops and people are needed to serve the community in general. It may be possible to ask students to examine the way someone in the family may function as the cooker of meals, maker of beds and cleaner of the house. This person or these persons do not increase the total earnings of the family by performing these services just as the settlement as a whole does not increase its total income by selling goods and services to one another. Similarly the settlement derives its income by exporting the timber products from its mills. And just as the people in a family who work for wages or some other payment support the non-working members (usually the younger children or grandparents) so it is the timber-felling, milling and processing which supports the whole settlement and enables each family to buy groceries or motor cars. Activities supporting a settlement are called *basic activities*. They are basic to the life of the settlement just as the money which certain members of a family bring home is basic to the life of that family. The activities which simply serve the settlement within itself are called *non-basic*. The diagram (Fig. 7.18), summarizes the point and could in fact be used with discussion to introduce the two important concepts of basic and non-basic activities.

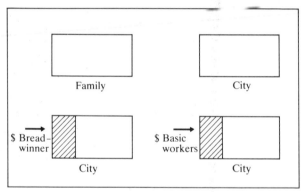

Fig. 7.18 Basic, non-basic activities

Every settlement is likely to have basic and non-basic activities. Figure 7.19 is dominated by an important man-made feature. Make suggestions about the kind of need that has promoted the development of a settlement there. Are there then other possible activities which may now be developed in the area as a result of one change? The photograph (Fig. 7.20) is of another small settlement. Again, what is likely to be the main occupation of the people? Figure 7.20 is perhaps the most obvious example where several plausible hypotheses obtain – the chairlift, mountains and rivers suggest a tourist spot, the wooded slopes, timber-milling, and the expanse of water might support a fishing industry. What further evidence is needed to test and come to some conclusions about these suggestions? The partial evidence afforded by the photograph highlights a significant constraint which must be recognized in the use of both maps and

Fig. 7.19 Settlement B: 'What is most likely to provide the livelihood of the people living here?'

photographs. Statistical and other documentary evidence is essential. As a resource for starting a lesson, as a focus for study, photographs have great value, but perhaps raise more questions than they answer.

Like the settlement in Fig. 7.20, the settlement in Fig. 7.21 has probably more than one basic activity, but its main function could be the transport of goods and people from this area to another. In what way does this function differ from that of the hypothesized main functions of the settlements in the other photographs? Are people

Fig. 7.20 Settlement C: 'What is most likely to provide the livelihood of the people living here?'

Fig. 7.21 Settlement D: 'What is most likely to provide the livelihood of the people living here?'

here to cut timber or dig coal? Perhaps the most important resource of this settlement is its location at the head of a sheltered sound between two islands?

Figure 7.22 is a town surrounded by farmland and in the distance farmhouses dot the countryside. What might be the main occupations of the people here? What do farms and farmers need? The basic function may be guessed to be that of providing services to the people working the land to produce not timber but food. They need their

Fig. 7.22 Settlement E: 'What is most likely to provide the livelihood of the people living here?'

machinery repaired, perhaps their animals slaughtered or sold at a central collecting point or their milk made into butter. So the basic activity is serving the farmers and a non-basic activity is the time the motor mechanic spends repairing the grocer's car or the seed merchant's car, but not the farmer's truck or lorry.

What is strange about the last photograph in Fig. 7.23? What seems to be missing? Why might settlements grow and die? This photograph shows a reconstruction of the kind of buildings and services – a stationer and newsagent, mining office, a general store, a colonial cottage and a stable – which were once part of a flourishing town. Just over 100 years ago, hundreds of people were mining for gold here. The gold ran out. The town died. It became a ghost town. Could this happen to any of the other settlements discussed? Will we always need power generated from water? Will we always need timber and its products? What could happen to the farming land or to the port? Should settlements which are dying be revitalized by government intervention, or should the people be assisted to move elsewhere?

This set of photographs – similar sets could be collected for any country – in exemplifying a range of settlement situations is intended to help develop the notion that settlements grow in response to the exploitation of a resource – soil, timber or pleasant scenery which has the effect of bringing in money from outside the settlement. An associated idea is that of renewable and non-renewable resources and

Fig. 7.23 Settlement F: 'What is most likely to provide the livelihood of the people living here?'

settlements could be classified according to these criteria. Do all postulated activities fall completely into one category or the other? How might the values of different societies at different stages of development or societies having different priorities affect the use of resources? What other resources, renewable and non-renewable, give rise to settlements? There is not, for example, an iron mining town shown in any of Figs 7.17 and 7.19–7.23. These rather more advanced and other questions may be asked of a class depending on their background in settlement geography and cultural geography.

The photographs generally suggest one main function. But is this characteristic of all towns? If we recall the notion of a hierarchy of settlements, then we realize that some larger towns will perform many functions. Students could be asked to list some of the important functions of settlements and to consider what kinds of single-function and multi-function settlements exist in their country.

Judgements from limited evidence

While a study of the photographs has been used to introduce the relationship between resource utilization and settlement function, it becomes apparent at the same time that a tier of occupational groupings exists. The tier or hierarchy is based on the fact that there are those people who are working in closest contact with the resource – the farmer, the timberjack, the construction engineer and those people in occupations serving workers in basic occupations – for example, the garage mechanic, the banker and the grocer. Man makes a special utilization of resources and man in society specializes in different activities to serve those resources directly and indirectly. It is therefore difficult to make a sweeping judgement about who is most important in society, yet we make all kinds of sweeping statements or judgements in our everyday lives, and the next photograph and map exercise (Figs 7.24–7.27) is designed to test a judgement which many people hold.

Analysing patterns in the city

This exercise was developed by the High School Geography Project of the Association of American Geographers. Maps, aerial photographs and census material provide the essential data. It emphasizes the hazards of drawing conclusions from limited evidence and it is designed to shatter or disturb students' stereotypes or inaccurate generalizations.

Students are asked to hypothesize about the socio-economic characteristics – the level of income, education, value of homes and

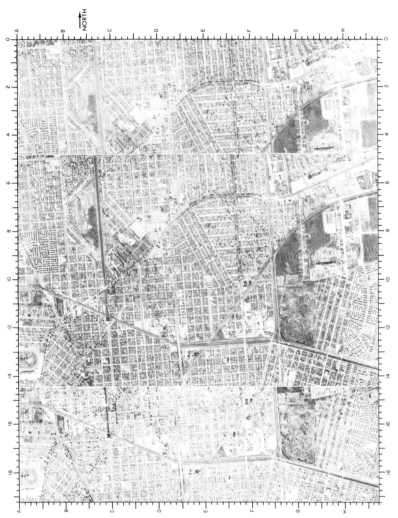

Fig. 7.24 New Orleans: neighbourhoods 1 and 2. (*Source:* HSGP 1970)

ethnic composition – of three adjacent neighbourhoods in New Orleans. A set of slides and topographical maps of each of the neighbourhoods accompanied the original version, but these are not reproduced here. Obviously they provide students with further clues for their analysis of the neighbourhoods. The topographical map is replaced by a sketch map (Fig. 7.27) to give an outline impression.

Using stereograms (Figs 7.24 and 7.25), neighbourhood 1 is examined to determine the following:

(a) size of buildings;

(b) size of housing lots or sections;
(c) age of buildings;
(d) amount of open space;
(e) types of buildings;
(f) street patterns.

Neighbourhood 2 (Fig. 7.25) and neighbourhood 3 (Figs 7.25 and 7.26) are analysed according to the same criteria. Other criteria which could be applied equally validly to these or similar photos include:

(a) density of buildings;

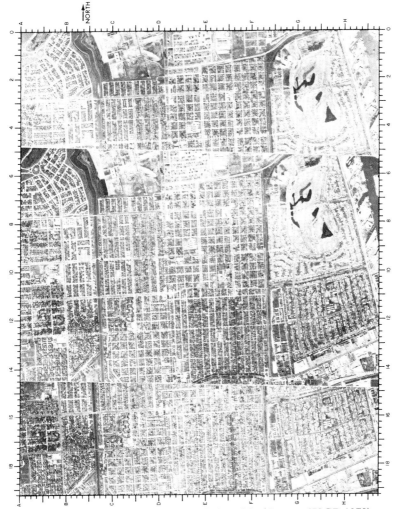

Fig. 7.25 New Orleans: neighbourhoods 2 and 3. (*Source:* HSGP 1970)

(b) width of streets;
(c) number of cars;
(d) number of trees;
(e) presence of swimming-pools;
(f) street patterns.

Neighbourhood 1 has a large public housing project with many small houses on small crowded lots or sections. Many of the houses are old and there are several factories in the area. The houses in neighbourhood 2 seem newer and have larger dots or sections. The street pattern is curved and the area is mostly residential with a large

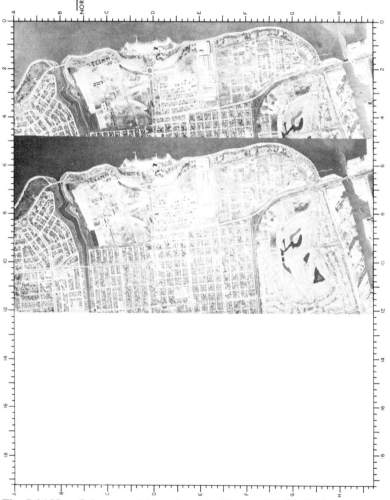

Fig. 7.26 New Orleans: neighbourhood 3. (*Source:* HSGP 1970)

shopping centre and a college. The third neighbourhood looks like a rather new suburban neighbourhood built around a park. The houses are large and have fairly spacious gardens. There is a large amount of open space, a golf course and developed recreation area. All buildings, apart from the university, are residential.

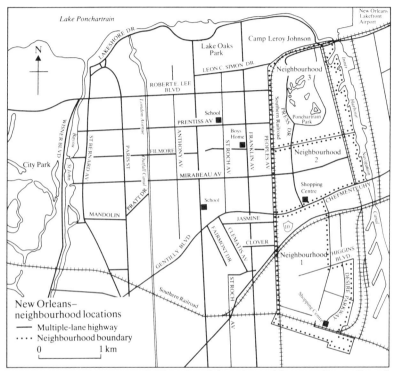

Fig 7.27 New Orleans: neighbourhood locations. (*Source:* Carswell and Cason 1970)

Students can be asked (1) what they would expect to see on a walk through these neighbourhoods, so that they have a chance to suggest some of the cultural features likely to be associated with the type of neighbourhood, and (2) what the expected social and economic characteristics of the inhabitants are likely to be. They are being required to make inferences based on their previous knowledge and experience. They are probably going to generalize about the residents' education and income level, racial background, size of families, occupations and cost of housing. The class will probably associate low income, low level of education, low value of housing and a minority group population with the dilapidated neighbourhood. As each neighbourhood is examined the students fill in a chart (Table 7.2) to estimate the characteristics of the three neighbour-

	Median value of Housing		Median family income	
	Estimated	*Actual*	*Estimated*	*Actual*
Neighbourhood 1	Low	Low	Low	Low
Neighbourhood 2	Moderate	Moderate	Moderate	Moderate
Neighbourhood 3	Moderate		Moderate	

Table 7.2 Neighbourhood characteristics. (*Source:* Carswell and Cason 1970)

hoods. While the original exercise asked for specific figures, here estimates based on a high, medium and low rating system are asked for. As each neighbourhood is studied, estimates of characteristics are filled in on the chart.

After the final two neighbourhoods have been studied, then the actual ratings for each characteristic can be supplied to the students. The majority of them are likely to have made guesses or inferences which are in line with the actual characteristics of the first two neighbourhoods. In judging neighbourhood 3, chances are high that students will not have guessed that this neighbourhood is made up of well-educated, middle-income Negroes. What has promoted the discrepancy between their expectations and the actual situation in the third neighbourhood? Partly this is due to the limited information which the maps and stereograms provide. Students could not know that a university in the vicinity, Southern University, is a predominantly Negro university and they have probably overlooked that the neighbourhood is close to an army camp, an airport and industrial land. An erroneous conclusion about the population characteristics of neighbourhood 3 has been reached because of an idea dominating student thinking. At the back of their minds, students may have had the idea that: 'Negroes are not in the majority in what appears to be a high-income area', or 'Certain groups of people are associated with certain kinds of neighbourhoods.' Class discussion will hopefully lead to a revision of the generalization. For example: 'Some Negro and some white middle-class areas look very much alike', or 'Although value of housing, income and schooling seem to be associated with certain kinds of neighbourhoods, ethnic groups are not.' Figure 7.28 summarizes the discrepant data teaching procedure of which the New Orleans exercise is but an example.

One of the purposes of the discrepant data procedure is to help students examine ideas they hold and to give them an opportunity to develop more precise and accurate generalizations. Because a person

Median school years completed		Per cent Negro		
Estimated	*Actual*	*Estimated*	*Actual*	
	Low	Low	High	Moderate/High
Moderate	High	Low	Low	
Moderate		Low		

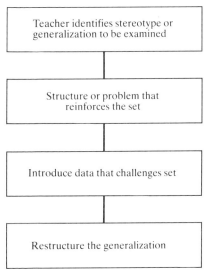

Teacher identifies stereotype or generalization to be examined

Structure or problem that reinforces the set

Introduce data that challenges set

Restructure the generalization

Fig. 7.28 Discrepant data technique. (*Source:* Carswell and Cason 1970)

has a certain stereotype in his mind, he would expect certain things to be so. If a person, for example, believes particular groups of people are associated with particular socio-economic areas, then he could well classify lower socio-economic areas as mostly Negro. In this case, then he might also believe that almost no Negroes would be found in upper-middle-class areas. This mind set or expectation would tend to guide thinking as a person worked through data. Carswell and Cason (1970) emphasize that the discrepant data approach (1) motivates students because they realize they were wrong about certain things and that they have an opportunity to study the topic more fully; (2) may be used to help students understand that they have certain values and that they also hold biases or prejudices; (3) helps make students aware of the tentativeness of hypotheses and the need to check *all* sources of data before arriving at conclusions which seem certain.

A much modified and simplified version of the discrepant data technique which is linked to the third point above is the idea of setting students tasks of intelligent guessing and explaining changes in patterns. The Geography 14–18 Project (Schools Council of England and Wales), developed a number of exemplars using maps and other data around which three questions were asked. Similar to their exemplars is the following.

Given the six patterns in Fig. 7.29 a class may be asked to (1) try to guess what the changing patterns are; (2) what other information would be needed to confirm your guess? (3) say what you think is the best explanation of the changes. The patterns are, in fact, the population densities in Flint, Michigan, at selected times during a 24-hour period. The maps should be presented to students without information on the time of the day or night appropriate to each pattern and without the key words explaining the intensity of shading. What other exercises could be developed from this?

The mapping of a variety of socio-economic data for areas ranging in size from the city to the nation and indeed to the whole world has been very much a part of the human geographer's sphere of interest for many years and gives further opportunity for studying patterns and changes in patterns. However, while in the past such maps have been difficult and time-consuming to prepare, the development of computer mapping offers the possibility that these maps will not only be more readily available but also based on more accurate and recent information.

The four maps, Figs 7.31, 7.32, 7.33 and 7.34 showing the distribution of the population of the Australian city of Sydney according to various socio-economic criteria, have been produced by such a computer process (Davis and Spearitt 1974).

With all maps of this type students can be expected to undertake at least three major tasks:

1. description of the spatial pattern shown on each map;
2. correlation of these spatial patterns through map comparisons;
3. the derivation of generalizations and/or hypotheses which can then be tested against similar data for other cities and epecially for the cities in one's own country.

It may be desirable to make use of other data such as maps of land-use, income distribution and population distribution in order to add to the variables brought into the discussion. However, given these four maps only, it would seem reasonable that students should be able to conclude their study with statements of the following type:

1. In any metropolis, social and economic groups tend to congregate in distinct and separate areas of districts. For example, the professional workforce will be resident in different areas of the city from labourers.

2. In some cities in certain cultures, particular religious and/or ethnic groups will be strongly associated spatially with distinctive occupational groups. For example, in Sydney the distribution of Catholics tends to be strongly and positively correlated with the

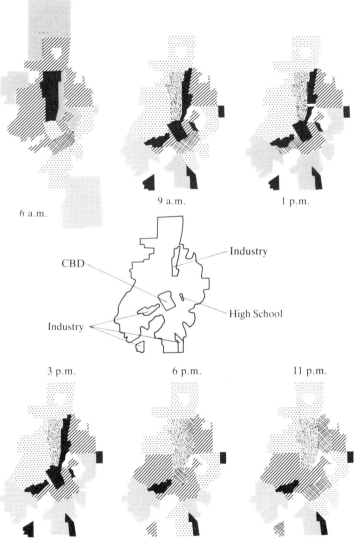

Fig. 7.29 Population densities in Flint, Michigan, at selected times during the day and night, June 1950. (From Chapin 1965, fig. 6.) Students should not be given this information relating to the source and nature of the diagrams until the exercise has been tried.

distribution of blue-collar workers (labourers). In this exercise students are being asked to make judgements based on visual inspection of the maps rather than the more sophisticated statistical correlation methods discussed in Chapter 6.

3. In many cities, the spatial distribution of people with tertiary (beyond high school) education will tend to be positively and strongly correlated with the distribution of upper-class white-collar (professional) workers, and we may hypothesize that the distribution of tertiary-educated people will be positively correlated with the distribution of the higher-income groups in society and with the higher-status suburban districts.

4. In most Western cities, the higher socio-economic status groups will tend to reside in those areas which are perceived by the population of those cities as being environmentally more pleasant than other areas – for example, near to the harbour or to seaside beaches, or in areas of undulating rather than flat terrain and not close to industrial districts. To what extent does this generalization apply to your country's cities?

Two other activities follow: firstly, the social, political and planning implications of these generalizations can be discussed with particular reference to the students' own cities; and, secondly, the students may be introduced to the various models of urban structure (the Concentric Theory, the Multiple-Nuclei Theory, and the Sector Theory). As a useful extension of this latter aspect, students may be asked to postulate the type of regional differentiation which may be expected to occur in a new city sited on uniform terrain and allowed to develop with the free operation of economic and social forces. Students then might well be encouraged to question whether governments or local authorities ought not to counter the tendencies for similar social and economic groups to cluster together. How far should policies to mix social groups residentially be pursued?

As a matter of teaching technique, teachers should be aware of the value of drawing, or photocopying, maps of the type shown in Figs 7.31–7.34 on to transparent sheets suitable for use with the overhead projector. The use of transparency overlays also discussed in Chapter 8 is a most effective method for showing students how variables correlate spatially; for example two maps of the same scale may be placed on the projector so as to compare two distributions which appear connected.

From maps to models

The following exercises based on Melbourne's Central Business District (CBD) illustrate and lead on to a model-building exercise. In this instance from a map (Fig. 7.30) and an aerial photograph

(Fig.7.35), a model will be designed to show the spatial interrelationship of form and function in the CBD of the typical Western city.

Students should be asked to use tracing paper to prepare a more general map of land-use in the CBD from Fig. 7.30 and then to compare the details of their general map with the details of the photograph (Fig. 7.35).

It should be possible for students to recognize the following zones of functional homogeneity within the CBD:

1. The inner or primary retail zone.
2. The outer or secondary retail zone.
3. One of two office or commercial zones – usually associated with the tallest buildings; and to observe the focusing of roads and rail transport in the district – a reflection of its actual or perceived centrality in the city.

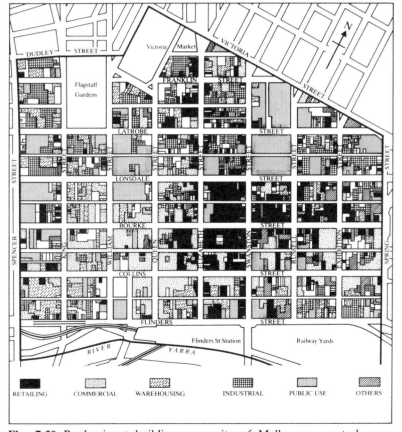

Fig. 7.30 Predominant building uses, city of Melbourne, central area. (*Source:* Spicer 1973)

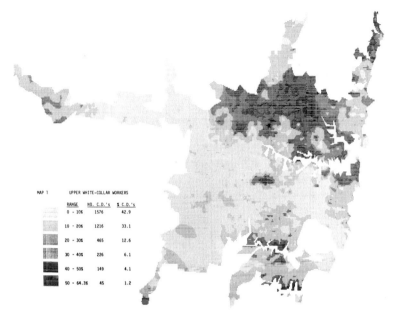

Fig. 7.31 Sydney: distribution of upper white-collar workers

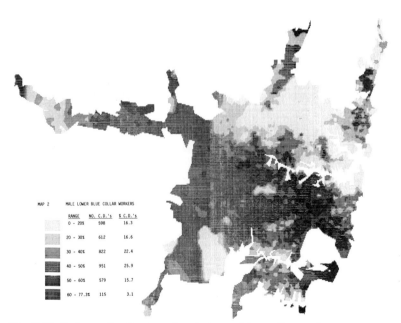

Fig. 7.32 Sydney: distribution of male lower blue-collar workers

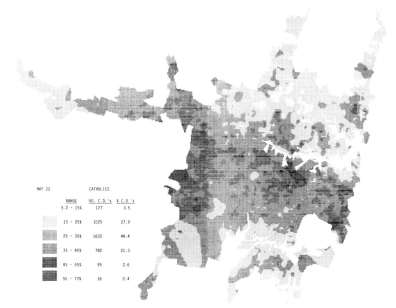

Fig. 7.33 Sydney: distribution of Catholics

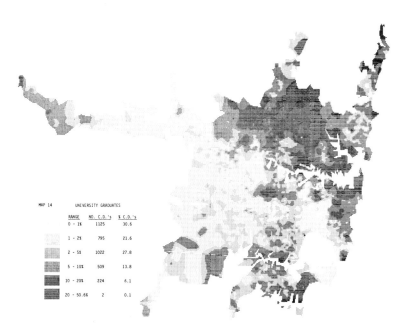

Fig. 7.34 Sydney: distribution of university graduates

Fig. 7.35 Oblique aerial view of Melbourne CBD

Following this students should then be asked, either individually or in groups, to prepare a diagram or model representing the spatial structuring of the CBD similar to that shown in Fig. 7.36 which shows the clustering of some activities in the CBD and associated areas of blight (requiring urban renewal) and assimilation where CBD functions are spreading outwards.

Conclusion

In this chapter we have developed the idea of data gathering, data processing and analysing approaches to teaching with its emphasis on student involvement and the development of the capacity to go beyond the information given to formulate hypotheses, obtain insights into decision-making and reach generalizations or develop models. The wealth of information stored in maps and photographs assists a teacher to follow such a teaching strategy. It should be stressed, however, that we are aware that the suggestions and exercises outlined here will have to be carefully and judiciously modified, adapted, perhaps pruned or expanded before being transformed into successful, enjoyable classroom lessons. The inputs will necessarily be different for each and every class and teachers may

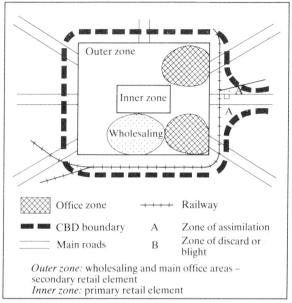

Office zone • • • ┼┼┼┼┼ Railway

▬ ▬ CBD boundary ⟶ A Zone of assimilation

────── Main roads B Zone of discard or blight

Outer zone: wholesaling and main office areas – secondary retail element

Inner zone: primary retail element

Fig. 7.36 A CBD model. (*Source:* Spicer 1973)

well wish to go to some of the sources indicated in order to refresh their knowledge of a particular topic or concept, for nothing courts disaster so certainly in the classroom as the partially thought-out lesson. Similarly, students cannot reach an understanding of general principles out of thin air, and hence we have sought to provide a balance between materials (maps, photographs and diagrams) which supply information (the data storage component) and suggestions for their use (the move towards generalization and theory as storage devices), so that the teacher becomes a manager of resources, a guide, a provider of signposts which lead from knowledge to understanding and thus expands his role beyond that of being the giver of information only. From the detail in the maps and photographs, understanding in the general sense of that term may be unravelled by teacher and students in a collaborative exercise. Equally, the theoretical understandings may be subjected to modification and refinement when other evidence is examined.

Landsat imagery may be obtained from EROS Data Center, Sioux Falls, South Dakota, USA.

Handling agents who can also be of assistance and also supply teaching sets include:

Nigel Press Associates:	Apex House
	97 High Street
	Edenbridge
	Kent
	England
Space Dimensions:	PO Box 3022
	Station C
	Ottawa K1Y 4J3
	Ontario
	Canada
TAC:	University of Mexico
	Albuquerque
	New Mexico
	USA

Acknowledgements

We wish to express our gratitude to Nigel Press (Apex House, 97 High Street, Edenbridge, Kent, England) for his help and advice in the preparation of the section dealing with remote sensing and satellite imagery.

Figures 7.17 and 7.19–23 were supplied by the courtesy of the New Zealand High Commission in the UK.

CHAPTER 8

Managing resources for learning

CHANDRA PAL SINGH

In recent years there have been many changes in geography, both in the conceptual structure of the subject and in the instructional techniques and equipment. Barring monetary constraints, the students can have learning resources ranging from such traditional items as the textbook to instructional television, different types of projectors, transparencies, films and even computers. The addition of new learning resources has brought with it problems of storage, of handling the equipment and of the management of space for using them. The geography room and the library with the traditional catalogue system can no longer cope with the situation. It demands suitable modifications in the geography room and a library-cum-resource centre with an efficient retrieval system. Geography teachers and students now have to learn to handle all kinds of costly equipment.

The expensive learning resources of today are beyond the reach of a large number of schools in the world. Many in the developing countries cannot afford them. But the objective of including a consideration of modern and expensive instructional equipment here is that geography teachers everywhere should have an idea of the innovations available. The diffusion of these innovations may not be uniform in all directions and at all levels, but these are going to be used increasingly by more and more schools as funds become available. It should be noted here that schools which are not aware of the new learning resources are generally also those which remain untouched by conceptual changes in geography. It is intended that the information given in these pages should serve as a guide for making a careful selection of equipment and other resources. It will also help in deciding the priorities of individual schools.

Learning resources come in many forms, from the more familiar press cuttings and duplicated sheets to the slide-tape package, the multi-media kit or the computer. The definition of a resource, in this context, is anything which may be an object of study or which assists or stimulates the student in his learning. It includes printed material, such as books, periodicals, newspapers, press cuttings, pictures; displayable material like maps, diagrams, charts, models and specimens; projectable material like slides, filmstrips, film loops, films, acetate transparencies and microfiche; combinations of sound and films like audio-tapes, slide-tapes, records, radio and television programmes, videotapes, slide-tape and film-record combination; programmed materials, such as computer-assisted instruction (CAI), etc. Field centres which help in organizing regular field trips are included in learning resources. Some people would like to include in this list individuals, objects in the community, zoological and botanical living items, physical features and natural phenomena, without which there can be problems of comprehension among the students. In this chapter we shall be concerned mainly with secondary rather than primary resources.

Much more space is needed to store, display and use such a wide variety of resources than an ordinary geography room and the traditional school library. The geography room should be spacious enough to display and use some of the resources. The school library could be the right place to store them, or it could be turned into a library-cum-resource centre. Resources produced by the teachers and students of one subject could be pooled together with those of other subjects. A resource centre is becoming a necessity in modern teaching.

The geography room: its layout and equipment

There is a need for a special room for teaching geography for various reasons (Fig. 8.1). Some of the learning resources are bulky and costly, and they need to be kept in one place, since movement from one place to another is difficult, time-consuming and risky. Apart from storage of such items the geography room serves as a kind of laboratory, with provides an atmosphere for working and learning. In this room chalkboard diagrams, which are sometimes made so laboriously, can be preserved for use in the next lesson. Other materials such as different types of hardware models can be displayed permanently there.

In a geography room there should be space for considerable movement – to draw and construct maps and diagrams, for model-making, to consult reference books and big atlases, to use equipment such as slide and film projectors and the episcope. A geography room, therefore, has to be allotted more space than a normal classroom (UNESCO 1965). In designing the geography room the following considerations should be kept in mind:
1. Adequate seating space for the class.
2. Adequate working space.
3. Adequate storage and office space.

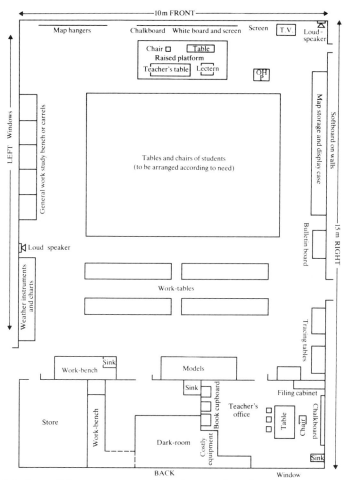

Fig. 8.1 A possible arrangement of furniture and equipment in a geography room

Seating space for students

A geography room should be large enough to accommodate a class of thirty students with their seats and tables, which should be comfortable to sit at and large enough for their books, atlases and mapsheets. This furniture should be so designed that it may be used both by the individual student during or after a lesson and by groups in group study by putting tables together without much commotion and damage to furniture. Placement of tables for various arrangements of students and groups will require a larger seating space. Ideally, a student should have a table-top of 100 cm × 80 cm. This flexibility of furniture is especially critical for air photos, weather maps and charts, models and topographic maps that must be placed for group use. The type of chairs or stools to go with the tables will depend on choice and upon the money and space available. It would be best if a chair for each student could be provided; otherwise short stools would serve the purpose well. Here the posture of sitting which a particular design of furniture permits should be kept in mind. It should be comfortable to sit in, keep the students alert and not harmful for their backbone.

Working space

The front of the class should have the main teaching space, though teaching may be done elsewhere in the room. A slightly elevated platform in the front may be preferred by some teachers as it may enable them to keep contact more easily with the students at the far corners of the room. More than 3 m should be allowed between the front row of tables and the wall behind the teacher, otherwise students sitting at the sides will not have a proper view of the chalkboard, wall maps, projection screen or television. A lectern may be placed on the right-hand corner near the first row, on which the teacher can keep papers needed during the lesson. It could be provided with a covered light to make it usable during blackout for screening slides or films. But many teachers prefer 'daylight' projections so that students can work at their papers during projection.

The teacher may make frequent use of the chalkboard or whiteboard (used with spirit markers) during a lesson, for drawing maps and diagrams, and may like to preserve them for use in the next lesson. The selection of the chalkboard can be from:
1. the roller board, this gives the largest total area for the smallest space taken up;
2. the folding board, which can give as many as four surfaces;
3. the counterpoise sliding board arranged like a sash window, where as many as four surfaces can be provided;
4. a wall fitting to hold three medium-sized boards 107 cm × 122 cm in slots, which can be taken out, interchanged or stored until the diagrams are required again.

The last kind is particularly useful, as on some boards it may be possible to paint a permanent outline of the continents or countries most often required, or a permanent map of the world. It is often useful to have one board with a squared surface. Some teachers prefer green rather than black boards and some may wish to use white board with water-based pens for clarity of drawing and vivid colour. Others which may be used are magnetic boards for metal objects and letters and felt boards for flannelgraph work.

The board should have a light projecting on it. The teacher may like to switch from writing to showing slides or film and vice versa.

Other walls may be partly faced with softboard, or some such material on which pins can be used. The entire softboard space can be used for permanent or temporary display of maps, diagrams, charts, air photographs, etc. A space on the front wall may be reserved for the maps and diagrams needed during the lessons.

The globes, specimens and models can be assigned space on the tables and in cupboards. The globes may be of three types – 40 or 60 cm globes with physical features, 40 cm slated globes with continental outlines painted with light colour and 15 or 20 cm globes for individual student use. The specimens should be stored in cupboards with doors so that they are free from dust and need to be taken out only when they are required. A model of the local area with a topographic map near a window overlooking the area would be very useful. Relief and other hardware models may be stored as required.

The geography teacher will frequently need to use slides, filmstrips, films, television programmes, projection of pictures and diagrams from books and magazines. It would be better if he can project slides, films and pictures in half-light. There are many types of rear projection screens especially designed for use in daylight. If these are not available, blackout should be provided to darken the room, taking care to maintain proper ventilation inside. There are other methods of blackout, such as dark blinds fitting into shutters, but these are expensive, slow and shut a great deal of air from the room. A rear projection screen needs to be in a corner, but if a hanging or portable screen is used it should be next to the board, so that the screen and board can be used in combination if needed. Sometimes a rolling chalkboard has a white surface on part of its total area which may be used as a screen or whiteboard.

Special mention should be made of the overhead projector (Fig. 8.2). The benefit of the overhead projector is that it can be used without disruption of normal class or geography room arrangements. It is light in weight and can be easily transported from one room to another. It can be used both in full daylight and artificial light. It utilizes the basic principles of transmission of light through a transparent material. It can project, in any colour, on to a viewing screen, large and bright pictures of drawings, printed or written matter prepared quickly and easily on a transparency. The teacher can make use of diagrams or printed material, or he can make up his own material on the spot to be projected on the screen. Such material can be stored for future use. The overhead projector can be used like a chalkboard also, as writing on the acetate is projected instantly on the screen.

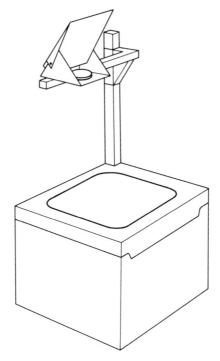

Fig. 8.2 An overhead projector

Class working area

Working space should be provided in a geography room for other activities outside the routine, such as tracing and making models. An area at the back of the room could perhaps be partitioned and kept reserved for these activities. The tracing table can be fitted on top of a map storage cabinet to save space. But they should be away from the model-making section and the sink. The materials and water used in that section could damage the glass of the tracing table and spoil the wood over a period of time.

A work-bench both for students and teacher is useful in any geography room. The students can be encouraged to make models and use their hands creatively. Moreover, the teacher may wish to make models to illustrate his lessons. The work-bench can be in the same section of the partitioned area as the dark-room (see Fig. 8.1), and used for routine maintenance of geography equipment. Wall maps have to be repaired, some maps may need protective edges, geological specimens labelled and hosts of other jobs may need to be done. The bench, therefore, should have a solid top, be about 75 cm high and 65 cm wide, be as long as the available space allows, and have ample cupboards underneath for modelling materials and the storage of half-completed models. It should be fitted with a woodworker's vice, a supply of tools suitably stored, a sink with hot and cold water and a slate slab or zinc top for modelling purposes.

General work-benches or study carrels, could be provided along part of a wall. The precise orientation of the room will probably already be given by the building. In any case, the base orientation will vary according to the locality of the school and its position latitudinally. The feeling of openness will help the student work in a cheerful atmosphere, though the extent of window space will again depend on the location of the school and the nature of the local climate. Many windows also limit the wall pin-up space available.

Storage and office space

The geography teacher will need adequate storage space for resources borrowed from the resource centre, maps and equipment and personal collection of resources. The portion in the rear section could be divided into three small rooms, one of which could be used as store, another for dark-room and work-bench and the third as office for the teacher (see Fig. 8.1). The teacher can make his own decisions regarding what is to be kept in the store and what should go to his office. It is possible that the teacher would like to consult books or resources to plan out his lesson. In this case it would be better if the books are kept in his office. He may also like to keep the more costly equipment in his room. The store and the office together should essentially have a filing cabinet, wall-map cupboard, map chest, card-index cabinet and a general cupboard with shelves for storing drawings, instruments, meteorological instruments, drawing materials, stationery, filmstrips, slides, etc. The office of the teacher should also have a small chalkboard of the size of 2.5 m × 1.5 m, which can be used for teaching small groups in his office. A sink unit should also be provided in a corner of the office, as well as in the students' area.

Electrical arrangements in the geography room

It is of utmost importance that special attention should be paid to the lighting arrangements in the geography room to make best use of such a variety of equipment. The electric switchboard should be fixed within the easy reach of the teacher to enable him to control lights in all parts of the room. The chalkboard and the lectern should be provided with adequate lighting for writing and reading without the light escaping to other parts of the room. A rheostat for dimming the lights to the desired intensity should be installed. It is essential that there should be several power points in different parts of the room so that the projectors may be used from several suitable angles and for plugging in other electrical equipment such as a micro-computer. A long cable may be needed for the remote control of a slide projector.

The resources centre

The idea of a resource centre has grown up recently in several countries in the West (Beswick 1972; Wyatt 1973). It is likely to spread because increasingly schools in most parts of the world are going to be faced with the problem of storing all kinds of resources. Newspapers in all countries print news items and articles which can be used in teaching many subjects. The use of instructional equipment is on the increase. Television instruction in different subjects is given in most countries which have this facility. There is the common requirement of all the subjects for equipment like the slide projectors, film projectors, tape recorders, duplicating machines, television sets and so on. Then there are the special requirements of each subject. For instance, geography needs topographic and weather maps, air photographs, etc. These items can also be used in other school subjects. There is no reason why resources produced or acquired by one subject cannot be used by others who need them.

In future there is likely to be more inter-disciplinary borrowing, which will bring in economies by reducing duplication of resources in the same school. It is wasteful to produce the same resource in different parts of the school, or to buy a resource which already exists in the school and is lying idle. For instance, a duplicating machine and photocopier are needed by all at one time or other, and it may be more efficient and cheaper to have the work done in a central place.

The answer to this decentralization and duplication of resources is the establishment of a resource centre in the school. There resources used by a large number of subject teachers can be kept, or it can give information regarding the resources available in different parts of the school. Since there will be an enormous number of resources in the school and the centre, it is of utmost importance that an efficient retrieval system is in use. This is considered later in the chapter. Thus the idea of resource centre is a logical step forward from the library.

Production of resources

Some resources are supplied by commercial suppliers, but others can be produced in the school by individual teachers and students. Each teacher knows about his requirements and should plan, devise and produce some of his own resources. He can work out his lessons in a systematic way and visualize the resources needed: notes, maps, information sheets, pamphlets, photocopies, slides, tape commentaries, etc. The teacher can himself produce some of these, if they do not exist in the resource centre, or can ask the centre to get them for him. Groups of students can be usefully employed in preparing resources.

It should, however, be kept in mind that teachers are busy people and ought not to be burdened by tasks which can be done by others. The school should try to procure as many resources as possible within its financial reach. The staff of the resource centre should be capable of advising teachers on educational and technical facets of resource production, to order, receive and store the resources, classify and index the items and help teachers and students in finding the resources they need.

Acquisition of resources

The acquisition of learning resources may be centralized in the resource centre. A librarian, or media resource officer, who may already be dealing with the purchases for the library, can be assigned the job of receiving the requirements of the teachers, placing orders with commercial firms or writing for the loan of the resource from other sources, receiving them, making payments and indexing and giving accession numbers to the resource. The job can be facilitated if the order file is made up of individual cards or slips, kept in alphabetical order. The slip should have full details of the item ordered, name of the supplier, date of the order and such basic information which the staff need. A copy of the slip can serve as the order to the supplier and another copy can be retained with the school, which can help in making an accession record after the item has been received.

Similar slips can be made for recording loans from other institutions. They should be arranged in subject order to facilitate searching for them when required. To avoid confusion later, all bulk loans and subject loans should have their contents listed on arrival. Otherwise they will get mixed up with the other resources of the school, or may be lost.

Retrieval of resources

The staff and students of a school may produce or acquire resources in their initial enthusiasm, but it may all end up in piles of papers, models, tapes and in utter confusion, if a proper retrieval system is not adopted. The teachers and students must know what materials the school possesses or to which it has access. For this indexing of all the resources is necessary.

An index is not a mere catalogue, which can be a list written down in a register. The index tells the inquirer much more about the material – its author, producer or illustrator, its location in the centre, the other titles under which it can be found and such other vital information. It should be kept in mind that a resource centre is different from a library in many respects. It contains many kinds of flat papers, both printed and duplicated, pictures, all kinds of audio-visual software, models, specimens and realia. Without a systematic indexing system it can baffle its users.

There are two retrieval systems commonly in use: the classified catalogue and the alphabetical or dictionary catalogue systems. Other systems like co-ordinate indexing are being experimented with. It should be noted that many teachers and students are not experienced persons in library science. Advice of the library staff should be taken in adopting a particular system of indexing or better still, a media resource specialist employed. However, a brief account of the two systems is given below.

The classified catalogue

In this system the cards are arranged in two ways – alphabetically and subject-wise. The alphabetical section contains an author/title index arranged alphabetically along with the headings of the subjects under which the subject index has been arranged. It leads the inquirer to the work of an author without any difficulty. But if the author is not known the inquirer will have to make a guess of the subject under which that title may be found. Each subject is given a classification number, and all books belonging to that subject are arranged at one place in the subject part bearing its respective classification number. The following illustration should make the point clear (Fig. 8.3).

A specific book by Emrys Jones can be found by looking through the alphabetical section. But all books on human geography would be found together under U47, in the above example. Thus for each item at least two cards are made – one for alphabetical index and the other for subject index. The alphabetical index has a few more cards for various subjects. This is a very simple and efficient system to locate books. With suitable modifications it can be used in a resource centre. The subject index, in addition to the author index, can have cards regarding all materials falling under different subjects, giving the location of each item in the resource centre.

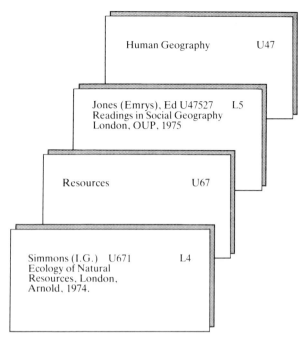

Fig. 8.3 Library catalogue and resource classification cards

The alphabetical or dictionary catalogue

In this system the cards are arranged alphabetically, like a dictionary, under authors as well as titles. The cards contain a full description and location of the material. One such card is filed alphabetically under author (or each author, editor, translator, illustrator, etc.) and another under title. The subject heading is always as specific as possible. There is no separate subject catalogue in this system and books belonging to a subject may be found scattered at different places. The other problem which the inquirer can sometimes face in this system is that he may not always pick on the form of subject heading which the cataloguer has chosen. In a resource centre where there will be so many resources of different kinds this system may not be efficient.

Location and layout of the resource centre

It is desirable that the resources are stored adjacent to, or in a part of, the central building of the school which is accessible to the entire school. The allocation of space to different subjects should be such that those subjects which need to use the resource centre more frequently are kept near it. Geography should normally expect to be near the centre. A large school, or a school with scattered premises, may like to locate the material of the resource centre in different parts of the building, keeping the materials needed by a subject close by, either in the classroom or the study room allocated to that subject. But this is detrimental to the idea of a central pool of resources where there is no compartmentalization according to subjects.

Most school libraries provide the focal point where all students of the school can come regularly. It would be appropriate to develop the school library as a resource centre, where apart from the books, all other kinds of resources can be kept. It will require extra space for storage of non-book materials and essential equipment.

Layout

The layout of the resource centre (see Fig. 8.4) will depend mainly upon the learning materials available and the future policy of the school. The major items, apart from the books, which a school must have in its resource centre are:
 1. Audio-visuals: slides, filmstrips, a previewer and a small slide projector, a film projector, portable cassette tape recorder or tape players, preferably with headphones, filmstrip projector, overhead projector, episcope.
 2. Shelves for books.
 3. Space for keeping reprographic and audio-visual equipment.
 4. Tables and carrels for study.
 5. Counter to issue and receive books.
 6. Librarian's office.
 7. Card catalogue.
 8. Map cabinet.
 9. Section for production of resources.
10. Filing cabinets.

The resources after they have been grouped subject-wise or given an accession number should be assigned a fixed place to which they can be returned after use. They can be obtained either through an open access system, in which the material can be found and examined by the user, or through a closed system, in which a resource is fetched by the staff of the centre.

The book stacks, study tables and carrels should be kept away from the listening and viewing section to keep the noise away from the reading section. The production centre is another area which is likely to be noisy and it should also be kept away from the reading room. The sounds from the non-reading room can be effectively cut down

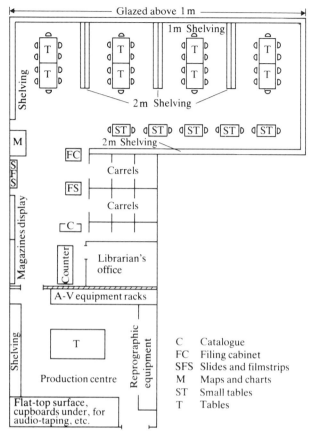

Fig. 8.4 Plan of a resource centre. A fixed and somewhat formal layout is sometimes dictated by circumstances. Here, an L-shaped library room is used for all media storage, grouped into subject bays. Carrels for use of equipment are near issue counter and away from other areas. Resources not easily integrated on shelves are stored within sight of issue counter. A classroom next door has been adapted for a production centre, though not for photographic purposes for which a small dark-room is often sufficient. Plan is not to scale, and amalgamates elements found in several resource centres visited. (*Sources:* Beswick 1972)

by partitioning the resource centre with soundproof material. The windows of the centre should be double glazed, especially near the study section.

A final, but important, point which can generally be ignored is providing toilets in the resource centre. It is important that once a person has entered the centre he does not have to leave it before his job is over, or the class returns for the next period.

Field centres as resource centres

The importance of fieldwork in geography hardly needs any elabora-
tion. It is agreed that fieldwork leads to a greater appreciation of
fundamental geographical ideas. But there are three main problems
in conducting any fieldwork:
1. conducting fieldwork during school time;
2. the difficulty of examining the fieldwork;
3. the financial expenditure involved.

These problems can be effectively tackled if the school has a
permanent base in the area where the students are generally taken
out to fieldwork every year. Such a field centre could be any place in
the area of study, which is permanently at the disposal of the school.
It should provide the students with all the necessary requirements
and accommodation during fieldwork.

For this purpose an unused building in the area could be acquired
by the school. For instance, a Bristol school in England bought an
unused railway station to be used as a field centre. If the purchase of a
building is not possible, the school can enter into a contract with a
hotel or a camping site or a tourist centre to reserve permanent
accommodation for regular use by the school. Clearly such a place
will have other guests also, and some adjustments with them and the
staff of that place will have to be made.

The advantage of a field centre will not be to one subject alone, but
to all subjects in the school which have fieldwork as part of their
curriculum, like botany, zoology, geology and geography. A mutually agreed timetable for fieldwork can be worked out and put up on
the notice-board for information to all concerned. It will help in
planning the visits by each subject ahead of time. The timetable of
the school can be suitably modified to accommodate fieldwork by
different departments. For such regular visits the school should have
a vehicle for transporting the students and their baggage to the field
centre and back. If it is not possible for a school to have a vehicle of
its own, it can engage a private bus on a regular basis (Boardman
1969). In many cases contracting with a transport organization is
cheaper.

The possession of the field centre will enable the examination of
students in the field, by which they will take fieldwork more seriously.
Considering the combined expenses of different departments on
fieldwork at the present, and the advantages of long-term planning
for fieldwork, it may be cheaper for the school to own a field centre.
It could be used as a resource centre by allocating space in the field
centre for specimens, maps, topographic maps and weather instruments. A study room provided with selective books on different
subjects which the students may need to consult in the field will be
very useful. It can, of course, be used for many subjects other than
geography.

Textbooks as resources

In spite of the development of new learning resources the importance of the textbook has not diminished. It still remains a major learning resource. The textbook may provide a logical order of arguments regarding the topic to be studied. It can pose questions to be answered by the student and help him in drawing conclusions. In appendices, there may be suggestions for relevant texts, personal readings, statistics and subjects for practical exercises. Therefore, special care should be given to prescribing and recommending a textbook.

Teachers will find a wide range of instructional technologies complementary to geography. These include programmed instruction, self-paced instruction, audio-visual tutorial, radio and television. Programmed instruction is demonstrated in Chapter 3. Self-paced instruction is a mastery-learning system whereby the student interacts with textual materials and behavioural objectives in order to attain a mastery score on examination criteria referenced to the objectives (Keller 1968). It represents an instructional management system readily perfected by the classroom teacher. Audio-visual tutorial (AVT) instruction involves equipment stations, usually containing a cassette tape player, a slide projector and study manual. The lesson is co-ordinated so that the students receive the content both in visual and audio form. The study manual enables the student to address significant content questions and problems, while a small group tutorial presents an opportunity for students to clarify issues regarding the materials. AVT may be supplemented by a textbook and lectures. Radio and television continue to present numerous opportunities for distant and self-contained instruction. While the cost of TV recording and play-back equipment prohibits its widespread use, geography teachers may find it advantageous to use regular programming and structure supplemental lessons to build upon pertinent audio-visual content delivery through the electronic media.

Computer terminals as resources

Apart from their utilization for analysing the massive data for higher research in geography, computer programs are being used as active elements in teaching and learning geography. The computer can play the role of a challenger to the student and tell him whether his responses to the questions put by the computer are right or wrong. The computer may serve not only as a high-speed calculator, but also as a learning resource where it guides the student in instructional processes. The student may sit at an inquiry station and communicate directly with the computer through an electric typewriter, using the typewriter as an input and output device. The computer presents programmed information, asks questions, analyses responses and maintains records of student performance.

Computer-based learning (CBL) helps the students to check their knowledge of geographical concepts and facts. The student participates in the learning process almost in a tutorial situation, where he can actively check his comprehension of the material covered or the skills involved. If he fails to achieve the programmed objective he is 'branched' off to a remedial loop, or he must repeat the initial material. The teacher is thus relieved of some basic exercises. Computer-assisted instruction (CAI) relieves him to devote his attentions to other important activities.

The computer can also facilitate learning by making the student perceive and respond to geographical problems by playing roles and games in given situations. For instance, the student can examine certain aspects of land-use decision-making among members of a hypothetical society in a tropical subsistence setting at the console of the computer and choosing the allocation of specific crop types and hectares. The computer here gives immediate feedback as to the consequence of such decisions. Or the student is assigned to play the role of a peasant farmer in South America with the object of maximizing his yield. He manipulates a number of variables which govern production and the computer system estimates the production attained. His wrong decision will give him low yield. Such games, in which the computer gives results quickly, help the student understand the constraints and consequences of decisions in given conditions. This way the student is involved in real situations, and learning in this manner can be fun and stimulating.

Besides, the computer can store and process a vast amount of data quickly. It can serve as a data bank, in which the data can be stored on punched cards, magnetic tapes, etc. and which can be used by different persons for different purposes. The computer can also plot maps of any desired characteristics by an automated plotter. In addition, with a cathode-ray tube, maps and graphs produced from data stored in the computer can be displayed on a television tube which can be photographed to provide permanent copies.

The computer this way has a great utility in storing vast amounts of data, analysing and mapping them, assisting the students in playing roles and games and in simulation; but it does not replace the teacher. It is merely one of the several other learning resources used by the teacher and students (Association of American Geographers 1967; Shepherd *et al* 1980).

Producing cheap resources for students and teachers

Once the necessary equipment and other material for a resource centre and for the geography room have been bought, it will need additional money and effort to maintain resources. The teachers and students may have to take the responsibility of producing additional resources. The students can participate in producing newspaper cuttings, making models, charts and diagrams, keeping weather records, taking and printing photographs, collecting books and documents, etc. The teachers, on the other hand, have to produce resources like duplicated sheets, information sheets, arranging slides with a tape commentary and notes, developing computer-assisted instruction programmes, planning field trips and so on. The production of such resources may not entail much expenditure on the part of the individuals or the school. Once produced they can be used by all the students and teachers of the school.

In this way the school can build up a rich collection of resources. Most schools have the basic infrastructure available to them and it is only a matter of suitable modification in the building and reallocation of the existing resources.

CHAPTER 9

Course planning in geography

DONALD S. BIDDLE

In their daily experiences in the school, geography teachers are involved in finding answers to questions such as:

1. What topic in geography have I planned to introduce to the next group of students?
2. Which educational objectives will I attempt to achieve?
3. How will I select appropriate geographical content for these students?
4. What learning experiences will I emphasize?
5. How will I organize resources to maximize each student's learning experiences?
6. To what extent will I concentrate on individualized learning, small group or class activities?
7. How will I know whether my teaching has been effective?

That is, the teacher is involved in finding immediate solutions in the classroom to curriculum problems associated with the teaching of geography as a discipline, or as part of a multi-disciplinary or an inter-disciplinary course.

The nature of the curriculum problems the teacher has to solve is dependent to a large extent on the kind of educational system in which he or she is employed. Some systems have not moved into the application of curriculum theory to the development of courses and still supply teachers with prescriptive syllabuses in which aims are expressed in terms of external examination requirements (see Fig. 9.1). Other systems, that apply curriculum theory to the design of geography curricula, differ in their views concerning the extent that teachers should be involved in formulating the curriculum. Consequently, some teachers receive the minimum of guidance, while other teachers may be given what many regard as too much assistance in the form of a curriculum document based on instructional units plus 'teacher-proof' packages for each of these units.

In the last quarter of this century finding solutions to curriculum problems has become more difficult because of the explosive growth of information about world environments; the commercial production of a variety of educational resources which the teacher has to evaluate before purchasing; the diffusion of information and value systems to students through the mass media, particularly radio and television; the lack of agreement among psychologists about the way students learn and the way learning experiences should be organized; and the controversy among educationists about the purposes of schooling. The complexity of these problems has led to a ferment of ideas about:

1. the nature of curriculum;
2. the question of who should be responsible for its design and evaluation;
3. the criteria to be used in its formulation.

The nature of curriculum

There are many definitions of 'curriculum' and its meaning appears to have changed through time. The earlier definitions referred to the total educational experiences of the student and the later definitions tended to restrict the experiences to those organized by the school. In recent years more specific definitions have been used to facilitate dialogue among groups of people, such as teachers, parents, students, lecturers in tertiary institutions and producers of educational resources, who are interested in curriculum questions.

In this chapter the curriculum is defined as *a document containing the guidelines for developing a course or courses in an educational institution.* These guidelines provide statements about long-term aims; objectives stated in terms of knowledge, skills and values; organizational structures such as concepts, themes and units; learning experiences; and techniques of evaluation (Johnson 1967; Beauchamp 1968).

The use of the term 'curriculum' is further clarified by using a preceding adjective to define the level at which decision-making occurs and the specificity of the details included in the document (Eisner 1963). For example, it is possible to identify four kinds of curriculum document using these criteria:

1. *A national education system's curriculum*
   which is exemplified by an educational document summarizing a course or courses prepared by a centralized authority for all the schools in a country as is found in France, Sweden and New Zealand.

2. *A state or regional education system's curriculum*
   which is prepared by state or regional authorities such as those found in the states of the USA and Australia, and in the provinces of Canada.

3. *A school curriculum*
   which is the total curriculum organized by the staff for a particular school with or without the assistance of students and of parents.

4. *A subject curriculum*
which is a document prepared by a curriculum committee at the
national, state, regional or school level for a subject in the school
curriculum, e.g. a curriculum based on a discipline, such as
geography, or a multi-disciplinary course, such as environmental
studies.

It might be noted that numerous questions of a systematic nature
arise in curriculum and course planning. While the author does not
view the analysis of curriculum materials as critical to this chapter,
the various systematic schemes which have evolved in past years
provide a marked advantage to the curriculum and course planner.
Survey schemes which have been developed and implemented with
success are:
1. Curriculum Materials Analysis System, Social Sciences Education
   Consortium, University of Colorado, Boulder, Colorado, USA.
2. Berkeley Scheme, Far West Laboratory for Educational Research
   and Development, Berkeley, California, USA,
3. St Gallen Scheme, Educational Resource Centre, St Gallen
   Canton, Switzerland.
4. Haussler and Pittman Scheme, Institut für die Padagogik der
   Naturwissenschaften, University of Kiel, Germany.
5. Swedish Scheme, National Board of Education, Stockholm,
   Sweden.
6. Sussex Scheme, Centre for Educational Technology, University of
   Sussex, Brighton, UK.
However, in this chapter attention is focused on the curriculum
processes associated with the design, implementation and evaluation
of a variety of geography curricula at two levels of organization: the
level of a curriculum committee consisting of practising teachers,
tertiary lecturers in geography and education, curriculum consultants
and other resource personnel working at the national, state or
regional level, and the level of a smaller group of teachers working
within a particular school.

Responsibility for design and evaluation of the curriculum

Some teachers argue that they should have complete freedom to
organize courses for their students on the assumption that they know
best what the needs of these students are. That is, they support the
concept of school-based curriculum development. There are, no
doubt, some teachers who are capable of formulating worthwhile
curricula without the assistance of people outside the school system,
and they could profitably use the curriculum process models described in this chapter or use them to develop a model to suit their
own purposes.

However, investigations of the development of geography curricula in a number of countries indicate that the complex processes associated with the design of a worthwhile curriculum in geography require far more time, energy and expertise than the average teacher possesses. In addition, the spiralling costs of education have reduced the possibility of teachers obtaining a reduction in teaching commitments in order to gain the expertise to plan curricula and, at the same time, to maintain their knowledge of the continuing changes in geography and in education.

It seems reasonable to suggest, therefore, that in the majority of school systems teachers should, under their present conditions of employment, have the support of curriculum planning teams consisting of practising teachers, tertiary education specialists in geography and curriculum studies and any other resource personnel who can make a contribution. These planning teams should be organized in accordance with the needs of students and teachers at national, regional or local levels to formulate geography curricula to be pilot tested in selected schools before being implemented in a section of, or in the whole of, an educational system.

The diffusion of information about a new curriculum can be channelled through conferences and workshop sessions in which teachers evaluate the viability of the curriculum in their school situation and assist each other in developing instructional units. Other means of disseminating information about a curriculum are publications sponsored by the curriculum committee, the journals and newsletters of geographical societies, educational supplements in newspapers and visits to schools by curriculum consultants.

Finally, each geography curriculum must be regarded as an experiment in curriculum design, which is based on particular educational assumptions, and on a dynamic curriculum process system that emphasizes the need for continuous change and development. As teachers acquire the necessary expertise and confidence in curriculum planning the establishment of local groups can be a means of sponsoring continuous curriculum renewal and encouraging experimentation with innovative practices in geography and in education. This process has been developed in some countries and has resulted in the publication of stimulating ideas and materials for the teaching of geography in disciplinary, multi-disciplinary and inter-disciplinary courses.

Criteria to be used in the formulation of a geography curriculum

In the last 50 years there has been an increasing interest shown in the criteria to be used in the design, implementation and evaluation of curricula, and many conceptual models have been developed by research workers to provide graphic representations of the components and the processes considered to be essential in the formulation of a curriculum.

The earliest curriculum models, in contrast to methods used in syllabus construction which were content-centred (see Fig. 9.1), were designed to indicate how teachers could balance the needs of students against the kind of learning experiences and knowledge which could be provided from the discipline of geography. Attempts were made to express general aims in terms of knowledge to be gained by students; to select learning experiences which would assist students to achieve these aims; and to develop assessment procedures that would indicate the extent to which the aims had been achieved. That is, teachers became more interested in selecting content and skills from geography which were appropriate for students with varying interests and abilities than in teaching the discipline for its own sake.

Because so little research had been done on each of the components of the curriculum, aims continued to be expressed in general terms and were not translated into more specific educational objectives; factual content was emphasized within the broad structure of the regional geography of the world; learning experiences were reduced to the development of a limited number of skills associated with maps, photographs and field studies, and the memorization of factual information from set textbooks; and the assessment methods used were based on obtaining satisfactory responses from pupils to non-structured or loosely structured essay questions (see Fig. 9.2).

Many secondary schools are at present using geography curricula formulated by committees who have based their planning on the relationships among the components in a cyclic curriculum model similar to, or the same as, that depicted in Fig. 9.2 (Taba 1962; Tyler 1949; Wheeler 1967). However, although fundamental questions about curriculum development may be answered by reference to this model, many refinements have been made, in the last decade, to its components and processes as a result of research done by specialists in geography and in education, in association with teachers preparing experimental courses in particular school systems (Cromarty 1975; Deer *et al* 1977; Hickman *et al* 1973; SGEP 1975; Rolfe *et al* 1974; Smith 1976b; Young 1977).

Figure 9.3 is a curriculum process system which combines the major features of a number of cyclic models and incorporates most of the refinements suggested by research (Biddle 1976a). An analysis of the components in Fig. 9.3 can be used to identify the questions which have to be answered by teachers and consultants in curriculum planning committees when they are involved in the formulation of geography curricula.

The curriculum process system provides the framework for for-

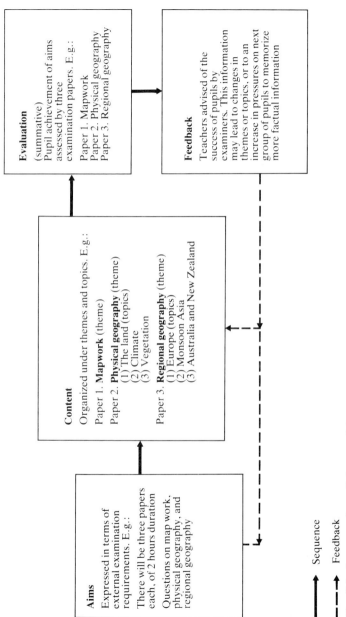

Aims

Expressed in terms of external examination requirements. E.g.:

There will be three papers each, of 2 hours duration

Questions on map work, physical geography, and regional geography

Content

Organized under themes and topics. E.g.:

Paper 1. **Mapwork** (theme)

Paper 2. **Physical geography** (theme)
  (1) The land (topics)
  (2) Climate
  (3) Vegetation

Paper 3. **Regional geography** (theme)
  (1) Europe (topics)
  (2) Monsoon Asia
  (3) Australia and New Zealand

Evaluation

(summative)
Pupil achievement of aims assessed by three examination papers. E.g.:

Paper 1. Mapwork
Paper 2. Physical geography
Paper 3. Regional geography

Feedback

Teachers advised of the success of pupils by examiners. This information may lead to changes in themes or topics, or to an increase in pressures on next group of pupils to memorize more factual information

→ Sequence

--→ Feedback

Fig. 9.1 A geography syllabus model

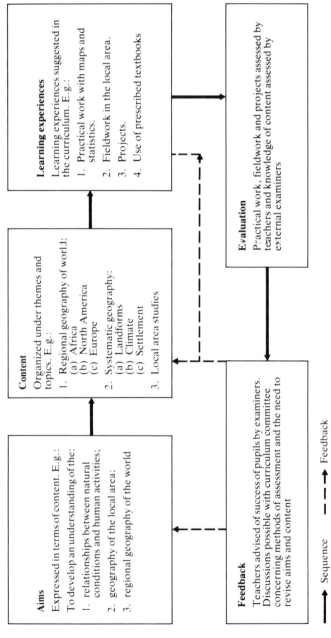

Aims

Expressed in terms of content. E.g.:

To develop an understanding of the:

1. relationships between natural conditions and human activities;
2. geography of the local area;
3. regional geography of the world

Content

Organized under themes and topics. E.g.:

1. Regional geography of world:
   (a) Africa
   (b) North America
   (c) Europe
2. Systematic geography:
   (a) Landforms
   (b) Climate
   (c) Settlement
3. Local area studies

Learning experiences

Learning experiences suggested in the curriculum. E.g.:

1. Practical work with maps and statistics.
2. Fieldwork in the local area.
3. Projects.
4. Use of prescribed textbooks

Evaluation

Practical work, fieldwork and projects assessed by teachers and knowledge of content assessed by external examiners

Feedback

Teachers advised of success of pupils by examiners. Discussions possible with curriculum committee concerning methods of assessment and the need to revise aims and content

→ Sequence   - - → Feedback

Fig. 9.2 A geography curriculum model

mulating a curriculum document. Initially the planning committee has to analyse the research evidence supporting the need for change in the educational system and in the geography curriculum. It has to be aware of constraints associated with:

1. the availability of specialists in geography and of accommodation for teaching geography;
2. the social and cultural background of the parents which affect their life styles and value systems;
3. the interests and abilities of students;
4. problems of disseminating information to schools about curriculum innovations;
5. any administrative difficulties in the school which could be created by special requirements in the curriculum, such as fieldwork.

The selection of long-term aims for the curriculum should be related to the stated purposes of education where these exist, and to the educational environment of which the school is a part. These aims assist the planning committee to select a structure of geography which provides an organizational framework for developing a curriculum.

Since the structure selected will be related to the achievement of the long-term aims it should assist the curriculum committee to translate these aims into educational objectives which may be classified, for example as in Fig. 9.3, into knowledge, skills and values. These educational objectives then provide the guidelines for selecting the themes or problems which are used to combine the content and methods of geography with selected learning experiences in order to achieve the intended learning outcomes (see organized learning centres in Fig. 9.3).

Finally, evaluation is an integral part of the curriculum process. The techniques of evaluation used must be flexible enough to incorporate the chain of repercussions which occur within the learning environment when a new curriculum is introduced. In addition, the evaluator must be just as concerned with the effects of changes in the curriculum on teachers and parents as with the cognitive, psychomotor and affective development of students.

Evaluation can be applied in the initial, formative and summative stages (Bloom *et al* 1971). Initial evaluation is an aspect of the analysis of the need for change in the curriculum; formative or ongoing evaluation is related to interaction between the curriculum committee and teachers who are either involved in pilot-teaching the course, or in discussing its viability in different learning environments at conference and workshop sessions; while summative or terminal evaluation is the result of an investigation of the impact of the curriculum on students, teacher and parents by an evaluator who has not been involved in formulating or pilot-teaching the curriculum. Each of these forms of evaluation are an essential component in the

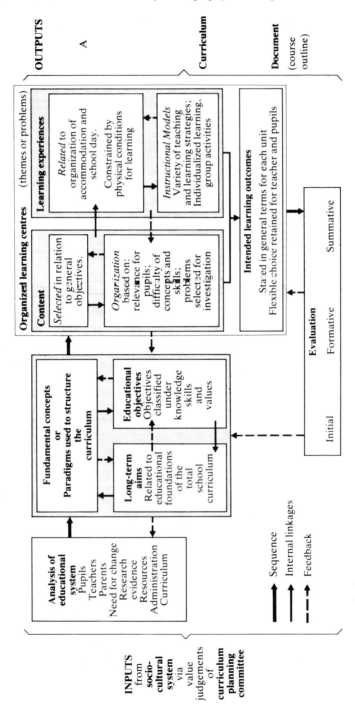

Fig. 9.3 A curriculum process system

formulation and implementation of geography curricula (see Ch. 10 ·on the evaluation of geographical education).

Ways of structuring geography curricula

One of the major advantages of using the disciplines of knowledge as the basis for selecting subjects to be studied by students in the secondary school is that each discipline has one or more structures, which provide research workers with guidelines in their investigations and teachers with a means of gaining cohesion in a syllabus consisting of a variety of themes and topics. There are a number of organizational frameworks used in the development of geography curricula, but the principal structures to be discussed in this chapter are:
1. the continental and regional structure;
2. the conceptual structure of geography;
3. research paradigms as structures.

1. Continental and regional structure

Probably the best known and most universally accepted organizational framework up to the 1960s, but still found frequently in school programmes, was based on geography viewed as the study of areal differentiation. The structure used is the study of world continents and their subdivision into regions, which may be identified in a number of ways. For example, regional boundaries can be delineated by the spatial distribution of an element or combination of elements of the natural environment or of the dominant type of agriculture or of the impact of people's cultural heritage and social organization on their use of the land. An example of the kind of syllabus which emanated from this approach is the *regional geography of the world syllabus* (Long and Roberson 1966).

In this syllabus, emphasis is on the subdivision of countries or continents into regions and on the explanatory description of these regions. In the first year the local district is included as a field laboratory in which students are introduced to skills of observation, recording of data and explanatory description of the landscape. In most cases a general descriptive coverage of the home country is included. In the second year the continents most remote from the home country are studied because teachers assume that their regions are not as relevant for students as are neighbouring regions, or because they are believed to be easier for students to study. As the course progresses in the third and fourth years the more densely populated regions are analysed and problems of resource utilization considered. In the final year the home country is studied in detail in conjunction with a revision of world regional geography, although the latter topic is usually found in educational systems where the students are candidates for an external examination in geography.

If this approach is used in an English school the pattern of the course may be as follows:

Year 1. The local district and the British Isles
　　　2. The southern continents: *Africa, Australasia and South America*
　　　3. North America and Asia
　　　4. Europe
　　　5. British Isles and world revision

This type of syllabus has been accepted as a model by teachers for many years because it is easy to plan school programmes based on the continents, and there is a plentiful supply of regional textbooks written for students which indicate the order of treatment of each continent and provide revision questions. In effect for some teachers, the textbook becomes the school programme and it provides their lesson summaries.

There are some problems with the continental and regional approach. Because of the large number of regions it is possible to study during a secondary school course, and the pressures on students to memorize considerable quantities of factual information to satisfy the requirements of external examinations, regional description can develop into a stereotyped approach commencing with elements of the physical and biotic environments, which frequently take a disproportionate amount of the time available, and ending with studies of human responses to environments within selected regions. Consequently, this approach has been criticized in recent years by students, parents, research workers in geography and teachers who have studied in universities where the emphasis in geographical studies has been on systematic geography and/or on the development of skills in investigating spatial problems.

This criticism of a regional approach which emphasized the unique characteristics of each region led to more emphasis on systematic geography, but still within a regional framework (Biddle 1972). The study of the *systematic and regional geography of the world* takes the following form:

Africa

General physical structure;

Climatic forces in operation and regional climates; climate–vegetation relationships and biogeographical regions in low and middle latitudes;

Modes of land-use and relation of land-use regions to biogeographical regions;

Nature and distribution of chief mineral deposits;

Distribution and density of population.

Asia

General physical structure;

Climate–vegetation relationships; monsoon climates and climate–vegetation relationships in monsoon areas; modification of natural vegetation by man; land-use methods and population densities in monsoon lands;

Population densities and standards of living. Distribution of population between urban and rural areas;

Urbanization; functions of villages, towns and cities; rural–urban relationships;

Analysis of regions based on land-use characteristics.

The intention is that each continent is included in the course and that the emphasis is on the study of the systematic geography of each of the physical, biotic and cultural elements and of their interrelationships at world, continental and smaller areal scales.

The belief of some students and teachers that the geography course should be made more relevant for students, by explaining spatial distributions in the local environment and the home country before introducing foreign examples, led to the development of the *concentric syllabus* (Briault and Shave 1960). This approach commences with studies in the local district, moves to studies of regions in the home country, regions in the home continent and then to regions in more distant parts of the world. In addition, an aspect of systematic geography is included in the study of these regions, and students are given practice in the research techniques of geography. The unifying thread running through this concentric pattern of regional studies is a theme or topic linking them together and associating them with the systematic geography topic selected. An example of a syllabus based on this approach in an Australian school is:

Theme:	*Mid-latitude deserts*
Local district:	Greengrocer's shop (dates). Plotting location of food shops on maps. Suggesting reasons for the location of food shops in relation to other types of shops.

New South Wales:	Broken Hill – A city in the desert.
Australia:	The Centre – cattle grazing and mining.
World:	Kerman Desert, Iran – irrigation farming; the *qanat* system.
	Saltan Trough, Imperial and Coachella valleys, California, USA – irrigation farming; the large-scale dam and water reticulation system.
Systematic geography:	World climatic patterns and the location of deserts. Desert resource systems.

Theme:	*Population*
Local districts:	Population statistics. Finding information in census returns.
New South Wales:	Distribution of population – coastal locations versus the inland.
Australia:	Percentage of population in capital cities; primate cities; centralization and decentralization.
World:	Population studies of the United Kingdom, India and Japan – areas of high population density.
Systematic geography:	Problems of population pressure on food and raw material resources.

These two themes could be allocated all the scheduled lessons in geography for a period of 10 to 12 weeks. In order to retain cohesion in this kind of syllabus teachers have to prepare summaries or matrices to ensure a regional coverage of the world, the inclusion of a study of each of the elements in systematic geography and of the techniques and procedures used in solving geographical problems.

Each of these three syllabus examples are based on a continental and regional structure, or to be more precise on the view that geography is concerned mainly with the study of areal differentiation. Each of these approaches can be identified today in the educational systems of both developing and developed countries, and regional textbooks are available for teachers who prefer these kinds of courses.

2. Conceptual structure of geography

In the 1960s the tremendous growth in factual information, due to the increase of expenditure on research and the improvements in technology for processing data, led philosophers and psychologists in education to question the emphasis on factual learning in the schools. Their conclusions were that the memorization of facts in a discipline or subject placed too much emphasis on the end-products of other people's thinking and not enough on the process of their own thinking; that disciplines were not to be defined by the objects they study but by the kinds of questions they asked and the conceptual structures they used; and that students should learn the skills of thinking and the ways of ordering reality so they could learn more efficiently in the future (Greco 1967; Graves 1980; McCaskill 1977).

Geographical educationists, who were looking for alternative approaches to geography curricula, became interested in these views and began to focus attention on the identification of the fundamental concepts in geography (Stringer 1975). Many lists of these concepts were prepared and an analysis of these lists provide the basis for formulating a model of a conceptual structure of geography as in Fig. 9.4 (Shortle 1975). This model may be used as a means of structuring a geography curriculum for students of varying age and ability levels.

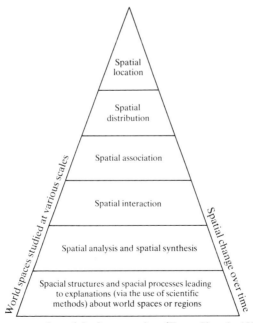

Fig. 9.4 A conceptual model of geography. (From Shortle 1975)

One of the aims of a curriculum based on this approach would be to lead students to the formulation of concepts appropriate to a study of geography which could be derived from the pupils' experience and understanding during the course. The other aims can vary considerably, for outside the general relationships of the concepts shown in a conceptual structure of geography there is no organizing framework which limits the selection of content and skills in the curriculum. In most cases this problem is overcome by the selection of organized learning centres based on themes and the division of these themes into topics.

For example, a curriculum committee could, after analysing the educational system, decide that the aims of the geography curriculum could be:

1. To identify the relationships that exist between people living in society and the environments in which they live.
2. To develop attitudes that will provide a basis for students' understanding of different cultures and of world problems.
3. To lead students to the formulation of concepts derived from experience and understanding appropriate for identifying and solving spatial questions.
4. To encourage students to systematize and give coherence to data through classification.
5. To develop students' skills in the application of data to the solution of problems.

These aims may be achieved by developing an organized learning centre based on a theme such as *Human Responses to Resources*. The kind of educational objectives which could be achieved through this theme are:

1. A *knowledge* of:
   (a) organizing concepts such as spatial location, spatial distribution, spatial association, spatial interaction, spatial change over time, conservation, energy and movement;
   (b) human responses to resources in the home country;
   (c) human responses to resources in other countries;
   (d) the implications of the use of resources for future generations.

2. *Skills* in:
   (a) the use of problem-solving techniques;
   (b) the application of these techniques to the solution of problems associated with human responses to resources;
   (c) the presentation of these solutions so as to influence individuals who can initiate activities to implement them.

3. *Values* which will provide the basis for developing:
   (a) an attitude of objectivity in inquiry;
   (b) an appreciation of cultural differences;

(c) respect and responsibility for the quality of the environment;
(d) an awareness of the need for planned use and conservation of resources.

From these educational objectives the following types of instructional units could be organized on the theme: *Human Responses to Resources* for a school in a region or country, e.g. Nigeria.
1. the nature and distribution of resources in Nigeria;
2. environmental impact of agricultural activities in Nigeria;
3. industrial activities and natural resources in Nigeria;
4. human responses to urban systems in Nigeria;
5. the individual, the environment and the future.
Each of these units could be extended by reference to, and comparison with, human responses to resources in other regions and/ or countries.

This approach to curriculum development in geography has gained the support of educationists who are continually searching for ways of integrating the social sciences. They argue that by identifying the fundamental organizing concepts of each discipline it is possible to formulate multi-disciplinary or inter-disciplinary curricula based on the solution of problems. The integrating elements are the major ideas or concepts in each discipline which they claim can be orchestrated in the solution of particular world problems.

3. Research paradigms as structures

Some geographical educationists have not supported the use of a single conceptual structure of geography as a basis for curriculum development on the grounds that it is a reductionist approach with the inherent disadvantage that it effectively camouflages the diversity of interests of research workers and could, therefore, eliminate a number of interesting approaches to the organization of geography curricula. Consequently, they have preferred to use research paradigms which are structures of beliefs which guide research workers in the selection and solution of problems, and in the evaluation and critical analysis of the solutions to these problems (Biddle 1976b). For example, the ecosystem paradigm and problems associated with environmental quality, or the environmental paradigm and problems associated with decision-making. It follows that the selection of a paradigm by a research worker in geography focuses attention on certain kinds of spatial problems which emanate from a particular image of the world and a particular interpretation of perceptual experience.

In Fig. 9.5 six intersecting paradigms have been suggested to be appropriate for providing cohesion in geography curricula. Each of

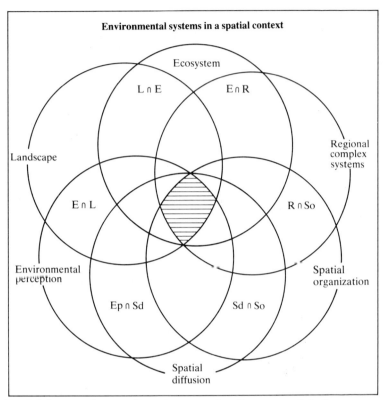

Fig. 9.5 Intersecting paradigms in geography. One approach to the representation of the interrelationships among the major paradigms employed by research workers in geography is to use a Venn diagram and to regard the paradigms as six intersecting sets within an environmental systems set. That is, the complement to the E (ecosystem) set would be R (regional complex systems), So (spatial organization), Sd (spatial diffusion), Ep (environmental perception), L (landscape), and the intersecting sets, within the overarching Es (environmental systems) set.

these paradigms is supported by a community of scholars who publish their research findings and attract students in tertiary institutions to their approach to spatial problems.

An investigation of research publications using these paradigms, or a combination of them, provides information for constructing conceptual models, based on the interrelationships among a number of organizing concepts, to guide the organization and format of curriculum documents.

By selecting a paradigm to achieve long-term aims the teacher is beginning a process which should lead students to concentrate their attention on identifying significant variables for solving particular problems. That is, these students would be learning to find solutions to problems using a structure of geography which would be similar to that used by some research workers.

The paradigm selected by the teacher provides the guidelines for translating aims into educational objectives under the categories of knowledge, skills and values, and from these objectives instructional units can be organized. For example, if the curriculum planning committee believe, after analysing the educational system, that students are at the stage of development where they can apply logical thinking to problems of maintaining an ecological balance in the environment, they may decide that the aims of geography should be to develop skills in the formulation and testing of hypotheses as a means of finding solutions to these problems. In this example it is obvious that the ecosystem paradigm could be used as the basis for a conceptual model (see Fig. 9.6) to provide a structure for this kind of curriculum because it emphasizes inputs, processes, linkages, flows of energy, information and matter, outputs and feedback mechanisms. Examples of the kinds of educational objectives which may be achieved through this approach are the development of:

1. *Knowledge:*
   (a) of concepts such as inputs, energy, information, matter, processes, linkages, feedback, outputs, spatial interaction, movement, resources, environments, regional systems;
   (b) that people are an inseparable part of a system consisting of the physical, biological and socio-cultural environments;
   (c) that people are centrally placed in the system and can alter the interrelationships within it;
   (d) that the nature and magnitude of changes in the system are a result of people's decisions and activities;
   (e) that people's decisions and activities can adversely affect the quality of present and future environments;
   (f) that since man produces these changes in the environment it is possible to take action to improve or maintain the quality of the environment;
   (g) that there are democratic procedures that can be used for the solution of environmental problems.

2. The development of *skills* for solving problems occurring in ecosystems by:
   (a) formulating hypotheses;
   (b) testing each hypothesis by:
      (i) analysing the hypothesis to discover the type of information required;
      (ii) collecting information from resource materials and/or from fieldwork;

INPUTS: Matter – Energy – Information

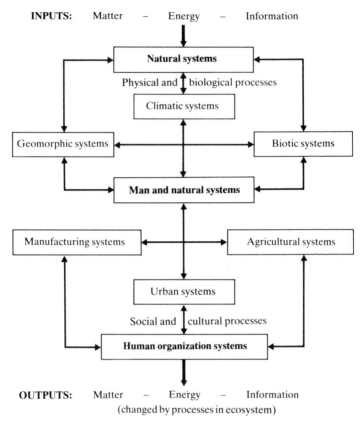

OUTPUTS: Matter – Energy – Information
(changed by processes in ecosystem)

Fig. 9.6 A conceptual model for curriculum development based on the ecosystem paradigm. (Emphasis is on process, on the flows of energy, information, matter and on feedback mechanisms)

    (iii) interpreting the information;
    (c) presenting a solution to the problem within the framework of the information available.
3. *Values revealing:*
    (a) a concern for the quality of life in local, national and global human ecosystems which will motivate students to participate in solving these problems;
    (b) an understanding of the need for objectivity in inquiry;
    (c) a respect for other people's opinions, and for their right to express different opinions from those held by the students;
    (d) an awareness of the importance of co-operation with other members of the community for the purpose of solving problems in human ecosystems.

These educational objectives provide guidelines for selecting organized learning centres based on themes such as:
1. areal studies of environmental impact;
2. environmental changes initiated by man;
3. conflicts in man–environment relationships;
4. future prospects for man and the environment.

Each of these themes may be further subdivided into topics which may be used as the basis for planning instructional units. For example, possible topics to be studied as part of *Theme 3: Conflicts in Man–Environment Relationships* could be:
(a) beach mining in recreational areas;
(b) pollution and congestion in cities;
(c) construction of major highways through residential areas;
(d) forest-clearing by farmers on steep slopes; and
(e) the expansion of urban settlements in rural areas.

Similarly in *Theme 4: Future Prospects for Man and the Environment* possible topics could be:
(a) population pressures on resources in selected areas;
(b) conservation of resources;
(c) global patterns of waste disposal;
(d) allocation of space for leisure activities and recreation;
(e) development of more efficient means of communication and transportation;
(f) the world distribution of wealth; spatial disparities in wealth and human welfare.

It is obvious, therefore, that by using the ecosystem approach it is possible to identify a number of topics which would be relevant for students of varying age and ability levels (Biddle 1976a).

At a later stage in student development the curriculum committee might select aims which are achieved more effectively through a conceptual model based on the spatial organization paradigm (see Fig. 9.7). This paradigm emphasizes the study of spatial structures and processes contributing to spatial organization and the formulation of spatial theories with predictive functions. Examples of the kinds of educational objectives which may be achieved through the spatial organization paradigm are the development of:

1. *A knowledge of:*
   (a) fundamental organizing concepts in the study of urban spatial systems such as spatial location, central place, spatial distribution, spatial association and interaction, spatial structure, spatial order;
   (b) the tendency for the size and spacing of urban systems to take on distinctive and recognizable patterns;
   (c) the importance of mental maps and the diffusion of innovations on decision-making in urban systems;

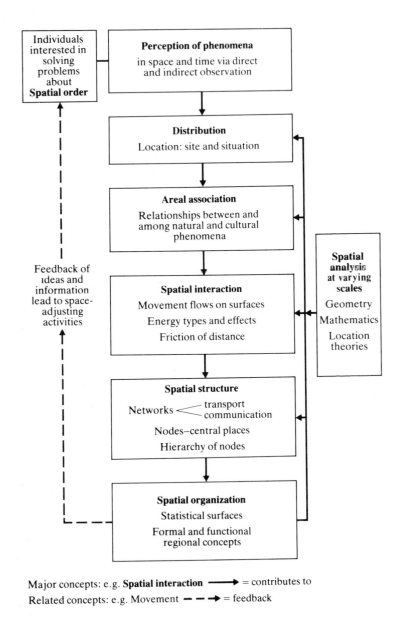

Major concepts: e.g. **Spatial interaction** ──────▶ = contributes to

Related concepts: e.g. Movement ─ ─ ─▶ = feedback

Fig. 9.7 A conceptual model for curriculum development based on the spatial organization paradigm. (Emphasis is on the study of spatial structures and processes contributing to spatial organization and formulation of spatial theories with predictive functions.)

(*d*) how changes in the urban system can lead to social problems and the deterioration of the quality of the urban environment.

2. *Skills in:*
   (*a*) decision-making through participation in role-playing games;
   (*b*) the appraisal of the implications of the decisions reached for urban systems;
   (*c*) the presentation of these solutions so as to influence individuals who can initiate activities to implement them;

3. *Values which indicate:*
   (*a*) an awareness of modes of conduct which enable discussion to proceed smoothly and constructively in group situations;
   (*b*) a recognition of the importance of objective procedures in problem-solving and decision-making;
   (*c*) a recognition of the effect of value judgements in the interpretation of data and on decision-making;
   (*d*) a willingness critically to examine the rationale for internalized personal values;
   (*e*) an appreciation of the need for individuals and groups to co-operate in the maintenance and improvement of urban environments.

The following themes provide the basis for organized learning centres which could assist the teacher to achieve these educational objectives:

1. the development of urban areas;
2. the urban area as a central place;
3. spatial patterns in cities;
4. social implications of planning in cities;
5. problems of urban areas.

These themes can then be divided into instructional units by reference to specific urban areas.

The translation of aims into educational objectives can be demonstrated in a similar manner using the landscape, spatial diffusion, environmental perception and regional complex system paradigms to develop conceptual models (Biddle 1976b). This approach to curriculum development in geography is a flexible one in which curriculum committees or teachers may choose to use different paradigms or a combination of them, to formulate curricula for one or more years, or develop courses for shorter periods based on the organization of the school year. The paradigms provide structures for organizing instructional units which give cohesion to the geography curriculum; they add to the interest and relevance of geographical studies for students by indicating a variety of ways of looking at spatial problems; and they should lead pupils to an awareness of the importance of value judgements in decision-making.

In this section three major approaches to structuring geography curricula have been described and illustrated. They represent a sequential development of ideas about the changing nature of geography and of the need for teachers to retain close links with research workers in both geography and education. Once the curriculum committee has made a decision on the appropriate structure to be used the next step is to consider the preparation of a curriculum document.

A curriculum document

The content and format of a curriculum is dependent on the curriculum committees' assessment of the needs of teachers in the educational system. In any case, to be identified as a curriculum the document must contain:

1. Aims (long-term) of the curriculum.

2. Description of the structure used to give cohesion to the geography course.

3. General educational objectives categorized as:
   (a) knowledge (concepts and principles);
   (b) skills (cognitive, psychomotor, social);
   (c) values (social norms, personal disciplines).

4. Organized learning centres based on the selection and organization of:
   (a) content of geography;
   (b) learning experiences;
   (c) statement of intended learning outcomes in general terms.

5. Suggestions on methods of assessment to provide data for evaluation of the achievement of objectives in relation to:
   (a) fieldwork;
   (b) individual assignments;
   (c) group projects;
   (d) other learning activities.

   In some countries syllabuses are issued by central educational authorities and contain statements of aims which are not translated into educational objectives. Organized learning centres in these syllabuses consist of themes divided into topics for study with detailed statements of the content to be learned, while evaluation of the course is usually illustrated by a trial examination paper. It is frequently argued that this kind of curriculum is necessary because of the limited professional qualifications of many of the teachers in the education system. Two themes from this type of syllabus illustrate the approach:

Physical geography

Theme 3: Water and the world pattern of climate and vegetation

Topic 3(a) The energy basis of the water cycle
Heat balance of the atmosphere and the earth's surface; exchange of energy.

Topic 3(b) Local accumulations of energy
The significance of latent heat; condensation and the form of clouds; stability and instability; air masses and source regions; frontal activity and characteristic frontal situations; weather sequences and the climatic pattern in the local area.

Topic 3(c) Climatic variations throughout the world
Climatic types; importance of the interplay of air masses.

Topic 3(d) Relationship of climatic types to types of vegetation
Serial progression, climax associations, dynamic change; major associations and their distribution; the significance of fire, man and domestic animals in vegetational systems.

Human geography

Theme 6: Urban studies

Topic 6(a) Urban development
Broad world patterns of urban development; trends of urban concentration.

Topic 6(b) Urban hierarchies
Forces affecting size, spacing and character of towns; towns in their regional settings; impact of technological changes on the size and spacing of towns; towns in relation to transport nets and transport nodes.

Topic 6(c) Force of internal differentiation
Regions within towns; individual nodes and distinctive regions; functional differentiation of area; trend of continued change in pattern and population; problems for the future.

Types of examination questions

Question 1 'The interplay of air masses determines the climate of an area.' Discuss this statement with reference to any two mid-latitude climates.

Question 2 To what extent have changes in the technology of transport contributed to changes in the land-use patterns within cities?

Question 3 'The rapid growth of cities in developing countries is creating many problems for the inhabitants of these cities.' Discuss this statement with reference to one large city in either south-east Asia or India.

In a situation where teachers feel the need for considerable support from the educational authorities, the development of a curriculum research division in the education department to meet these needs would appear to be a logical alternative. This division could produce a more detailed curriculum document containing examples of a school programme based on a theme and its subdivision into instructional units as shown in Table 9.1. In some educational

Table 9.1 Theme: Interaction of people and environment in areas of high rural population density. Unit: Intensive subsistence agriculture based on rice

Content

Concepts	Methods and topics	Case studies
Spatial Location Distribution Association Interaction Analysis Synthesis Processes	1. Map *interpretation* with inferences, e.g. highest population densities and maximum rice production occur in fertile river valleys.	Monsoon Asian landscape
	2. Soil *experiments*, e.g. soil permeability	Yadaw – an irrigated rice-growing village of Asia
	3. River studies	The Baga Serai Triangle
	4. Patterns of agriculture	
	5. *Interaction* Use of rivers through time by various socio-cultural groups: Modification of soil Effect on landscapes Conservation	Growing rice in Thailand Growing rice in southern Bihar

systems explanatory notes and suggested approaches to particular units are supplied to teachers, usually at the request of the teachers' representatives on the curriculum committee. In other systems educational research projects and commercial interests prepare curriculum packages which interpret the units. These packages contain educational objectives, teaching resources, learning experiences appropriate for the unit, criterion-referenced tests and other techniques of assessment to enable the teacher to evaluate the achievement of objectives.

Package-type curricula are exemplified by the American High School Geography Project (Gunn 1972) and the Schools Council Project Geography for the Young School Leaver (Beddis *et al* 1972–1975). Each of these projects is based on a curriculum process model and contains references to aims, educational objectives, learning experiences and evaluation; each contains collections of teaching

Resources

Books	*Materials*
B. O'Rourke and R. J. Frisken, *Skills and Systematics of Landscape Geography*, p. 88, Ex. 3	Bunnett, *Map Reading for Malaysian Students*, Map 2
P. Lant, *Agricultural Geography*, Vol. 1, p. 16	NSW Geography Teachers Association, *Landscape Picture Study Sets.*
P. G. Irwin, *Monsoon Asia*	Unesco Geography Series for Asia: No. 2 Indonesia
C. S. Freestone, *The South East Asian Village*, p. 62	3 and 4 The Philippines 5 Burma
A. B. A. Hutson, *Sample Studies Around the World*, p. 99	6 India 7 Cambodia
H. G. Roepke (ed.), *Readings in Economic Geography*, p. 100	SVE filmstrip: Modern Indonesia and the Philippines
M. Simons, *Poverty and Wealth in Cities and Villages*, p. 62	Unipack: Indian Village
	National Geog. Soc. Enc. Britannica kit: South-east Asia – includes seven filmstrips and records.

Table 9.2 Summary of a geography curriculum for the 7th to 10th years of school

1. **Introductory statements**
    (a) *The place of geography in school years 7 to 10*
        (i) Emphasis on preparing students to live in contemporary society.
        (ii) Variations in place of geography in disciplinary, multi-disciplinary and inter-disciplinary courses.

    (b) *Geography today*
        (i) Geography is concerned with spatial problems, behavioural problems and patterns of interaction of people and environments around the world.
        (ii) Various approaches to the structuring and presentation of geography are used, such as the landscape, systems, ecosystem, regional studies, spatial organization, environmental perception and behaviour.

    (c) *Advantages of structuring the geography curriculum*
        (i) Necessary in a flexible, pupil oriented curriculum.
        (ii) Cohesion of units.
        (iii) Variations in geographical viewpoints possible.

    (d) *Implementation of the aims and objectives of the curriculum*
        (i) Aims.
        (ii) Translating aims into specific objectives in instructional units within a course structure.
        (iii) Organizing concepts and principles.
        (iv) Skill development.
        (v) Evaluation of the achievement of aims and objectives.

2. **Aims and objectives**
    (a) Aims are broad intentions providing guidelines in a curriculum.
    (b) Objectives are specific intentions underlying an instructional unit categorized as knowledge, skill and value objectives.

3. **Planning the course**
    (a) Planning based on models of research paradigms in geography with knowledge, skill and value objectives suggested.
    (b) Selecting and planning of themes and units.
        (i) Definition of themes.
        (ii) Possible themes.
        (iii) Definition of units.
        (iv) Possible units.
    (c) Criteria for the selection of themes and units.
        (i) Learner-based.
        (ii) Teacher-based.
        (iii) Community-based.

(d) Developing a course.
 (i) Determine length of course.
 (ii) Look at the total curriculum of the school.
 (iii) Consider the aims and objectives of the curriculum.
 (iv) Select the paradigm, or combination of paradigms, to provide the structure of the course.
 (v) Prepare a plan of themes and units.
 (vi) Prepare sequence of skills to be developed.
 (vii) Prepare unit outlines to include a statement of objectives, selection and organization of content including concepts and principles, selection of learning experiences and techniques of evaluation of learner progress.
 (viii) Make a time allowance for course and pupil evaluation procedures.

4. Concepts
(a) Explanation of use of concepts in everyday experience.
(b) Definition of concepts.
(c) Types of concepts.
(d) Designing courses around concepts.
(e) Order of difficulty of concepts.

5. Skill objectives
(a) Features of skills.
(b) Types of skills.
(c) Skill objectives for the curriculum.
 (i) Observation and recognition of phenomena.
 (ii) Collecting and recording relevant information.
 (iii) Selecting questions and framing hypotheses.
 (iv) Interpretation, analysis and synthesis of phenomena.
 (v) Interpretation of data.
 (vi) Effective communication.

6. Evaluation
(a) What is evaluation?
(b) Why evaluate?
(c) When to evaluate?
(d) How to evaluate?

Table 9.3 Guidelines for course construction

1. The students
Readiness of students to be assessed in terms of:
(a) stage of development;
(b) prior learning;
(c) present interests.

2. What are appropriate issues to be considered by students?
Refer to:
(a) interests of students;
(b) stage of development of students;
(c) educational aims of the school;
(d) possibility of translating these educational aims into general objectives to be achieved through geography.

3. What learning experiences would be most beneficial to students?
Decisions about these learning experiences would be based on:
(a) time available;
(b) readiness of students;
(c) interests of students;
(d) nature of the issue or problem to be investigated;
(e) resources available inside and outside the school:
    (i) materials;
    (ii) staff and other resource personnel;
    (iii) accommodation;
    (iv) equipment including audio-visual.
(f) Dimensions of balance in the curriculum.
    (i) Area balance in terms of real and hypothetical areas; local and foreign areas; areas studied at various scales; changing criteria for the selection of areas.
    (ii) Topic balance in terms of physical, biological and socio-cultural elements in the environment.
    (iii) Organizing concept balance. Each of the major organizing concepts to be used.
    (iv) Problems balance based on description, explanation, speculation and normative judgements.

Each of these dimensions of balance can be checked by preparing matrices with the time available on the vertical axis and the dimensions on the horizontal axis.

Table 9.4 Suggested format of an instructional unit

---

1. Name of topic.

2. Reason for selection of this topic.

3. General objectives.
    (a) Knowledge (cognitive domain).
    (b) Skills: processes and skills related to abilities (cognitive, psychomotor and social).
(c)   *Values (affective):*
        (i) norms;
        (ii) predilections.

4. Organized centres for learning.
  (a) Selection and organization of content:
  (i) facts;
  (ii) concrete concepts;
  (iii) abstract concepts;
  (iv) generalizations;
  (v) procedures.
  (b) Selection and organization of learning environments:
  (i) large groups;
  (ii) small group;
  (iii) individual.
  (c) Intended learning outcomes (behaviourally or procedurally defined)

5. Evaluation.
  (a) Preparation of pre-test items, or initial evaluation.
  (b) Continuous assessment to guide remedial work, or formative evaluation.
  (c) Fieldwork and assignments.
  (d) Preparation of post-test items, or summative evaluation.

6. Bibliography of multi-media resources.

---

resources sufficient in number to cater for the needs of students; and each suggests approaches to the use of these materials in the classroom in both disciplinary and inter-disciplinary courses. It is unwise, however, for teachers to use these packages without significant modifications if they are teaching in another country, for the curriculum is a product of the values and resources of the socio-cultural system in which it is developed, as evidenced by Fig. 9.3.

In these examples the teacher has few decisions to make and it could be said that the developers aspired to produce reasonably 'teacher-proof' packages, especially for teachers not adequately prepared to use the new approaches to instruction. Although this approach is not acceptable to many teachers, particularly those who have high qualifications and strong commitments to education, they may use the packages to gain other points of view and to develop new teaching strategies.

In countries where teachers are well qualified and feel professionally competent to formulate school-based geography curricula, and where terminal assessment of students is the responsibility of each school, two approaches have been used based on the wishes of parents and teachers.

The first is the preparation by a curriculum committee of a document which provides guidelines only for each of the curriculum components and allows the teacher considerable freedom in the selection of content. This kind of curriculum document is summarized in Table 9.2 (Smith 1976b).

The second approach is to provide no guidance to the teacher but to appoint curriculum consultants to regions containing up to ten schools and to arrange for the geography teachers from these schools to meet in workshop sessions to develop their own guidelines for course construction (see Fig. 9.3 and Table 9.3) (SGEP 1975).

It is evident from this review of approaches to the content and format of curriculum documents that the approach selected is related to the teachers' professional qualifications in geography, to their knowledge of curriculum theory and their expertise in translating general aims into the practical situation in the classroom; and to the amount of freedom in curriculum planning society is prepared to give its teachers through its educational authorities.

Table 9.5 Instructional Unit 1: Desert landscapes (content and skill oriented)

Date	Case studies	Analyses
Start	1. Kerman Desert, Iran	Analysis of each desert landscape case study
	2. Saltan Trough, Imperial and Coachella valleys, USA	*Natural systems:* Explanatory description of vegetation and animal life, climate, soil and landforms. Interrelationships of natural elements in desert systems. Effects of climate change.
4 weeks	3. The Centre, Australia	
	World distribution of desert landscapes with particular reference to the:	
	1. Iranian Desert	*Human organization systems:* Variations in the interrelationships of socio-cultural elements in desert systems. People's perception of desert resource systems
	2. Deserts of California, USA	
	3. Deserts of central Australia	
		Problems of maintaining quality of desert resource systems. Problems for people living in deserts – water, transport, health linkages between desert resource systems and other world systems

Planning instructional units

No matter what approach is used to formulate the curriculum document the teacher has to analyse both the curriculum and the class situation before he or she prepares each of the instructional units which make up the course for a school term or a year. There are three principal factors to consider in the analysis of the class situation. These are:

1. *Students*
   (a) Stage of development including levels of ability and aptitude.
   (b) Prior knowledge of topic.
   (c) Present interests.
   (d) Attitudes to learning.

2. *School organization*
   (a) Time allocation for geography.
   (b) Length of lessons – single or multiple lessons.

Techniques and skills	Concepts
Reading and interpreting topographic maps, aerial photos and regional maps of desert areas	Examples of major concepts *Abstract concepts*
Reading and interpreting statistical tables and diagrams prepared by investigators of desert areas	Ecosystem Landscape Natural systems Human organization systems
Developing problem-solving skills in relation to desert resource systems	Spatial analysis: distribution and pattern, association, interaction, change over time
Presentation of materials to support arguments about the appropriate relationships between people and desert resource systems	Spatial synthesis: regional, concept, structures *Concrete concepts* Referred to as they arise in discussions

(c) Flexibility of the timetable.
(d) Geography in relation to the total school curriculum.
3. *Resources for learning*
   (a) Size of classrooms.
   (b) Types of furniture.
   (c) Availability of multi-media resources.
   (d) Qualifications of teachers.
   (e) Teaching aids and other resource personnel.

On completion of this analysis the teacher has to decide on the design of the instructional unit. There are many designs used in practice and Table 9.4, which is based on a curriculum process model (see Fig. 9.3), incorporates most of the major components generally found in units. The greatest contrasts exist in the amount of information that teachers include in the units, and this is illustrated in Tables 9.5, 9.6 and 9.7.

Table 9.5, an instructional unit on desert landscapes, is content- and skill-oriented, whereas Table 9.6 on the same topic includes information on the educational objectives, organizing concepts in the unit, instructional objectives defined in behavioural and procedural terms, learning activities, learning resources and evaluation. Table 9.7 is a more detailed attempt to state behavioural and procedural objectives in general terms and as specific intended learning outcomes.

The kind of unit design used by geography teachers depends on the preference of the teacher; the time he/she has available for planning; the availability of resources for research and the nature of the library resources in the school; and the teacher's knowledge and skills in geography and in curriculum.

Multi-disciplinary and inter-disciplinary units

Multi-disciplinary units are those in which each of the disciplines is studied in parallel so that interrelationships may be stressed, but differences between the disciplines are preserved. The use of team teaching is usually associated with this approach. One example of a multi-disciplinary unit could be a study of 'Environmental problems in a city'. This study would require knowledge of geology, biology, meteorology, technology, geography, economics, sociology and political science and could be taught by a team of teachers from the science, industrial arts, art, social science and history departments. One of the objectives of this unit would be the identification of the contribution of each discipline to an understanding of environmental problems. In addition each member of the team could clarify the interrelationships between his discipline and the other disciplines by using a variety of teaching strategies.

Table 9.6 Instructional Unit 2: Desert landscapes (educational objectives oriented)

THEME: Landscapes of minimum human impact	UNIT: Desert resource systems
TIME ALLOCATION: 4 weeks × 4 40-minute periods per week (16 periods)	LEVEL: Year 11

Educational objectives:
Knowledge and values: To develop pupil understanding of:
1. Desert landscapes in Asia, North America and Australia.
2. The interrelationships of the elements of desert landscape systems.
3. The effects of climatic change on desert landscapes.
4. The impact of people on desert landscapes.
   (a) Influence of people's perception of the environment on desert resource systems
   (b) Problems associated with people's use of desert resource systems.
   (c) Maintaining the quality of desert resource systems.
Skills: To develop in pupils the ability to:
1. Read and interpret topographic maps, aerial photos and regional maps at different scales of desert areas.
2. Abstract, interpret and use written materials, such as reports, tables, census data, graphs, newspaper reports, extracts from relevant journals, magazine articles about desert landscapes.
3. Construct and test hypotheses concerning problems associated with people's use of desert resource systems.
4. Present material and arguments used to solve environmental problems in deserts in an orderly and logical manner.

Organizing concepts in unit
In each case study the following organizing concepts and their associated concepts will be emphasized:
1. Landscape, ecosystem, open system, natural system, human organization system, desert resource system.
2. Spatial analysis of desert landscape systems: spatial distribution and pattern, association, interaction, change over time.
3. Spatial synthesis of desert landscape systems: regional concept, spatial structures.

Instructional objectives
On completion of this unit pupils should be able to:
1. Describe two or more desert landscape systems.
2. Account for the distribution and spatial characteristics of desert landscapes.
3. Analyse desert landscapes using an open system framework.
4. Suggest reasons for variations in people's perception and utilization of desert resource systems.

5. Find solutions to problems of people living in desert landscapes in relation to resource management, isolation, health, transport and capital investment.
6. Recognize linkages between desert resource systems and other world systems.

Learning activities
Introductory:
1. Broadening pupils' perceptual experiences of deserts through film, slide and picture interpretation.
2. Guided discussion on perception of desert environments.
3. Reading and discussing skilled observers' descriptions of desert landscapes.

Developmental:
1. Student research on desert resource systems.
2. Developing models of desert resource systems.
3. Group projects on people's responses to desert resource systems.
   (a) Hunting and gathering groups in central Australia.
   (b) Nomadic herding in the Iranian Desert.
   (c) Cattle-grazing in central Australia.
   (d) Irrigation in the Kerman Desert, Iran.
   (e) Irrigation in the Coachella Valley, USA.
4. Role-play simulation games in relation to a desert resource system to analyse problems of resource management for short-term and long-term gains.
5. Assignments on instructional objectives.
6. Discussion on linkages between desert resource systems and other world systems.

Ongoing and integrative:
1. Comparison of desert landscape systems with other landscapes of minimum human impact.
2. Comparing landscapes of minimum human impact with those of medium and maximum human impact.

Learning resources
Books
1. Barrett, D. T. et al., *Arid and Tropical Lands*, Herman, 1971.
2. Dasmann, R. F. et al., *Ecological Principles for Economic Development*, Wiley, 1973.
3. Faull, J. F., *Desert Lands*, Jacaranda, 1970.
4. Heathcote, R. L. and Twidale, C. R., *The Arid Lands*, Longman, 1972.
5. Hills, E. S., *Arid Lands: A Geographical Appraisal*, Methuen, 1966.
6. Langman, R. C. *Selected Studies in the United States: The Imbalance between People and Water*, McGraw-Hill, 1971.

7. McGinnies, W. G. *et al*, *Deserts of the World. An Appraisal of Research into their Physical and Biological Environments*, University of Arizona Press, 1968.
8. Simons, M., *Deserts: The Problem of Water in Arid Lands*, Oxford University Press, 1968.
9. Van Dyne, G. M. (ed.), *The Ecosystem Concept in Natural Resource Management*, Academic Press, 1969.

Films

> *Back of Beyond*, Shell Oil Co.
> *Man in the Desert*, Commonwealth Film Unit.
> *Man in the Desert*, Australian Visual Education Commission.

Multi-media

> J. Moody, *Arid Lands Study Unit*, Educational Media, Melbourne, 1971.
> *Life in Outback Australia* (slides, study guide, sound cassettes), Educational Media, Melbourne, 1978.

Evaluation

Initial:

1. Written and oral tests of pupils' knowledge of desert landscapes.
2. Assessment of pupils' attitudes to exploitation of resources in deserts.

Formative:

Evaluation of pupils' responses to desert landscape unit using:

1. Questionnaires, rating scales and teacher's perception of pupils' responses.
2. Objective and short answer tests of skills and content.
3. Structured essays to assess knowledge and values on selected topics in the unit.

Summative:

1. Objective tests, structured and open-ended essays as a means of assessing achievement of instructional objectives of this unit.
2. Evaluation of the achievement of educational objectives through cumulative assessment of pupils and terminal assessment of instructional objectives.

Table 9.7 An alternative format for an instructional programme based on units

UNIT TITLE: Environmental Pressure Generated in Southwark and London
TIME ALLOCATION: 8 weeks × 6 40-minute periods per week (48 periods)

Objectives		Content	
Knowledge and values	*Techniques and skills*	*Concepts*	*Topics*
1. Identify the main physical characteristics of built environment and describe the purposes they serve 2. Describe the natural elements which man endeavours to modify or control 3. Analyse the problems of waste disposal 4. Analyse and evaluate the dynamic aspects of urban centres and the consequent problems of growth and sprawl which increase environmental pressures and contribute to deterioration in the quality of life	Formulate hypothesis for each objective then test hypothesis by: 1. Consulting resources in library – reports, books, maps, pictures, slides, films 2. Making direct observations when possible 3. Discussions with authorities such as town planners 4. Critical review of collected information in class seminars 5. Comparison with other possible hypotheses. Accept or reject hypothesis	Built environment, waste disposal, pollution, environmental pressures, congestion, urban sprawl, urban blight, recreational resources.	Examine the nature of the built environment in relation to man's needs for shelter, transport and environmental control Contrast skyline profiles and spatial structure of London with other cities Discuss implications of spatial structure for commuters Describe man's endeavours to control natural elements such as surface run-off, stream banks, high tides and floods, temperature (air conditioning), drought (relate to city water supply) Examine problems associated with disposal of waste

Intended learning outcomes (sample only)	Teacher's resources (examples)
Analyse the problems of waste disposal. Analysis requires division of problem into: *(a)* define types of waste, e.g. materials exhausted into the atmosphere, solid waste, sewage *(b)* describe types of pollution, e.g. of air, land, water and man's senses *(c)* compare the nature of the problems in the cities studied	Jones and Sinclair (eds), *Atlas of London and the London Region*, 1968 Ormsby, 'The London Basin' in *Great Britain: Essays in Regional Geography*, 1928 Dury, 'The London Basin' in *The British Isles: A Systematic and Regional Geography*, 1968 Wise, 'The London Region' in *Great Britain: Geographical Essays*, 1962 Clayton (ed.), *Guide to London Excursions*, 1964 Clayton (ed.), *The Geography of Greater London*, 1964 Martin, *Greater London: An Industrial Geography*, 1966
Topics (cont.)	SE Joint Planning Team, *Strategic Plan for the S.E.*, 1970
Analyse types of pollution affecting quality of life	Barr, *The Assaults on Our Senses*, 1970 Goldsmith (ed.), *Can Britain Survive?*, 1971
Evaluate the consequences of urban growth and sprawl. Suggest future problems and possible solutions	Johnson, *The Politics of Environment, The British Experience*, 1973

Variations
For example: discuss newspaper reports on environmental arguments against third airport at Foulness

Table 9.8 is an example of a multi-disciplinary theme on *population control*. Pupils are introduced to the theme through a focus question: 'Two babies or three?' Questions from five disciplines are selected which could contribute to finding the solution for the focus question. Organizing concepts are also identified for each of the disciplines.

Inter-disciplinary units are those in which content and processes of inquiry from the disciplines are fused around themes, topics, areas, concepts or questions in an attempt to integrate a number of the social sciences and/or the humanities. Many social problems, particularly those which are accentuated by technological change, run across existing boundaries of disciplines. Some teachers prefer to use an inter-disciplinary approach, particularly in the junior years of the secondary school, to investigate these kinds of problems, although the educational assumptions for continuing this approach throughout the year are frequently questioned. In general, process is emphasized and content is selected from various disciplines, but no attempt is made to draw pupils' attention to the disciplines concerned (Bolam 1972; Fenton 1966; Warwick 1973; Williams 1976).

Table 9.9 is an example of an inter-disciplinary theme which is concerned with *river pollution*. The focus question is, 'Why is our river polluted?' and contributing questions are selected at random in an attempt to find a solution to the focus question.

Since the publication of the *Unesco Source Book for Geography Teaching* in 1965 (Brouillette 1965) there has been a tremendous growth in knowledge of the components of the curriculum process and of the effects of the application of this process to the design, implementation and evaluation of geography curricula. This chapter has attempted to explore the significance of these changes for the geography teacher seeking solutions to the questions he has to answer each day in order to be an effective educator.

Table 9.8 A multi-disciplinary theme: *population control.* (*Source:* Smith 1976b)

FOCUS QUESTION: Two babies or three?

Geography	Economics	Sociology and demography	Asian studies	History
Where is the world's population distributed?	How do changes in population affect the needs and wants of society?	What effect does an increase in family size have upon other members?	Is Asia over-populated?	At what times has population increased or decreased?
What regions of the world are most heavily populated?			Are parts of Asia over-populated?	What factors cause increases or decreases?
	How do these changes affect the workforce and employment?	What is the optimum family size?	Is there an imbalance in the population and resources ratio of Asia?	What effect has population change had upon social organization of different groups of people?
How does the distribution vary from area to area?		How do parents' roles differ in different families?		
Why is population distributed in this way?	How is the balance between population and resources changed by changes in population?		Can Asia feed itself?	
		Should population be controlled, in Australia, in the world, generally?	How large is the Asian family?	Will the world starve itself in the future?
What factors influence the distribution?			Why are they this size?	
What is the result of this pattern?	Is population a resource?	What are government attitudes towards birth control?	Is population a resource for Asia?	Does this matter, or is it just another evolutionary step?
How can population be measured and mapped?	Is labour a resource?	Should abortion be legalised?	What methods of population control are used in these countries?	

table continues overleaf

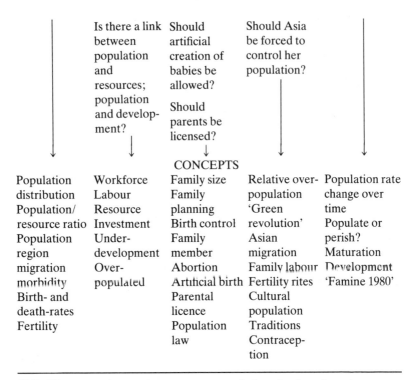

		CONCEPTS		
Population distribution	Workforce Labour	Family size Family	Relative over-population	Population rate change over
Population/ resource ratio	Resource Investment	planning Birth control	'Green revolution'	time Populate or
Population region	Under-development	Family member	Asian migration	perish? Maturation
migration morbidity	Over-populated	Abortion Artificial birth	Family labour Fertility rites	Development 'Famine 1980'
Birth- and death-rates		Parental licence	Cultural population	
Fertility		Population law	Traditions Contraception	

N.B. These questions and concepts are not designed to be exhaustive or exclusive.

Table 9.9 An inter-disciplinary theme: *river pollution*

FOCUS QUESTION: Why is our river polluted?
1. Who is responsible for the control of waste materials into this river?
2. Is it profitable for companies to pollute rivers?
3. Should rivers be used by factories to get rid of wastes?
4. Is pollution just a question of money?
5. What is the role of the individual in helping to prevent the river becoming dirty?
6. Why do people throw rubbish into rivers?
7. How could governments control waste disposal?
8. Can wastes be recycled?
9. Can we afford pollution?

CHAPTER 10

The evaluation of geographical education

NORMAN J. GRAVES

Introduction

In previous chapters we have considered such matters as values in geographical education, the problems of learning geography in relation to mental development, teaching strategies and learning techniques and the organization of resources for learning. It is now time to examine the question of the evaluation of geographical education and in doing this we shall look at:
1. the relation of evaluation to the curriculum;
2. curriculum development and evaluation;
3. the evaluation of student learning by various techniques such as continuous and course work assessment, essay assessment, oral testing, objective tests and the questions of validity and reliability.
   In considering these problems and techniques of evaluation I shall attempt to use examples which are appropriate to students ranging from ages 11 to 18 years. It should be borne in mind by the reader that my own experience is that of teaching in a Western European setting, and that consequently applying such techniques in a different cultural environment may require appropriate modifications.

Evaluation and the curriculum

The term 'evaluation' is often thought of as another word for assessment which itself is a concept denoting that students are tested by one means or another to ascertain whether they have learned certain skills, concepts, principles, or facts. But the concept of evaluating geographical education is considerably wider than this since it is related not just to the students' learning, but to the whole geography curriculum.

Further, the idea of evaluating the curriculum nationally is becoming acceptable. The reasoning behind this idea is that governments (and therefore taxpayers) are investing huge amounts of resources in education and that schools and teachers should therefore be accountable for the use they have made of these resources. The problem lies in measuring whether such resources have been wisely used. In England and Wales the Department of Education and Science has set up an Assessment of Performance Unit whose purpose is to devise nationally acceptable tests of performance which can be used to test the progress of individual schools. However while progress has been made in the fields of mathematics, science and reading, no such nationally acceptable test exists for geography. There are fundamental problems in accepting national forms of performance in subjects, particularly in subjects like geography, where the location of the school may well affect the nature of the curriculum.

Let us first remind ourselves what we mean by the word 'curriculum'. It is important to be clear about this word since it has evolved in meaning in the English language and may not even have an equivalent in some languages. In educational theory, the word tends now to mean the total of the activities within a school or college whose purpose is to contribute to the educational aims of the institution (note that Biddle's definition in Ch. 10 relates to a curriculum document). Consequently to write about the geography curriculum is to describe the objectives of the course, the kinds of activities (or learning experiences) in which students will be engaged in order to attempt to reach those objectives and the evaluation of those activities and of student learning to find out whether the objectives are being achieved. Thus the curriculum can be thought of as a system in which there are various interacting parts, these parts being essentially:

(a) the objectives;
(b) the learning experiences of students and teachers;
(c) the evaluation.

This system may be shown in simple form diagrammatically (Fig. 10.1).

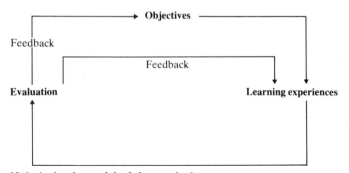

Fig. 10.1 A simple model of the curriculum system

The objectives suggest that teachers should organize certain activities for their students; the evaluation of those activities will take two forms, the evaluation of the activities themselves and the evaluation of student learning. Both these forms of evaluation will lead to the feedback of information about the objectives (e.g. whether they are being realized or whether they are incapable of being realized and therefore need to be changed) and about the learning experiences (e.g. whether these need to be modified to achieve the objectives).

Let us take a simple example. Suppose the teacher has set his students the objective of finding out, as part of the topic 'Using energy wisely' (see Ch. 5) what difficulties exist in increasing the production of petroleum rapidly. The teacher may have in mind such constraints as the conservation policies of the producing countries, the costs of increasing the outflow from old oil wells, the time and capital needed to search for and exploit new resources. He may ask the students to find out for themselves what these constraints are by suggesting they look for information in textbooks, encyclopedias, newspapers, pamphlets from oil companies and so on. Now when he comes to check on what his class has in fact achieved, he may find that only a small proportion of the class has in fact found out what these main constraints are. In other words his evaluation of the learning activities tells him that his objective has not been achieved by a majority of the class. He then has to decide whether this is because the objective is inappropriate for the group, for example because the students are too young to appreciate what is meant by the ideas mentioned above, or whether it is because the learning experiences were organized in such a way that the students were unable to discover what the teacher had planned they should discover. Perhaps it was because they were not yet trained to look up on their own a wide variety of sources of information and needed closer guidance in their search activities. This is a well-known process to most teachers and needs little emphasizing. In a situation where the teacher and his class have been working together on a familiar curriculum, the constant adjustment which takes place among the objectives and the learning experiences is a product of the teacher's continuous monitoring of the curriculum process. It takes place almost automatically. But when the curriculum objectives are tending to change rapidly owing to changes in knowledge or in society's requirements or both, then the teacher may be dealing with a less familiar situation and the curriculum process needs to be more consciously understood and manipulated.

Suppose that it has been suggested that the geography curriculum for 16-year-old students should include the learning of the rank–size rule, that is the idea that there is a regular relationship between a city's rank in the list of the country's cities ordered by their population, and its own population; a relationship which may be expressed symbolically by the expression:

$$Pn = \frac{P1}{n} \quad \text{or} \quad Pn = P1.n^{-1}$$

where *Pn* is the population of the *n*th city and *P*1 is the population of the first city. Although this may seem a precise enough statement of an objective, in fact it requires elaborating. Among the many possible objectives, is the objective
(a) that the students shall learn the theoretical relationship expressed above $(Pn = P1/n)$?
(b) that the student should apply it to a set of cities in a given country to test whether the relationship holds true, and if so, find out how closely the empirical situation matches the theoretical statement?
Or is it
(c) to explain why such a relationship might be true?

   If the teacher were to choose objective (a) he might be successful in achieving it, though the students might know little more than a formula which would hardly illuminate their understanding. If he chose objective (b) he might find that some of the class failed to understand the relationship because they were unfamiliar with the algebraic notation $Pn = P1.n^{-1}$, in which case he could use the simpler $Pn = P1/n$, but they might still be unclear as to how they could judge how closely an empirical situation fitted the theoretical statement. Consequently the teacher might need to demonstrate the use of the logarithmic graph paper as shown in Figs 10.2 and 10.3. It would be advantageous if the geography and the mathematics teachers were to co-operate over such an objective since mathematical skills are involved. In both cases the teacher has fed back his evaluation of the students' performance into the curriculum process and adjusted the learning experiences. Of course had he set such objectives for 11-year-old students he might well have found that no matter how he adjusted these learning experiences, the students would never have achieved the goals set and in such a case his evaluation could result in his realizing that the objectives were inappropriate for those students.

   The concept and purpose of evaluation are perhaps becoming clearer. Evaluation is the activity of making value judgements about a curriculum with a view to improving that curriculum. I realize that the word 'improving' subsumes all kinds of unexamined ideas about what is an improved curriculum. One answer is that it is a more efficient curriculum in which objectives appear to be achieved. However, this cannot be the whole answer; evaluation must involve an appraisal of the objectives, since a curriculum could be efficient but strive after objectives which are not worth achieving. It is probably true that much geography taught has often concentrated on

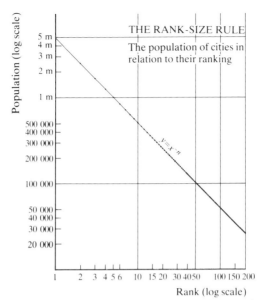

Fig. 10.2 The rank-size rule: the hypothetical size of the population of cities in relation to their ranking. (*Source:* Johnson 1967)

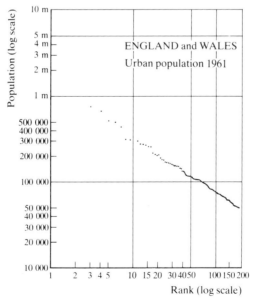

Fig. 10.3 The size and ranking of urban areas in England and Wales, 1961. (*Source:* Johnson 1967)

giving factual information about areas, and such an objective is now seldom deemed worth while since it does little by itself to transform the students' view of the world. Consequently an 'improved curriculum' is also one in which the objectives sought are deemed worthwhile and capable of being learned so that students' minds have in some way been changed to give them a deeper and wider understanding of life. Inevitably this involves the evaluator in making value judgements, since there is probably no general agreement about what are worth-while objectives (Tawney 1976).

Curriculum development and evaluation

As I indicated earlier, the geography curriculum is probably much more dynamic than it once was. A manifestation of the need for curriculum change is the effort made by educational authorities to engender curriculum development through various curriculum projects. Within the field of geography we have examples of the Earth Science Curriculum Project in the USA (1963–67), the American High School Geography Project (1961–70), The British Projects on Geography for the Young School Leaver (1970–75), Geography 14–18 (1970–75), History, Geography and Social Science 8–13 (1971–75) and Geography 16–19 (1976–84). In all these examples the basic idea was to attempt to stimulate curriculum development in geography through the action of teams of teachers who experimented with new curricula and then tried to disseminate such curricula among other teachers and schools. The American High School Geography Project developed a course entitled 'Geography in an Urban Age' which concentrated on problem-solving approaches to the spatial aspects of an industrial urban society, and this project considerably influenced similar projects in the United Kingdom and in Germany where the Association of German Geographers (Zentralverband der Deutschen Geographen) have developed their own geography project.

The very existence of such curriculum projects implies that evaluation of the geography curriculum proposed must take place, but the evaluation process has a special significance here, since such projects are intended as models of what teachers in general might undertake in their own schools. Thus curriculum evaluation of this type must give information on the following:

(a) Whether the proposed curriculum is feasible in the circumstances in which it is intended to apply it. For example, the American High School Geography Project contains a unit on farming which has examples from Poland. It is important to decide whether such a unit would be appropriate for geography classes in West Africa or Latin America.

(b) Whether the procedures and teaching strategies developed by the project teams are effective in the sense that they appear to be contributing to the objectives of the curriculum. This is not a simple question since there are short-term and long-term aspects to teaching strategies. Some which appear successful in the short term may have few long-term beneficial effects, as for example procedures which concentrate on the teaching of information. The problem is that it is difficult to evaluate the long-term effects of a curriculum in an objective way except of course, by waiting for these long-term effects to manifest themselves; and most curriculum projects have too short a life to make this possible. There is also a more fundamental question which needs to be asked about procedures, and this concerns not just the teaching procedures of the curriculum, but the very model of curriculum development that the project team have in mind. There is, for example, a fundamental distinction between the manner in which curriculum development was undertaken by the team concerned with the Geography for the Young School Leaver Project and the team concerned with the Geography 14–18 project. In the first case the project team developed a curriculum on three main themes: Man, Land and Leisure, Cities and Peoples, and People, Place and Work (Schools Council 1975–76), and then tried it out in various schools. In other words the teachers were provided with packs of curriculum materials in which the objectives and learning activities were specified; their job was to organize the curriculum along pre-planned lines and report on its workings. In the case of the Geography 14–18 Project, the team attempted to make the teachers in the schools propose the objectives and content of the curriculum. The team saw themselves as 'change-agents' attempting to supply ideas and give support, but not as providers of a pre-packaged curriculum to be applied in all schools, except in providing certain 'starter-kits' to give teachers a lead. The question inevitably poses itself: Which of these two models of curriculum development is the more effective? Or alternatively, which is the more effective in certain circumstances? Could it be that the first model is the more effective where teachers have had a limited initial training and cannot easily have access to a variety of teaching resources, while the second is more appropriate to teachers who are very well qualified and can command a wide variety of teaching resources?

In learning from each other, the two projects eventually came closer together in policy and practice than is suggested here.

(c) Whether the curriculum has some educational value for the students for whom it is intended. Clearly such a question must be considered by those who initiate a curriculum project, but it needs to be asked again once the project is in operation since it is fundamental to the educational process.

Since curriculum development is an evolutionary process taking place over a number of years, curriculum evaluation may be seen as a more or less continuous process monitoring the activities of the curriculum development team and the reactions of the students and teachers involved. Scriven (1967) suggested that the term *formative evaluation* might be used to denote the kind of evaluation which occurs during the development stage of the curriculum, and the term *summative evaluation* for the evaluation taking place at the end of the curriculum project's life span. Other terms suggested for the same ideas are *concurrent* and *subsequent* evaluation. But evaluation should go on beyond the life span of a project since it is of great importance to know what happens to a curriculum once the project team's work has ended. Does the curriculum go on developing and spreading throughout schools in the country, or does it wither away?

Who, however, is to do the evaluation? Some projects, like the American High School Geography Project and the British History, Geography and Social Science 8–13 Project appoint official evaluators whose special function is to monitor the team's progress and feed back information to the team and to those who ultimately will make decisions about the project. Others rely on feedback from teachers and a consultative committee whose function is to give advice to the project team and the decision-takers in the education system. Professional evaluators are becoming more common, but their attitudes to their tasks vary considerably. They may look upon themselves as employees of the education system whose function is simply to give information about whether a particular curriculum project is achieving objectives which are taken as given. On the other hand, some may see themselves as experts whose advice on curriculum development projects would normally be accepted and followed by the education authorities. Finally, some see themselves as information providers for decision-takers, that is, they study the curriculum development process in action, make judgements about what is happening and who is benefiting and put this information before those who have power in the education system, recognizing that given the plurality of values, an evaluator has no special right to insist that these recommendations should be implemented. It is plausibly argued that, if it is to be useful, the information provided by evaluators must be available in a form readily accessible to those who are not experts and do not possess an intimate knowledge of technical terms and of educational research.

But how may curriculum evaluation be undertaken? We have already discussed the wide-ranging nature of the concept of curriculum evaluation, but we now need to concentrate on the ways in which an evaluator may work. A simple way of dealing with the problem is to attempt to measure the 'output' of the curriculum. For example, if the objective is to enable students to learn the concept of urban hierarchy including Christaller's $K = 3$, $K = 4$ and $K = 7$ (the market, transport and administrative principles), then evaluation is the task of measuring what students knew before a particular curriculum was put into operation (the pre-test) and what they knew after having had the appropriate learning experiences (the post-test) and then making judgements about what they have learned and what they have not learned and in the latter case indicating how the curriculum may be changed to remedy the situation. This is a well-known method of undertaking educational research, strongly supported by a number of eminent educational psychologists, among them Scriven who feels that it is an appropriate method to use in curriculum evaluation.

Such a method of undertaking curriculum evaluation imposes certain rigid conditions in its application. First the objectives need to be accepted as given. Unfortunately, curriculum development projects in geography, as in other subjects, do not begin by having simple, straightforward, clear-cut objectives which can then be incorporated into an achievement test. Indeed many curriculum projects devote part of their energies to devising worth-while objectives, some of which may not be susceptible to measurement. For example, one objective in most geography curriculum projects is the development of students' curiosity about the spatial regularities in the landscape so that they may continue to ask questions about these after their formal schooling is over. But such an objective is difficult to measure precisely. Further, it may well be that certain objectives are what Eisner (1969) has called *expressive objectives*, that is, a situation in which the student is given an educational experience and is asked to react to it, but there is no means of knowing precisely in what way he will react. For instance, a student might be given certain data about a new neighbourhood and asked to plan the street layout, the social services and the housing. While there may be a certain pattern about the response of students to such a task, it is difficult to specify ahead of the experience precisely what the student should produce. Part of what he does produce will be an expression of his feelings and value judgements, but there is no precise way of measuring such objectives by the pre-test–post-test method.

Secondly, the classical method in educational research involves the use of either large randomized samples (which is very expensive) or the use of small samples where the conditions affecting the performance of students must be strictly controlled. Let us take a simple example. Suppose that the evaluator is trying to find out whether the processes of erosion by wind are better taught to a 15-year-old class by means of an inquiry method using moving film and documentary evidence (in the form of maps, pictures and written texts) or by means of an inquiry method using fieldwork and documentary evidence. Since the same ideas are being taught, two sample classes must be used, but if the classical research design is adhered to, then the classes must be equally matched as to ability, age, social composition and so on. Further, the conditions under which the classes are taught must be the same in all respects except for the variable of the teaching methods used; therefore the teacher must be the same, the time devoted to the learning experience must be the same, the documents used must be the same and so on. Students in both classes are given a pre-test to show what they knew already and a post-test after the learning experiences to find out what they have gained in learning. If there is a difference in the gains between the two samples then it is necessary to find out whether this difference is significant or could have been obtained by chance. If it is significant then the group which has obtained the greater gain in scope is the group taught by the more successful method. Unfortunately, the elaborate controls which need to be maintained with an experiment of this type to make its results credible are seldom possible in a curriculum development situation, where a large number of conditions are likely to be changing. Further, the kinds of findings obtained with such an elaborate experimental framework are not always of such magnitude as to warrant the time and energy expended on them.

Some curriculum evaluators have abandoned the idea of being able to measure accurately the benefits of certain curricula, though they have continued faith in the activity of evaluation using more subjective and descriptive methods. This is what Trow (1970) has called *illuminative evaluation*. The process is essentially one of monitoring the curriculum development process and analysing what appears to happen. For example a curriculum development project may have as its main aim the development of a course in geography for able 14–18-year-old pupils in order to incorporate some of the new ideas which became manifest in the 1960s. However, owing to the interest of some of the project team involved in the sociological aspect of curriculum development, the emphasis may be placed *not* on providing a new course but on facilitating curriculum development as a socio-cultural process by attempting to make teachers in schools the prime agents of the process. Thus the aims are transformed and likelihood of a 'course' emerging becomes remote. Another example is one provided by Marten Shipman (1974) who monitored the Integrated Studies Project at Keele University from 1968 to 1972. He shows that teachers modified in their practice the kinds of procedures that the curriculum developers had in mind, so that instead of teachers providing specialist guidance for building the geographical aspects of the integrated curriculum being developed, they attempted to become polyvalent teachers of all subjects. Yet another example is provided by the kind of teacher–pupil interaction which is engendered by a decision to incorporate into a curriculum work which may result in greater feedback from students to teachers, leading to a subsequent change in the curriculum. The evaluator is therefore attempting to describe the kind of interaction which goes on during curriculum development and to provide information about this to all those involved: the financing body, the education authorities, the school administrators, the teachers and, of course, the curriculum developers themselves.

Besides observing and recording his perceptions of what happens in a curriculum project, the evaluator may also interview those involved, get teachers and pupils to answer questionnaires and also use various tests and documentary evidence. He will not, however, place all his faith in test results, but use these as part of the total evidence he will put forward to the decision-makers. An example of *illuminative evaluation* is provided by Dana Kurfman (though he does not use that term) who was evaluator for the American High School Geography Project (Kurfman 1968). He argues that three evaluation functions were foreseen for the project:

(a) the clarification of the objectives of each section of the units devised for the course 'Geography in an urban age';

(b) the use of tests and questionnaires to find out about the efficiency of various teaching materials used;

(c) a summative evaluation of the whole course before it was marketed.

In the event, the first function proved useful since it resulted in the course unit writers being much more specific about the kinds of learning outcomes which they anticipated for each unit. It also became clear, as Eisner has insisted, that there were many unintended learning outcomes. An educational encounter inevitably gives results which cannot entirely be predicted given the variability of human reactions. Thus the project team were able to modify both the objectives and contents of the course in the light of the evaluation of course objectives and outcomes.

The second function involved two distinct evaluation techniques:

(i) the use of achievement tests to find out how effective certain teaching materials and procedures were in getting students to learn concepts, skills and principles in the 'Geography of cities' unit;

(ii) the use of questionnaires to find out students' and teachers' reactions to the materials, that is, whether they had enjoyed using them or not, and why.

In practice it proved difficult to attach much weight to the achievement test results. The problem is that any particular teaching unit will contain numerous materials making reference to the skills, concepts and principles which the students are intended to learn, and it is difficult to ascertain which of the materials is the more effective from the results of achievement tests. On the other hand the results of questionnaires proved much more useful. Students were able to indicate how much a particular unit had succeeded in involving them in the learning process, therefore giving the evaluator a measure of the effectiveness of a unit. Teachers were able to show evaluators where units required revision and why.

The summative evaluation of the whole course was never undertaken due to lack of time and resources. Thus Kurfman began his evaluation with the idea that it might be possible to use, at least in part, the traditional methods of educational research, but as the project developed he found that the conditions were too dynamic to make such research possible and fell back on what was essentially *illuminative evaluation*. In the last analysis, what mattered was what students and teachers felt about the curriculum, rather than some apparently scientific measure of gains in knowledge under conditions which are not normally obtained in schools, particularly when a new curriculum is being tried out.

Examples of evaluation questionnaires

Two examples of evaluation 'instruments' are given below. The first attempts to obtain from teachers their estimation of the value of a teaching unit and what suggestions they have for improving it. The second tries to gauge student reactions to the same unit. Both questionnaires refer to a unit on Japan from the American High School Geography Project, but could be adapted to any other teaching unit, whether that unit was part of a curriculum development project or simply part of a commercially produced teaching programme.

The teacher questionnaire *(adapted from Kurfman 1968)*

This questionnaire will be of use to curriculum project developers.

Please tick the appropriate spaces or answer the questions.

A. The reading materials

	Yes	No
1. Were the readings understandable to		
(a) the average student	___	___
(b) the below-average student	___	___
2. There should be		
(a) more reading materials	___	___
(b) fewer reading materials	___	___

3. From the teacher's point of view was the reading
matter well organized? _____ _____

4. Please make suggestions or comments about the reading materials:

....

....

....

....

B. The teacher's guidelines

Please state whether the guidelines could be more effective in:

	Yes	No
1. providing clearer instructions	_____	_____
2. stating the objectives of the unit	_____	_____
3. suggesting more varied activities	_____	_____
4. giving more background information needed to teach the unit	_____	_____
5. indicating supplementary reading for the students	_____	_____
6. being more directive	_____	_____
7. being less directive	_____	_____

Please make any suggestions or comments about the teachers' guidelines:

....

....

....

....

C. The content of the unit

	Yes	No
1. Is the content of the unit		
(a) too difficult for average students	_____	_____
(b) too difficult for below-average students	_____	_____
(c) too easy for average students	_____	_____
(d) too easy for below-average students	_____	_____
2. Is the content well organized?	_____	_____

3. Make suggestions or comments about the content:

....

....

....

....

D. The individual activities of the unit

1. Please give each activity one of the following ratings:
   1 = could be omitted
   2 = could be optional
   3 = is essential to the unit

   Introduction to Japan   ———

   Modernization and population growth   ———

   Life of a Japanese family man   ———

   Population in pre-modern Japan   ———

   The redistribution of population in modern Japan   ———

   Distribution of economic activities and population   ———

   Case studies: Mitaka and Nuike   ———

2. What do you believe is the most important thing your students learned from the unit?

....

....

....

....

3. If you were to teach the unit again, what changes would you make?

   (a) in the activities

....

....

....

....

(b) in the order of teaching these activities

....

....

....

....

(c) in the time you would spend on each activity

....

....

....

....

The student questionnaire (see Renner and Slater 1974)

The results of the original questionnaire to teachers on the Japan unit of the High School Geography Project were used to modify the unit substantially from its original form. Thus by the time it was published it consisted of four major activities:
1. an introduction showing similarities and differences between Japan and North America;
2. a description of life in traditional Japan;
3. an exploration of the process of change from a traditional to an industrial society;
4. a simulation game in which students use the knowledge gained on Japan's economic development to suggest to a UN committee how developing countries might speed up their own development.

The questionnaire printed below (Table 10.1) was one teacher's (Dr F. A. Slater) method of gauging the attitude of her class to the unit. The class was one of 15-year-old above-average girl students. The results of the questionnaire are also given (Table 10.2).

It can be seen that from the students' point of view the filmstrip in the first activity was ineffective since 55 per cent of the students could not remember it. On the other hand, some of the reading and the simulation were deemed generally interesting.

Evaluating student learning

I have concentrated so far on curriculum evaluation because I see this as the prime function of evaluation. Nevertheless, tests and examinations have loomed large in education and are still an important aspect of most education systems. It is necessary, therefore, to spend some time looking at the evaluation of student learning. To begin, let us attempt to classify the various types of evaluation at present in vogue.

First there is the day-to-day informal evaluation given by the teacher to his students as they are working on an exercise, course or project. This may consist of no more than a verbal indication to the student that he is on the correct track in an exercise and is achieving success, or vice versa that he may need to try another approach. Secondly, there is the more formal evaluation of an exercise or homework or project where the teacher may not only append comments and suggestions, but also give a mark or grade. This may sometimes be called *course work assessment.* Thirdly, there is the informal *class test* during which the teacher may set a series of oral or written questions to which the students must answer by one- or two-word answers, the results of the tests then give the teacher an indication of how his teaching has succeeded. Fourthly, there are the more formal termly, half-yearly examinations, when students are systematically tested to find out what progress they have made during a particular period of time. Such *internal school examinations* are fairly common in Europe, Africa and Asia, but less widespread in North America where more reliance is placed on various forms of course work assessment. Fifthly, there are the very formal *external examinations* set by an authority outside the school whose purpose is to measure the standard of knowledge and understanding of the students in a region or a state or a federation. For example, the General Certificate of Education in England and Wales, and the College Entrance Examination in the USA are examinations of this type. They have often been pass/fail examinations in which students obtaining certain grades are deemed to have qualified and others to have failed. These examinations have assumed enormous importance in the education system because they have been used to give access to higher education or to certain occupations. It is important to bear in mind that practice varies from country to country and that the classification given here may not fit every case.

From this list it may be seen that tests and examinations serve more than one purpose and this is why there is often confused thinking about the nature and purpose of examinations. For example, in France one examination known as 'l'agrégation' is essentially a competition for selecting a number of secondary school teachers for a small number of posts for which highly erudite teachers are said to be

Table 10.1 The evaluation form

1. *How did our study of Japan compare with our study of other topics in geography this year?*
   ☐ **Much poorer**   ☐ Somewhat poorer   ☐ Much the same   ☐ Somewhat better
   ☐ **Much better**

2. *How interesting did you find the study of Japan?*

	Work as whole	Reading parts	Graphical illustrations	*Part One* Filmstrip	*Part Two* Traditional Japan	*Part Three* Japanese family man	*Part Four* Modern-ization
Don't remember							
Dull							
Uninteresting							
Generally interesting							
Extremely interesting							

3. *What do you consider was the main objective (reason) for studying*
   (a) *The topic as a whole?* To _____
   (b) *The reading sections?* To _____
   (c) *The graphs?* To _____
   (d) *Part One?* To _____
   (e) *Part Two?* To _____
   (f) *Part Three?* To _____
   (g) *Part Four?* To _____

4. *How much do you think you learned from*

	Nothing	Little	Quite a lot	A great deal
(a) *The topic as a whole?*				
(b) *The readings?*				
(c) *Graphs?*				
(d) *Part One?*				
(e) *Part Two?*				
(f) *Part Three?*				
(g) *Part Four?*				

5. *Make any general comments, favourable or unfavourable, on any part of the work, if you wish.*

_____
_____
_____
_____
_____

Table 10.2 A summary of students' responses

1. *Student comparison of Japan unit with other work*

   Number responding 22

	Number	Percentage
Much poorer	1	4
Somewhat poorer	4	18
Much the same	5	23
Somewhat better	8	36
Much better	4	18

2. *Student assessment of interest*

	Work as a whole	Reading parts	Graphical illustrations	Part One Film-strip	Part Two Traditional Japan	Part Three Family man	Part Four Modernization UN Conference
Number responding	22	22	22	22	22	22	22
	%	%	%	%	%	%	%
Don't remember	4·5	9 0	0·0	55·0	13·5	13·5	0·0
Dull	4·5	4·5	9·0	4·5	4·5	9·0	13·5
Uninteresting	4·5	9·0	31·5	4·5	9·0	4·5	13·5
Generally interesting	77·0	64·0	46·0	36·0	46·0	46·0	50·0
Extremely interesting	10·0	13·5	13·5	0·0	27·0	27·0	23·0

3. *Student awareness of objectives*

	Topic as a whole	Reading sections	Graphs	Part One	Part Two	Part Three	Part Four
Number responding	21	21	22	19	21	18	22
	%	%	%	%	%	%	%
Not aware	18·0	32·0	0·0	32·0	9·0	18·0	18·0
Vaguely aware	13·5	36·0	18·0	55·0	13·5	18·0	4·5
Generally aware	13·5	4·5	32·0	9·0	68·0	41·0	13·5
Clearly aware	55·0	27·0	50·0	4·5	9·0	23·0	64·0

4. *Student estimate of own learning*

	Topic as a whole	Reading sections	Graphs	Part One	Part Two	Part Three	Part Four
Number responding	22	22	22	22	22	22	22
	%	%	%	%	%	%	%
Nothing	0·0	0·0	4·5	27·5	9·0	4·5	0·0
Little	13·5	23·0	23·0	32·0	9·0	27·0	27·0
Quite a lot	89·0	77·0	59·0	36·0	68·0	64·0	41·0
A great deal	27·0	0·0	14·0	4·5	13·5	4·5	32·0

needed. Thus its function is essentially that of selecting a predetermined number of teachers from available candidates with the number varying from year to year according to availability of posts. Such an examination has little to do with curriculum improvement. On the other hand, class tests which indicate clearly whether pupils have or have not grasped certain ideas and skills are mainly intruments to enable teachers to evaluate their courses. Broadly, it is possible to think of student evaluation as having two main functions:

1. that which is concerned with the improvement of the curriculum;
2. that which is concerned with student assessment.

In general, it is the latter function which has tended to dominate, with great emphasis being placed on the measuring of precise levels of achievement, on predicting future attainment and on the selection of certain students from their fellow candidates. But the same examinations have often been used for both main functions. It is also useful to bear in mind another classification of tests and examinations. This classification is one based on the kind of response made by the student:

1. The open-ended test or examination, where a question is asked but the candidate is free to interpret and answer it as he wishes.
2. The closed-ended or so called objective test, where the question asked is so structured that the candidate can only respond in a certain way to give a correct answer. In practice, certain kinds of tests or examinations are best suited to certain objectives. Thus in choosing an evaluation instrument, the teacher should be guided by the kind of objectives which he is trying to achieve.

Let me digress briefly on the question of objectives. First, I shall use the term *objective* to refer to those short- or medium-term learning outcomes which the teacher is trying to achieve, and reserve the term *aim* for those more general and long-term outcomes of the educational process. Thus one may refer to the *aims* of the secondary school geography curriculum, but to the *objectives* of a particular lesson or group of lessons. Secondly, there is a difference between an objective and a learning outcome in the sense that an objective refers to an intention whereas a learning outcome is an achievement. For example, I may set a class the objective of explaining why an international date-line is necessary, but only 10 per cent of the class may succeed in so doing. Thirdly, objectives may be more or less precisely specified. If we consider the objective of explaining the need for an international date-line, it is specific up to a point, but no further. What do we mean by 'explain', do we want a specification of how the convention of having an international date-line came about, of what were the advantages and disadvantages of not having an international date-line, of why the 180° line of longitude was chosen, of why the date-line diverges from the 180° longitude in certain places, or what the date-line implies for ships and aircraft crossing it from east to west and from west to east? Do we want the explanation to be in words only, or in words with a diagram, or with a globe? This may seem rather pedantic to some teachers, but it corresponds to what some educators and psychologists have called 'behavioural objectives', that is objectives which can be specified in terms of the particular behaviour required at the end of a period of instruction. Specifying particular objectives of this nature can be a very elaborate process since one has to bear in mind, for example, in relation to instruction on networks:

(a) the person for whom the objective is designed, e.g. his or her age;

(b) the kind of behaviour which will demonstrate that the objective has been reached, e.g. writing down an index number;

(c) the kind or product of performance by which the objective can be measured, e.g. being able to measure the index of a network;

(d) the sort of conditions under which the operation takes place, e.g. with a network of between 15 and 20 edges on a map showing no other information;

(e) the standard to be used in evaluating the achievement, e.g. getting at least 8 out of 10 indexes correct (Clegg 1970).

In classroom practice it is seldom found that teachers spell out their objectives in such an elaborate way, though the devisers of 'programmed learning tests' in drafting their 'frames' have had to resort to such tactics. In general, one can say that the more distant objectives are, the more vague they appear, but the more proximate they are, then the more specific their formulation must be. However, this can only apply to instructional objectives and not to expressive objectives (see earlier discussion).

The relevance of this digression on objectives is that on the whole the so-called 'objective-type' tests are more suited to short-term objectives which can be precisely specified, but much less suitable to testing an individual's understanding of the more general aims of geographical education. Let us, however, deal with the objective type of tests first, since they are being increasingly used to test geographical knowledge, particularly in public or external examinations.

It is as well to distinguish between two types of tests: (1) norm-referenced tests, and (2) criterion-referenced tests. A norm-referenced test is one which has been tried out on a large sample of a given population and the performance of that sample on the test is recorded. Thus any particular group of students subsequently tested will have their performance compared with that of the trial sample, the latter providing the 'norm'. As a result a group of students may be described as performing above or below the norm, hence the term 'norm-referenced test'. But if one is interested not in how well or badly a group of students do compared with a norm, but in their mastering certain ideas and skills, then criterion-referenced tests are more useful. Essentially students' performances are measured in terms of a set of criteria, which are the ideas and skills to be learned – hence the term 'criterion-referenced tests'. If the teacher is interested in whether his students have mastered Christaller's ideas on settlement hierarchy, then an appropriate criterion-referenced test should be used and not a norm-referenced test. In general, criterion-referenced tests will deal with a limited area of knowledge and in a way appropriate to the learners' state of academic development.

Objective tests in geography

First it is important to bear in mind that the term 'objective' refers only to the marking of such tests. In other words, the test is marked objectively, because the marker has no discretion as to whether an answer is right or wrong. If a multiple-choice question states:

Tick the correct answer in the box provided –
The β index in a network is defined as:

(a) $\beta = \dfrac{\text{edges}}{\text{nodes}}$

(b) $\beta = \text{edges} \times \text{nodes}$

(c) $\beta = \dfrac{\text{nodes}}{\text{edges}}$

(d) $\beta = \text{nodes} \times \dfrac{\text{edges}}{2}$

(e) $\beta = \text{nodes} \times 2 \text{ edges}$

then the marker can only mark correct those responses which select (a) as the appropriate answer. The other answers are known as *distractors*. On the other hand there is clearly a subjective element in the setting of that question. The writer has presumed that being able to recognize the correct definition of a β index is a behaviour worth evaluating in a student of geography. Secondly, and arising out of what was stated above, many objective-type tests in geography tend to test fact or information because of the ease of devising questions with factual answers. For example, it is easy to draft a question such as:

Tick the correct answer in the box provided –
The capital of Argentina is:

(a) Mendoza

(b) Rosario

(c) Bahia Blanca

(d) Buenos Aires

(e) Santa Fe

but a little more difficult to devise one like the following:

Study the map (Fig. 10.4) which shows the percentage of each region's exports handled by the port of London and tick which one of the following statements is correct.

Percentage represents
London's share of EXPORTS

Percentage represents
London's share of IMPORTS

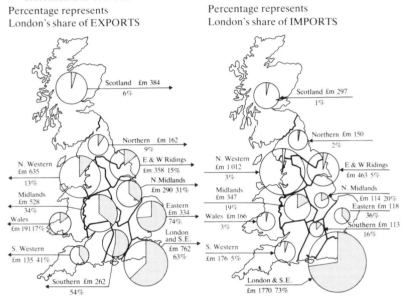

Fig. 10.4 Importance of the Port of London to each region of Great Britain (a) exports and (b) imports by value. (*Source:* Port of London Authority)

(a) most of Great Britain's exports go through London

(b) most of Scotland's exports pass through Liverpool

(c) the Eastern region has a greater percentage of its exports go through London than any other port

(d) more than half of the Midland region's exports go through the Port of London

(e) less than half of the Southern region's exports go through London

and even more difficult to devise the following question:

> The map of England and Wales (Fig. 10.5) shows the flow of electric power along the main grid lines; using the map information, which of the following statements about the relationship between production and consumption of electricity and the distribution of population can be inferred to be correct?
>
> Tick the correct answer in the box provided.

(*a*) Most electricity is produced in the Midlands, but consumed in the Lancashire industrial towns.

(*b*) A great deal of electricity is produced in Wales, but it is all exported to England because the density of population in Wales is low.

(*c*) Electrical power is sent to the South-West Peninsula from the South East of England because there are no power stations in South West England

(*d*) Owing to the large population of south-eastern England and the greater generating capacity in the Midlands, the net flow of electrical power is from the Midlands to the South East.

(*e*) There is a net flow of electrical power from the Midlands to the South East of England because there are no large power stations in the London area.

Whereas it took approximately a minute to write the question about capitals, it took about 20 minutes to develop the last question. On the other hand, whereas the earlier question merely tests factual recall, the last question tests the ability to:
 (i) read information on a map;
 (ii) analyse maps and written information;
(iii) reason, since candidates must decide whether the statements made can be inferred from the map evidence or whether they must be rejected as invalid or not warranted.

Objective-type tests in geography have a number of other advantages, besides those of being marked objectively. Perhaps the most important is that since candidates need only respond by ticking an answer (or shading a box), many questions can be answered in a given time and therefore a much greater coverage of a curriculum is possible than when candidates are writing answers to essay questions.

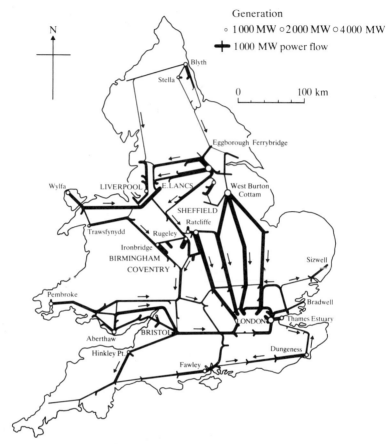

Fig. 10.5 The power flow in England and Wales

This is important because the test then becomes much fairer to candidates. A student who has to answer a hundred questions on a test is more likely to do himself justice than if he has to answer three questions, since the three questions will merely be a small sample of the content he has studied and he may be unlucky in his choice. Other advantages are that the test is one of geographical knowledge; the ability to write essays, to spell or to be grammatically correct do not enter into the assessment. Further, the test can be designed carefully to match the population of candidates for whom it is intended.

The questions given as examples above are known as *multiple-choice questions*, which by having five possible answers, tend to cut down to 20 per cent the chance of a correct answer being obtained by guesswork. Another similar type of question is the *matching type*, an example of which follows:

The following types of farming are described in the right-hand list. Write the appropriate number in the boxes provided next to the descriptions.

1. Intensive farming	A. Land is cultivated for a few years and abandoned when yields begin to decrease.	
2. Plantation agriculture	B. The output per hectare is high, but the output per man may be low. Much fertilizer is used and careful cultivation occurs.	
3. Extensive farming	C. One crop is usually grown on a large estate with a view to a predominantly export market.	
4. Shifting cultivation	D. One crop is grown, usually grain, year in year out.	
5. Market gardening	E. The output per man is high but the output per hectare may be low.	
6. No name given	F. Animals are kept and crops grown, the animals produce milk or meat and the crops are usually fodder crops.	
	G. Many crops are grown to satisfy a not too distant urban population.	

(ANSWERS: A = 4, B = 1, C = 2, D = 6, E = 3, F = 6, G = 5)

In such questions, there must be more possibilities among the letters, so that the student is not able to fill in the last space by a simple process of elimination. In the question above, choice D and F are not usable by someone who answers correctly.

Yet another type of question is the *alternative response* type also called the *True/False* type. As shown below the student responds by ticking the correct box:

An anticyclone is an area of descending air.

TRUE ☐   FALSE ☐

Another example is:

The greater the size of a town, the smaller the number of functions.

TRUE ☐   FALSE ☐

It is important that the statement can be clearly seen to be true or false by an able student; an ambiguous statement does not make a good question, neither does one containing both correct and incorrect information such as:

An anticyclone is an area of descending air which consequently brings rain.

TRUE ☐   FALSE ☐

True/false questions have a great disadvantage, namely that a candidate who merely guesses the answer has a 50 per cent chance of being correct. Thus in totalling marks from such tests it is necessary to use a technique whereby the marks for incorrect answers are deducted from those for correct answers. For example, a candidate who answered questions purely by guesswork might get, in a test where the maximum mark was 100, 52 correct answers and 48 incorrect ones. Applying the above technique, his adjusted mark would then be 4. A candidate who was much more knowledgeable on the test might get 80 correct answers and 20 incorrect answers and his adjusted mark would then be 60. The difference between the two marks would then more correctly reflect the performance of the two candidates. Owing to the need for such corrections to the raw scores, true/false items are seldom used in tests containing other items such as multiple-choice items.

Devising an objective test paper is a fairly complex task and is best done by two or more teachers in collaboration. In the first place it is important to see to it that the instructional objectives tested cover a wide range and that factual recall is not overemphasized. An instrument specifically designed to classify instructional objectives was Bloom's *Taxonomy of Educational Objectives: The Cognitive Domain*, (Bloom 1956). Bloom's *Taxonomy* arranges objectives into the following classes:

1. Knowledge   e.g. knowledge of facts, of principles, of theories.

2. Comprehension   e.g. the understanding of a written or graphical statement, i.e. on a map or diagram.

3. Application   e.g. the ability to apply a given principle or theory to a new situation.

4. Analysis   e.g. the ability to break up a statement into its constituent parts.

5. Synthesis   e.g. the ability to put together various elements in a situation to form a pattern or a recognizable whole.

6. Evaluation   e.g. the ability to make a judgement about a situation given all the necessary evidence.

This classification is a hierarchy in the sense that it is arranged in increasing order of complexity and the higher levels of the hierarchy include the lower levels. For example, if an instructional objective is classified as involving 'synthesis', then it must also involve knowledge, comprehension, application and analysis. But an objective which is classified as 'knowledge' only involves the ability to recall a certain fact or principle and does not involve the rest of the hierarchy.

Test items should, therefore, be designed to cover the range of Bloom's objectives, though clearly, in a test designed for the younger age groups, say up to 14 years, there will tend to be relatively more items in the 'knowledge', 'comprehension' and 'application' categories than in the others. Conversely, a test for older students should contain proportionately more items in the 'analysis', 'synthesis' and 'evaluation' categories. In practice it is difficult to devise test items which can be marked objectively which fall in the 'synthesis' and 'evaluation' categories since these involve a subjective element in the response.

Here are a few examples of such test items. I shall leave out 'knowledge' since clear examples of these have already been given earlier.

Comprehension

Tick the correct *one* of the following statements in the box provided –

The *map* (Fig. 10.6) of part of The Netherlands shows:

(a) that most of the land is below sea-level

(b) all the Dutch rivers

(c) all the Dutch polderlands

(d) the two main conurbations of The Netherlands

(e) the main hydroelectric installations

Although most of the answers are plausible, the map only really shows (d).The students need to *comprehend* what the map shows and

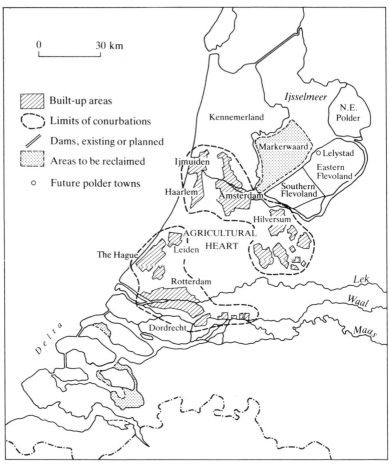

Fig. 10.6 The Randstad, Netherlands

does not show. This is an important objective as experiments have shown that students often do not understand the limitations of map information (Sandford 1972).

Application

Study Fig. 10.7 and indicate by a tick which of the following statements are correct:

1. The air flowing over town A is likely to be

(a) dry all the year round

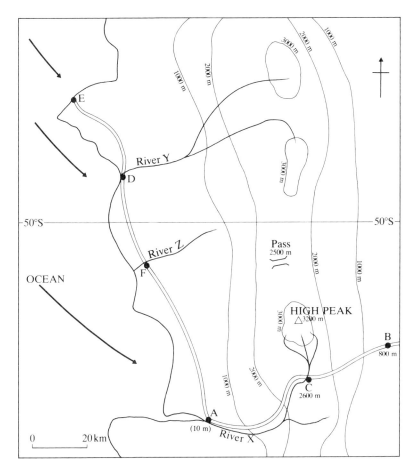

Fig. 10.7 Hypothetical map of a coastal area of a continent

(b) dry in the summer only

(c) humid most of the year

(d) humid in the summer only

(e) humid in the winter only

2. River X is likely to have a rate of flow of water which is

    (a) greater than that of river Z

    (b) less than that of river Z

    (c) less than that of river Z in summer

    (d) less than that of river Z in winter

    (e) negligible

3. The mean annual precipitation of town C is likely to be

    (a) less than that of town B

    (b) greater than that of town B but less than that of town A

    (c) greater than that of towns A or B

    (d) negligible during the summer months

    (e) negligible during the winter months

4. Snow is likely to fall

    (a) in January around town A

    (b) in July on the hills above 2 000 m

    (c) in January in the northern part of the west lowland

    (d) in February in the area to the east of the main mountains

    (e) in December along the coast

5. A road from town D to town B is likely

    (a) to be impossible to construct because of high relief

    (b) to rise to over 3 000 m

    (c) not to go above 2 500 m

    (d) to go through the High Peak area

    (e) to cross the mountains by using the Y river valley throughout its length

6. A large port is more likely to have developed at

   (a) settlement E

   (b) settlement D

   (c) settlement F

   (d) settlement A

   (e) at none of these

Here the student is being asked to *apply* his knowledge of meteorological, hydrological and transportation principles to an imaginary situation portrayed on the map. He needs also to have *knowledge* of the principles and *comprehension* of the map.

Analysis

The figures in Table 10.3 give the iron ore production for the world's main producers.

Using these figures, tick which of the following statements can be inferred to be correct.

1. (a) India and Liberia produce equivalent quantities of steel

   (b) India and Liberia produce the same quantity of iron ore

   (c) the iron content of India's iron ore production is less than that of Liberia's

   (d) Liberia produces more pig iron than India

   (e) Liberia is a greater steel producer than India

2. China's output of iron ore (measured in metal content) is

   (a) used mainly for making soldiers' helmets

   (b) used mainly to make agricultural implements

   (c) exported to Japan

   (d) used to make iron and steel for export

   (e) over twice that of Venezuela's

Table 10.3 World production of iron ore (iron content). (*Source: United Nations Statistical Yearbook*)

	Tonnes (iron content) (1974)
USSR	135 000
Australia	59 623
USA	47 256
Brazil	40 408
China	39 000 (1973)
Canada	30 000
Liberia	24 500
Sweden	22 176
India	20 884
France	17 364
Venezuela	16 635
Total World production = 510 000	

The student is here being asked to examine the figures and decide whether the statements made can reasonably be inferred from the figures provided. For example in 2(c) it will be clear that China's output of iron ore is high, in fact higher than Canada's, though Canada is a much more highly industrialized nation than China. But the figures themselves state nothing about the use of the iron ore so that one cannot infer that China exports most of its iron ore. In fact it does not. This is where problems arise in such tests because some questions which can be answered through a reasoning process can also be answered from factual knowledge if the student happens to know the facts. But no tests will ever be perfect. No attempt will be made to give examples of 'synthesis' and 'evaluation' questions, since these involve the logical difficulty that any ability so tested must lead to divergent answers which cannot be labelled as definitely correct or incorrect.

Once it has been decided that the instructional objectives covered by the test give a fairly wide spread of objectives from knowledge through comprehension, and application to analysis, it is then necessary to find out whether the items devised are too easy or too difficult and perhaps, according to the purpose of the test, whether they discriminate between candidates. The only way to find out whether test items are too easy or too difficult is to try them out on a group of students similar to those who are to take the test. A *facility index* can be calculated for each item to give an indication of how easy an item has been. If an item is tested on 300 students (the maximum number which needs to be used for such item analysis) and 100 get the correct answer then the facility index is

$$\frac{\text{Nos. answering correctly}}{\text{Nos. attempting item}} = \frac{100}{300} = 0.33 \text{ or } 33 \text{ per cent}$$

An easy item could have a facility index value of 0.9, and a difficult item a value of 0.1. If a figure of 0 is obtained it is usually an indication that there is something wrong with the item, even if that is merely a printing error. The facility index value to strive for will depend on the teacher's purpose. If he is merely wishing to confirm that what has been taught has in fact been learned, then a high facility index will result since the general expectation is that pupils will be able to tackle the questions set, i.e. a facility index of between 0.6 and 0.9 will be aimed at. If, however, the purpose is to select a few candidates from a large group then a large number of difficult items will be devised with facility indices of between 0.14 and 0.5.

If the teacher's objective is to make the test discriminate between students to produce a rank order, then it is advisable to calculate a *discrimination index* for each item. A simple way of doing this is to give a test containing the items to be tested and work out the rank order of students. Then count how many of the top 27 per cent of students answered the item correctly (N_t) and subtract from this the number of students in the bottom 27 per cent who answered the item correctly (N_b) and divide by the number representing 27 per cent of the entry to the test (N), i.e.

$$\text{discrimination index} = \frac{N_t - N_b}{N}$$

For example, if 100 candidates sit the test then

$$N = 27$$
if
$$N_t = 17$$
and
$$N_b = 10$$

$$\text{discrimination index} = \frac{17 - 10}{27} = \frac{7}{27} = 0.26$$

If all candidates in the top 27 per cent have the item correct but none in the bottom 27 per cent then the

$$\text{discrimination index} = \frac{27 - 0}{27} = \frac{27}{27} = 1.0$$

indicating that the item discriminated perfectly between the top and bottom group and by implication, between the knowledgeable and not so knowledgeable candidates.

If the top 27 per cent all got the item wrong but the bottom 27 per cent got the item right, then

$$\text{discrimination index} = \frac{0 - 27}{27} = -1$$

which indicates a situation of reverse discrimination.

In practice, it is usual to reject from such tests all items which have a discrimination index of below 0.3. Such low values usually indicate that there is something wrong with the item. Possibly more than one response is correct, or the wording is not clear, or the distractors are so obviously wrong that the correct answer is patent, or the answer may be much too difficult for the group being tested or again that the item is in fact incongruous in that it is testing an objective which is quite different from the other items in the test. For example, it could be testing historical rather than geographical knowledge.

It is, of course, essential to ensure that a test covers the objectives which the teacher is teaching to, and this may mean also ensuring that certain aspects of content are covered For example, a general aim which the teacher may wish to see implemented is that the students come to think scientifically about the natural landscape. His more specific objectives may be to get students to understand the processes of erosion, transport and deposition of rock material. It therefore follows that the test cannot test for understanding of scientific method only, but for such understanding in the context of the denudation of natural landscapes. It is therefore useful for the teacher to devise a table indicating the number of items to cover each topic for each level in the hierarchy of objectives. Let us take an illustration from urban geography, where the main areas to be covered might be shown at the top of each column (see Table 10.4). This table would indicate in the columns the relative importance attached to each topic in the geography curriculum. For example it is clear that I value the topic on the 'Functional zoning in towns' much more than the 'Rank–size rule', since I allocate 12 as against 4 items for each respectively. I am recognizing that at 16 years of age, many students are not very sophisticated analysers and my test items are consequently not so numerous in that category; on the other hand I can expect them to recall and comprehend information and to some extent apply principles to a new situation. Similarly, the areas of synthesis and evaluation have not been included in the table. Such higher-order cognitive questions might be included, depending upon the students in the class.The same table may be drawn up for other aspects of geography like *economic geography* or *climatology* or *geomorphology*. If it is found necessary to cover topics dealing with particular areas like Africa or Asia or North America, then the appropriate areal coverage must be written into the table.

There remain the twin problems of the *validity* and *reliability* of

Table 10.4 Number of items planned for an objective test on urban geography for 16-year-old students

	Rank–size rule	Town size in relation to functions	The spacing of towns in a political area	Func-tional zoning in towns	Urban growth	Urban decay	Total
Knowledge	1	2	2	4	3	2	14
Comprehen-sion	1	2	2	4	3	2	14
Application	1	2	1	3	2	1	10
Analysis	1	1	1	1	1	1	6
Total	4	7	6	12	9	6	44

these tests. *Validity* is a concept denoting the extent to which a test is measuring what it is meant to measure. If a test is meant to measure a student's ability to use a topographical or survey map to find his way across a piece of country, then the test must do just that to be valid. The fact that questions could be set to find out what he could infer about the geology of the area from the map is irrelevant. It follows that the more narrowly the objective of the test is defined, the more likely it is to be valid. But this is an ideal which is seldom reached. Broadly there are two aspects to validity: one is known as *content validity* and the other as *criterion validity*. Content validity describes the extent to which the items test the objectives and content which it is desired to test. For example, would the items devised as a result of Table 10.4 actually test the behaviours and contents specified? One way to determine this is to ask colleagues to scan the items and indicate what behaviours and content these appear to test. If you are in reasonable agreement then the content validity is probably high. Criterion validity refers to the way the test under construction may be compared with another instrument which purports to measure the same behaviours and content. For example it may be possible to compare the results of the test under scrutiny with the results of a previously administered end-of-year examination. If there is good agreement between them, then the criterion validity of the test may be said to be high. This would involve working out the correlation coefficients between the results of the two tests. In practice this is seldom done, for it presumes that the end-of-term test (or any other equivalent measure) is a good criterion to compare your test with for its predictive validity; but this is problematic. Thus no really satisfactory way of measuring the criterion validity of a test exists, since the very concept of one test being able to predict the kinds of behaviour to be tested by a second test is a doubtful one.

Reliability is a description of the extent to which a test performs consistently on different occasions with a population of students. Thus if a test is reliable a student sitting the test on two occasions, say a month apart, should get nearly the same mark or grade on each occasion. Reliability is very important, since a test is of no use if it gives different results at different times. Thus a good test which is valid must be reliable. But a reliable test may not be valid, that is, it may be consistent in its scoring of students, but it may not in fact test what it is meant to test.

There are several ways of estimating the reliability of a test, but probably the simplest is to use the Kuder–Richardson formula 20 or KR 20, though you will have to take it on trust that it works. The calculation is:

$$\text{reliability coefficient (KR 20)} = \frac{n}{(n-1)} \times \frac{s^2 - \Sigma pq}{s^2}$$

where p is the proportion of students answering the test item correctly, q is the proportion of students answering the test item incorrectly, n the number of items in the test and s the standard deviation of the test score (see Ch. 6) (s^2 = the variance). The standard deviation is a means of measuring the extent to which individual scores vary from the mean and is calculated in the following way:

$$s = \sqrt{\frac{\Sigma d^2}{n}}$$

where Σ means sum of, d is the deviation of each score from the mean (if the mean is 50 and an individual score is 40 then $d = 10$) and n the number of scores. Since s^2 is required, there is no need to work out the square root:

$$s^2 = \frac{\Sigma d^2}{n}$$

If there were 100 students and $\Sigma d^2 = 10\,000$ then $s^2 = 100$. If there were 100 items on the test and the mean score was 50/100, and $\Sigma pq = 25$ then:

$$\text{reliability coefficient} = \text{(KR 20)} = \frac{100}{100 - 1} \times \frac{100 - 25}{100}$$

$$= \frac{100 - 25}{99}$$

$$= \frac{75}{99}$$

$$= + 0.76$$

As in most of these coefficients the possible range is between 0 which would indicate that the test is completely unreliable and 1.0 which is a measure of complete reliability. In the case worked out above, a reliability of 0.76 is quite good since most classroom tests have a reliablity of between 0.60 and 0.80 worked on the Kuder–Richardson formula. Most published standardized tests advertise a reliability coefficient of 0.90 or greater. A simple visual means of ascertaining the reliability of a test is to divide the items into odd and even items and plot the scores of each student on each axis of a graph as shown in Fig. 10.8. This is known as the scatter diagram means of judging *split-half reliability*. The procedure is to add up the total score of each student on the even items of the test and the total score on the odd items of the test and then use one dot to plot that student's score. For example a student may have 45/100 marks for the odd items and 55/100 for the even items. (His total score on the test would therefore be 100/200.) But a dot would be placed on the graph opposite 45 of the horizontal (or odd) axis and opposite 55 of the vertical (or even) axis. The same procedure would be repeated for all other students. The result would be a scatter-graph such as those shown in Fig. 10.8. If the students performed absolutely consistently and the test items were utterly reliable, then all the dots would be along a central diagonal line going from 0 to 100. That is, a student scoring 10 on odd items would also score 10 on even items, a student scoring 80 on odd items would also score 80 on even items and so on. In practice a reasonably reliable test is more likely to produce a result like that in Fig. 10.8(a) where the distribution of dots is 'cigar-shaped'. An unreliable test is more likely to produce a distribution like that shown in Fig. 10.8(b). This would show that the test could not be relied upon to measure whatever it was intended to measure. Thus an unreliable test can never be valid.

In general, if a test shows up as not having a high reliability, this means that the test items need to be re-examined. Usually this will show up in the facility index and the discrimination index. A test can have its reliability improved by increasing the number of items, replacing items which discriminate poorly, increasing the number of distractors per item and making sure that the language used in the test is clear and unambiguous.

Objective tests in geography may be used in all sorts of different circumstances; for internal school tests and examinations, for external examinations of various types and levels. It is perhaps not practicable for the hard-pressed school-teacher to ensure that his own self-devised tests are rigorously pre-tested and assessed for validity and reliability, but it is vitally important that any geography objective tests which are used for giving qualifications or for selecting students for higher education or jobs should be adequately pre-tested and should be as valid and reliable as possible given the instruments available at present for measuring these qualities.

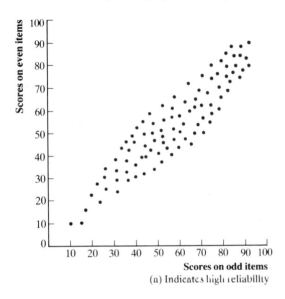

(a) Indicates high reliability

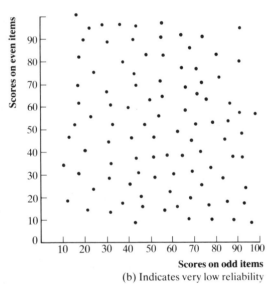

(b) Indicates very low reliability

Fig. 10.8 Scatter diagrams of split-half scores

Non-objective tests and examinations

It is often objected that the kind of test illustrated in the previous section does not test much beyond factual recall. I think I have demonstrated that such tests can be constructed to test comprehension application and analysis, that is, mental operations which require thinking or reasoning in one form or another. It is true, however, that such tests cannot measure a student's capacity for expressing geographical ideas in his own way (verbally or graphically) or for being creative. This is one reason why the traditional essay-type examination is still widely used, though another is that it is much easier to set an essay-type examinaton than an objective one. The main problem is that such examinations are very difficult to mark in a way which is entirely fair to candidates. No matter how carefully the questions are chosen and worded, markers will differ in their assessment of answers. One way of overcoming this is to have each candidate's work marked by a number of different examiners. While this ensures that a candidate's work is not dependent on one person's opinion, it is a very expensive process since all examiners have to be paid. Traditional practice in some school examinations has been for all examiners of a particular examination paper to meet under a chief examiner and agree upon a marking scheme. Groups of examiners then mark sample scripts and discuss among themselves the marks which they have given each script and try to agree on common marks. This attempts to harmonize marking standards. When some sort of agreement has been reached, examiners then mark an allotted batch of scripts, but their performance is monitored from time to time by a chief examiner who by rereading samples of scripts ensures that examiners are keeping to the agreed marking scheme and to the standard. In practice such a scheme can work reasonably well, though the extent to which it can ensure absolute parity between examiners is limited, since the subjective element is always present. What is often done is to compare the total performance of all examiners and to note where there are significant differences – for example, one examiner may be marking to a higher standard than another, that is, his scripts get lower marks. When this is clear a decision may be taken to raise all the marks by a certain percentage to bring these scripts into line with a norm set by the chief examiner (Bruce 1969).

In the ultimate analysis, what matters is the performance of all candidates in the examination. If the marking seems to indicate that, with a large number of candidates, the general peformance is higher (or lower) than with similar candidates (for example those who took the same examination in the previous year), then it is presumed that this is statistically unlikely, and an adjustment will be made to bring the distribution of grades in line with a distribution which has been acceptable in the past.

Whatever the methods used to ensure fairness in the allocation of marks and grades, it is important to select questions which make such an examination educationally worth-while. Certain principles may be adhered to in setting such examination questions:

1. The language should be clear and appropriate for the students who are to sit the examination. There is little point in setting a question that the majority of candidates will not understand. Thus 'Evaluate a systems approach to the study of geomorphological processes' would seem an inappropriate question for most students up to the age of 17. It is better to avoid such words as 'geography' or 'geographical factors' which tend to be vague.

2. Questions should not be such as to require only the regurgitation of previously learned information. For example a question such as 'Describe ground nut-growing in Nigeria', is not likely to produce answers which test anything beyond factual recall. Questions should therefore be set which involve the candidate in problem-solving or relational thinking. This may be done by setting such a question as 'How can you explain that the functional zones of some towns are arranged in a concentric pattern?' Of course it is always possible for someone to answer such a question from a remembered but not understood explanation, though this tends to be evident in the answer.

3. Questions are better if they do not rely unduly on remembered information. In other words questions which supply information but ask students to reflect upon the significance of that information are better at testing thinking rather than memory. For example 'Study Fig. 10.9 and indicate what it tells you about the distribution of manufacturing industries in the United States. Explain why this kind of spatial distribution exists.' In this question the distribution of employment in manufacturing industries is indicated by a statistical diagram on a map, so that the candidate can use the map to answer the first part of the question. For the second part of the question he has to use his knowledge of the United States' relief and size, his knowledge of the way the area was peopled as well as the distribution of power and mineral resources. In other words he is using his knowledge of principles of industrial location.

4. The younger the candidates the more advisable it will be to break a question up into a series of constituent parts, since such candidates will find it difficult to compose an analytical or synthetical essay. For example, 16-year-old students might well be set a question like the following:

Figure 10.10 is a map of the United States of America which shows the main uses of land in the major regions.

(a) Which region has the biggest total area?

(b) Which region has the biggest proportion of land under crops?

(c) Which region has the greatest area of forest land?

(d) Which regions have more than half their land under pasture? In what part of the USA are these regions?

(e) What physical factors help to explain the general distribution of pasture land in the USA?

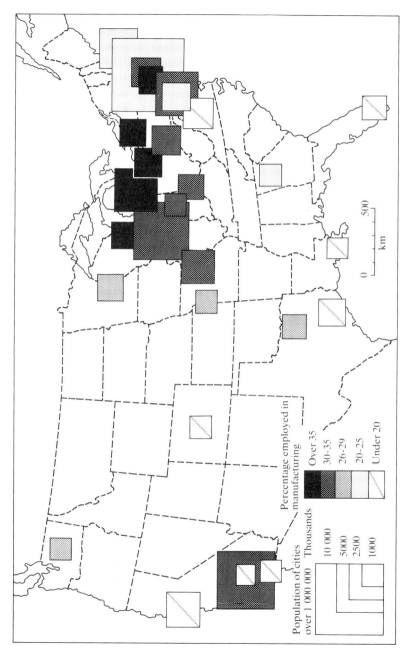

Fig. 10.9 Large standard metropolitan statistical areas by proportion of employment in manufacturing, 1969. (*Source:* Estall 1972)

Such a question directs the candidate's attention to particular aspects of the evidence on the map, makes him aware of some spatial patterns and asks him to explain an areal distribution in terms of physical factors. Clearly a question of this sort, sometimes known as a structured essay question, approximates to an objective test question, though because the candidate is asked to supply answers the marking can never be completely objective. It is sometimes known as a 'restricted response question', whereas the true objective-type question is known as 'controlled response question', and a completely open-ended question is known as a 'free response question'. Another variant of such examining techniques is the so-called 'open-book' examination, in which essay questions are set and candidates are free to bring into the examination room certain books and documents.

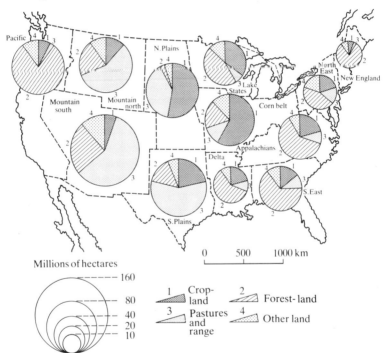

Fig. 10.10 Major regional uses of land in the USA, 1964. (*Source:* Estall 1972)

Course work assessment

Because tests and examinations only occur from time to time and because they may give a false picture of a student's true worth, it has often been suggested that the assessment of a student should be made on the basis of the work which he does during the course of his studies. In this way, it is argued, his performance is not hampered by the special conditions affecting examinations, and the grades recorded for his work sample his normal learning behaviour instead of the rather untypical behaviour produced by examinations. Thus *course work assessment* is the giving of marks or grades for a selection of the work done by a student during his course and their addition to give an overall grade. If *all* the student's learning behaviour is graded, then this tends to be called *continuous assessment*, that is, it is an aggregate of all class work, homework, oral tests, written tests and practical work including fieldwork which the student has obtained over a period of time. Continuous assessment tends to be used mainly for feedback purposes, that is, it gives the teacher an indication of how the student's learning is developing. Most continuous assessment is therefore used for internal school purposes and not intended for publication. Its use outside the school, for example for employers, is generally in a synthesized grade or general mark. Course work assessment, however, is often used with or instead of traditional examinations as a means of assessing a student for what is a public qualification.

The problem of course work assessment is similar to that of assessing essays, namely that the assessment is bound to some extent to be subjective. Further, the course work may be disparate in nature consisting of essays, projects and fieldwork. Let us therefore examine ways of attempting to minimize the difficulties of course work assessment, bearing in mind that no method of assessment is ever likely to be perfect.

Essays

A student's essay is his attempt at organizing his thoughts around a topic or problem in a coherent and relevant way and to give him scope for being creative, albeit in a small way. To grade such an essay involves a judgement which can be made either from a general impression or as a result of using an analytical scheme. An impression mark is one which enables a teacher to take into account all the qualities of an essay which are not easily specifiable in advance of its being written, such as its originality. But an impression mark will tend to vary from teacher to teacher and from the same teacher at different times. A mark based on an analytical scheme will tend to be less variable, but such a scheme can only be drawn up when the topic lends itself to it. For example, supposing that the topic is 'The factors affecting the location of hydroelectric power installations' (assuming a market exists for the power and capital for the construction is available) then if 20 marks are to be given to the essay one could allocate the marks as follows:

Marks

5 Site considerations (deep valley, firm foundations, accessibility).

3 Catchment area for water (many tributaries to main river, size of catchment area).

4 Climatic factors (rainfall, evaporation, winter temperatures).

2 Distance from market (location of main users of electricity).

5 Environmental considerations (flooding of arable land and villages, effect on natural flora and fauna, disease spreading, landscape quality).

20

It will be an advantage if teachers in the same department can each mark several essays and compare marks and then agree on some reasonably common standard. In a case where a question involves values, then multiple marking is a necessity, since marks allocated for each marker will reflect his own set of values. For example a question which asks 'Draw a plan for a small housing estate of 500 people indicating what services you would provide and where you would place them', clearly involves values and should be marked by more than one person. It is also as well to remember that a mark of 20 means the best that one can expect of a student of that age, not what the teacher considers a perfect essay on the topic.

Projects

These are attempts at gathering data on a particular theme or problem and putting this together in the form of an exhibition or a folder of maps, pictures and diagrams with an accompanying text which exposes the theme or problem. Consequently, a project is a manifestation of a student's ability to work independently and find appropriate information, to put information together in a coherent way and to display this information in several forms (verbal and graphic). It may therefore be useful to mark the project using the following criteria (Deale 1975):

(a) Presentation (neatness, clarity, appropriate illustrations, etc.).

(b) Research (references, bibliography, personal investigations).

(c) Content (coherence, relevance, continuity and significance).

(d) Conclusions (interpretation of evidence presented).

What weight is given to each is up to the teacher, but I would suggest that if 10 per cent is given to *Presentation*, then 30 per cent can be given each to *Research*, *Content* and *Conclusions*. It is probable that students produce the best individual studies in geography when:

(a) a manageable problem is defined;

(b) a hypothesis or generalization or model is formulated;

(c) data are collected either from direct fieldwork or from secondary sources;

(d) data are analysed and presented;
(e) conclusions are reached which enable the hypothesis, generalization or model to be evaluated.

This, of course, applies to fieldwork as much as to projects.

Fieldwork

Fieldwork presents special problems in that assessment can take place at two stages:

(a) when the fieldwork is being carried out,
that is, in the 'field' itself;
(b) when the fieldwork has been written up,
that is, in the notebook or folder.

The assessment of fieldwork in the 'field' is analogous to the assessment of a practical examination in the laboratory. The teacher should be assessing processes which cannot be assessed elsewhere. In the case of geographical fieldwork, this means assessing the ways in which students go about the process of gathering the data which they need to test a hypothesis or to complete a survey. For example, in physical geography they may be making slope measurements, testing rock hardness, collecting field samples of rocks and vegetation, making field sketches, measuring distances, monitoring run-off and so on. In human geography, they may be gathering information from visible evidence (e.g. land-use surveys, traffic surveys, dating buildings etc. ...) or from questionnaire surveys, or again from public documentary sources. It is probably useful to assess such qualities as:

(a) ability to organize the observations to be made;
(b) ability to observe and record observations;
(c) ability to manipulate equipment (if relevant);
(d) attitude, i.e. persistence, resourcefulness, enthusiasm.

Each quality could be marked on a 5-point scale such as:

5 Outstanding
4 Good
3 Average (in relation to other candidates)
2 Weak
1 Poor

Such assessment would clearly be more reliable if it were given for more than one field exercise, for example, on three separate occasions and by different teachers.

The assessment of the results of a fieldwork exercise is a similar operation to the assessment of a project and the same suggested breakdown of the assessment given above for a project may be used (presentation, research, content, conclusions).

Oral examinations

One further method of assessing a student's work is to give him an oral examination. Although this is a favoured method of examining secondary-school students in geography in such European countries as France and Belgium, there are certain difficulties associated with this method. In the first place any thorough sampling of the student's knowledge and abilities in geography is likely to be time-consuming. Even if each student is only given a 10-minute oral examination, this means that a class of 30 students will need 5 hours of the examiner's time. Secondly, students are often more nervous in an oral than in a written examination, though this will vary enormously from student to student. An inarticulate student may yet be able to produce an excellent piece of written work, and similarly a student responding well to an oral examination may not perform so well in a written examination. It is therefore very important that the oral examiner should put the student at his ease. I have conducted oral examinations in secondary schools and was particularly conscious of the nervous state of certain candidates, and although I did my best to indicate that the student could relax and feel at ease, a few remained tense during the interview. Thirdly, it may be difficult in the conversation between student and examiner for the examiner to remain sufficiently detached to be able to mark objectively the student's performance. For this reason, some examiners prefer to record an interview on magnetic tape and then to assess the candidate's performance later. This, however, is even more time-consuming and even more expensive.

In view of these disadvantages, you may wonder whether there can possibly by any valid reason for conducting an oral examination in geography. Clearly, where students have some difficulty in expressing themselves in writing, an oral examination is of some use. But there is the added advantage that an oral examiner can guide a student's responses and avoid the kind of total disaster which sometimes occurs in essay questions when a candidate in an examination accidentally misreads a question. I well remember watching powerless during a public examination when a student who had been asked to answer a question in the context of South America, proceeded to answer the question in the context of North America! Further, an examiner may probe into work done by a student in a project or in fieldwork, in such a way that he is better able to judge the conception and execution of the project. Thus to my mind oral examinations are best used as supplements to, rather than as replacements for, written assessments. Just how an oral examination is structured must depend on what objectives are being tested and in what context. If an oral test is being used to probe into a project or fieldwork exercise, then the examiner is looking for ability in:

(a) justifying the procedures used to collect data;
(b) understanding the analysis to which the data were subjected;
(c) interpreting the results in different ways.
If 20 marks are being given for the oral examination then the division of marks could be *(a)* 6, *(b)* 6 and *(c)* 8. I would suggest that the marks given for the oral part of a geography test or examination where such is desirable, should form about 20 per cent of the total. For example in a fieldwork exercise the distribution of marks could be:
(a) practical work in the field   20%
(b) fieldwork folder or notebook   60%
(c) oral examination   20%
Teachers may, of course, find that they can only use the evidence of the fieldwork folder or notebook.

The problem of moderation

If objective tests are used in testing candidates from many different schools, then since the marking is objective, the marks and/or grades obtained will be strictly comparable. If essays are marked by different examiners, then a problem arises about the different standards of different examiners. We discussed earlier what measures could be taken to minimize those difficulties. But if a large number of schools undertake course work assessment and if such assessments are to have a common meaning for all schools, then some means must be found of harmonizing the assessments given by individual tutors, particularly if the grades given to candidates are to feature as part of a school-leaving examination which will have currency over a national area. This process of making marks or grades by different teachers (or examiners) comparable is known as moderation. It is as well to understand that such a process involves human judgement and is therefore short of perfection.

If it is possible to combine course work assessment with the administration of an objective test of attainment in geography which is common to all students, then the results of the attainment test may be used to 'moderate' (or standardize) the marks given for course work by different teachers. Broadly, what is implied by such a technique is that there is a fairly strong correlation (0.7 or more) between the results of the attainment test and those of course work assessment. Put in another way, the rank order of students in the two tests will be broadly similar though not identical. However, the absolute level of marks in the test is probably going to be different from the absolute level of marks given by different teachers on the course work. The test marks are used to standardize marks of the course work so that the absolute levels are not very different. It is as well to bear in mind that since the test is being used in this way it must be valid and reliable and be seen to be testing roughly the same sort of abilities as the course work.

Let us take the example of two schools, which have ten candidates each for an examination in geography. All candidates take a common attainment test, but course work in each school is marked by the resident teacher. The distribution of marks could be as shown in Table 10.5, the maximum mark being 100. As you can see, the

Table 10.5 Distribution of marks for course work and test in two schools

School Y

Student	Test rank	Course work mark	Course work rank	Test mark
A	1	65	3	90
B	2	85	1	70
C	3	70	2	60
D	4	60	4	55
E	5	50	6	50
F	6	45	7	45
G	7	55	5	40
H	8	36	9	35
I	9	30	10	30
J	10	38	8	20
Mean		53.4		49.5

School Z

Student	Test rank	Course work mark	Course work rank	Test mark
K	1	90	1	95
L	2	70	4	75
M	3	75	3	60
N	4	68	5	58
O	5	80	2	49
P	6	65	6	46
Q	7	60	7	42
R	8	46	10	36
S	9	50	9	31
T	10	55	8	22
Mean		65.9		51.4

average or mean course work mark is higher in both cases than the test mark. But the course work marks for school Z are much higher than those for school Y, though the mean test marks for each school are fairly close to each other. It follows, therefore, that something needs to be done to make the course work marks of school Y and school Z more comparable. For example student E and student S both get 50 marks, but are they really of the same calibre?

Now the rank correlation coefficient between the test order and the course work order in school Y is 0.89 and in school Z it is 0.87. These are high enough to be able to use the attainment test to standardize the course work mark. This is shown in Table 10.6. For each school the students are arranged first in their test order then in their course work order. The test marks allocated to the students in test order are

Table 10.6 The scaling of course work marks by test marks in two schools

School Y

Test order	Test mark	Course work order	Scaled course work mark
A	90	B	90
B	70	C	70
C	60	A	60
D	55	D	55
E	50	G	50
F	45	E	45
G	40	F	40
H	35	J	35
I	30	H	30
J	20	I	20

School Z

Test order	Test mark	Course work order	Scaled course work mark
K	95	K	95
L	75	O	75
M	60	M	60
N	58	L	58
O	49	N	49
P	46	P	46
Q	42	Q	42
R	36	T	36
S	31	S	31
T	22	R	22

then allocated in to the course work order. Thus the order established by the original course work marks is not changed, but the marks have been effectively scaled to present the same distribution as the test marks. You can see now that although student E has a scaled mark of 50 for course work, student S now has a scaled mark of 31 for course work which more closely represents his rank. Since students will probably be given a total mark based on both test and course assessment, the scaled marks can be added together to give a final result. For example student A's total marks are 150 out of 200, i.e. 90 + 60, student B's marks are 160 (70 + 90), student C's marks are 130 (60 + 70) and so on. But if teachers feel that course work marks should count for more than test marks, then these can be appropriately weighted. For example, it may be decided that, because course work covers a year's work, it should count for three times the test mark. In that case student E's total mark becomes 185, i.e. (3 × 45) + 50 = 185. This can be reduced to a percentage if necessary by dividing by 4, i.e. 185/4 = 46.25 per cent.

When students do not sit a standardized attainment test, the process of moderation is much less precise. It depends essentially on the judgement of a *moderator*. The moderator is an experienced teacher who compares samples of work from students in differing schools and verifies the standards of marking or grading. In general, a moderator when examining the work of a school's students in geography will accept the rank order provided by the teachers who teach those pupils. He will, however, on the basis of his knowledge of other students' work in other schools, decide whether the marks or grades should be raised or lowered as a whole, Since it is important that the moderator understands the nature and purpose of the course work being done, it is usual for him to visit the schools concerned on several occasions. Thus, in looking at the work of students, he might see, for example, the following set of marks and moderate them as shown in Table 10.7. Sometimes moderation can be achieved by groups of teachers in the locality meeting, reviewing each others' student assignments and agreeing on their grading.

Table 10.7 The moderation of course work marks

Candidates' marks											
School X	Original	90	70	60	55	50	45	40	35	30	20
	Moderated	No change									
School Y	Original	60	55	50	45	40	40	35	32	30	25
	Moderated	75	65	60	55	50	40	35	30	25	20
School Z	Original	80	75	70	65	60	55	50	45	40	25
	Moderated	80	70	65	60	55	45	40	35	30	25

Conclusions on evaluation in geography

Having examined various methods of evaluating geographical education, it is important to bear in mind that the main purpose of evaluation is to improve the curriculum, that is, ultimately to achieve a greater level of understanding among all pupils. Although it is possible to go to great lengths to measure the achievement of students, all is of little avail unless something positive and worthwhile is achieved. Thus the evaluation of student performance should always be fed back to the teachers and the students so that they can appreciate what progress has been made, or if little has been achieved, then some inquiry can begin to find out why. The great advantage of course work assessment and teacher moderation is that teachers from different schools meet to discuss their work and problems. Curriculum improvement often occurs as a result of better communication between practising teachers. But knowledge of the student's reaction to a curriculum is equally important since they are the teachers' clients!

Glossary

Accommodation: Adjustment of a child's understanding of past experiences in the light of new perceptions. Previous learning is accommodated so as to assimilate the new. Thus past learning and new experiences are considered and mutually adjusted leading to the development of *new* schemata or conceptual structures.

Aims in education: The term 'aim' is now generally reserved for those general aims which give direction to a teacher's work, but which are broad and non-specific. The term 'objective' is given to the more specific goal which a teacher may have in a lesson or teaching unit. Thus to promote international understanding may be an aim of geographical education, but to show that the attitude to cattle of Indians and Americans differs for cultural reasons is an objective.

Assimilation: The taking in of new experiences and fitting these into *existing* schemata or conceptual structures.

Baseline data: Information describing pertinent aspects of a situation prior to a study. These data provide a point of reference against which later data may be compared.

Behavioural objectives: Objectives for a curriculum which are very tightly defined in terms of the students for whom they are meant, the kind of behaviour required, the kind of performance by which the objective can be measured, the standard to be used in evaluating whether the objective has been met and the conditions under which the learning experiences may take place.

Bloom's taxonomy of educational objectives: A system of classifying educational objectives into hierarchical categories in which the later categories subsume the earlier ones. It may be used to judge whether questions in a list are testing simple or more complex learnings.

Coefficient of correlation: Measure of the strength of a relationship (*see* **correlation**).

Cognitive growth (cognitive development, mental development): Development of thinking from birth to adult life; development of mental skills which are qualitatively different through chronological phases of development.

Cognitive perspective: A term used by, *inter alia*, R. S. Peters in the philosophy of education to indicate that an educated person should not only have some in-depth knowledge of a particular discipline, but also a broad but more superficial knowledge of a number of other disciplines. Having cognitive perspective involves having both depth and breadth of understanding.

Concept: A notion held in the mind which is built up by abstracting common attributes of events, situations, objects or ideas, and which is given a name. Simple concepts refer to concrete objects, difficult concepts refer to ideas.

Conceptual model: Is a model describing or illustrating an imaginary but possible structure of a system or process which provides a basis for scientific research or is a guide to practice.

Concrete operations: Mental operations which characterize the thinking of children aged about 7 to 12 years. Thinking is linked to concrete reality more than to abstract ideas, and some operations may be carried out in a concrete way, e.g. using counters or an abacus.

Confidence level: Amount of confidence with which a statement can be accepted. For example, a 99 per cent confidence level means that the statement would be likely to be true in 99 cases in every 100.

Conservation of weight, quantity and volume: The understanding that weight, quantity, volume and number remain constant even though shape or pattern or arrangement may be altered.

Continuous assessment: The assessment of all the activities undertaken by a student during a course study, i.e. not selected pieces of course work.

Correlation: Mutual relationship between sets of variables. Correlation is usually expressed in terms of a number which can vary from -1.0 (perfect negative relationship) to 1.0 (perfect positive relationship).

Course work assessment: The assessment of specified pieces of work undertaken by students during a course of study. These may include fieldwork, essays, projects, maps.

Curriculum (Biddle's definition): Is a document containing a structured series of intended learning outcomes which have been organized for pupils by an educational institution. This document would include statements about aims, educational objectives, organized learning centres and methods of evaluation.

Curriculum development: The activity of attempting to change the curriculum by engaging in experimental activities in educational establishments. This activity usually has as its aim the development of new objectives, the use of new content and teaching/learning methods. Curriculum development may be carried out by individual teachers or by teams specially appointed for this task. Curriculum development projects are specially financed projects to promote curriculum development in a subject or group of subjects. The American High School Geography

Project was an example of such a project in the USA and the Geography 16–19 Project is an example of such a project in England and Wales.

Curriculum system or process: The way in which the aims, objectives, content, methods and evaluation of an educational experience interact. The curriculum can be thought of as a description of what happens in schools or other educational institutions. It should be borne in mind that older uses of the term also exist, as when a curriculum is used to indicate (a) a course of study, or (b) the combinations of subjects taught in a school. The term 'hidden curriculum' is used to denote those aspects of the curriculum process which are not planned but from which learning takes place, as for example, when a student learns not to query what a teacher states because he knows the teacher may object to his authority being questioned. It is important to remember that no generally agreed definition of the term 'curriculum' exists. The above definition can be thought of as the 'curriculum process in action'. Restriction of the term to a document (see Curriculum) can be thought of as the 'planned or intended curriculum'.

Degrees of freedom: That maximum number of observations that can vary without automatically determining the rest.

Dependent variable: May be considered as the effect in the cause–effect relationship. It is the attribute, property or characteristic which manipulation of the independent variable is meant to change. It is also called the criterion or criterion variable because it is the phenomenon with which the researcher is ultimately concerned.

Discrimination index: A way of evaluating how far a test item discriminates between those candidates who perform well and less well on the test.

Distractors: The plausible but incorrect responses to a multiple-choice question in an objective test.

Double-barrelled question: A question on a questionnaire or interview form which contains two or more ideas. The answer cannot be interpreted because there is no way to determine to which idea the subject was responding.

Ecosystem approach: An approach to geography which views man and his relationships with his total environment as a dynamic system.

Educational objectives: Statements of intentions or intended outcomes to be achieved as a result of the educational process. An *instructional objective* is a statement by the teacher of the learning outcomes he expects students to attain. It may be defined in behavioural, procedural or expressive terms.

Egocentrism: Distortion of an individual's perception and conception caused by viewing experience purely in terms of his own schemata.

Embedded shapes: Complex arrangement of lines, points and patterns, where patterns overlap and interweave (as on topographical maps).

Enactive representation: An early stage in the development of the way a child represents his understanding of the world. This early stage involves the actual manipulation of concrete objects, e.g. modelling with bricks or clay.

Equilibration: Putting experiences into relation with one another to achieve balance between past learning and new experiences.

Essay-type examination: These are examinations in which the questions are open-ended and the student must construct his answer. These questions are also called 'free response questions'. Although they test the student's ability to compose an answer and marshal facts and arguments, they are very difficult to mark reliably because a strong subjective element is involved in evaluating the answers.

Euclidean stage: Stage in the understanding of spatial concepts when the child has a grasp of the relationships between objects in space; their relative proportion, size and distance. He is aware of perspective, and of the different sets of spatial relationships which will occur from different viewpoints.

Evaluation: The act of making a value judgement about any aspect of the curriculum process. This is usually divided into *(a)* curriculum evaluation, that is, providing information for decision-making about a curriculum, and *(b)* student assessment, the process of measuring the learning which a student has achieved.

Expository methods: These are mainly deductive methods of teaching/ learning in which facts, concepts, relationships and generalizations are described by the teacher or printed in a book with a view to students understanding and assimilating them. For example, the teaching method used for a lecture is an expository method.

External examination: An examination organized by a body (e.g. a university or special examination board) which is not concerned directly with teaching the students examined. External examining boards usually award qualifying diplomas like the General Certificate of Education in England or the Baccalauréat in France.

Facility index: A means of judging how easy or difficult is a test item. It is defined as the ratio of the number of correct responses to an item to the number of attempted responses.

$$FI = \frac{\text{number of correct responses}}{\text{number of attempted responses}}$$

Formal operations: The final stage in the development of thinking, according to Piaget. Concrete operations have been internalized, so that they can now be carried out mentally and thinking in the abstract becomes possible, i.e. hypothetic-deductive thinking takes place (see below).

Formative evaluation: The activity of evaluating the curriculum process as it is developing.

368 New Unesco Source Book for Geography Teaching

Hypothesis: A statement of an outcome or relationship which a study is designed to test. In the declarative form, null form or question form, it is the basis for inquiry objectives and the procedures which follow.

Hypothetico-deductive reasoning: Hypotheses are set up as possible solutions to a question or problem. Hypotheses are then tested in turn by collection and analysis of data. The hypothesis which is best supported by the evidence may be accepted as the best solution. This kind of reasoning in a student is evidence that he is at the Piagetian stage of formal operations.

Iconic representation: Stage in the development of the way a child represents his world. In this stage the use of images, examples from concrete reality, remain an important aid to understanding, e.g. drawings, models or maps.

Idiographic geography: Is concerned with the study of the particular event and phenomenon. Monographs, case studies and sample studies may be classified as parts of idiographic geography. The investigating way of this 'school of geography' is more inductive, factual and descriptive and the explanation is often 'contained in the description'.

Independent variable: Refers to the cause in the cause–effect relationship. It is the attribute, property or characteristic which, when changed in some way, is thought to cause a change in some other attribute, property or characteristic.

Illuminative evaluation: This term usually refers to methods of evaluating curriculum which do not rely solely on assessing student learning by classical research designs, but on a variety of approaches which owe much more to phenomenology than to logical positivism. Descriptions of the ways students and teachers react to a new curriculum are linked to more traditional assessments of pupil performance. The aim is to give an analysis of what is going on in a curriculum development situation, and to make value judgements about this for those who will ultimately have to take decisions about the process.

Inductive mental process: Part of inquiry/discovery methods where students from a series of questions reach stages of:
1. concept formation;
2. inferring and generalizing;
3. applying principles in new situations.
Inductive mental processes are essentially focused on the *acquisition of concepts* where they can be seen as generalizations of data.

Inquiry/discovery methods: Are essentially inductive methods from a given case to a generalization, from a hypothesis to a principle, from a problem to a solution. Many findings in cognitive psychology (Piaget, Bruner) suggested the importance of using such methods for primary and secondary education.

Inquiry learning: Where teachers provide resources for analysis by pupils engaged in finding out for themselves. Teacher control varies from strict direction of pupil work to genuinely open pupil inquiry.

Intended learning outcome: Is a planned learning experience consisting of an activity component and a content component which has been organized to suit the levels of ability and interest of pupils at a particular stage of cognitive development. A *structured series of intended learning outcomes* refers to the organizational relationships for effective learning among the intended outcomes.

Inter-disciplinary units: Are those in which content and processes of inquiry from the disciplines are fused around themes, topics, areas, concepts or questions in an attempt to integrate a number of sciences and/or humanities.

Internalization: The process of translating concrete actions into mental activities. Experiences are internalized and help the child to carry out activities in the imagination. For Piaget, thought is internalized action.

Interview: A variation of the survey method in which information is obtained from the respondent directly, that is, through face-to-face interaction.

Intuitive stage: A subdividion of Piaget's pre-operational stage in the development of thinking. In this stage ideas are formed impressionistically, or intuitively, because the child's perceptions of his environment are still superficial. A number of basic concepts, e.g. conservation, remain incompletely understood.

Learning experiences: The kind of experiences which students have in a classroom, laboratory or on fieldwork. These experiences are usually wholly or partly organized and structured by the teacher. They consist of the content of a subject structured in an exercise which enables the students to learn a concept, principle and/or skill, or to apply these in a new situation.

Mental maps: Maps which are held in mind, e.g. a mental picture of how to reach a certain destination, or a mental image of the spatial arrangement of a certain urban district. Mental maps may be expressed as drawn maps, e.g. in Fig. 7.7(b).

Mental operation (operations): The ability to carry out activities in the imagination, that is mentally.

Moderation: The process of harmonizing the marks or grades given by different teachers or examiners in such a way that all students' marks conform to the same standard. This may be done statistically or by judgement depending on the available information.

Multi-disciplinary units: Are those in which disciplines are studied in parallel, so that interrelationships may be stressed, and differences preserved.

Nomothetic geography: Is concerned with theories, principles and generalizations. This geography is often called *NEW*; and since 1950, it has been much developed by several geographers in the USA, Great Britain, Sweden, Canada and also from other countries (Berry, Bunge, Haggett, Hägerstrand, Burton).

Null hypothesis: A statement that the relationship or outcome predicted in the related declarative hypothesis will not occur. The null hypothesis is used because it corresponds to the statistical procedures, that is, the procedures directly test the null hypothesis.

Objectives in education: These refer to the more immediate goals which a teacher may have in teaching an idea concept, principle or skill. An objective is always a target which may or may not be reached. The term 'outcome' is usually reserved for what has in fact been achieved. An objective may be cognitive, i.e. concerned with knowledge; affective, i.e. concerned with emotions and attitudes; or expressive, denoting an objective whose precise outcome is uncertain, i.e. the student is asked to react to an educational encounter.

Objective tests: Tests of knowledge or thinking skills which can be marked objectively since only one correct response is acceptable. These are usually in the form of multiple-choice questions, matching-type questions, alternative-response questions. These are also known as closed-ended questions, since the student does not compose an answer but merely chooses the one he thinks is correct. They are also called controlled response tests.

Open question: A question in an interview, on a questionnaire or on an examination paper for which the respondent constructs an answer; opposite of closed question, in which possible responses are predetermined.

Oral examination: A method of evaluating student performance by an examiner putting questions orally to students. Best used in geography as a complement to other forms of assessment.

Organized learning centres: Are the topics or problems which are used to combine the content and methods of geography with selected learning experiences in order to achieve the intended learning outcomes.

Organizing concept (central concept, key idea): A major concept of broad scope which subsumes many other concepts under it, and relates to other concepts. It is of such general importance that it forms one of the central ideas of a discipline, e.g. spatial interaction in geography.

Perception: The 'contact' of an organism with its environment, established, in the case of humans by the senses of smell, touch, hearing and sight. A percept is made when certain stimuli received by the organism are given some kind of recognition by being singled out for attention from a mass of undifferentiated stimuli.

Used colloquially, viz. 'my perception' – 'the way I see it'. Thus, 'environmental perception' – 'the way the environment is seen'.

Population: All of the elements – people, events, situations, etc. – about which a research study is designed to produce information. A sample is a part of or a subset of the population. Studies are usually conducted with samples, and the external validity of a study is the extent to which findings achieved with a sample can be generalized to the population.

Post-test: A test designed to measure a student's knowledge of a topic after a course of study on that topic.

Potential concept stage: According to Vygotsky, the stage in the development of concept formulation immediately preceding full attainment. In this stage the learner can recognize some, but not all, the attributes which define a certain concept.

Practical significance: The extent to which research findings are meaningful in terms of application to educational practice, that is, in terms of the ability to produce desired changes in behaviour. To be practically significant, a finding must be statistically significant, and it must be stable. However, it can be statistically significant, but not practically significant.

Pre-conceptual stage: Early stage in the development of thinking, from about 2 to 4 years, when the child is not able to form concepts by inductive reasoning. Instead the child tends to reason by going from one particular instance to another.

Pre-test: A test given to students to measure their knowledge of a particular topic prior to a course of study on this topic.

Primary source: Information directly concerned with a particular study. It is usually a journal, article or book in which the author is reporting on his own work. It differs from a secondary source, which involves a second person interpreting the work of someone else.

Problem-solving approach: This is a part of inquiry/discovery methods which deals with a problem, an issue and/or a concern for which students may find some solutions or/and formulate further problems. Various classroom strategies can be used to achieve such an approach, as for example a *simulation game*, where students can solve a problem or test an hypothesis based on something real or unreal by *simulating* facts and data. Role-playing and gaming are mainly used as means to illustrate the problem-solving approach.

Projective stage: A stage in the development of spatial conceptualization, transitional between the topological and the Euclidean stages. In the projective stage, the ability to deal with relationships between objects in space increases as the learner becomes more able to cope with configuration, location and order.

Pseudo-concept: A 'primitive' concept based on superficial attributes rather than truly characteristic attributes of an object or idea, e.g. 'all streams are rivers because they have bridges'. Further discrimination of the attributes which distinguish streams from rivers is required.

Questionnaire: An instrument by which information is obtained from a respondent in written form. Used as one variation of the survey method, it is different from the interview in that information is obtained from the respondent through a pencil-and-paper device.

Random assignment: A method of selecting elements of a population for a study sample, also of dividing a sample into two or more similar groups. This is the only method of assignment which assures that the sample is representative of the population or that one group is similar to another group in every respect within specifiable limits.

Regional geography: Study of units of area of the earth's surface.

Reliability: As applied to a test, the term describes how consistent a test is in measuring the qualities it is designed to measure. A reliable test will give the same result when applied on two occasions to the same test population. Reliability can be measured quantitatively by the Kuder–Richardson formula, or by the split-half test.

Reversibility: Property of a mental operation, that it can be annulled by the reverse operation, e.g. $a + b = c$ can be annulled by $c - b = a$.

Sample: The group of individuals, events, situations or the like which will be involved in a study. The sample is always a part or a subset of a population; a usual concern is to assure that the sample is representative of the population so that results can be generalized.

Sampling unit: The entity which is selected or chosen in the sampling process. It is the unit with which the sampler works.

Schema (pl. schemata): A pattern of knowing which is built up, according to Piaget, by the processes of assimilation and accommodation leading to equilibration. Through equilibration, experiences are placed in relation with one another so as to produce a schema which is stable, consistent and non-contradictory. Schemata can then be applied and tested out when the child is faced with a novel situation. A schema is a sequence of mental or physical operations.

Secondary source: Information about a study or studies which is provided by someone other than the one who conducted the study. The information, usually presented in summary form, involves an interpretation of study results by a person not directly involved.

Significance: Meaning or inference.

Significance level: The level at which one can say, with a stated amount of confidence, that a correlation or any other relationship has not occurred by chance.

Socratic method: For most teachers, the Socratic method is a mode of oral questioning. *Strictu sensu*, the Socratic method is based on four points:
1. the student states a proposition,
2. but, the student's proposition or statement is by no means so simple –

and the teacher leads him to doubt it,
3. the student admits he did not know or perceive the complexity of his proposition,
4. he guides the student to the discovery of truth on the issue.

In the reality of a classroom, the teacher does not use the Socratic method in its pure form because it is a long way to find out the 'truth'. But on social issues, moral behaviour, international understanding, where the answer is complex, the use of the Socratic method might be a good way to reach and understand problems and issues.

Statistical significance: The assurance that the results obtained in a study are not likely to have occurred by chance. High statistical significance provides confidence that the results, and therefore the effects which produced them, are real. However, it says nothing about the nature of the explanation for the findings.

Statistics: The science of collecting and classifying facts and of treating these in ways which allow valid summary statements to be made. Also, it is the mathematical treatment of facts so that stable relationships which are free from chance influences are discovered. The former are referred to as descriptive statistics; the latter as inferential statistics.

Structured interview: An interview in which a specific order and a specific set of procedures is followed. A structured interview is relatively inflexible, for the interviewer does not have freedom to depart from the specified interview plan.

Summative evaluation: The activity of evaluating curriculum development after it has occurred. It usually refers to the evaluation which makes a final judgement on all the aspects of the curriculum process at the end of a curriculum development project's life. There is the inevitable problem that if the curriculum process is still proceeding then no evaluation can ever be final. For this reason some prefer to use the terms *concurrent* evaluation instead of formative evaluation and *subsequent* evaluation instead of summative evaluation.

Survey: A set of research techniques through which subjects actively provide information about themselves. This is one of the descriptive research methods. Surveys are conducted through either interviews or the questionnaire.

Syllabus: A document which may have remote aims but is essentially a summary of the *content* of a course of study.

Symbolic representation: Final stage in the development of the child's ability to represent his world, when he can think in abstract terms and represent reality by symbolic means. Language is a major form of symbolizing.

Syncretic stage: An early stage in concept learning when, according to Vygotsky, concepts may be easily confused because there is little recognition or understanding of their respective attributes. Thus exemplars of concepts may be grouped in a random rather than a reasoned manner, e.g. cats, otters and bears may all be classed as dogs. Unrelated attributes are linked by the child.

Teaching/learning methods: Ways and processes of teaching educational objectives. Teaching methods deal with HOW, for instance, a concept, a notion, a skill can be taught and learned.

Teaching or curriculum unit: An assembly of content, suggestions for teachers and students whose purpose is to teach a limited body of knowledge and skill. Development projects often produce curriculum units as a result of their activities. Thus the American High School Geography Project produced a whole series of units on geography consisting of documents, maps, tables, photographs and teachers' guides. The programme in Chapter 3 is one example of such a unit. A teaching unit might consist of written and/or audio-visual materials. Generally, a teaching unit is divided into several parts, such as objectives, description of activities, strategies, contents, audio-visual materials and evaluation techniques. The HSGP is composed of six teaching units and can be applied for a period of one academic year for 14–16-year-old students.

Topological stage: An early stage in the development of spatial conceptualization, from about 2 to 7 years. The child has ideas of proximity, separation and order of objects, and of enclosure and continuity, but he has no system of co-ordinates with which to relate objects in space and has difficulty in understanding a spatial arrangement from any viewpoint but his own.

Typology: A hierarchical classification of groups of classes of concepts, regions, etc.

Validity: As applied to a test, this term describes how well a test measures the qualities it is meant to measure. There is no entirely satisfactory quantitative way of measuring validity. Comparative value judgements by two or more teachers are a useful means of estimating the validity of a teacher-devised test.

Values: Beliefs that certain things, phenomena or behaviour are held to be worth while.

Variable: A quantity which varies from one point, or time or area, to another.

Bibliography

1. General works on geographical education

Books

(a) English language

Bacon, Ph. (ed.) (1970), *Focus on Geography*, 40th Yearbook National Council for the Social Studies in Education, Washington DC, USA.

Bailey, P. M. J. (1974), *Teaching Geography*, David and Charles, Newton Abbot, UK.

Ball, J. M., Steinbrink, J. E. and Stoltman, J. P. (eds), (1971), *The Social Sciences and Geographic Education: A Reader*, Wiley, New York, USA.

Biddle, D. S. (ed.) (1968), *Readings in Geographical Education*, Vol. 1, Whitcombe and Tombs, Sydney, Australia.

Biddle, D. S. and Deer, C. E. (eds) (1973), *Readings in Geographical Education*, Vol. 2, Whitcombe and Tombs, Sydney, Australia.

Bloom, B. S. (1956), *Taxonomy of Educational Objectives: The Cognitive Domain*, Longman, London, UK.

Graves, N. J. (1980), *Geographical Education in Secondary Schools*, Geographical Association, Sheffield, UK.

Graves, N. J. (ed.) (1972), *New Movements in the Study and Teaching of Geography*, Temple Smith, London, UK.

Graves, N. J. (1980), *Geography in Education*, Heinemann, London, UK.

Graves, N. J. (1979), *Curriculum Planning in Geography*, Heinemann, London, UK.

Hall, D. (1976), *Geography and the Geography Teacher*, Allen and Unwin, London, UK.

Long, M. (ed.) (1974), *Handbook for the Teaching of Geography*, Methuen, London, UK.

Marsden, W. E. (ed.) (1976), *Evaluating the Geography Curriculum*, Oliver and Boyd, Edinburgh, UK.

Walford, R. (ed.) (1973), *New Directions in Geography Teaching*.

(b) French language

Debesse-Arviset (1968), *La géographie a l'école*, PUF, Paris, France.

Unesco (1966), *L'enseignement de la géographie*, Ipam, Paris, France.

(c) German language

(A) Federal Republic of Germany

Bauer, L. (1976), *Einführung in die Didaktik der Geographie*, Wissenschaftliche Buchgesellschaft, Darmstadt, FRG.

Bauer, L. and Hausmann, W. (eds) (1976), *Geographie*, Oldenbourg, Munich, FRG.

Birkenhauer, J. (1971), *Erdkunde, Eine Didaktik für die Sekundarstufe*, Parts 1 and 2, Schwann, Düsseldorf, FRG (4th edn, 1975).

Birkenhauer, J. (1976), *Bibliographie Didaktik der Geographie*, Schöning, Paderborn, FRG.

Ebinger, H. (1971), *Einführung in die Didaktik der Geographie*, Rombach, Freiburg, FRG (3rd edn, 1976).

Haubrich, H. *et al* (1977), *Konkrete Didaktik der Geographie*, Westermann, Braunschweig, FRG.

Schmidt, A. (1965), *Der Erdkundeunterricht*, Klinkhardt, Bad Heilbrunn, FRG (5th edn, 1976).

Ernst, E. and Hoffman, G. (eds) (1978), *Geographie für die Schule, Ein Lernbereich in der Diskussion*, Westermann, Braunschweig, FRG.

(B) German Democratic Republic

Barth, L. and Schlimme, W. (eds) (1976), *Methodik Geographieunterricht*, Volk und Wissen, East Berlin, GDR.

(C) Austria

Sitte, W. and Wohlschlägl, H. (eds) (1975), *Schulgeographie im Wandel, Beiträge zur Neugestaltung des Geographieunterrichts in Österreich*, Schendl, Vienna, Austria.

(D) Switzerland

Roth, H. (1956), *Unterrichtsgestaltung in der Volkschule – Geographie*, Sauerländer, Aarau, Switzerand (2nd edn, 1967).

(d) Russian language

Bibik, A. E. (ed.) (1968, 1975), *Metodhika Obucheniya geografiy v Sredney Shkole*, Prosveshchenie, Moscow, USSR.

Bibik, A. E., Matrusov, I. S. and Solov'ev, A. I. (1970), *Izuchanie geografiy po novoy programme*, Prosveshchenie, Moscow, USSR.

Shorabiera, I. M. and Panchesnikova, L. M. (Translators and adaptors) (1975), *Novie Tendentsiy v Izucheniy, i prepadavaniy geografiy v Shkole*, Progress, Moscow.

Voprosy geografiy (1971) (Book Collection No. 86), *Problemy shkolnogo Kuroa geografiy*, MYSL, Moscow, USSR.

Voprosy geografiy, (1977) (Book Collection No. 103), *Novoe soderzhanie shkolnoy geografiy*, MYSL, Moscow, USSR.

(e) Spanish language

Unesco (1966), *Metodo para la Enseñanza de Geografia*, Teide/Unesco, Barcelona, Spain.
Unesco (1975), *Geografia de America Latina*, Unesco/Teide, Barcelona, Spain.

(f) Italian language

Unesco (1967), *L'Insegnamento della geografia*, Unesco/Armando, Rome, Italy.

Periodicals

(a) English language

Geography, Geographical Association, Sheffield, UK.
Journal of Geography, National Council for Geographic Education, USA.
Journal of Geography in Higher Education, Carfax, Oxford, UK.
Teaching Geography, Geographical Association, Sheffield, Longman, London, UK.

(b) French language

Historiens et géographes, Bulletin de l'Association des professeurs d'histoire et de geographie de l'enseignement public, Paris, France.
Information géographique, J. Baillière, Paris, France.

(c) German language

(A) Federal German Republic
Geographische Rundschau, Westermann seit, Braunschweig, FRG (1949).
Geographie und ihre Didaktik, Schöning, Paderborn, FRG (1973); Fachbereich 2 der Universität seit, Osnabrück (1977).
Geographie im Unterricht, Zeitschrift für die Unterrichtspraxis in der Sekundarstufe I, Köln, Aulis seit, 1976.

(B) German Democratic Republic
Zeitschrift für den Erdkundeunterricht, Volk und Wissen, East Berlin, GDR (1950).

(C) Austria
Wissenschaftliche Nachrichten, Informationsblätter zur Fortbildung von Lehrern an höheren Schulen, Stadtschulrat, Vienna, Austria (1963).

(D) Switzerland
Geographica Helvetica, Kümmerly und Frey, Berne, Switzerland (1946).

(d) Russian language

Geografiya v shkole, Moscow.

(e) Spanish language

Boletin, Centro de Investigaciones geodidacticas, Caracas, Venezuela.
Revista de Geografia, Departmento de Geografia de la Universidad de
Barcelona, Barcelona, Spain.

(f) Italian language

La geografia nella scuola, Rome, Italy.

2. References contained in the text in alphabetical order by authors

Alexander, J. W. (1963), *Economic Geography,* Prentice-Hall, Englewood
  Cliffs, NJ, USA.
Almy, M. (1967), *Research Needs in Geographic Education: Suggestions and
  Possibilities,* Geographic Education Series No. 7, National Council for
  Geographic Education, USA.
Appleyard, D. (1970), 'Styles and methods of structuring a city', *Environ-
  ment and Behavior,* **2** (1), June, 100–17, Beverly Hills, California.
Association of American Geographers (1967), *Computer Assisted Instruction
  in Geography,* Technical Paper No. 2, Washington DC, USA.
Association of American Geographers (1968), *Field Training in Geography,*
  Technical Paper No. 1, Washington DC, USA.
Association of American Geographers (1970), *Geography in the Two-Year
  College,* Publication No. 10, Washington DC, USA.
Association of American Geographers (1972), *Computerized Instruction in
  Undergraduate Geography,* Technical Paper, No. 6, Washington DC,
  USA.

Beard, R. M. (1969), *An Outline of Piaget's Developmental Psychology,*
  Routledge and Kegan Paul, London, UK.
Beauchamp, G. A. (1968), *Curriculum Theory,* 2nd edn, Wilmette, Ill.,
  USA.
Beddis, R. *et al* (1972–75), *Geography for the Young School Leaver,*
  Teachers' Guides, Schools Council, London, UK.
Beswick, N. W. (1972), *School Resource Centres,* Schools Council Working
  Paper No. 43, Evan/Methuen Educational, London, UK.
Biddle, D. S. (1972), 'Curriculum development in geography in the second-
  ary schools of New South Wales, 1911–1971', *Australian Geographer,* **12**,
  99–114, Sydney, Australia.
Biddle, D. S. (1976a), *Translating Curriculum Theory into Practice in
  Geographical Education: A Systems Approach,* Australian Geography
  Teachers Association, Melbourne, Australia.
Biddle, D. S. (1976b), 'Paradigms in geography: implications for curriculum
  development', *Geographical Education,* **2** (4), 403–49, Sydney, Australia.
Biddle, D. S. and Shortle, D. (eds), (1969), *Programme Planning in
  Geography,* Martindale Press, Sydney, Australia.
Bloom, B. S. (1956), *Taxonomy of Educational Objectives: The Cognitive
  Domain,* Longman, London, UK.
Bloom, B. S., Hastings, J. H. and Madaus, G. F. (1971), *Handbook on*

Formative and Summative Evaluation of Student Learning, McGraw-Hill, New York, USA.

Boardman, D. J. (1969), 'The place of the school field centre in the teaching of geography,' *Geography*, **54**, 319–24, Sheffield, UK.

Bolam, D. (1972), *Exploration Man: An Introduction to Integrated Studies*, Schools Council and OUP, London, UK.

Brearley, M. and Hitchfield, E. (1966), *A Teacher's Guide to Reading Piaget*, Routledge and Kegan Paul, London, UK.

Briault, E. W. H. and Shave, D. W. (1960), *Geography in and out of School*, Harrap, London, UK.

Brouillette, B. (ed.) (1965), *Source Book for Geography Teaching*, Longman/Unesco, London, UK.

Brown, G. and Desforges, C. (1979), *Piaget's Theory: A Psychological Critique*, Routledge and Kegan Paul, London, UK.

Bruce, G. (1969), *Secondary School Examinations: Facts and Commentary*, Pergamon, Oxford, UK.

Bruner, J. S. (1960), *The Process of Education*, Vintage Books, New York, USA.

Bruner, J. S. (1967), *Towards a Theory of Instruction*, Belknap Press, Cambridge, Mass., USA.

Carswell, R. J. B. and Cason, R. M. (1970), *Using Media to Stimulate Inquiry*, Association of American Geographers, Washington DC, USA.

Catling, S. J. (1976), 'Cognitive mapping: judgements and responsibilities', *Architectural Psychology, Newsletter*, **VI** (4), New York, USA.

Catling, S. J. (1973), *A Consideration of the Relationship Between Children's Spatial Conceptualization and the Structure of Geography as a Theoretical Guide to the Objectives in Geographical Education*, unpublished M. A. dissertation, University of London.

Catling, S. J. (1978), *The child's spatial conception and geographic education*, Journal of Geography, Vol. 77, No. 1, pp. 24–28.

Catling S. J. (1978), *Cognitive mapping exercises as a primary geographical experience*, Teaching Geography, Vol. 3, No. 3, pp. 120–123.

Chapin, F. Stuart (1965), *Urban Land Use Planning*, 2nd ed., University of Illinois Press, Urbana, Ill., USA.

Child, D. (1973), *Psychology and the Teacher*, Holt, Rinehart and Winston, London, UK.

Christaller, W. (1966), *Central Places in Southern Germany*, translated by C. W. Baskin, Prentice-Hall, Englewood Cliffs, NJ, USA.

Clegg, A. A. (1970), 'Developing and using behavioural objectives in Geography', *Focus on Geography*, 40th Year Book, National Council for the Social Studies, Washington DC, USA.

Cromarty, D. (1975), 'Reconstructing the syllabus', *Teaching Geography*, **1** (1), Edinburgh, UK.

Dale, P. F. (1971), 'Children's reactions to maps and aerial photographs', *Area*, **3**, London, UK.

Dalton, R. *et al* (1973), *Networks in Geography*, Philips, London, UK.

Davis, J. R. and Spearitt, P. (1974), *Sydney at the Census: 1971: A Social Atlas*, Urban Research Unit, Australian National University, Sydney, Australia.

Davis, W. M. (1954 edition), *Geographical Essays*, Dover, London, UK.
Deale, R. N. (1975), *Assessment and Testing in the Secondary School*, Schools Council Examinations, Bulletin No. 32, Evans/Methuen, London, UK.
Deer, C. *et al* (1977), *A Handbook for Australian Geography Teachers*, Section 1, Sorrett for the Australian Geography Teachers Association, Melbourne, Australia.
De Jonge, D. (1962), 'Images of urban areas', *Journal of the American Institute of Planners*, **28**, 266–76.
Dewey, John (1916), *Democracy and Education*, Macmillan, New York, USA.
Doggett, A. (1975), 'Teaching central place theory from a topographic map', unpublished lesson plan, University of London Institute of Education, Postgraduate Certificate in Education course.
Dolfus, O. (1970), *L'Espace Géographique*, PUF, Paris, France.
Donaldson, M. (1978), *Children's Minds*, Fontana, Glasgow, UK.
Dosman, E. J. (1976), *The Arctic in Question*, OUP, Toronto, Canada.

Eisner, E. W. (1963), *Towards Improved Curriculum Theory: is the Past Prologue?*, University of Chicago, Chicago, USA.
Eisner, E. W. (1969), 'Instructional and expressive educational objectives: their formulation and use in curriculum, *Curriculum Evaluation*, AERA Monograph No. 3, Rand McNally, Chicago, Ill., USA.
Eliot, J. (1970), 'Children's spatial visualization', in Bacon, P. (ed.), *Focus on Geography*, 40th Year Book, National Council for the Social Studies in Education, Washington DC, USA.
Emery, J. S. *et al* (1976), *A Handbook for Australian Geography Teachers*, Sorrett for the Australian Geography Teachers Association, Melbourne, Australia.
Estall, R. (1972), *A Modern Geography of the USA*, Penguin, Harmondsworth, UK.

Fairgrieve, J. (1926), *Geography in School*, University of London Press, London, UK.
Fenton, E. (ed.) (1966), *Teaching the New Social Studies in Secondary Schools: An Inductive Approach*, Holt, Rinehart and Winston, New York, USA, Chs. 25 and 26.

Gagné, R. M. (1966), 'The learning of principles', in Klausmeier, H. J. and Harris, C. W. (eds), *Analyses of Concept Learning*, Academic Press, New York, USA.
Gagné, R. M. (1970), *The Conditions of Learning*, Holt, Rinehart and Winston, New York, USA.
Gardner, John W. (1969), *No Easy Victories*, Harper Colophon Books, New York, USA.
Getis, A. and J. (1966), *Trial Unit 2, Inside the City*, High School Geography Project, Association of American Geographers, Washington DC, USA.
Gulick, J. (1963), 'Images of an Arab city', *Journal of the American Institute of Planners*, **29** (3), 179–89.
Gould, P. and White, R. (1974), *Mental Maps*, Penguin Books, Harmondsworth, UK.
Graves, N. J. (1980), *Geography in Education*, Heinemann, London, UK.

Greco, P. (1967), 'Fundamental ideas in geography' in Morrissett, Irving (ed.), *Concepts and Structure in the New Social Science Curricula*, Holt, Rinehart and Winston, New York, USA, pp. 35–7.

Gunn, A. (ed.) (1972), 'High School Geography Project: legacy for the seventies', Centre Educatif et Culturel, Montreal. French adaptation by B. Robert, in *Didactique-Geographie*, Montreal, Canada, 1974.

Halford, G. S. (1972), 'The impact of Piaget on psychology in the seventies', in Dodwell, P. C. (ed.), *New Horizons in Psychology*, Vol. 2, Penguin Education, Harmondsworth, UK.

Hart, R. (1979), *Children's Experience of Place*, Irvington, USA.

Hart, R. A. and Moore, G. T. (1973), 'The development of spatial cognition, a review', in Downs, R. M. and Stea, D. (eds), *Image and Environment*, Arnold, London, UK.

Harvey, D. (1972), 'The role of theory', in Graves, N. J. (ed.), *New Movements in the Study and Teaching of Geography*, Temple Smith, London, UK.

Heamon, A. J. (1973–4), 'The maturation of spatial ability in geography', *Educational Research*, **16**, Windsor, Berks, UK.

Hickman, G. *et al* (1973), *A New Professionalism for a Changing Geography: Schools Council Geography 14–18 Project*, London, UK.

High School Geography Project, Association of American Geographers (1970), *Geographers in an Urban Age, Unit 1, Geography of Cities*, Macmillan, New York, USA.

Hyman, R. T. (1974), *Ways of Teaching*, Lippincott, New York, USA.

Inhelder, B. and Piaget, J. (1956), *The Child's Conception of Space*, Routledge and Kegan Paul, London, UK.

Johnson, M. (1967), 'Definitions and models in curriculum theory', *Educational Theory*, **17**, Urbana, Ill., USA.

Johnson, J. (1967), *Urban Geography*, Pergamon, Oxford, UK.

Joyce, B. and Weil, M. (eds.) (1972), *Models of Teaching*, Prentice-Hall, Englewood Cliffs, NJ, USA.

Kansky, K. J. (1963), *Structure of Transportation Networks*, Research Paper No. 84, University of Chicago, Department of Geography.

Keller, F. S. (1968), 'Goodbye Teacher', *Journal of Applied Behavior Analysis*, **1**, Kansas, USA.

Kohlberg, L. (1975), 'The cognitive-development approach to moral education', *Phi Delta Kappa*, **56**, 10, Bloomington, Ind., USA.

Kurfman, D. (1968), *Japan. Evaluation Report from a Limited School Trial of a Teaching Unit of the High School Geography Project*, Association of American Geographers, Washington DC, USA.

Lacoste, Y. (1976), *Géographie du sous-développement*, PUF, Paris, France.

Ladd, F. C. (1970), 'Black youths view their environment', *Environment and Behavior*, **2** (1), June, 74–99, Beverly Hills, California, USA.

Lloyd, P. E. and Dicken, P. (1972), *Location in Space: A Theoretical Approach to Economic Geography*, Harper and Row, New York, USA.

Long, I. L. M. (1953), 'Children's reactions to geographical pictures', *Geography*, **38**, Sheffield, UK.

382 *New Unesco Source Book for Geography Teaching*

Long, I. L. M. (1961), 'Research in picture study', *Geography*, **46**, Sheffield, UK.
Long, I. L. M. and Roberson, B. S. (1966), *Teaching Geography*, Heinemann, London, UK.
Lunnon, A. J. (1969), 'The understanding of certain geographical concepts by primary school children', unpublished M Ed. thesis, University of Birmingham, UK.
Lynch, K. (1960), *Image of the City*, MIT Press, Cambridge, Mass., USA.
Lynch, K. (ed.) (1977), *Growing up in Cities*, MIT Press, Cambridge, Mass., USA and Unesco, Paris.

McCaskill, N. (1977), *Patterns on the Land: Basic Concepts in Geography*, 2nd edn, Longman Cheshire, Melbourne, Australia.
McNaughton, A. H. (1966), 'Piaget's theory and primary school social studies', *Education Review*, **19**. Also in Ball, J. M. *et al* (eds) (1971), *The Social Sciences and Geographic Education*, Wiley, New York, USA.
Martin, N., D'Arcy, P., Newton, B. and Parker, R. (1976), *Writing and Learning Across the Curriculum, 11–16*, Ward Lock Educational, London, UK.
Milburn, D. (1969), 'The understanding of vocabulary in geography by primary and secondary school children', unpublished M. Phil. thesis, University of London. See also Milburn, D. (1972), 'Children's vocabulary', in Graves, N. J. (ed.), *New Movements in the Study and Teaching of Geography*, Temple Smith, London, UK.
Mowat, F. (1976), *Canada North Now: The Great Betrayal*, McClelland and Stewart, Toronto, Canada.

Okunrotifa, P. T. (1974), University of Ibadan (Nigeria), is the author of the series of frames in contour line interpretation.

Pattison, William D. (1964), 'The four traditions of geography', *Journal of Geography*, **63**, May, USA.
Peel, E. A. (1971), *The Nature of Adolescent Judgement*, Staples Press, London, UK.
Piaget, J. (1929), *The Child's Conception of the World*, Routledge, London, UK.
Piaget, J. (1932), *The Moral Judgement of the Child*, Routledge, London, UK.
Piaget, J. (1962), 'The stages of the intellectual development of the child', *Bulletin of the Menninger Clinic*, **26**. Also in Wason, P. C. and Johnson-Laird, P. N. (eds) (1968) *Thinking and Reasoning*, Penguin, London, UK.

Renner, J. and Slater, F. (1974), 'Geography in an urban age: trials of HSGP materials in New Zealand schools', *Geographical Education*, **2** (2), New Zealand.
Robert, B. (1974), The teaching unit on railway building was designed by a group of teachers under the direction of B. Robert and R. Nadeau.
Robert, B. (1975), The teaching unit on the Canadian North was designed by a group of teachers under the direction of B. Robert and R. Nadeau.
Rolfe, J. *et al* (1981), *Oxford Geography Project, 1–3*, OUP, London, UK.
Rhys, W. (1966), 'The development of logical thought in the adolescent with

reference to the teaching of geography in the secondary school; unpublished M.Ed. thesis, University of Birmingham.

Rhys, W. (1972), 'The development of logical thinking', in Graves, N. J. (ed.), *New Movements in the Study and Teaching of Geography*, Temple Smith, London, UK.

Saarinen, T. F. (1970), 'Environmental perception', in Bacon, P. (ed.), *Focus on Geography*, 40th Year Book National Council for the Social Studies in Education, Washington DC, USA.

Sandford, H. A. (1966), 'An experimental investigation into children's perception of a school atlas map', unpublished M.Phil. thesis, University of London.

Sandford, H. A. (1972), 'Perceptual problems', in Graves, N. J. (ed.), *New Movements in the Study and Teaching of Geography*, Temple Smith, London, UK.

Satterly, D. J. (1964), 'Skills and concepts involved in map drawing and map interpretation', *New Era*, **45**, UK.

Schools Council Project (1975), *Geography for the Young School Leaver*, Nelson, London, UK.

Schools Council (1977), *Curriculum Design and Management in Geography: A Handbook for School-based Curriculum Renewal*, Macmillan Educational, Basingstoke, UK.

Scriven, M. (1967), 'The methodology of evaluation', in Stake, R. (ed.), *Perspectives of Curriculum Evaluation*, Rand McNally, Chicago, USA.

Secondary Geography Education Project (1975), *Geography Course Construction Rationale*, Glenbervie Teachers Centre, Education Department, Victoria, Australia.

Shepherd, I. D. H., Cooper, Z. A. and Walker, D. R. F. (1980), *Computer Assisted Learning in Geography*, Council for Educational Technology, London, UK.

Shipman, M. (1974), *Inside a Curriculum Project*, Longman, London, UK.

Shortle, D. (1975), 'Geography as a discipline of knowledge: some curriculum implications', *Geographical Education*, **2** (3), 281–303, Australia.

Sigel, I. E. and Hooper, F. H. (1968), *Logical Thinking in Children*, Holt, Rinehart and Winston, New York, USA

Slater, F. A. (1970), 'The relationship between levels of learning in geography, Piaget's theory of intellectual development, and Bruner's teaching hypothesis', *Geographical Education*, AGTA, June 1970, Australia.

Smith, D. (ed.) (1976a), *Geography Teaching in the 70s*, Geography Teachers Association of New South Wales, Sydney, Australia.

Smith, D. (1976b), 'Curriculum theory and geography teaching years 7–10', *Geography Bulletin*, **8** (8) (2), 35–48, Sydney, Australia.

Spicer, B. J. (1973), *The Melbourne Central Business District*, Jacaranda Press, Milton, Queensland, Australia.

Stringer, W. N. (1975), 'The conceptual structure of geography, *Geography Teacher*, **15**, 10–24, Clayton North, Vic., Australia.

Taba, H. (1962), *Curriculum Development: Theory and Practice*, Harcourt, Brace and World, New York, USA.

Taba, H. (1967), *Teacher's Handbook for Elementary Social Studies*, Addison-Wesley, California, USA.

Tansey, P. J. and Unwin, D. (1969), *Simulation and Gaming in Education*, Methuen, London, UK.

Tawney, D. (ed.) (1976), *Curriculum Evaluation Today: Trends and Implications*, Macmillan Education, Basingstoke, UK.

Trow, M. A. (1970), 'Methodological problems in the evaluation of innovation', in Whitrock, M. C. and Whiley, D. E. (eds), *The Evaluation of Instruction*, Holt, Rinehart and Winston, New York, USA.

Turner, J. (1975), *Cognitive Development*, Methuen, London, UK.

Tyler, R. W. (1949), *Basic Principles of Curriculum Instruction*, UCP, Chicago, USA.

Unesco (1965), *Source Book for Geography Teaching*, Longmans, London, UK.

Vygotsky, L. S. (1962), *Thought and Language*, MIT Press, Cambridge, Mass., USA.

Walford, R. (1969), *Games in Geography*, Longman, London, UK.

Walker, M. J. (1975), *Location and Links*, Blackwell, Oxford, UK.

Walker, M. J. (1976), 'Changing the curriculum', *Teaching Geography*, 1 (4), UK.

Warwick, D. (1973), *Integrated Studies in the Secondary School*, ULP, London, UK.

West, E. (1971), 'Concepts, generalizations and theories', in Ball, J. M. *et al* (eds) (1971), *The Social Sciences and Geographic Education: A Reader*, Wiley, New York, USA.

Wheeler, D. K. (1967), *Curriculum Process*, ULP, London, UK.

Williams, M. (1976), *Geography and the Integrated Curriculum: A Reader*, Section 3, HEB, London.

Wonders, W. C. (1971), *Canada's Changing North*, McClelland and Stewart, Montreal, Canada.

Wonders, W. C. and Mills, D. (1976), *The Arctic Circle*, Longman, Don Mills, Ontario, Canada.

Wyatt, H. (1973), 'A resource centre in geography teaching', *Geography*, **58**, 260–2, Sheffield, UK.

Young, I. (1977), *The Curriculum Development Process: Forms 5 to 7 Geography in New Zealand*, National Geography Curriculum Committee, Wellington, New Zealand.

Further Reading

Bale, J., Graves, N. J. and Walford, R. (eds) (1973), *Perspectives in Geographical Education*, Oliver and Boyd, Edinburgh, UK.

Bartz, B. S. (1970), 'Maps in the classroom', *Journal of Geography*, **69**, Houston, Texas, USA.

Bayliss, D. G. and Renwick, T. M. (1966), 'Photograph study in a junior school', *Geography*, **51**, Sheffield, UK.

Beddis, R. et al. (1972–75), *Geography for the Young School Leaver* Teachers' Guides, Schools Council, London, UK.

Biddle, D. S., Milne, A. and Shortle, D. A. (1974), *The Language of Topographic Maps*, The Jacaranda Press, Milton, Queensland, Australia.
Blaut, J. M. and Stea, D. (1971), 'Studies in geographic learning', *Ann AAG*, **61**. See also in Bale, J., Graves, N. J. and Walford, R., *Perspectives in Geographical Education*, Oliver and Boyd, Edinburgh, UK.
Bloomfield, B., Dobby, J. and Duckworth, D. (1977), *Mode Comparability in the CSE*, Schools Council Examination Bulletin No. 36, Evans/ Methuen, London, UK.

Calland, A. R. (1973), 'An investigation of the images held by a small sample of primary school children of their local environment', unpublished MA Dissertation, University of London.
Chorley, R. J. and Haggett, P. (1967), *Models in Geography*, Methuen, London, UK.
Clark, M. J. (1970), 'Physical geography on films', *Geography*, **55**, Sheffield, UK.
Cole, J. P. (1975), *Situations in Human Geography*, Blackwell, Oxford, UK.
Cole, J. P. and Beynon, N. J. (1968), *New Ways in Geography*, Book 1, Book 2, Blackwell, Oxford UK.
Cole, J. P. and Beynon, N. J. (1972), *New Ways in Geography*, Book 3, Blackwell, Oxford UK.

Dalton, R., Garlick, J., Minshull, R. and Robinson, A. (1972), *Correlation Techniques in Geography*, Philip, London, UK.
Dalton, R., Garlick, J., Minshull, R. and Robinson, A. (1973), *Networks in Geography*, Philip, London, UK.
Downs, R. M. and Stea, D. (eds) (1974), *Image and Environment*, Arnold, London, UK.
Downs, R. M. and Stea, D. (1977), *Maps in Mind*, Arnold, London, UK.

Everson, J. (1969), 'Some aspects of teaching geography through field-work', *Geography*, **54**, Sheffield, UK.

Goodlands, J. I. *et al* (1966), *Changing the School Curriculum*, Fund for the Advancement of Education, New York, USA.
Gregory, R. L. (1966), *Eye and Brain, the Psychology of Seeing*, World University Library, Weidenfeld and Nicolson, London, UK.
Gregory, S. (1963), *Statistical Methods for the Geographer*, Longman, London, UK.

Hickman, G. *et al* (1973), *A New Professionalism for a Changing Geography: Schools Council Geography 14–18 Project*, London, UK.
Howling, P. H. and Hunter, L. A. (1974), *Mapping Skills and Techniques*, Oliver and Boyd, Edinburgh, UK.
Hurst, M. E. (1974), *A Geography of Economic Behaviour*, Prentice-Hall, London, UK.

Inhelder, B. and Piaget, J. (1958), *The Growth of Logical Thinking from Childhood to Adolescence*, Basic Books, New York, USA.
Inhelder, B. and Piaget, J. (1964), *The Early Growth of Logic in the Child*, Harper and Row, New York, USA.

Kurfman, D. G. (ed) (1970), *Evaluation in Geographic Education*, Fearon, Belmont, California, USA.

Lawton, D. (1973), *Social Change, Educational Theory and Curriculum Planning*, University of London Press, London, UK.
Logan, M. I. and Missen, G. J. (1971), *New Viewpoints in Urban and Industrial Geography*, Reed, Terrey Hills, NSW, Australia.

McCullagh, P. (1974), *Data Use and Interpretation*, Oxford University Press, Oxford, UK.
Macdonald, B. and Walker, R. (1976), *Changing the Curriculum*, Open Books, London, UK.
Maclure, S. (1972), *Styles of Curriculum Development*, OECD Report, Paris, France.
Mercer, Charles (1975), *Living in Cities – Psychology and the Urban Environment*, Pelican Books, UK.
Mills, D. (ed.) (1981), *Geographical Work in Primary and Middle Schools*, Geographical Association, Sheffield, UK.
Monkhouse, F. J. and Wilkinson, H. R. (1956 and later editions), *Maps and Diagrams*, Methuen, London, UK.
Moore, P. G. (1958), *Principles of Statistical Techniques*, Cambridge University Press, London, UK.
Murphy, R. (1966), *The American City*, McGraw-Hill, New York, USA.

Nicholls, A. and H. (1972), *Developing a Curriculum: a Practical Guide*, Allen and Unwin, London, UK.

Pemberton, P. H. (ed.) (1970), *Geography in Primary Schools*, Geographical Association, Sheffield, UK.
Piaget, J. (1952), *The Child's Conception of Number*, Humanities Press, Atlantic Heights, NJ, USA.
Piaget, J. (1954), *The Construction of Reality in the Child*, Basic Books, London, UK.
Piaget, J. (1955), 'The development of time concepts in the child', in Hock, P. H. and Zubin, J. (eds), *Psychopathology of Childhood*, Grune and Stratton, New York, USA.
Piaget, J. and Inhelder, B. (1941), *Le Développement des Quantités chez L'Enfant*, Delachaux et Niestle, Geneva, Switzerland.
Piaget, J. and Inhelder, B. (1956), *The Child's Conception of Space*, Routledge and Kegan Paul, London, UK.
Piaget, J. and Inhelder, B. (1960), *The Child's Conception of Geometry*, Basic Books, London, UK.

Rushdoony, H. A. (1968), 'A child's ability to read maps', *Journal of Geography*, **67**, Houston, Texas, USA.

Salmon, R. B. and Masterton, T. H. (1974), *The Principles of Objective Testing in Geography*, Heinemann, London, UK.
Schools Council (1966), *The Certificate of Secondary Education: Trial Examinations, Geography*, HMSO, London, UK.

Senathirajah, N. and Weiss, J. (1971), *Evaluation in Geography*, Ontario Institute for Studies in Education, Toronto, Canada.

Slater, F. A. (1975), 'Questions and answers: implications for geographical education', *Geographical Education*, **2** (3), Sydney, Australia.

Spicer, B. J. (1973), *The Melbourne CBD*, The Jacaranda Press, Milton, Queensland, Australia.

Spicer, B. J. (1976), *HSC Geography*, Sorrett, Malvern, Victoria, Australia.

Spicer, B. J., Achurch, M., Blachford, K. and Stringer, W. (eds) (1972), *The Global System 1, Man and Space*, The Jacaranda Press, Milton, Queensland, Australia.

Spicer, B. J., Achurch, M., Blachford, K. and Stringer, W. (eds) (1973), *The Global System 2, Space in Change*, The Jacaranda Press, Milton, Queensland, Australia.

Spicer, B. J., Achurch, M., Blachford, K. and Stringer, W. (eds) (1979), *The Global System 3, Production and Space*, The Jacaranda Press, Milton, Queensland, Australia.

Spicer, B. J. *et al* (eds) (1978), *The Global System 4, Space for Living*, Jacaranda-Wiley, Milton, Queensland, Australia.

Stenhouse, L. (1975), *An Introduction to Curriculum Research and Development*, Heinemann, London, UK.

Stoltman, J. P. (ed.) (1976), *Spatial Stages Development in Children*, International Research in Geographical Education, Western Michigan University, Kalamazoo, USA.

Taba, H. (1962), *Curriculum Development: Theory and Practice*, Harcourt, Brace and World, New York, USA.

Taylor, L. C. (1969), *Resources for Learning*, Penguin, London, UK.

Taylor, P. H. (1970), *How Teachers Plan their Courses*, NFER, Slough, UK.

Tyler, R. W. (1949), *Basic Principles of Curriculum and Instruction*, University of Chicago Press, Chicago, USA.

United States Geological Survey (1976), *ERTS I, A New Window on our Planet*, Professional Paper No. 929.

Vernon, M. D. (1971, 2nd edn), *The Psychology of Perception*, Pelican, London, UK.

Walton, J. (ed.) (1971), *Curriculum Organization and Design*. University of London Press, London, UK.

Wheeler, D. K. (1967), *Curriculum Process*, University of London Press, London, UK.

Yeates, M. and Garner, B. (1976), *The North American City* (2nd ed.), Harper and Row, New York, USA.

3. Books on geography

Abler, R., Adams, J. and Gould, P. (1971), *Spatial Organisation: The Geographer's View of the World*, Prentice-Hall, Englewood Cliffs, NJ, USA.

Bradford, M. G and Kent, W. A. (1977), *Human Geography: Theories and their Application*, Oxford University Press, Oxford, UK.

Chorley, R. J. and Kennedy, B. A. (1971), *Physical Geography: A System Approach*, Prentice-Hall International, London, UK.

Daugherty, R. (1974), *Data Collection*, Oxford University Press, Oxford, UK.

Davis, P. (1974), *Data Description and Presentation*, Oxford University Press, Oxford, UK.

Fitzgerald, B. P. (1974), *Developments in Geographical Method*, Oxford University Press, Oxford, UK.

Haggett, P. (1979), *Geography: A Modern Synthesis*, Harper Row, New York, USA.

Hurst, M. E. E. (1974), *A Geography of Economic Behavior: An Introduction*, Duxbury Press, Belmont, California, USA.

McCullagh, P. (1974), *Data Use and Interpretation*, Oxford University Press, Oxford, UK.

McCullagh, P. (1978), *Modern Concepts in Geomorphology*, Oxford University Press, Oxford, UK.

Morrill, R. L. (1970), *The Spatial Organisation of Society*, Duxbury Press, Belmont, California, USA.

Pocock, D. and Hudson, R. (1978), *Images of the Urban Environment*, Macmillan, London, UK.

Ralph, E. (1976), *Place and Placelessness*, Pion, London, UK.

Smith, D. (1977), *Patterns in Human Geography*, Penguin, Harmondsworth, UK.

Smith, D. (1979), *Where the Grass is Greener*, Penguin, Harmondsworth, UK.

Yi-Fu Tuan (1974), *Topophilia*, Prentice Hall, Eaglewood Cliffs, USA.
Yi-Fu Tuan (1977), *Space and Place*, Arnold, London, UK.

Index

abstract spatial reasoning, 50
accommodation, 364
acquisition of resources, 263
action based on problem solution, 137–8
activities, basic and non-basic, 234–8
adults, mental mapping, 199
aims of geographical education, 1–10, 14–15, 279, 294, 331, 264; *see also* objectives
Almy, M., 29, 43, 378
alternate hypotheses, 189–90
American geography *see* United States
analysis; environmental, 6–8; testing of, 339, 343–4
Appleyard, D., 215, 217, 378
application, testing of, 338, 340–3
assessment, continuous and course work, 194, 254–9, 328, 365; *see also* evaluation
assignment, random, 372
assimilation, 364
Association of American Geographers, 378
Association of German Geographers, 318
atlas *see* maps
Australia, urban studies, 246, 248–52
average, 179

Barrett, D. T., 306
baseline data, 364
basic and non-basic activities, 234–8
Beard, R. M., 28, 378
Beauchamp, G. A., 273, 378
Beddis, R., 297, 378, 384
behavioural objectives, 364
Beswick, N. W., 262, 267, 378
Biddle, D. S., xv, xxi, 268, 270, 272, 276, 282, 314, 375, 378, 384–5
Bloom, B. S., 279, 338, 375, 379; his taxonomy of educational objectives, 364
Boardman, D. J., 268, 379

Bolam, D., 310, 379
Brearley, M., 52, 379
Briault, E. W. H., 283, 379
Brouillette, B., 210, 379
Brown, G., 28, 379
Bruce, G., 351, 379
Bruner, J., 41, 56, 226, 379

Canada: Northlands study, 55, 70–7; railroad game, 77–88
Carswell, R. J. B., 243, 245, 379
Cason, R. M., 243, 245, 379
catalogues, 264–5
Catling, S. J., 17, 44–5, 50, 379
central concept, 370
central tendency, 175–7
centralized curriculum, 294–6
chaining, 42
changes in geographical teaching, 2–5
Chapin, F. S., 247, 379
Child, D., 22, 28, 40, 379
chi-square test, 201–3
Christaller, W., 321, 333, 379
city *see* settlements; urban studies
Clegg, A. A., 332, 379
closed-ended questions, 158, 167
coding, 167–8
coefficient: of correlation, 364; reliability, 348–9
cognitive development, 16–54 *passim*, 364–5
collation, data, 167–8
collection, data, 144–5, 162–7
community, social characteristics of, 131–4
competence, spatial, 13–14
comprehension, testing of, 338–40
computers, 269–70
concepts/conceptual, 35–49, 303, 305, 365; hierarchy of, 36–9; learning, 17–22, 35–49, 58; models, 285, 290, 292, 365; perception, 20–2, 58; revolution, 4; spatial, 43–6; structure of geography, 281, 285–7